MOST SECRET

DAVID O'KEEFE
ONE DAY IN AUGUST

THE UNTOLD STORY BEHIND CANADA'S TRAGEDY AT DIEPPE

ALFRED A. KNOPF CANADA

PUBLISHED BY ALFRED A. KNOPF CANADA

Copyright © 2013 David O'Keefe

www.randomhouse.ca

Knopf Canada and colophon are registered trademarks.
Pages 452–457 constitute a continuation of the copyright page.

LIBRARY AND ARCHIVES CANADA CATALOGUING IN PUBLICATION

O'Keefe, David R., 1967– , author
One day in August : the untold story behind Canada's tragedy in Dieppe / David O'Keefe.
Includes bibliographical references and index.
Issued in print and electronic formats.

ISBN 978-0-345-80769-4

1. Dieppe Raid, 1942. 2. World War, 1939–1945—Cryptography. 3. World War, 1939–
1945—Military intelligence. 4. Canada. Canadian Army—History—World War, 1939–
1945. I. Title.

D756.5.D5O54 2013   940.54'21425   C2013-901551-5

Text, maps and cover design by Andrew Roberts
Printed and bound in the United States of America

2 4 6 8 9 7 5 3 1

"For those who never knew"

Private Ron Beal, photographed in 2012 holding a picture of himself as a young soldier before embarking for Dieppe.

CONTENTS

Contents

ONE DAY IN AUGUST

AN ODE TO C.P. STACEY

"**N**o respectable historian would dream of writing a Naval history of the late war unless he was given access to our sources of information," mused John Godfrey at the end of the Second World War. His successor as Director of Naval Intelligence, Rear Admiral Edmund Rushbrooke, elaborated on the system adopted in the United Kingdom. "The Head of the Historical Section (Royal Navy) had been indoctrinated into Special Intelligence," he wrote, and "it may be found necessary to indoctrinate others of the Historical Staff, such as the writer of any history of the U-Boat Campaign which was influenced in a dominating way by Special Intelligence."

The British realized that skilled historians would question the multitude of inconsistencies, open-ended questions and all-encompassing excuses for various events—including Dieppe. Fearing that their curiosity would lead to unintended revelation of the source—one that continued to be used in the Cold War—both the British and the Americans adopted a hybrid approach: historians would be indoctrinated into Ultra, but the use of the material would be severely restricted. Official army, navy and air force historians were then instructed to use this knowledge to sidestep any historically dangerous areas—a process similar to the way the Admiralty used Ultra to reroute convoys from the clutches of U-boat wolf packs. This privilege was not made available to the official historians in Canada, although Canadians took part in Ultra-inspired missions, worked at Bletchley Park, and were indoctrinated in and used the material in the field.

When the brilliant patriarch of Canadian military history, Colonel Charles P. Stacey, set his official historical team to work on Dieppe in the days following the raid, he was fighting a historical battle with one hand tied behind his back. The story line fed to the war correspondents to protect the true intent of the raid spilled over into the historical realm, creating an impenetrable fog. Forced to rely on the personal testimonies of men sworn to secrecy to lay the cornerstone for our understanding of the raid—sanitized after-action reports, official communiqués, war diaries and snippets of message logs—Stacey lacked the essential ingredients and contextual knowledge to achieve a firm understanding of Dieppe. But Stacey was no fool: as the war went on, he realized that the Allies did have something up their sleeve, but he had no clue at that time about the nature of Ultra, how pervasive it was, how it was used, or the sources and methods used to maintain the flow. Regardless, he was able to cobble together a truly accurate "human" account of the battle—one that will never fade from history.

After the revelation of Ultra in the late 1970s, the initial expectation that it would rewrite the history of the Second World War soon faded as the British government released only a tiny portion of the perhaps billions of pages of material created under that security stamp during and after the war. On the fiftieth anniversary of the war's end, in 1995, both the British and the American governments embarked on a protracted release of these documents, which continues to this day. Although I began my research that same year, the story has emerged slowly over the past two decades. I had no single "eureka" moment that suddenly allowed me to fit all the pieces of the puzzle into place. Rather, it was the painstaking assembly of minuscule pieces of evidence—balanced, sorted and weighed against other evidence—that has finally allowed me to tell the "untold" story of Dieppe. New technologies such as the Internet, the microchip and digitization—ones that would have delighted Charles Babbage, Alan Turing, Frank Birch and Ian Fleming—have allowed me to consult more than 150,000 pages of documents from archives on two continents and over 50,000 pages of published primary and secondary source material for this book.

The methodology I employ is straightforward, based in large part on the sage advice of a multitude of mentors in the historical realm and, perhaps rather ironically, on the musings of Colonel Peter Wright, the man who served as General Ham Roberts's intelligence officer aboard the *Calpe*. After the Dieppe fiasco, Wright went on to become the highly respected and Ultra-indoctrinated intelligence master at General Harry Crerar's First Canadian Army throughout the battles in Normandy and northwest Europe. On his return from the war, he resumed his legal practice and was eventually appointed a judge on the Ontario High Court of Justice. He believed that the primary job of the intelligence officer is first to assess what the enemy is doing and then what he *should be* doing—sage advice I adopted as my general approach to historical inquiry. In other words, the evidence must drive the story. In this case, because there is much "white noise" surrounding the Dieppe saga, I placed greater weight on the documents created before or during the raid than on those written later. Because the Dieppe scholarship is vast, much of this material had to be left on the "cutting-room floor," though I used it during my research phase to eliminate possibilities, myths and conjecture, and to balance and shape my analysis. A full bibliography is available on my publisher's website for further consultation: see http://www.randomhouse.ca/onedayinaugust.

On the fiftieth anniversary of the end of the Second World War, one historical commentator proclaimed that nothing more could be said about this war and that it was time to move on to the history of the Cold War. The remarkable revelations in this account are but one example of the short-sighted nature of that comment. As long-classified materials on Ultra and on other conflicts make their way into open archives around the world, we realize that the book never closes on history and that only now can the real history of the Second World War begin to be written.

Although this new interpretation answers many of the old questions about Operation Jubilee, it also raises new ones that emerge from our unfolding understanding. Essentially, it provides a firm foundation from which to build a more complete picture of the Dieppe Raid and the reasons behind it. In the coming years, more information will undoubtedly grace the vast wealth already available. The various agencies responsible for SIGINT material—the Government Communications Headquarters in England, the National Security Agency in the United States and, to a lesser extent, the Communications Security Establishment Canada—along with the respective arms of the ministries or departments of defence—continue to release documents into the public domain year after year.

Like the generations of skilled historians who passed the torch to me many years ago, I turn this interpretation of Dieppe over to a new generation of young scholars. I hope they will be as inspired as I have been to dive into the realm of historical research—regardless of the subject or the challenge.

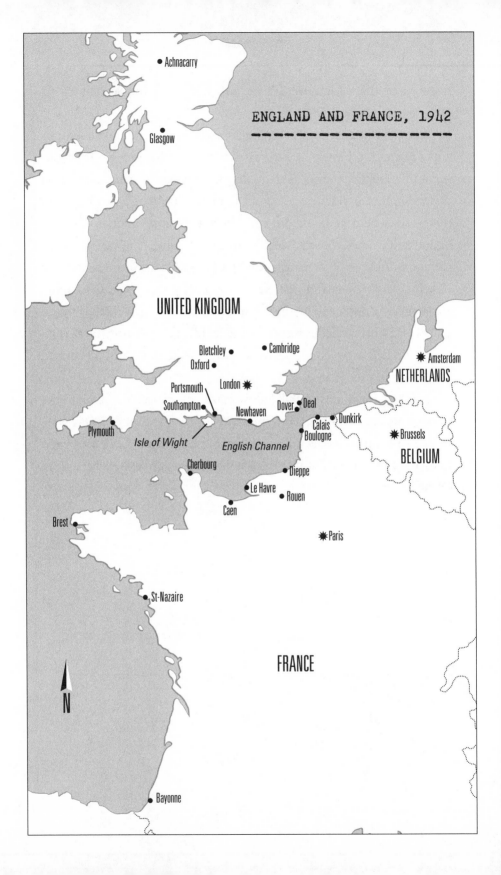

PROLOGUE

August 19, 1942, 0347 hours, English Channel off Dieppe, Normandy, France

Moving swiftly across the slick deck of the drab grey British destroyer HMS *Fernie* and up onto the bridge, a peacoat-clad Royal Naval Voluntary Reserve officer from Special Branch discarded his hand-rolled cigarette and pressed his binoculars to his eyes, adjusting the focus wheel to account for the darkness. In the distance, a series of fire-red mushroom-shaped explosions merged with the silver glow of bursting star shells and a carnival of red, orange and green tracer fire that darted back and forth just above the ink-black waterline. Then came the echo of staccato machine-gun and high-powered cannon fire, punctuated at irregular intervals by the whiplash crack of larger-calibre naval gunfire.

Straining to discern friend from foe, Commander Ian Fleming stood among a group of Allied journalists, broadcasters and photographers and American military observers expecting to witness the successful execution of the largest amphibious raid of the war to date, known as Operation Jubilee. But it was now clear to all aboard that something had gone wrong, and that the carefully synchronized raid, planned by Lord Louis Mountbatten's Combined Operations Headquarters and involving a largely Canadian force, had begun sixty-three minutes prematurely.

Ian Fleming—who a decade later would write *Casino Royale* and launch his immortal James Bond dynasty—was listed innocuously on the ship's manifest that day as a "guest." For years, historians and biographers have asserted that the normally desk-bound member of the British Naval Intelligence Division played no role other than that of observer, and that Fleming's natural desire for action and adventure, fused with an innate talent for bureaucratic machination, had landed him a prize seat on the *Fernie*, the backup command ship.

But this "guest" was in fact present in an official capacity—to oversee a critical intelligence portfolio, one of many he handled as personal assistant to the Director of Naval Intelligence, Rear Admiral John Godfrey. He was on board to witness the launch of a highly specialized commando unit that had been created specifically to carry out skilled and dangerous operations deemed of the greatest urgency and importance to the war effort. Fleming's crack commando unit was set to make its debut under cover of this landmark raid on the coast of German-occupied France.

With the dawn, however, came the sober realization that the raid had gone off the rails in truly epic fashion. As the sky lightened, Fleming could see heavy German fire coming from the hotels that lined the beachfront and ribbons of flame flaring out from the towering clifftops. Below, the main beach—which had hosted generations of English vacationers, including Fleming himself, who had won and lost at the tables of its seaside casino before the war—had become a killing field for the assaulting troops. Catching quick glimpses of the scene through the swirling smokescreen, he could make out small black, motionless dots on the rocky beach where countless Canadian soldiers now lay dead and wounded, and scores of tanks and landing craft sitting abandoned or burning alongside them. Above the town hung an ominous black, acrid cloud, periodically pierced by German and British fighters swooping down to search out quarry, while rapid-firing anti-aircraft guns from both sides swept the sky with bright yellow and orange tracer fire. The roar of aircraft engines, the sounds of machine-gun and cannon fire, and the explosion of artillery and mortar shells shook the air, as British destroyers attempted to assist the men pinned down on the beach, and now holding on for dear life.

Just seven hundred yards offshore, Fleming watched helplessly as his fledgling commando unit headed through the heavy smokescreen in their landing craft towards the deadly maelstrom. Tragically, what was about to occur was not simply the final act in the darkest day in Canadian military history but the beginning of one of the most controversial episodes of the entire Second World War. This one day in August—August 19, 1942—would haunt the survivors and leave the country struggling to understand why its young men had been sent to such a slaughter on Dieppe's beaches.

But what was known only to the young Commander Ian Fleming and a few others was that the raid on this seemingly unimportant French port had at its heart a potentially war-changing mission—one whose extreme secrecy and security ensured that its purpose would remain among the great mysteries of the Second World War. Fleming's presence on board the *Fernie* connected the deadly Dieppe Raid with the top-secret British intelligence-gathering operation dubbed "Ultra," one of the most closely guarded secrets of wartime Britain. And understanding exactly why Ian Fleming was on board the *Fernie* that day was a key that helped me finally to unravel the mystery behind the raid.

Over almost two decades I combed through nearly 150,000 pages of historical documents and interviewed participants in the raid (as well as filming them for the documentary *Dieppe Uncovered*, aired simultaneously in England and Canada on August 19, 2012). The pieces of the jigsaw puzzle are at last largely in place.

Locked away until now in dusty archives, the story unfolded and took shape over time as intelligence agencies and archive facilities in Britain, the United States and Canada released long-classified documents withheld for seven decades from public view. Slowly, each piece was added to the puzzle until, at the end of my journey, I found a story that rivalled a Tom Clancy or a James Bond thriller—although this saga was all too true. And this stunning discovery, kept under wraps until now, necessitates a reconsideration of this phase of the Second World War and a reassessment of the painful legacy of Dieppe.

As Ron Beal, a Dieppe veteran, said to me after I laid out the story for him: "Now I can die in peace. Now I know what my friends died for . . ."

ONE

THE CANADIAN ALBATROSS

This was too big for a raid and too small for invasion: What were you trying to do?

—GERMAN INTERROGATOR TO
MAJOR BRIAN McCOOL, AUGUST 1942

During his intensive interrogation in the days following his capture, the exhausted prisoner, Major Brian McCool, the Principal Military Landing Officer for the Dieppe Raid, was subjected repeatedly to one burning question from his German interrogator: "What were you trying to do?" Still at a loss, the bewildered McCool lifted his head and replied, "If you could tell me . . . I would be very grateful."

For nearly three-quarters of a century, that same query has remained unanswered despite numerous attempts by historians, journalists and politicians to explain the reasons behind the deadliest amphibious raid in history. The veterans of that fateful day have themselves never understood the abject failure they experienced and the staggering loss of life their comrades suffered on the blood-soaked beaches of Dieppe. Over the decades since, a pitiful legacy of sorrow, bitterness and recrimination has developed to frame the collective

Canadian memory of an operation seemingly devoid of tangible purpose and intent.

The cost to Canada of Operation Jubilee, as the Allies' raid on Dieppe on August 19, 1942, was code-named, was appalling: 907 men killed—roughly one man every thirty-five seconds during the nine-hour ordeal—a rate rivalled only by the charnel-house battles on the Western Front in the First World War. To place that number in current perspective, Canadian losses from over a decade of combat in the Afghan war would fill one row in the Dieppe military cemetery, where twenty rows of dead, all lost in just one morning, now lie. Adding to that sobering toll, a further 2,460 Canadian names filled the columns of the wounded, prisoners of war and missing in the formal casualty returns. By nightfall, a total of 3,367 men—68 percent of all the Canadian young men (mostly in their teens and early twenties) who made the one-day Channel crossing to France—had become official casualties in some form. Units such as the Royal Regiment of Canada from Toronto, which suffered 97 percent casualties in less than four hours of fighting on Blue Beach at Puys, virtually "ceased to exist."[1] To varying degrees, the same was true of the other units of the raiding force: bodies of men from army regiments in Quebec, Ontario, Alberta, Saskatchewan and Manitoba fell in piles alongside men from the east and west coasts who toiled in the signals, medical, provost, intelligence or service corps.

The catastrophe would strike a deep chord throughout Canada, seared into the country's psyche as both our greatest historical mystery and our supreme national tragedy. For decades, Dieppe has been Canada's albatross.

The losses on that day in August 1942 represented a snapshot of Canadian society. The lasting images were stark and unforgiving: the dead—once husbands, fathers, sons, brothers, managers, janitors, students, fishermen, farm workers and clerks, who had risked their lives in the name of Canada—lay motionless on the pebbled beaches

On September 1, 1944, members of Canada's Royal Hamilton Light Infantry returned to kneel at the graves of their comrades killed at Dieppe after the port's liberation from the German occupation. Twenty rows of graves holding more than nine hundred men lost in one morning fill the military cemetery there.

or slumped along the narrow streets of the town, their often mangled bodies used as fodder for German propaganda. Brothers in arms for that campaign, they now rest in the cemetery close by for eternity, bonded and branded by the name "Dieppe." For those fortunate enough to be taken prisoner, their reward was almost three years of harsh captivity, their hands and feet shackled night and day for the first eighteen months, and a cruel forced death-march in the winter of 1945 over the frozen fields of Poland and Germany. Only after that did the survivors among them reach home.

For many, coming home did not end their Dieppe experience. By then the regiments they had once viewed as family had rebuilt, and they found few there who had shared their particular experience. Unlike so many other veterans, they had no "band-of-brothers" stories to share, of storming the beaches on D-Day, slugging it out in Normandy, progressing through France and Belgium, or delivering the Dutch from the twin evils of starvation and Nazi Germany. Although the Canadian Army fought successfully and heroically through Italy and northwest Europe later in the war, nothing dislodged the Dieppe stigma. A few of the lucky ones managed to move on, reminded of the "shame and the glory" only at chilly Remembrance Day ceremonies, on muggy August anniversaries, or during an occasional night terror. Without proper care for what we now recognize as Post-Traumatic Stress Disorder (PTSD), some who could not exorcise the Dieppe demons found temporary solace by lashing out in numerous and at times self-destructive ways instead.

The raid, it should be remembered, was not strictly "Canadian": conducted under the overall command of Lord Louis Mountbatten's Combined Operations Headquarters, close to five thousand other Allied soldiers, sailors and airmen, mostly from the United Kingdom, with a smattering of Americans, French, Poles, Belgians and Norwegians, shared the same fateful ordeal in Operation Jubilee. They too were left with lingering frustration about the apparent lack of purpose behind the raid, a vexation captured on the web page of the Juno Beach Centre in Normandy—one of Canada's military history ambassadors to the world:

"Dieppe was a pathetic failure," it reads, "a bizarre operation with no chance of success whatsoever and likely to result in a huge number of casualties."[2]

The historical struggle that followed has proven almost as nasty and inconclusive as the battle itself, with the finger pointing beginning not long after the sounds of conflict faded. Accusations ranged from incompetent leadership to Machiavellian intent, after those involved with the planning and conduct of the raid offered up what many felt were deeply unsatisfactory excuses for the disastrous results. The central issue remains, as it has for seven decades, the lack of any clear rationale for the raid. That absence has left a legacy not only of sorrow but of suspicion, intrigue, mistrust and even conspiracy. The common denominator—that Canadian men had been sacrificed for no obvious or tangible reason—led to a sentiment of unease that quickly built up steam in historical accounts, in the press and in public discussion.

Attempting to rationalize what has defied rationalization, researchers and commentators over the decades have sought to make sense out of the seemingly nonsensical. Historians have searched valiantly through the Allied planning papers, after-action reports, personal and official correspondence, and other ancillary documents available in the public domain, looking for any scrap of evidence that would lead to discovering the driving force or imperative behind the Dieppe Raid. Although the planning documents revealed a list of desired objectives for the raid, they remained nothing more than a grocery list of targets that offered little clue to what achieving them would actually mean in the end.

Officially, Prime Minister Winston Churchill would maintain that the raid was merely a "reconnaissance in force"—an explanation that Mountbatten and others associated with the planning and implementation of the raid expanded upon. Before long, another standard excuse emerged: the Dieppe Raid was simply to test Hitler's vaunted *Festung Europa* (Fortress Europe) and, as such, it was the necessary precursor to future amphibious operations such as the D-Day landings. After that came the "sacrificial" excuses: the Dieppe Raid had been designed by Great Britain specifically to placate its new ally, the beleaguered Soviet Union, by creating the "second front now" that the Russians were demanding, and thereby drawing German air and land forces away from the East and into Western Europe. These excuses never satisfied the soldiers involved and led to a healthy skepticism among professional and amateur historians alike. Soon, fingers began to point, with suggestions that the main players in the Dieppe saga all had something to hide.

They were indeed a motley crew, some highly distinguished, others less so, and the reputations of these men have only added to the furore. Lord Louis Mountbatten, the chief of the Combined Operations Headquarters, is traditionally pegged as the main culprit, not so much for his headquarters' handling of the planning and conduct of the raid —as "inexperienced enthusiasts"—but more for his personality.[3] A vainglorious and ambitious character from royal bloodlines, "Dickie" Mountbatten is traditionally accused of operating far above his ceiling, a man primarily interested in courting the press for favourable headlines designed to put him and his headquarters on the map. But nobody in the chain of command has been spared—all have been painted to varying degrees with the same brush of suspicion and guilt. Were the force commanders who called the shots from the distant bridge of the headquarters ship HMS *Calpe*, offshore from Dieppe, responsible—Canadian major general John Hamilton "Ham" Roberts and Royal Navy captain John "Jock" Hughes-Hallett? Or were the highest authorities in wartime Britain, the Chiefs of Staff Committee and, ultimately, Prime Minister Winston Churchill, responsible?

It's a truth of human nature that any void in our understanding tends to force open a Pandora's box of wild, seductive and intriguing theories. In this case, they span the spectrum from bureaucratic bungling and inflated ambition to treasonous intent; from "raiding for the sake of raiding" to the intentional tipoff of the Germans as an act of betrayal by the French to gain favour with their occupiers. Or perhaps, some surmise, Dieppe was part of a clever game of foxes—an Allied deception to cover the upcoming invasion of North Africa—or, alternatively, an unauthorized action by Mountbatten to win praise and secure his place in history. Some commentators, citing the relative lack of firepower in the raid, for instance, and the overreliance on the element of surprise, coupled with the unprofessional approach to planning and execution, suggest that the entire operation was sacrificial in nature, intended to fail right from the start, to demonstrate the foolhardiness of American and Soviet calls for a second front in 1942.

Some theories are merely silly and irresponsible, such as the urban legend making the rounds in the cafés along Dieppe's beachfront today that the raid was an "anniversary present" from Winston Churchill to his beloved wife, Clementine, who had summered in that delightful Channel port town in her youth—a favourite seaside holiday spot for English families.

Despite all these efforts to make sense of the Dieppe Raid, however, the mystery has remained intact for seventy years, taunting us with the pain of its legacy.

That was my own experience, almost two decades ago, in 1995, when I called up a recently declassified file in the British National Archives in London. This wartime British Admiralty file, which at first did not appear to have any connection with the Dieppe Raid, contained an appendix to an "Ultra Secret" classified report concerning the exploits of a highly secret Intelligence Assault Unit (IAU) that,

One of the main objectives of 30 Commando, from
its inception, was the capture of current German and Italian
cypher material, including specimens of the wheels used on
the ENIGMA cyphering machine, particulars of the daily
settings for wheels and plugs, code books and all documents
relating to signals and communications. On the counter-
espionage side, requirements included information in regard
to German book-breaking, 'Y'-work, the capture of persons
engaged in the CHI service and up to date intelligence
relating to the priorities accorded by the Germans and
Italians to Allied signals for intercept purposes.

2. With the object of furnishing the Unit with
detailed and up to date briefings in regard to the location
of SIGINT targets, a special room was set up in B.P. under
Commander N.A. BACON, O.B.E., R.N.V.R., an Officer with
considerable experience of Commando raids and cutting out
parties.

3. Before the invasion of North Africa, and again
before Sicily and Salerno, the Officers and Senior N.C.Os.
were given a thorough, albeit limited, briefing on the most
urgent current requirements in enemy cypher material. These
were:

    (a) wheels for Enigma machines, especially GAMMA
        and KAPPA, with their associated "return"
        wheels,

    (b) particulars of current daily wheel and plug
        settings,

    (c) Code books 19, 56 and 65,

    (d) any documents relating to enemy signals and
        communications, or from main intercept and
        'Y' stations.

No notes were allowed to be taken in regard to these
requirements and Officers and men of 30 A.U. were not allowed
to visit B.P. or to have any knowledge of progress made in
breaking enemy cyphers or of the methods and machinery used
in British crypto-analytic procedure.

4. As regards captures, the party concerned at DIEPPE
did not reach their objective. NORTH AFRICA yielded a new
machine relating to a high grade ABWEHR link which had
hitherto remained unbroken. This capture resulted in the
immediate reading of about six weeks traffic on this link.
In addition a notebook containing particulars of a high grade
Italian code was captured.

5. During the landings in SICILY, a complete set of the
cyphers used by the Italian Air Force homing beacons for the
months of July, August and September 1943 was picked up.
These were sent to MALTA by hand of Officer and used
operationally by the T.A.F. who were thus enabled to fly in
to their objectives in North Italy with the guidance of the
Italian homing beacons themselves.

because of its clandestine activities, was known during the war by a variety of names, most notably No. 10 Platoon, 30 Commando or 30 Assault Unit. Until the release of that file, there had been nothing to confirm the commando unit's existence, rumoured to be the brain-child of Royal Naval Volunteer Reserve Commander Ian Fleming. Barely a decade later, Fleming would forge another lasting creation—the super-spy James Bond, the most famous, enduring character in espionage literature. The Intelligence Assault Unit was raised and trained with one specific purpose in mind: to steal, or "pinch," the most sensitive of intelligence materials from the Germans, items needed to break their top secret codes and ciphers, including the Enigma cyphering machine, allowing the Allies to read enemy message traffic and to wage the war effectively.

It was a short passage in the fourth paragraph that started me on my journey of discovery: "As regards captures, the party concerned at DIEPPE did not reach their objective." The connection was startling: for the first time here was direct evidence that linked one of the greatest and most closely guarded secrets of the entire Second World War—Enigma—with the deadliest day in Canadian military history. Never before had anything similar appeared in the vast corpus of literature dealing with the Dieppe saga. Something that had remained classified as "Ultra Secret" for over half a century by British intelligence

---

OPPOSITE: A single cryptic sentence in this appendix to a wartime Admiralty report on SIGINT (signals intelligence) operations, classified "Ultra Secret," began my inquiry almost twenty years ago. The report concerns the exploits of the clandestine "30 Assault Unit," the commando unit created by Ian Fleming. The brief comment in paragraph 4—"As regards captures, the party concerned at DIEPPE did not reach their objective"—raised immediate questions: Why was that unit, highly trained in the capture of German cipher material, especially Enigma-related code books and documents, involved in the Dieppe Raid? What had it been tasked to "capture"? And what was the "objective"?

appeared to be lurking beneath the veneer of the traditional interpretations of Dieppe.

In June 1941, British intelligence adopted the term "Ultra" as a security classification for intelligence derived from tapping into enemy communications, most notably their encrypted radio and later teleprinter traffic. Considered prize intelligence—or, as Winston Churchill called it, his "golden eggs"—"Ultra Secret" went above the traditional top-level classification of Most Secret, or, as the Americans referred to it, Top Secret. Logically enough, the term quickly became a security "catch-all" that not only denoted the end product used by Churchill and his commanders to formulate their decisions on the field of battle, but also extended to the technology, processes, policies, operations and even history centred around the secret British code-breaking facility known as Bletchley Park.

Purchased by the Secret Intelligence Service (SIS, or MI6 as it became popularly known) at the outset of the war, this sprawling Victorian estate in Buckinghamshire, just an hour's drive north of London, was the main site for the Government Code and Cypher School (GC&CS), which was responsible for signals intelligence (SIGINT) and code-breaking. By military standards, it was a most unusual place: the requirements of the job called for the utmost in intellectual prowess, which meant recruiting some of the most "beautiful" minds that Great Britain, and later the Allies, could offer. The head of operations, Alastair Denniston, had served in British intelligence during the First World War, and now he recruited "men of the professor type," as he called them, for the new challenge. Drawn mostly from elite universities such as Oxford or Cambridge, these men and women came from a variety of disciplines—mathematics, the sciences, linguistics, classics, history, to name but a few—literally the best and the brightest of the academic world. In this large mansion,

Captain Ridley's Shooting Party: The brightest minds in England were recruited to serve at Bletchley Park, the sprawling country estate north of London. Here, a group visits the new code-breaking headquarters for the first time in August 1938, soon after it was purchased by the Secret Intelligence Service. Because of the nature of their top-secret work, on this introductory visit they were referred to only as "Captain Ridley's shooting party." Anne Hamilton-Grace, aged twenty-seven, described Bletchley in her own secret diary (reproduced by her daughter Elisa Segrave in *The Girl from Station X*) as "one of the most amazing places of this war" as well as "the most peculiar place, masses of odd-looking civil servants and men with orange shirts and long hair about." The important work done on the estate would not come to light until many years after the war.

Although most of the Enigma work at Bletchley Park took place in Huts 4 and 8, this photograph of civilian and service men and women at work in Hut 3 in 1942 gives a sense of the work atmosphere. Anne Hamilton-Grace was one of the girls in Hut 3, first allocated a job as an indexer, then promoted to 4th Naval Duty Officer in Hut 3N. The month before the Dieppe Raid she wrote in her diary: "There was masses to do and I found a whole lot of inaccuracies, which drives me frantic, as it is dangerous now not to be dead right. As every little thing matters enormously . . ."

they joined forces with gifted intelligence officers (again British and later Allied) from the navy, the air force and the army to produce something that up to that point no other country in history could boast: a relatively consistent and comprehensive ability to tap into a direct information pipeline to monitor their enemy's strengths, weaknesses, intentions, capabilities, hopes, fears, desires and dreams. It was an incredible "ace up the sleeve" for a nation at war.

As the importance of their work to the overall war effort increased, so too did the size of Bletchley Park, with numerous numbered "huts" springing up around the grounds which visitors can still see today. These nondescript plywood barracks housed the offices of the naval, air, military and diplomatic sections, which toiled not only to break into, or decrypt, enemy messages intercepted by numerous radio intercept stations located around the British Empire, but then to turn what they intercepted and decrypted into sensible and accurate intelligence to be used by the decision makers to help win the war.

By the end of the Second World War, Sir Harry Hinsley, the official historian of British intelligence, who as a twenty-three-year-old undergraduate in history played an influential role in Bletchley's Naval Section, concluded that Ultra may not have been the "war winner," but it was certainly a "war shortener." By his reckoning, it shaved at least one year, if not two, off the duration of the war, thereby saving millions of lives.[4] However, with all its bumps and bruises, the road was not a smooth one. Although victory ultimately prevailed, mistakes were made along the way.

Information is power, and everyone involved in the Ultra Secret process knew it. In all such cases, then as now, it is imperative that the enemy never realize that his supposedly secure communications have been successfully penetrated. For this reason, signals intelligence and code-breaking, or cryptography, must be conducted in the strictest secrecy, or the enemy will catch on and change the codes and ciphers that guard his message traffic.

Because of its vital military importance and potential, Ultra became one of the most cherished and closely guarded secrets of the war, surpassing even the development of the atomic bomb in the postwar era. Ultra required elaborate precautions to maintain its security, given that more than ten thousand people played various roles connected with it by war's end. Such was the secrecy surrounding the work in Bletchley Park that all those who worked and lived there—from the clerks and young female secretaries to the brilliant code-breaking "boffins"—knew that to talk about their work informally, even to dorm mates or colleagues outside their hut, was treasonous and could result in lifetime imprisonment or even execution. Accordingly, the security surrounding Ultra was to be maintained indefinitely.

As things turned out, the very existence of Ultra remained under wraps for over thirty years following the conclusion of the war. In the late 1970s, for reasons that are still unclear today, the British government officially, and some say unwisely, acknowledged Ultra. Even then, it took close to two more decades before the first batches of significant documents were released to the public—a release that began in 1995, on the fiftieth anniversary of the end of the Second World War, and continues in piecemeal fashion to this day.

Such was the nature of the recently declassified document I had unearthed in the British National Archives. As I continued to scan the pages of the document, the experience reminded me of a miner discovering his first nugget, wondering if he has indeed tapped into a lucrative vein or simply into "fool's gold." Thus began my nearly two-decade historical journey in search of the truth behind Dieppe.

The information contained in the document only increased my natural curiosity. What was the "objective" of this "party"? What role did the objective play in the overall context of the raid? Could it have been a long-concealed reason for the Dieppe Raid? The document offered nothing more direct than that one sentence—"the party concerned at DIEPPE did not reach their objective"—but it struck me immediately as a potential game changer. Included in the document was a general "target list" of items that Commander Ian Fleming's Intelligence Assault Unit had been asked to pinch in the summer and fall of 1942. Labelled "Most Urgent," the items on the list all related to the four-rotor Enigma cipher machine that the German navy (Kriegsmarine) had recently introduced to encrypt its messages before they were sent via wireless. Among these items were "specimens of the wheels used on the Enigma machine, particulars of their daily settings for wheels and plugs, code books, and all documents relating to signals and communications," as well as anything connected with the German signals intelligence effort against British communications. Given my background as a signals intelligenc and Ultra historical specialist for the Department of National Defence in Canada, those lists made perfect sense in the context of the times.

Mid-1942 was the desperate "blackout" period for the British Naval Intelligence Division (NID). Thanks to the cryptanalysts working around the clock in Bletchley Park, for nearly a year—from the spring of 1941 to February 1942—the British had enjoyed astonishing success in intercepting and decrypting German navy messages between its headquarters and its surface and U-boat fleets. During that period, German communications were encrypted on a three-wheel Enigma machine— a complex electromechanical rotor cipher machine belonging to a family of machines (the army, navy and air force each had their own version) first developed by the Germans at the end of the First World War. To do their work, the cryptanalysts at Bletchley Park relied on pinched material—Enigma machines captured from destroyed submarines, for instance, or, more important, the code books, rotor-setting sheets and instruction manuals used to unravel the German secret transmissions. So great was their success, both in stealing materials from the Germans and in intercepting and decrypting the German messages, that the Naval Section at Bletchley Park euphorically nicknamed 1941 the *annus mirabilis*, the "year of miracles."

But the miracle ended abruptly on February 1, 1942, when the German navy equipped its U-boat arm operating in the Atlantic with a new and vastly more complex four-rotor version of the Enigma machine that left the expert code-breakers at Bletchley hopelessly in the dark. The next ten months were a frantic and dangerous time for Great Britain—in particular for her Admiralty and Naval Intelligence Division. Due to a combination of factors, all exacerbated by the Bletchley code-breakers' sudden inability to read the German messages and locate enemy submarines before they attacked, merchant shipping losses in the Atlantic suddenly skyrocketed, seriously threatening Britain's supply and trade routes.

There was near panic in some circles over the perceived threat to the Allies' command of the vital sea lanes essential to ultimate victory in the war. Fortunately for the Allies, when the Germans introduced their updated four-rotor Enigma, they possessed only enough of these machines to equip their Atlantic fleet, leaving all the other areas of operation—the Mediterranean Sea, the Baltic, Norway and the German home waters—with the three-rotor machine and still vulnerable to Bletchley's code-breaking skills. But the clock was ticking: new four-rotor machines would obviously be produced and disseminated as soon as the Germans could manage it. It was this crisis surrounding Ultra that led to the creation of Ian Fleming's commando unit, operating under the aegis of British Admiralty Intelligence and focused solely on "the pinch."

As I read on, the document outlined the criteria for the commandos in Fleming's new Intelligence Assault Unit: they should be familiar with the materials targeted in a pinch but not indoctrinated into the mysterious world of Ultra and Bletchley Park in case, God forbid, they fell into enemy hands and cracked under interrogation. In addition, the unit would include a special adviser with experience in "commando raids" and "cutting-out parties" to guide in the selection of targets and later compile a list of lessons learned. Here, one cautionary note in the report stood out supreme for me: "No raid should be laid on for SIGINT purposes only. The scope of the objectives should always be sufficiently wide to presuppose normal operational objects."

That passage, in light of the Ultra Secret designation, raised some startling new questions: If Commander Ian Fleming's specially raised and trained commando unit was targeting Dieppe, was this pinch the purpose and intent behind Operation Jubilee, the raison d'être for the raid? Could the initial motive for the raid on Dieppe be, as that last passage suggested, to provide a cover under which the commandos could raid a specific target in Dieppe and then depart without rousing German suspicions? Could it even be that the pinch of the target materials, under cover of the other objectives, was the driving force for the entire operation—a scenario that seems ripped from the pages of an Ian Fleming or Tom Clancy spy thriller?

Fleming's inclusion in the raid to oversee his nondescript commando unit, which was making its combat debut, had earlier raised no questions. Traditionally, it has always been viewed as a lark or a "day trip" to Dieppe. But knowing now what his commando unit was targeting opened up an unexpected avenue for a fundamental reassessment of the Dieppe Raid. The potential implications were staggering.

Fully aware of the importance of Dieppe in the Canadian psyche, I realized that my theory required substantial investigation before it could even be proposed—something that proved daunting and near impossible in 1995 for the simple reason that few classified British intelligence files had been released into the public domain. It was true that millions of pages had become available to historians and researchers on the fiftieth anniversary of the war's end, but the British, American and Canadian governments still held back key intelligence files that they regarded as too sensitive or potentially too controversial to release at that time. So, over the next two decades, as more documents slowly became available, my investigation continued.

In 2010, with the vast majority of the research and most of the central pieces in place, it was time to take my journey to another level. I set out my argument to the historians at the Royal Navy's Historical Branch in Portsmouth and the Government Communications Headquarters in Cheltenham. My thesis came as a shock to both groups but they both separately offered that I was indeed "on to something," because they too were curious about the Dieppe mystery. The chief historian at the Government Communications Headquarters agreed to a further public release of classified files dealing with the contextual story of pinch operations, including reports of previous similar operations and vital documents on pinch policy or "doctrine." These documents provided a series of small but highly significant "eureka moments" that helped me to round out the Dieppe saga. Many times I felt I was building a complex historical jigsaw puzzle that had begun with just one tantalizing piece and grew year by year until I felt comfortable enough to come forward with the findings.

To paraphrase Bruce Cockburn, one of Canada's great songwriters, this work has kicked at the darkness until it has bled daylight. Now, after seventy years, we can lift the albatross from our shoulders and move past the initial sorrow, anger, excuses, recrimination and bitterness to achieve something essential—a genuine understanding of the reasons for the raid on Dieppe. In this way we can honour those who sacrificed so much on that bloody day in August 1942.

TWO

A VERY SPECIAL BOND

My job got me right into the inside of everything, including all the most secret affairs.
I couldn't possibly have had a more exciting or
interesting War.

IAN FLEMING, THE PLAYBOY INTERVIEWS

M any of us love to revel in all things James Bond, so the legend of
Ian Fleming's charismatic and unsinkable 007 has fused over the
decades with the legend of his creator. Was he a spy himself? Was
he a crack commando? Did he or did he not train in Camp X, outside
Whitby, Ontario, under the famous William Stephenson, the "man
called Intrepid"? Speculation and fantasy, all. Until recently, for the
serious historian, it seemed almost inconceivable that Bond's creator
played more than an ephemeral role in planning the tragic raid that
August day at Dieppe—and so it appeared to me too, initially. Yet the
information I began to unearth as I went deeper into this story reveals
a very different Ian Fleming *circa* 1942.

It all began three years earlier, in the late spring of 1939, when Rear
Admiral John Godfrey, the fifty-one-year-old, silver-haired though
balding new director of the Naval Intelligence Division, invited

Fleming, twenty years his junior, for lunch at the fashionable Carlton Grill—the restaurant in one of London's most luxurious hotels off Whitehall, once ruled over by the French master chef Auguste Escoffier. A year later, the Carlton Hotel itself was nearly destroyed by a German bomb during the Blitz, and today the site is occupied by the New Zealand High Commission (passersby are reminded of the hotel's previous glory only by a small plaque stating that the young Ho Chi Minh, the Communist founder of modern Vietnam, worked there in 1913). At that luncheon on May 24, Godfrey was just three months into his appointment, and he wanted to meet Fleming, a former journalist turned stockbroker, with the idea of appointing him as his personal assistant. Godfrey's mentor, Admiral Sir William "Blinker" Hall, the legendary spymaster from the First World War, had suggested he should hire someone to help him with his overwhelming pressures and responsibilities in a world verging on war, particularly in the now long-neglected Intelligence Division.[1]

John Godfrey immediately reached out for suggestions for a worthwhile candidate.[2] As with most things in the shadowy world of British intelligence and espionage in those days, Fleming's name reached him through the time-honoured old boys' network—specifically Sir Montagu Norman, the longest-serving governor of the Bank of England.[3] Fleming, like Norman, had been tempered at Eton, the

---

OPPOSITE: The dashing Commander Ian Fleming, RNVR, photographed in naval uniform in the famous Room 39 at the Old Admiralty Building. He appears here in the dark blue jacket of the "wavy navy," with three undulating gold and emerald-green stripes on his sleeves. His boss, Admiral Godfrey, recalled fondly that the large office, the "cave" as its inhabitants called it, was a "cheerful" place: "The atmosphere was more like that of a commune than one would expect in the nerve centre of an important division." His motley staff grew in numbers "in almost ragamuffin conditions": they "worked like ants, and their combined output staggered the imagination."

prestigious boys' school that had crafted the character of generations of the privileged class, preordained for positions of power within the British Empire. The brief resumé Godfrey received seemed impressive enough: the young journalist had achieved a modicum of notoriety dabbling as an "occasional informant" for the Secret Intelligence Service while covering the Russian beat for Reuters in the 1930s.[4] And he was made of the right stuff: he was the grandson of Robert Fleming, the founder of Robert Fleming & Company in Dundee, which produced jute-based products during the American Civil War years before moving on to investments in the lucrative American railroad industry. Eventually, he had transformed "the Flemings" into one of the last private merchant banks that focused on mergers and acquisitions, putting it on the financial map on both sides of the Atlantic alongside J.P. Morgan, Jacob Schiff, and Kuhn, Loeb & Co.

Robert's two sons, Valentine (Val) and Philip, followed in the family business until 1910, when Val, Ian's father, won a seat in Parliament. A product of Eton and Oxford, Val became a rising star in the Conservative Party, "a pillar of the landed squirearchy."[5] On the outbreak of war in 1914, he and Philip joined the dashing Queen's Own Oxfordshire Hussars.[6] After fighting through the second battle of Ypres the following spring, Val was twice mentioned in dispatches and earned the Distinguished Service Order before succumbing to German artillery shells in the fall of 1917, just one week before Ian's ninth birthday. Val's friend and parliamentary ally, the brash, outspoken Winston Churchill, penned his obituary for the *Times*.[7] Little did anyone know then that the former First Lord of the Admiralty, at that point disgraced for having staunchly backed the Gallipoli debacle one year into the war, would reappear two decades later out of the political wilderness. Less than a year after Fleming's introductory luncheon with Godfrey, Churchill reclaimed the political reins of power at the Admiralty and moved on to even greater heights as minister of defence and as prime minister in May 1940—at the darkest moment in British history.

The young Fleming, confident, sophisticated, and somewhat aloof in manner, no doubt sat comfortably at the table that day. Like many other trust-fund babies who came of age in the wake of his father's "lost generation," he lived a carefree life. He had left the Royal Military College at Sandhurst after allegedly contracting a venereal disease; the rumour cast a cloud over his character and general suitability for a King's commission. His distraught mother, fearing for his psychological well-being, sent him to a kind of finishing school for men in Kitzbühel, Austria, where, along with skiing and mountain climbing, he came under the influence of Ernan Forbes-Dennis, a former British spy, and his wife, Phyllis Bottome, a novelist. They encouraged Fleming's aptitude for languages and suggested he start writing. Considering a career in diplomacy, he next enrolled in universities in Munich and Geneva but soon developed a reputation as a playboy. He travelled through Europe at his family's expense, trying sporadically to write between visits to taverns, casinos and brothels, chain-smoking and already drinking too much. When he failed the competitive examination for the Foreign Office, his mother managed to secure him a position as a journalist with Reuters News Agency, where he reported from Moscow on the trial of some British engineers accused of spying. Given his charm, Fleming also made friends in influential circles. When he returned to England, he joined a prestigious brokerage firm.

Fleming's ability to operate in French, German and Russian impressed Godfrey, as did his "talent for spare and simple prose," developed while writing for Reuters.[8] But there was much more to Fleming than his social, linguistic and writing skills. Like many people who leave an indelible impression on their peers, he was a wealth of contradictions. "At the first encounter," recalled his friend William Plomer, who later became his editor at Jonathan Cape for most of the Bond books, "he struck me as no mere conventional young English man-of the-world of his generation; he showed more character, a much quicker brain, and a promise of something dashing or daring.

Like a mettlesome young horse, he seemed to show the whites of his eyes and to smell some battle from afar."[9] Fleming, tall and slim, moved gracefully and with purpose. His sad, bony face with its clear blue eyes was strong-featured, despite the disjointed nose he had acquired during his athletic days at Eton, which only added to "his rakish allure."[10]

Most unusually, Fleming had a special interest in typography and book collecting, and by 1939 he had built a remarkable library of first editions of important inventions, theories and scientific discoveries of modern times. In due course it turned out to be one of the best collections of its genre in England.[11] Part of what attracted Godfrey to Fleming was surely the younger man's intense interest in cryptography—an intelligence source that Godfrey knew all too well had been vital to the success of Naval Intelligence during the First World War. Half in jest, Fleming would later argue that the moniker "C," used to denote the head of the British Secret Intelligence Service, did not refer to Sir Mansfield Cumming, as everyone thought, but to Charles Babbage, widely referred to as the "father of the computer."[12]

In 1822, a century and a half before Bletchley Park unleashed the world's first computer, Babbage, assisted by parliamentary funding, embarked on the development of his "Second Difference Engine." Unfortunately, official patience soon ran dry, leaving the development of "the computer" on the sidelines until the Second World War, when Britain's very survival demanded assistance beyond human intelligence. The fact that Babbage's invention could have rivalled or even eclipsed Gutenberg's printing press as the most influential technological development in a millennium, affording Great Britain an unmatched industrial advantage, was not lost on Fleming. Babbage and his cryptographic passion became Fleming's own fervent intellectual pursuit: he studied his writings carefully, captivated by passages on the art and science of deciphering, which Babbage had compared to picking locks.[13] Various segments from Babbage's seminal *Passages* from a *Life of a Philosopher*, published in 1864, were, according to Fleming, the "most cherished" in his collection.[14]

Apart from his intellectual interests, there was a darker side to Fleming that Godfrey came to appreciate and even foster. One fellow student from Austria had remarked that Fleming was "a totally ruthless young man [who] didn't consider anyone"—a sentiment shared by Godfrey, who said that Fleming "had little appreciation of the effects of his words and deeds upon others."[15] He was best at dealing with things and ideas rather than people. "He was primarily a man of action," Godfrey wrote, whose "great ability did not extend to human relations or understanding of the humanities."[16] Fleming's Machiavellian flair flourished in the Naval Intelligence Division, where an "element of ruthlessness and perfidy, verging on the unscrupulous, [was] inherent in certain intelligence activities."[17]

Fleming was a civilian quite unlike "service-trained officers imbued with the instinct to 'play the game' . . . a maverick who had a gambler's instinct and a taste for adventure."[18] From Godfrey's perspective, Fleming possessed an intellectual flexibility that could easily transform, engage with and understand any problem, idea or concept with equal ease, whether in a formal work setting or over drinks and a meal. In many ways, Fleming reminded Godfrey of Churchill: he "had plenty of ideas and was anxious to carry them out, but was not interested in, and preferred to ignore, the extent of the logistic background inseparable to all projects."[19] Or, as Plomer put it, "He always seemed to take the shortest distance between two points in the shortest possible time."[20]

And so it happened that, in May 1939, Admiral Godfrey offered Fleming the job of personal assistant to the Director of Naval Intelligence (DNI). He had no obvious training or experience for the role, but neither did most of the men (and fewer women) recruited

The dignified Old Admiralty Building looks out onto Horse Guards Parade and Number 10 Downing Street, and lies just blocks away from the War Office, the Air Ministry and Combined Operations Headquarters in Whitehall. During the Second World War this was the operational headquarters for the Royal Navy and the Naval Intelligence Division. A bunker designed to withstand the Blitz, resembling an old brown fort, was built alongside it, housing the Operational Intelligence Centre and the Submarine Tracking Room that controlled the intelligence effort for the war at sea.

into the secret services at that time. Rather, the primary traits were initiative, imagination, brains, and a tireless commitment to winning the war, not so much on the battlefield as in the world of intelligence.

Fleming did not begin his work in Room 39 of the Old Admiralty Building until mid-July, almost two months after his lunch at the Carlton Grill, because his employer, the brokerage firm Rowe and Pitman, only then granted him leave. Godfrey wanted all his staff in uniform, so he appointed Fleming a lieutenant in the Special Branch of the Royal Naval Voluntary Reserve (RNVR). He appeared in the dark blue jacket of the "wavy navy," with three undulating gold and emerald-green stripes on his sleeves, and Godfrey placed him right outside the green-baize door to his own office (Room 38). The larger space, the "cave" as its inhabitants called it, was crowded, noisy, blue with tobacco smoke, with telephones before every man at his desk and secretaries clattering along on typewriters or arranging documents in the endless rows of filing cabinets. Every window was adorned with the obligatory blackout curtains. A few years after the war ended, Godfrey remembered the scene fondly:

> The staff in this room, which later developed into the coordination section, grew up from nothing in a very haphazard way. As far as I know it never had a head, nor would a "head," in the way that the word is usually accepted in the service, be tolerated. I believe this has never been said before, and may come as a surprise to some. "Room 39" consisted at one time of two stockbrokers, a schoolmaster, a K.C. relieved by a most eminent barrister, a journalist, a collector of books on original thought, an Oxford classical don, a barrister's clerk, an insurance agent, two regular naval officers, an artist, two women civilian officers, and several women assistants and typists. Ian had a brainwave and some other specimen arrived for trial and if he did not suit

was mysteriously spirited away. There were many transitory types, both male and female, that came and went if Room 39 did not take kindly to them. But, there were habitués who stayed and stayed and became the elders of this community.

The atmosphere was more like that of a commune than one would expect in the nerve centre of an important division.

The noise in this room was terrific. It got so bad that I had a green baize door installed between Room 39 and my room [Room 38].

Everyone had a telephone of their own; some had two or three; they used them incessantly and relentlessly—almost savagely. They enjoyed the click, and clank of typewriters, and the ebb and flow of humanity, and it was with the greatest difficulty that I persuaded them to banish the typists and to institute some control over the nomadic marauders from other sections who camped out in the narrow defiles between the desks, or crowded round the fireplace.

Few of them met outside Room 39 . . . They worked like ants, and their combined output staggered the imagination.

To this section of interesting, and incongruous ingredients must be added the fatigue, fog, and frustration of war in an arena where the bad news was always known but could not be revealed, bad working conditions, fuggy rooms during the blackout, night work for some, blitz, and the friction caused by frayed nerves, and unsatisfactory personal relationships.

Given all these stresses and strains . . . how was it that Room 39 achieved such phenomenal success, and was so much admired inside and outside the Admiralty[?] The answer may be found in the mutual respect and the close personal friendships which grew rapidly between the naval officer and the civilian, whether in the uniform of the R.N.V.R. or not.[21]

Few of Ian Fleming's close friends thought he would stay more than a month; the mundane administrative side of the work would, they said, "drive him mad."[22] It did not. Fleming was in his element and took everything in his lofty stride, later telling an interviewer, "I could not possibly have had a more exciting or interesting War . . . my job got me right into the inside of everything, including all the most secret affairs."[23] Sitting at his desk piled high with dockets stamped *Most Secret* or *By hand of officer only*, and with folders bristling with sheets of coloured paper to indicate a particular source or a security grading (such as orange for Ultra), Fleming was at the centre of wartime Britain. At any moment, one or both of his two personal phones—one red, the other green—could connect him internally with all branches of the NID or externally to many corners of the British war effort.

The view from his window overlooking Horse Guards Parade confirmed his position. From his perch, Fleming could survey the Foreign Office, which also housed the head of the Secret Intelligence Service, as well as the government offices of Great George Street, where the Air Ministry and Bomber Command toiled, and the neo-baroque War Office Building long used by the army and the Chief of the General Staff. Almost directly across sat Number 10 Downing Street, the unassuming official residence of the prime minister, and nearby Richmond Terrace, the eventual home of Lord Louis Mountbatten's Combined Operations Headquarters. In the distance he could just see Big Ben and the great clock tower of the Houses of Parliament, forever a symbol of London and the British Empire now fighting for its survival. In the long shadow of Big Ben, beneath Whitehall, lay the underground bunkers built to house, among other things, the Cabinet War Rooms, where the prime minister and the chiefs of staff gathered regularly to confer once Luftwaffe bombs began to fall in the summer of 1940. Surrounded by all this expanding power, Fleming knew he was at the hub.

It was an excellent appointment. Fleming had a flair for administration, and he was quickly promoted from lieutenant to commander.

Although they worked together for only three years, Godfrey became one of his lifelong friends and enthusiastic supporters. "Ian," he would later write, "has achieved a unique worldwide acclaim and more publicity, I believe, than any other human being this century."[24] He bewailed the fact that, by the time of Fleming's death in 1964, the man himself had been "overtaken by Bond," with little more "than a screen of lampoons and parodies erected around him." In short, he lamented, "Ian has disappeared."[25] And in some ways, Fleming the intelligence officer did disappear, cloaked by his own personal fame as a writer, while rumours, fallacies, half-truths and hyperbole have swarmed around his role in Naval Intelligence, leaving, perhaps on purpose, more than a hint of fantasy attached to all he touched in the discharge of his duties. He has been credited with carrying out dangerous and spectacular missions—kidnapping high-ranking Nazi officials, facilitating their defection as part of an Illuminati or other nefarious organization, performing political assassinations, sabotage and espionage missions or commando operations . . . The list goes on.

So polarized have the stories and arguments swirling around Fleming become that some historians have even denied that he had any knowledge whatsoever of the enigmatic world of signals intelligence, and particularly of Ultra. Nigel West, for instance, the renowned historian of the British secret services, wrote that "Fleming was almost certainly never indoctrinated into the valuable cryptographic source distributed as Ultra."[26] Yet in John Godfrey's words, Fleming "participated in practically all the intelligence projects" during the Second World War. Clearly, as Godfrey's personal assistant, Fleming handled a number of responsibilities, including Section 17 (the coordinating centre for Naval Intelligence in which staff used Ultra material in their daily operations), and he helped to plan pinch operations for the codebreakers at Bletchley Park. Fortunately, a document declassified only in 2002 clears up the confusion. According to this list, the only one of its kind in the public record, Fleming was among the fewer than seventy officers in the entire British Admiralty who knew of Ultra's existence, and among the fewer than fifty permitted to use the original messages to accomplish their daily tasks.[27]

One of the sources of this confusion was Fleming himself, who, Godfrey recorded, "teasingly floated" the idea of James Bond as a veiled autobiography treading a fine line between fiction and fantasy, a notion that immediately raised alarm in the intelligence community. The concern was real enough: constrained by the provisions of the Official Secrets Act and by the gentleman's agreement among members of Godfrey's staff, Fleming could not reveal the true nature of his work. And without some knowledge of Ultra, it would have been impossible for Fleming to carry out the objectives of his loosely defined job description as Godfrey's personal assistant. Fleming acted as gatekeeper, fixer and principal "go-to" guy for the Director of Naval Intelligence—historically the senior intelligence service in Great Britain, whose tentacles spread over the entire globe.

"I made a point of keeping Ian in touch with *all* aspects of NID work," Godfrey wrote. "He was the only officer who had a finger in practically every pie. I shared *all* secrets with him so that if I got knocked out someone else would, we hoped, be left to pick up the bits and achieve some sort of continuity."[28] Unlike others in the NID who "knew a great deal about one subject," Godfrey maintained that Fleming "knew a bit (and a big bit) about all."[29] Any misstep Fleming made with tongue or pen could inadvertently reveal the inner workings, even long-buried secrets, of British intelligence. As Godfrey would later record, had Fleming, who was only fifty-six when he died, known about the many attempts to write his biography, he would, like most of the senior intelligence operatives of integrity, "have drawn a veil" over his Second World War activities and been "100% uncooperative" or even "laid false trails."[30]

Godfrey too played his role in this obfuscation: when a young author was commissioned to pen Fleming's biography, Godfrey summoned him to lunch and explained firmly that certain aspects of his

protagonist's work, "such as sources of intelligence, cooperation with other intelligence agencies, and anything of a nature which could lead to political embarrassment or controversy . . . must never be revealed."[31] For all these reasons, a realistic version of Ian Fleming *circa* 1942 has remained cloaked in what Godfrey called a "security smokescreen of deception" where "reality and fantasy got so mixed up that those who ought to know better became deceived."[32]

Fleming did not rival 007—one was a secret service field operative, the other an intelligence officer—but there is much more to Ian Fleming than authorities were prepared to admit in the mid-1960s when he died and the spotlight shifted to the man who was, and remains, one of the world's most successful, bestselling authors. That is why it is crucial for any understanding of the Dieppe Raid to investigate Fleming's true character and his role within the mysterious world of British naval intelligence.

Ian Fleming's boss, Admiral John Godfrey, who was sacked as Director of Naval Intelligence following the failure of Dieppe, is perhaps one of the least known of the remarkable figures of the Second World War. A leader with wide interests, gifted with "an exceptionally powerful and original intellect," he could suddenly "assume a demonic relenting smile at the end of the grilling that could make a strong man wet in the palms and weak in the bowels."[33] He cut an imposing figure in his

---

OPPOSITE: Rear Admiral John Godfrey, Director of Naval Intelligence from 1939 to 1942, who hired Ian Fleming to be his personal assistant, right-hand man and go-to guy on intelligence matters. A maverick, hot-tempered and arrogant, he was much loved and respected by his staff, who considered him brilliant, while others outside NID found him difficult to deal with and an insufferable intellectual bore. He was removed as DNI by Winston Churchill following the Dieppe Raid and given command of the Royal Indian Navy, which revolted under his command in 1946.

smart admiral's uniform, vigorous, stern in profile, and with steely blue, penetrating eyes. A grammar school boy from Birmingham rather than Eton, a graduate of the British Naval Academy HMS *Britannia* rather than Oxbridge, he was an experienced and respected career naval officer who had already spent all his adult life in His Majesty's Royal Navy when the war broke out.

During the First World War, Godfrey served in the Mediterranean theatre, spending the entire Gallipoli campaign on board a cruiser before joining the staff ashore, where he earned high praise as an exceptional staff officer. He was mentioned in dispatches and awarded both the Légion d'honneur and the Order of the Nile. After the war, he served as the deputy director of the Naval Staff College and also as captain of several fighting vessels in the Pacific and on the China station. His last seagoing post was as commander of HMS *Repulse*, one of the darlings of the British fleet.[34] In short, Godfrey had advanced by his own merit, not privileged birth.

Much like his new protégé Ian Fleming, Godfrey was a maverick, a commander who made it clear he "did not conform to the usual pattern of senior naval officers."[35] His abrasive manner, hot temper and intellectual arrogance often led to clashes with those he encountered above him and below, and he had as many enemies as admirers: to some he was brilliant, to others an over-intellectualized bore.[36] After one frustrating session with Admiral Sir John Kelly, Commander-in-Chief, Portsmouth, in 1936, this item appeared in Godfrey's file:

> I cannot call to mind, since I reached Admiral's rank, any Captain who impressed me less favourably. A real "Heavy Weather Jack." He is reputed to be very "Brainy": the only evidence I have had of this is his propensity for seeing difficulties and obstacles which less "Brainy" people like myself are unable to see . . . He is the first Captain whom I have ever had to discourage from coming to see me. He made a habit of coming, almost daily, with questions

that a reasonably intelligent Lieutenant could have answered for himself—till I could stand it no longer. I was extremely glad to see the last of him and, consequently, of his Ship.[37]

Unfortunately, this brusque and uncompromising demeanour eventually turned his colleagues in the Joint Intelligence Committee against him, and after the Dieppe Raid they recommended that he be dismissed from his position.

Personally, however, Godfrey was a highly cultured man. His interests were reading and music rather than public school games. His wife, Margaret, a capable Cambridge-trained woman, went on to do valuable war work in intelligence herself, serving at Bletchley Park and later at her husband's pet project, the Inter-Services Topographical Department (ISTD) located at Oxford University.

Godfrey would stamp his individual leadership style on the Naval Intelligence Division in the first three years of the war, though he himself had been heavily influenced by two First World War admirals. He worked for five years under the first, Admiral Rudolf Burmester, who was at Gallipoli and served as chief of staff for the Mediterranean fleet. Burmester preached against the dominant "remote control" style of leadership common in the navy, choosing instead to take his staff and subordinates into his confidence and "throw on them full power and responsibility, avoiding any appearance of interference."[38] Godfrey adopted this style too, thinking it the "only method" likely to achieve success in the current fast-paced, multi-dimensional world of naval intelligence.

The second and more profound influence was "Blinker" Hall, who had headed Naval Intelligence from 1914 to 1919 and, with Churchill's help, put cryptography and signals intelligence on the map. In his famous Room 40 in the Old Admiralty Building, he and his team intercepted and decrypted coded German diplomatic, military and naval messages. He quickly became a legend when, almost immediately after

Admiral Sir William Reginald "Blinker" Hall, former Director of Naval Intelligence, who guided the division through the Great War and became its de facto godfather thereafter. He believed that situations were never hopeless—problems lay only with "men who become hopeless about them." He would strongly influence John Godfrey's actions, as the new director, when war was again imminent.

the first shots were fired in August 1914, they received a code book stolen from the German cruiser *Magdeburg* and, within days, cracked the code of the German High Seas Fleet. That breakthrough greatly aided the British in their command of the oceans and their efforts to keep the German fleet bottled up in home ports for most of the war. The team then turned to diplomatic traffic and, in 1917, intercepted and deciphered the famous Zimmermann telegram, in which the Germans urged Mexico to declare war on the United States. That invitation so enraged the Americans that they too entered the war, enabling the Allies finally to defeat the Central Powers.

At his first meeting with Blinker Hall, in 1917, Godfrey, then a young staff officer, was taken by the older man's gambling nature. As he later recalled, Hall's mantra "boldness always pays" struck him to the core. "Mistakes," Hall used to preach, "may be forgiven, but even God himself cannot forgive the hanger-back."[39] Godfrey shared his mentor's vision that situations were never hopeless. The problem lay, rather, with "men who become hopeless about them."[40]

Godfrey soon put this philosophy to use when he was appointed Director of Naval Intelligence in 1939. This division, along with the intelligence arms of the other two services—air and land—had been much neglected in the years since the Great War. The 1919 Treaty of Versailles, which ended the war, had essentially scuttled the German navy, and Britain, exhausted by its enormous war effort, relaxed into passive complacency. With war imminent once again, Blinker Hall urged Godfrey to revive his division swiftly. The two men met regularly, with the septuagenarian Hall playing the role of patron and even lending Godfrey his flat at 36 Curzon Street—well serviced by his housekeeper—for the duration of the hostilities. It was just a short walk across Green Park from his office. As Godfrey wrote later: "He very unobtrusively offered me full access to his great store of knowledge and judgment on this strange commodity, Intelligence, about which I knew hardly anything."[41] His counsel would be crucial since intelligence, particularly signals intelligence, would again rocket to the forefront in the new war as England struggled to hold command of the seas.

Although Hall urged Godfrey to pick his own team and shape his division for the new war as he saw fit, he was anxious to help resuscitate his old fiefdom. Never fully out of the game, despite giving up active duty in 1919 and serving as a Conservative member of Parliament in Stanley Baldwin's postwar government, Hall introduced Godfrey to his old code-breaking team in Room 40—brilliant men such as Oxford scholar Dillwyn "Dilly" Knox—who were now in the process of setting up shop at Bletchley Park for the new war.[42] What fascinated Godfrey was the unique position of power and independence that Blinker Hall had carved out for himself during his time as director. His special position as head of Naval Intelligence had been recognized throughout Whitehall and had enabled him to deal directly with Cabinet ministers and high officials in various government departments outside his own. In what turned out to be sage advice, he counselled Godfrey to "act on his own initiative, obtaining permission, if necessary, afterwards . . . the DNI is entitled to enlist the help of anyone inside or outside the country from the Archbishop of Canterbury and the General of the Jesuits downwards," including leading bankers and corporate heads.[43]

From the beginning of their professional association, it was clear that Hall and Godfrey spoke the same language, sharing a common outlook and a "strange similarity of experience."[44] Both had commanded battle cruisers before becoming director; both for different reasons achieved an "anomalous sort" of independence inside the Naval Staff; both eventually shared anxieties about their respective Sea Lords, felt the adverse impact of hostility from outside the Admiralty, shouldered responsibilities, and sometimes made decisions without the help or knowledge of those in higher authority. Both, too, longed to see the return of the day when the Naval Intelligence Division had been the senior intelligence service and a "law unto itself."[45]

But the Intelligence Division Godfrey inherited was no longer the state-of-the-art organization Hall had left behind at the end of the Great War. In what some would categorize as the natural evolution of the trade, and others as an attempt to blunt the strength and influence of the senior service, most of the division's knowledgeable staff had found new homes in other armed branches of the service, in the rapidly rising Secret Intelligence Service or in the Foreign Office.[46] To Godfrey's dismay, he no longer had aerial reconnaissance, human intelligence, and the best British naval cryptographic minds under his immediate control, as Hall once had. Even the man who had run Room 40, Admiral Sir William "Bubbles" James, had been returned to regular duty as commander-in-chief of Portsmouth.[47] Realizing that Godfrey had far fewer of the "cutting-edge" intelligence sources under his direct control, Hall urged him to forge cast-iron links with rival services and the new government departments—in particular, the Government Code and Cypher School and the Foreign Office—and with foreign dignitaries, paying special attention to the then-neutral American ambassador. It was a tall order that required panache and the appropriate inside "machinery," or network, to carry out. As Godfrey saw it, his first duty was to make preparations for war that were at once practical and imaginative—practical in the sense of putting to use the knowledge, facilities and skilled personnel available; and imaginative in the sense that his whole intelligence empire could be adapted to the needs and opportunities of war.[48]

Hall's concept of "decentralization" proved Godfrey's saving grace—something he learned first-hand in the opening months of the war when two-thirds of his valuable time was taken up with "press investigations and post-mortems."[49] To remedy this drain on his time, he got approval from the Chief of the Naval Staff for the Sea Lords, as well as the directors of other intelligence branches, to deal directly with the heads of specific sections of his Naval Intelligence Division rather than with him. It was a smart move: as the war ramped up, his staff grew from about a handful to nearly a thousand by 1942.[50] He set out to select men with the "right sort of personality and knowledge . . . [and] to thrust responsibility on them even if they were not quite ready for it," on the principle that it is "only by experiencing responsibility that one can learn to be responsible."[51]

The Second World War differed vastly from the First in many respects, among them the executive direction of the war. The new war would be war by committee, where restraint would be imposed on formerly idiosyncratic policies and decision making. Godfrey, as Director of Naval Intelligence, sat on the Joint Intelligence Committee (JIC), a subcommittee of the chiefs of staff, along with his peers in the military and the air force.[52] To his relief, he soon found that "neither the First Lord, First Sea Lord nor the Vice Chief of the Naval Staff had time to keep in touch with the DNI's work," allowing him a fair degree of freedom to act as he liked.[53] He quickly set out to resurrect the division in the Hall tradition, hoping to "cut miles of red tape" and "get what he wanted in a few days instead of a few months."[54] He imaginatively took aggressive steps to recruit "barristers, dons, journalists and graphic designers, geologists and geographers" to work under him, "alongside R.N. hydrographs and Royal Marine majors."[55]

In this respect, Ian Fleming was the ideal personal assistant for Godfrey. He too had no use for pomposity and did not suffer from what his boss termed "very senior officer veneration." Godfrey expected Fleming to act as his intermediary with other branches of intelligence, to sort out potentially damaging flaps over policy, and to tackle problems of a sticky or perhaps less than gentlemanly nature, such as covering up the death of French double agent Captain Pierre Lablache-Combier at the hands of British intelligence.[56] As one intelligence officer later remarked, Fleming was Godfrey's "link with an appalling range of activities inseparable from modern war; from the cracking of codes to the practice of deception, from the preparation of topographical documentaries on the areas we have been driven from and would return to we hope. He had to keep an eye on these multifarious aspects of naval intelligence and report frequently to this always demanding Admiral."[57] Godfrey was vividly aware of all that Fleming accomplished. He recorded later, as the need for naval intelligence "changes from a sluggish brook to a raging torrent, war . . . changes the intelligence officer from Cinderella to the Princess."[58]

That summer of 1939, with tremendous efficiency, John Godfrey wasted no time in mobilizing for the expected war. His Naval Intelligence Division quickly grew into a labyrinthine organization. Room 39 was the helm, its workload divided among more than two dozen numbered sections, each one dealing with a range of intelligence duties and located in various rooms within the ever-changing layout of the Old Admiralty Building. Sections 1, 2, 3, 4, 16 and 20 were the geographically organized "country" sections: Section 1 covered Germany, Scandinavia, the Low Countries and occupied France; Section 2, the Americas; Section 3, the Mediterranean and Africa; Section 4, the Far East; Section 16 tracked Stalin's Soviet Union; and Section 20 hovered over unoccupied France, and portions of Africa, as well as the neutral countries—Spain, Portugal and their possessions. In addition, there were other sections: topographical intelligence, 5; the production of geographical handbooks, 6; enemy technical developments, 7; communications, 9; the security of British codes and ciphers, 10; the photographic library, 11; the intelligence summaries prepared for the chiefs of staff, the prime minister and the War Cabinet, 12; and propaganda, 19.

Section 14 was Godfrey's secretariat; and Section 8, the Operational Intelligence Centre (OIC), led by Lieutenant Commander Norman Denning, kept control of and disseminated a vast range of intelligence, from sightings of ships and aircraft from paid observers to information derived from captured documents and prisoners of war. Located in the claustrophobic, dungeon-like atmosphere of the Citadel—the concrete, brown bunker awkwardly attached to the Old Admiralty Building—the OIC handled the most vital of all intelligence traffic: Ultra—Signals Intelligence, or "Special Intelligence" as the navy also called it. Here, via a specifically dedicated underground cable from the Naval Section at Bletchley Park, staff kept their fingers on the pulse of the war at sea, tracking movements of deadly U-boat wolf packs, German raiders, and their super-battleships the Bismarck and the Admiral Von Tirpitz.

Despite weekly staff meetings and daily conferences of the "inner circle" of the NID, all these sections operated independently of one another. Section 17, Godfrey's personal staff, including Ian Fleming, was the essential link that conected the whole structure.

The task Godfrey gave Section 17 was to coordinate intelligence internally and to liaise between Naval Intelligence and the other intelligence bodies. Before long, as the demands of war increased, its role began to enlarge in scope and importance as it connected with the multiple arms of the entire Allied intelligence machinery. Section 17 in turn divided into subsections: 17P handled Ultra, the secret intelligence derived from breaking German and Italian naval ciphers; 17M specialized in German agents' traffic; 17Z focused on propaganda; and 17F, under Ian Fleming, coordinated and controlled them all.[59] Godfrey wasn't interested in a passive intelligence-collection body that waited for information to arrive on its doorstep from sources that might magically appear. Rather, he demanded that all his staff move aggressively to develop and maintain intelligence pipelines that provided the raw natural resources vital to the Empire's national interest. To meet that expectation, Section 17, and Fleming, had to maintain close contact with the full range of intelligence departments and committees, ensuring that Godfrey and his inner circle had access to all planning reports, memoranda, operational orders and signals, with advanced warning of all upcoming "futures," to use the naval parlance for these operations.[60]

Fleming's role in the NID quickly evolved into much more than that of personal assistant or liaison officer, with Godfrey increasingly counting on his dauphin to represent him officially on various interdepartmental committees and to put his operating vision for a decentralized intelligence division into action. Fleming handled both general and highly sensitive portfolios such as the Joint Intelligence Committee, which sent its advice to the chiefs of staff, the prime minister and the War Cabinet. He also maintained an intimate working relationship with the nascent Political Warfare Executive (PWE), designed to attack the German economy in particular, and the highly trained Special Operations Executive (SOE), which had been established by Cabinet in July 1940 "to coordinate all action, by way of subversion and sabotage, against the enemy overseas" and, as Churchill instructed, "set Europe ablaze!"[61] Likewise, he was required to meet with Sir Stewart Menzies, who had taken over as the new head, or "C," of the Secret Intelligence Service and the Ultra pipeline it provided. In addition, Fleming kept in touch with the Inter-Services Security Board (ISSB) and various joint operations and planning staffs—the Chief of Combined Operations (CCO), the Geographical Handbook Section, and one of Godfrey's beloved personal projects, the Inter-Services Topographical Department (ISTD) based in Oxford.[62]

As Fleming's responsibilities evolved, he took on more than his pay grade demanded, fulfilling in many ways what Godfrey hoped to take from the Blinker Hall tradition. According to Norman Denning, "Ian had enormous flair, imagination, and ability to get on with people . . . He could fix anyone or anything, if it was really necessary."[63] This talent was not lost on Godfrey, who strangely confided in his memoirs that "Ian should have been DNI and I his naval adviser," and that "if he had been ten years older and I ten years younger, this might have had the elements of a workable proposition."[64]

Winston Churchill, who told King George VI that "it was thanks to Ultra that we won the war," at his desk in the Cabinet Room at Number 10 Downing Street, the prime minister's residence.

Godfrey enlisted Fleming to act as his intermediary with Winston Churchill, but even then the strained relationship between the PM and the DNI continued to deteriorate throughout Godfrey's tenure. Churchill's determination to add "master strategist" to his role as "master statesman" led him to intrude on other people's responsibilities, and Godfrey had little patience with his constant interference or with his habit of massaging or intentionally misconstruing intelligence to fit his policy and public relations schemes. Early in the war Churchill inflated the number of U-boats sunk to boost public morale; and he constantly flooded Naval Intelligence with his "prayers"—nightly letters that began "Pray tell me . . ." or "Pray, why does this have to be?"—for which he insisted the explanations and answers must be provided the following day. Making matters worse, these requests usually came in the form of pointed, harshly toned attacks that Godfrey found condescending and challenging to answer. In an effort to placate the prime minister and keep him at arm's length, he turned the task over to Fleming, who, with his writer's skill, accomplished it with great aplomb.

The first eighteen months of the war were desperate times for Great Britain. Starting in September 1939, Hitler's Nazi Germany overran Poland in just six weeks; then in April 1940 invaded Norway and Denmark, followed by Holland, Belgium and France a month later. By the end of May, in the legendary "Miracle of Dunkirk," some 330,000 British and French troops were hurriedly evacuated from the beaches around the French Channel port and brought back to England in more than seven hundred vessels, large and small, many of them pleasure craft, fishing smacks, barges and even paddle steamers. The dramatic and historic events changed the balance of power in Europe, with Germany now in firm control on the continent. Soon, Hitler turned his focus to the British Isles, planning to defeat the defending Royal Navy and Air Force as a precursor to a cross-channel seaborne invasion of England known as Operation Sea

Lion. Great Brtiain would be the final—and triumphant—point in his expansion west. Beginning in August 1940, the Battle of Britain raged as RAF fighters tangled with the Luftwaffe over the Channel and southern England. On September 7 the first bombs fell on London, and the terrorizing Blitz began. Meanwhile, Italy had announced a blockade of Britain's Mediterranean and African territories and, one month later, invaded Egypt. The tough, long-drawn-out campaign in North Africa began.

How far could Britain's armed forces be stretched? Already fighting to the death to defend their own country, they had now to protect their strategically important interests and territories in the Mediterranean, the Middle East and North Africa—all without the support they had counted on from France and its navy. And there was more: the British Isles are small, but over several centuries they had built up a vast empire reaching into North America, East and Southeast Asia, the Antipodes and Africa. Their prosperity and their glory depended on exporting what they produced at home and importing the raw materials from their colonies or dominions abroad. Now their very survival depended on command of the sea lanes to bring in the food, oil, military supplies and troops they needed to win the war. An unexpected break came near the end of September 1941 when Hitler, his Luftwaffe stunned by the RAF, suddenly called off the Battle of Britain. That led Churchill famously to declare to the battered but resilient island, "Never in the history of human conflict has so much been owed by so many to so few."

Hitler, turning his forces to the east, launched an invasion of the Soviet Union in the summer of 1941. For Britain, even this momentous event came with a price: Stalin would join Great Britain in her fight against the Axis Powers, but to participate fully in the struggle, he demanded supplies—and in vast quantities for a vast nation. To seal this fragile new alliance, Churchill promised Stalin that convoys of ships would deliver essential military and other goods to the northern ports of Archangel and Murmansk. And so British command of the sea lanes suddenly extended northeast far into the Baltic as well.

In these dire circumstances, Churchill counted on men with imagination and daring to help shape the war effort. And characters such as John Godfrey and Ian Fleming were more than happy to play a role.

Godfrey had early on allowed Fleming the freedom to exercise his initiative and his creative abilities. Before long, the young assistant took over intelligence planning within the Naval Intelligence Division, "for which he had a marked flair." To Godfrey, Fleming was, above all, a classic "ideas man."[65] In truth, however, Fleming's original and creative approach to intelligence planning and gathering bounced between the professional and the amateurish. He believed in being open to "the unexpected" or "the chance remark" that might provide a shortcut to answer some unsolved riddle.[66] As Dennis Wheatley, the bestselling writer of thrillers and adventure stories, who was also one of Churchill's "Deception Planners" charged with developing ways to deceive the enemy, recalled, "I had quite a number of dealings with Fleming . . . he was full of ideas not only for helping to stop the invasion, but for our eventual plans to land on the continent."[67] Their relationship included the planning period for both the Dieppe Raid and Operation Torch, the Allied invasion of French North Africa in November 1942, where Lieutenant Alan Schneider, an American officer specifically attached to Fleming from the U.S. Office of Naval Intelligence, recorded that "we were both ideas men and would come up with all sorts of hare-brained schemes, making sure that someone else would have to carry them out."[68]

In the desperate and wild atmosphere of the war, schemes that today seem absolutely fantastic were regularly hatched by men and women—many of them very young—striving by any means to derail the Germans. Some were remarkably successful. Fleming began with modest yet devious ruses, such as employing an actor to create a character who would appeal to the vanity and snobbery of a particular highbrow German naval officer during interrogation, or disguising an officer as a priest to extract vital information from a U-boat captain during confession.[69] He then went on to more creative schemes, such as his plan with another writer, Aleister Crowley, an occultist and self-proclaimed "wickedest man in the world," to interfere with the reliance some in the Nazi hierarchy placed on astrology and the occult. He had two objectives in mind: to lure a high-ranking Nazi official to defect, and to buy time for Britain to recover from the fall of France by persuading German authorities through deliberately placed deceptive horoscopes that an invasion of England in the summer of 1940 was not in the stars.

In another scheme designed to hide the code-breakers' work at Bletchley Park and the signals intelligence funnelling into the Operational Intelligence Centre, Fleming introduced the cover story that British intelligence employed "Pendulum Practitioners" to find U-boat positions at sea by swinging pendulums over a map.[70] Encouraged, he initiated other, far more exotic plans that were approved by the admiring Godfrey and developed right through to the final planning stages. They never came to full fruition, however, or were scrapped at the last moment because the circumstances changed.

Operations Goldeneye and Tracer were two such plans from 1941. They were designed to enable Britain to keep monitoring what was happening in Spain and especially in the Mediterranean should Germany invade that country or General Franco enter into an alliance with Hitler. In February that year, as Fleming developed plans for Goldeneye, he visited Madrid, seeking ways to establish liaison offices in that city and also across the sea in Tangier with secure cipher leads to London. This operation seems to have had special meaning for Fleming: when the war was finally over, he bought an estate in Jamaica that he named Goldeneye, and there between 1951 and 1964 he wrote all twelve of his spy thrillers featuring the fictional MI6 officer James Bond.

Operation Tracer was far more elaborate, planned to cope with a possible takeover of the strategically important British colony and military base of Gibraltar—the island guarding the entrance to the Mediterranean Sea. Fleming had an underground bunker constructed there, carved into the towering rock face. If the Germans did manage to invade the island, a specially trained team of agents, including doctors and wireless operators, would be sealed into the cavern, with no chance of escape for at least a year and possibly much longer. Outfitted with provisions, wireless sets, and observation posts camouflaged from view, the team would report on Axis naval traffic squeezing through the narrow Strait of Gibraltar until the Allies could invade the island and rescue them. If time ran out, however, the agents would be left to their own devices. As things turned out, both Operations Goldeneye and Tracer were cancelled in August 1943, after the threat of a Nazi invasion of Spain had evaporated.

As the urgency to win the war intensified, Fleming became ever bolder in his schemes. "It was an atmosphere," Donald McLachlan wrote in his account of James Bond's origins in Naval Intelligence, "in which ordinary ideas of fair play and morality were not so much exploded as subtly and indeed pleasantly corrupted."[71] Fleming had found his niche: dreaming up intelligence-driven operations fostered by desperation and opportunity, harnessed to action with Godfrey's blessing and the formidable decentralized authority that came with it—all within a Churchill-inspired atmosphere that permitted and indeed encouraged the implementation of ruthless special operations.

In this environment, as Britain now strove to gather in the intelligence it needed to keep its sea lanes open and protect them from attack by Germany's navy, including its deadly U-boat fleet, the focus of the Admiralty took a new twist: to steal, or "pinch," materials—whether from the Kriegsmarine's ships at sea or, later, from their shore-based facilities—that were crucial to the code-breakers at Bletchley Park.

THREE

A RUTHLESS START

Public opinion seems to regard incendiary bombing, napalm and propaganda as respectable activities that can be indulged in by civilized powers without loss of face. Murder, arson, eavesdropping and the use of noxious gasses are not quite U. Where should the line be drawn, is there a moral issue, or are our perceptions of right and wrong permanently blunted?[1]

—Admiral John Godfrey, Director
Naval Intelligence Division (Retired), 1966

A solitary German Heinkel He 111 bomber, camouflaged with grey-green and sky-blue wash, dropped from the clouds to under fifteen hundred feet, trailing a long cone of smoke from what appeared to be its port engine, before levelling out temporarily, allowing the crew onboard to prepare for a dicey crash landing midway across the murky, frigid English Channel. The sight of a German bomber in obvious distress over the narrowest part of the Channel, near Dover, was not uncommon: during the previous eight weeks, beginning in September 1940, the Battle of Britain had shifted into its Blitz phase, which would last more than a year, with RAF fighters or British anti-aircraft gunners on the ground slowly racking up "kills" of German intruder aircraft with increasing frequency. Any German bomber unlucky enough to suffer damage over England, as this one surely had, might possibly be able to limp out to sea and into the waiting arms of a friendly German R- or M-boat—minesweeping vessels whose crews were generally on the alert to pluck downed men from the treacherous mid-Channel waters. With British cities ablaze, civilians dying or uprooted, the nation's children and some of its cultural treasures evacuated inland or abroad, and the spectre of an imminent German invasion looming over England, the fate of falling into British hands was not the preferred option for any enemy personnel.

On board the bomber, the crew of five prepared to "pancake" the wounded "bird" just as the second engine cut out, leaving the plane gliding silently in a permanent but gentle descent towards the water. At a thousand feet, one member threw caution aside and, abandoning the usual coded procedure, dispatched a distress call in plain German to any vessel in the area. A German patrol boat swiftly appeared. Crashing through the waves, it ploughed towards a position just a few hundred yards from what it expected would be the touchdown point of the falling bomber.

Breaking the near silence, calls to "hang on tight" joined the whistle of the wind snaking through the bullet-riddled fuselage and the cracked panes of the nose canopy. The plane bounced once on the water and spun clockwise almost ninety degrees in a slow-motion pirouette before settling with its nose pointing towards the oncoming rescue craft, just fifteen hundred feet away and closing in fast. In no time, it seemed, the crew regained their senses and, with clockwork precision, following the drill they had rehearsed in training, popped off the cover of the escape hatch and deployed the tiny dinghy. Clad in regulation khaki Luftwaffe flight suits, sporting bulky yellow Mae

West–style flotation devices, and with flight goggles hung around their necks, their wedge caps replaced by bloodied bandages, the men rowed hard towards their rescuers, waving frantically, shouting phrases in excited German clipped by the wind. The *Räumboote*, or R-boat, crew responded with the obligatory toss of a towline to draw them to the rescue craft.

Just as their deliverance seemed complete, a siren blared, summoning the R-boat crew to action stations, followed by shouts of "*Jabo! Jabo!*" (for *Jagdbomber*, fighter bomber) and the ripping sound of 20 mm and 37 mm flak guns on the aft deck discharging shells skywards. The rising stream of yellow tracers picked out a tiny black speck descending rapidly from four thousand feet above, revealing within seconds the distinctive mono-winged shape of an RAF Lysander reconnaissance aircraft making straight for the scene, firing all the while. With the attention of the R-boat crew fully engaged in fending it off as it swooped down, the Lysander suddenly banked left to drop its bomb load hundreds of yards from its intended mark. At that moment the "German" bomber crew sprang into action to launch their Trojan Horse ploy.

Pulling out weapons hidden on the rubber dinghy and tucked into their Luftwaffe flight suits, the British commandos boarded the R-boat, surprising the crew of seventeen and killing or capturing most in the first few seconds. After a cursory search of the boat to ensure they had subdued everyone on board, they located and seized their target: a three-rotor version of a German naval Enigma machine with its associated code books and setting sheets. Only then did they turn their attention to the captured crew members, whom they quickly ushered to the aft deck. In unison, the commandos raised their weapons and opened fire, eliminating all witnesses to the pinch, before unceremoniously tipping the bodies overboard and setting course for the nearest English port. This move indicated to the circling Lysander pilot above that the ruse, appropriately code-named Operation Ruthless, had succeeded and that the intelligence booty was en route to Commander Ian Fleming, the author of the scheme, waiting in the port of Dover to deliver the machine and its code books safely into the hands of the cryptographers at Bletchley Park.

In reality, Operation Ruthless never came off as planned. Fleming, with co-operation from the RAF, had indeed drawn up a highly detailed "script" for the mission, as outlined above—one that demonstrated his characteristic flair for the dramatic. At the time, Operation Ruthless was highly secret, and it has long been believed that the operation never took place; even in the context of what was becoming Britain's fight for survival, Ruthless crossed the line into the uncomfortable realm of war crimes. Some accounts have suggested that an official farther up the chain of command at Admiralty intelligence than his boss John Godfrey reined him in and forced the abortion of the mission. But those accounts are wrong: recently declassified files reveal that Ruthless did go ahead, following the script devised by Fleming, but twice it came up empty.

Ruthless was conceived in early September 1940, in the wake of Winston Churchill's "finest hour" speech, in which he warned that the very survival of Western civilization now rested with the British, who stood alone against Nazi tyranny. In this context, there can be little doubt that the "intelligence booty" Fleming sought in Ruthless was akin to the Holy Grail for the cryptographers at Bletchley Park. Fleming had dreamed up the operation to assist the gifted cryptographers who worked in Bletchley's Naval Section—brilliant mathematicians, physicists and classical scholars such as Dillwyn "Dilly" Knox, Alan Turing and Peter Twinn. These men now found themselves stymied in their critical struggle to break into German naval communications enciphered on a specially designed Enigma encryption machine. Despite their impressive intellectual efforts, they desperately needed "cribs," or "cheats"—plain-language German text—that they could match up with a stretch of cipher text and thus discover the daily "key" setting, or password, which would unlock the contents of the top secret

German messages. Depending on how quickly they could complete this process, they would provide Godfrey's Naval Intelligence Division with access to real-time enemy naval communications. That breakthrough would give a priceless advantage to an island nation facing German invasion—one increasingly forced to rely on its overseas empire and on troops drawn from its far-flung dominions for the raw materials and manpower necessary to fight on in the war.

Dilly Knox—the great Oxford classicist who had been recruited to work for the Royal Navy's First World War cryptographic bureau housed in Room 40 of the Old Admiralty Building in London—had suggested to Fleming that he send a bogus signal to the Germans asking them to resend the upcoming keys for the Enigma machines— keys that changed daily. Politely rejecting the idea, Fleming informed Knox that "the possibility should be examined and something got ready and kept ready for use in an emergency."[2] In fact, Fleming considered the idea foolhardy: not only would it alert the Germans to what they were after, forcing them to strengthen their signals security, but it would reveal how much the Allies depended on this intelligence source and their potential method of decryption. Rather, he thought, the material had to be pinched, and with a velvet touch so the Germans would never catch on that their encryption system had been compromised in any fundamental way. It was one thing for the Germans to suspect the British of attempting to crack their codes and ciphers, or even succeeding on a limited and temporary basis; it was another to have clear proof of systematic success or the likely method of achieving it. As long as the British could continue to cover or camouflage their pinch operations and any breakthroughs they made, they could benefit from a steady stream of bona fide intelligence drawn from the proverbial horse's mouth. The fundamental trait of any pinch operation is the need to "fox the enemy," and that in its extreme form is what Fleming planned by engaging in wholesale murder for Operation Ruthless.

On September 12, Fleming had outlined the plot for Ruthless in a memo to John Godfrey, who eagerly approved the plan. He then approached Mountbatten's predecessor at Combined Operations, Admiral Sir Roger Keyes, and asked him to organize Ruthless under the auspices of his headquarters. Fleming was quickly rebuffed: Keyes deemed the size of the operation "too small to come within their charter."[3] Undaunted, Godfrey decided to carry out the plan as an Admiralty operation and presented the scheme to the nascent Joint Intelligence Committee (where he sat as the navy's representative), which quickly sanctioned the endeavour. Godfrey then obtained full approval from Admiral Dudley Pound, the First Sea Lord, and from Air Chief Marshal Sir Cyril Newall, the head of the Royal Air Force, who offered support from No. 11 Fighter Group—which, two years later, would support the Dieppe operation. This co-operation was crucial because the RAF agreed not only to clear the vital airspace over the Channel needed at the height of the Battle of Britain but to provide the captured German bomber—the decoy—with a pilot to fly it. In addition, it would train the commandos who made up the rest of the crew, and supply their German uniforms and weapons. Newall also offered an operational base, a wireless net to track the events, and an RAF Lysander reconnaissance aircraft, plus a specially sequestered hangar to harbour the crew and the cover rumour that the crew were a special "spy party" set to land soon in Germany.[4]

The mission would start at dawn, when the captured bomber would take off and join the tail of other German aircraft making their way home across the Channel from their nightly raids on British cities. With German rescue boats working on a grid pattern, it was more than likely that the "German" crew or the Lysander would find a lone victim not long after getting airborne. Once spotted, the reconnaissance aircraft would vector the bomber onto a collision course with the vessel, and the ruse would unfold: in quick succession the crew would send a distress signal, cut one engine, light a smoke candle to simulate a fire on board, dive quickly, and crash-land the plane in the Channel in the path of the advancing rescue boat. Once down safely, they would deploy their raft, load their weapons, and scuttle the bomber so it would sink quickly and remove any temptation on the part of the rescue boat to call in additional reinforcements for salvage purposes.

With commandos in full paddle towards the rescue vessel, the Lysander would dive out of the sky, drawing the crew's attention, and make a half-hearted strafing run, just missing the ship. Taking full advantage of this diversion, Fleming's commando unit would then board the vessel, capture and kill the German crew, commandeer the vessel and its Enigma machine and code books, and hightail it back to the nearest British port, shadowed by RAF aircraft to prevent prying eyes from spotting the results of the privateering operation. In case things went wrong, Fleming prepared a cover story to obscure the pinch nature of the mission and prevent suspicion that the special party were after more "valuable targets than simply a rescue boat."[5] Should the commandos fall into German hands alive, their story— confirmed by follow-up communiqués dreamed up by Fleming— would be that the mission was "a lark by a group of young hot-heads who thought the war was too tame and wanted to have a go at the Germans. They had stolen a plane and equipment and had expected to get into trouble when they got back."

Contrary to historical accounts that claim Fleming's flight of fancy never passed beyond the planning stage and was in fact curbed in utero, Ruthless did in fact go into operation on October 16, 1940. However, with no potential victim sighted, the mission was postponed, and Fleming, who had joined the crew at their air base before takeoff, was summoned back to the Admiralty in London to await a better opportunity, likely in the Portsmouth area. The surviving records show that Fleming remounted the operation just five days later, but it too suffered the same inglorious fate, leaving the pinch on hold.[6]

Even though Operation Ruthless did not reach its desired dramatic climax, its authorization in as wild and cutthroat a fashion as Fleming originally conceived it clearly shows the lengths to which NID would go in order to obtain what the cryptographers at Bletchley needed to press on with their vital work. Perhaps more important, Ruthless demonstrates that operations of a Machiavellian nature had found official acceptance with the heads of both the Royal Navy and the RAF, along with the Joint Intelligence Committee, all eager to foster pinch operations of varying brands at one of the most desperate and pivotal moments in British history.

"Far be it from me to paint a rosy picture of the future," Winston Churchill told a worried House of Commons in the weeks following Operation Ruthless. "Indeed, I do not think we should be justified in using any but the most sombre tones and colours while our people, our Empire and indeed the whole English-speaking world are passing through a dark and deadly valley."[7] Britain, as the prime minister so eloquently expressed it, was "alone." The fate of the democratic world, not only of the British Empire, hung in the balance: an accumulation of recent events had fundamentally changed the complexion of the entire conflict, and in particular of the critical war at sea.

Just thirteen months before, in September 1939, Churchill had set out to "contain" the German fleet. A similar policy had been successfully adopted during the Great War of 1914–18, when a blockade had hemmed German surface and U-boat fleets into their home waters and prevented them from breaking out into the Atlantic Ocean, or elsewhere, to wreak havoc on British merchant shipping. For Great Britain, a small island nation with a far-flung empire, control of the sea routes has always been essential for its prosperity and, in times of conflict, its survival. Without an unfettered flow of imports and exports, it cannot—then or now—feed its people or maintain its economy. But as the

world once again veered towards the outbreak of war, the naval authorities did not seem particularly worried. The German navy, they said,
with fewer than thirty serviceable U-boats and only a small number of
modern and powerful surface raiding craft, presented a potential
rather than an imminent threat.

This complacent view changed radically when, shortly after the start
of hostilities, a handful of submarines skulked through the less than
hermetically sealed blockade and made a harsh impression on both the
Admiralty and the British psyche. On September 3, 1939, a lone
U-boat managed to sink the liner SS *Athenia* on its way from Glasgow to
Montreal, with some 1,420 on board. More than a hundred passengers
perished that day, including the first Canadian to die from enemy
action in the Second World War, ten-year-old Margaret Hayworth.[8] The
loss of the *Athenia* and the child's death deeply affected Canadians.
Newspapers publicized the story widely, some calling it "Canadians'
rallying point."

Two weeks later, submarine U-29 sank the British aircraft carrier
HMS *Courageous*, an event surpassed only by the actions of Günther
Prien, who, on October 14, slipped his U-47 into the home of the
British fleet at Scapa Flow in the Orkney Islands in Scotland and,
under the nose of the Royal Navy, sank HMS *Royal Oak* while at anchor.
Churchill, now in his second stint as First Lord of the Admiralty, was
apoplectic. One way to avoid catastrophe at sea, he then astutely realized, was to revive the ability British intelligence had possessed in the
First World War to read enciphered German naval messages in order
to reveal U-boat locations and, with luck, their plans for attack well in
advance of first contact.

Ultra or, as it was originally known in naval circles, Special
Intelligence, was initially dismissed by British naval commanders, who
either misunderstood its vast potential or were ignorant of its past
success. Relying on conventional and less profound sources of intelligence, such as aerial photographs, prisoner-of-war interrogations,

naval attaché reports and traditional espionage informants, or forgo-
ing it altogether, they blundered into a series of disasters in 1940
that thrust Special Intelligence back into the limelight. The first came
in April, when decrypted traffic clearly showed the German interest
in Norway; this intelligence went for naught, leading the British and
French to engage in a series of costly and ultimately futile actions that
paved the way for Hitler's conquest of that resource-rich country.
The next disaster was the sinking of the lumbering aircraft carrier
HMS *Glorious* and her two destroyer escorts at the hands of the German
battle cruisers *Scharnhorst* and *Gneisenau*. Despite warnings from Bletchley
Park's Naval Section that the two predators had left German ports and
were now on the prowl, the *Glorious* was left to their mercy on her
journey home from Norwegian waters.

But worse was still to come. By the fall of 1940, after the rapid
German advance through Norway, Denmark, Holland, Belgium and
France, the Kriegsmarine was able to establish a presence along the
entire coast of Western Europe, from the Arctic to the Bay of
Biscay—a position never seriously considered by the Admiralty, and
one that clearly threatened British survival. Luftwaffe aircraft and
German U-boats could now reach the sea lanes around the British
Isles, and their surface raiders could hide in French ports if they
chose to break out of their North Sea or Norwegian ports past the
now-crumbling British blockade. The French fleet, which the British
had counted on to provide additional escort vessels for its merchant-
ship traffic, surrendered to the Germans soon after the Italians
declared war on France and England in June. Almost overnight, these
events extended the Royal Navy's area of responsibility and stretched
its resources to the limit, if not beyond. The Admiralty now had to
contend in the Mediterranean with the Italian navy, which was
endangering the Suez Canal and British holdings in Egypt and the oil
fields in the Middle East. Moreover, on the other side of the world an
increasingly belligerent Japan, taking advantage of France's demise,

was making aggressive moves in Southeast Asia that threatened to spill over into the Indian Ocean, cutting Britain's lifeline to its Far East resources. Even more worrying, back in the English Channel, reports indicated ongoing preparations for a German amphibious invasion of England under the code name *Seelöwe* (Operation Sea Lion).

By October 1940, when Commander Ian Fleming was waiting in vain for Operation Ruthless to produce results, Great Britain had reached the lowest point in its history. At night, bombs rained down on British cities; by day, what was left of the British army units that had escaped from Dunkirk in June attempted to re-form and rebuild their depleted ranks, augmented by the Home Guard units that, for lack of weapons, drilled with broomsticks while expecting a German invasion at any moment. In London, plans went into effect to evacuate children, treasure and the British government to safer locations in the countryside or in other parts of the Empire, and to continue the fight even after the first Nazi jackboot landed near Dover. On the high seas, during this "Happy Time," as the German U-boat crews ghoulishly called it, increasing numbers of German submarines armed with potent torpedoes sent hundreds of thousands of tons of merchant shipping and their precious cargoes to the bottom. Meanwhile, seemingly indestructible German super-battleships—Bismarck and soon Tirpitz along with other formidable surface raiders—sat poised to pounce from their lairs and join the feeding frenzy. The overstretched and beleaguered Royal Navy and RAF were the last lines of defence. With England's survival hanging in the balance, breaking the Enigma codes was seen as nothing short of essential.

The failure of Ruthless and the subsequent postponement of further attempts struck through the hearts of the cryptographers labouring in the huts at Bletchley Park. "Turing and Twinn came to me like undertakers cheated of a nice corpse," Frank Birch, who had served in both the Royal Navy and Naval Intelligence in the First World War and who now headed Bletchley's Naval Section in Huts 4 and 8, wrote to Fleming.

"The burden of their song," he continued, was the "importance of a pinch." Did the authorities in the Naval Intelligence Division realize, he asked despairingly, that without a pinch "there was very little hope of their deciphering current, or even approximately current, Enigma for months and months and months—if ever"?[9] With the backdrop of the war at sea ever present in their minds, the cryptographers had toiled and struggled in vain to produce a breakthrough in decrypting the naval Enigma machine. Fleming reassured Birch that they "needed to have no fear that the value of a pinch was underestimated."[10]

The magnitude of all these developments in Europe and the Mediterranean, as well as at home, caught the Admiralty off guard. Nothing since the days of Napoleon Bonaparte had posed such a potent threat as the Axis air force, surface fleet and U-boat menace did now. For the British government, the ability to monitor an opponent's plans, intentions, capabilities and movements well before any action was under way was of prime concern, particularly for the Royal Navy. In naval warfare, the key feature that more often than not determines victory or defeat is surprise. With its resources stretched to the breaking point, the Admiralty could not afford to keep watch in the physical sense on all parts of its empire, and it now needed to develop and maintain a highly accurate intelligence weapon to ensure a cost-effective approach to imperial defence. Accurate insight into the enemy situation would allow the Royal Navy to effect an "economy of force," positioning its assets wisely around the globe and eliminating, or at least reducing, the odds of overspending in one area or being caught short in another.

To this end, the Admiralty spared little expense in developing the capability to monitor the Kriegsmarine's situation daily or even hourly, through cryptography and its "poor relations" in the signals intelligence family—direction finding, or DFing (establishing the direction from which a received signal was transmitted); radio finger printing, or RFP (identifying a transmitter by photographing its wave form); and traffic analysis, or TINA (analyzing the characteristics of the radio operator himself).[11] Intelligence defined the command structures and orders of battle among the Admiralty's enemies and could tap into the minds of their rivals—Kriegsmarine commander Erich Raeder and U-boat fleet commander Karl Dönitz, among others—gauging their strengths and weaknesses and the way they intended to play the game.

From various forms of SIGINT—signals intelligence—the staff at the Operational Intelligence Centre (OIC), located in the brown bombproof bunker connected to the Admiralty Citadel in London, could infer the number of enemy vessels in repair or under construction and project when and where they would make an appearance on the high seas. They could discover, often in advance, new technological developments that might swing the naval balance of power. Perhaps most important, in general terms they could locate and track surface raiders and U-boats from their bases right across the Atlantic Ocean, revealing where the giant surface raiders Bismarck, Tirpitz or others might suddenly appear or where U-boats were gathering in wolf packs to attack oncoming Allied convoys bringing vital supplies to wartime Britain. This same information, relayed by the OIC to the convoy's command with a simple "change course to . . ." message, allowed them either to scatter, in the case of raiders, or to sidestep the submarines lying in wait.

Within the mysterious world of naval intelligence, where signals intelligence reigned as the most vital of all intelligence sources, a pecking order developed. Ultra, a subset within SIGINT, dominated during the first half of the war. Reports from human sources—aerial photographs, traffic analysis and radio finger printing—which suggested that something was stirring with a particular vessel or group of vessels, were helpful and sometimes adequate, but Ultra went farther because it could provide direct or indirect information about Nazi Germany's intentions and capabilities, sometimes in great detail. When it was available, Ultra provided the most accurate and consistent form of intelligence, and in this sense it was priceless.

Fortunately, by the early months of 1941, Ultra did triumph—and it did so because of the changing nature of naval warfare. Unlike its army or air force counterparts, which restricted the use of the Enigma device to the upper echelons of high command, the Kriegsmarine relied on Enigma-encrypted communications for almost all classes of ships and its multitude of shore facilities. With the war at sea controlled for the most part by wireless communication since the turn of the century, the world's navies strove to develop codes and ciphers to protect their top secret communications from enemy cryptographic efforts. The seemingly impregnable Enigma machine appeared to be the answer for the German navy. Almost every vessel in the fleet was outfitted with this device—from their super-battleships, pocket battleships, cruisers, destroyers, torpedo boats and U-boats right down to their minesweepers, E-boats, R-boats and flak ships, as well as their anti-submarine and weather trawlers. They all enjoyed the anonymity of Enigma-encrypted communications not only with each other but with shore-based facilities as well. And it was this wide distribution that offered John Godfrey and Ian Fleming such fertile ground from which to pinch the materials so badly needed by the cryptographers at Bletchley Park.

The Enigma machine came to obsess anyone involved with decryption, no matter how marginal the association. It was an intellectual Everest, enticing, taunting, and at times seeming to ridicule its opponents as no other technology in existence had done. It posed impossible riddles and engaged some of the finest minds in England. It led to nightmares, emotional and psychological breakdown, and universal frustration; yet, given the secrecy surrounding it, for decades only muted glory came to those who eventually conquered it at Bletchley Park.

Originally designed in the closing months of the First World War by Arthur Scherbius, a German engineer, for commercial use to protect banking and industrial secrets, the aptly named Enigma encryption device was indeed a riddle, and it soon drew the interest of the German armed forces in the interwar period. Physically, the machine resembled a portable typewriter with a keyboard, a plug board, an illuminated lamp board, and a set of three (later four) rotors that protruded through the top, giving the appearance of a large combination lock. The machine could encipher each letter of the alphabet individually, as opposed to other machines and forms of encryption that encoded complete words, word for word. The Enigma machine was far more subtle and therefore more difficult to crack. It did not actually transmit messages itself, as a wireless or telegraphy set would do. Rather, it scrambled or enciphered each letter of each word of a message into unintelligible gibberish, before transmission to a recipient via wireless. The recipient then deciphered the received message letter for letter using an identical Enigma machine set to exactly the same specifications.

Early in the 1920s, the Enigma machine had made its commercial debut on a limited basis. It was sold domestically on the premise that its contrived internal set-up was so complicated that, should it fall into the wrong hands, it would remain impregnable unless that person also possessed the current setting sheets displaying the exact configurations of the rotor wheels and the plug-board settings that changed daily. The beauty of these code sheets was that, with these materials in hand, the machine was foolproof, allowing any secretary, clerk and, later, private or naval rating to encipher material quickly and accurately after a modicum of instruction. The staggering number of variations of ciphered text that could be produced was virtually unlimited and became the machine's main selling feature. As one account later claimed, it could encipher "every book on earth . . . differently without the machine settings having to be repeated."[12] By 1926 the German navy, followed quickly by the army, saw Enigma's massive potential benefits and adopted it wholesale, with each service improving on the basic design, particularly once the Nazis came to power.

The version employed by the Kriegsmarine was more complex than the German army's version of Enigma. Housed in a square wooden lidded box that resembled a silverware case stamped with the trademark Enigma, the machine required only three rotor wheels but offered eight removable wheels in all, each of which had its own distinct electrical wiring.[13] These wheels formed the basis of the multilayered or multi-step design that proved the hallmark of its security. When the signals operator wanted to begin transmission of a message, or to receive one, while at sea or on shore, he needed to consult a bigram table and a key sheet that contained what we would today call the daily "password," or "pin" number.

OVERLEAF, LEFT: The three-wheel Enigma machine in its wooden carrying case (the trademarked moniker ENIGMA stamped on the inside front panel and the German instructions in the lid), ca. 1930s. In addition to the main keyboard with its raised keys, it has a plug board (bottom), three rotor wheels (at the back, behind the keys), and an illuminated lamp board (top).

TOP RIGHT: Two sets of spare rotor wheels for the three-wheel Enigma machine, in their carrying box. With each rotor wheel designed with its own unique electronic wiring system, these wheels were at the top of the list as targets for pinch operations during the first phase of the war.

BOTTOM RIGHT: Three rotor wheels laid out on their sides. The alphabet is visible around the edge of the top rotor wheel. The three central rotor wheels were selected from a box of five for the army and air force versions of the machine and eight for the naval version. Monthly orders listed on key sheets, tables and code books specified a new combination every day (A-B-C, E-G-H) as well as their relative order in the machine (II-IV-V, III-I-IV), etc.

In the first step, the bigram table produced a random letter set known as the indicator. This set was sent as the plain-text heading of the enciphered message to instruct the receiver how to set up the machine. The next step involved the daily key setting, which usually came every month in the form of a booklet, called a K-book, or in a set of sheets and tables printed in water-soluble ink. This information was issued to both the senders and the receivers of messages. To make sure they were on the same page, all the operators on a given network, after receiving the indicator, consulted these materials to establish the starting position of the machine—specifically, which three of the eight possible rotor wheels to insert into the naval version of the machine, and in what order to place them in the slots at the top. Each rotor wheel was wrapped with a removable rubber ring with letters of the alphabet stamped on it, which was then clipped in a preordained position, also listed in the key sheets. The operator turned each rotor wheel separately until they all reached the given starting position for the day listed on the key sheet. With each wheel corresponding to a letter of the alphabet, the operator then lined up the letters, as if lining up the numbers of a combination lock, to produce the key setting itself.

At this point yet another security layer appeared: the operator inserted the plug cables—similar to patch cords on a TV or sound system—into the plug board at the base of the machine in a particular configuration provided by the daily key sheet or, sometimes, to strengthen security, by a completely separate key sheet. That done, the operator was ready to type the text message he wanted to send on the keyboard directly connected electrically to the rotor wheels, which in turn were connected to the lamp board. On the lamp board was another alphabet, as on the keyboard, but the difference was that each letter lit up once the machine was in operation. With every punch of a key, an electrical pulse would race into the individual wiring of each rotor and turn the right-hand rotor one position, to select in random fashion another letter of the alphabet, which would appear in illuminated form to replace the plain-text letter in the original message. With each keystroke, the rotor would turn, providing another unique encrypted letter for the operator to note and write down—by all these means eventually creating an encrypted version of the formerly plain-text message. The message was then transmitted via wireless using Morse code.

When the message arrived, or was intercepted, it seemed to be unintelligible nonsense—unless the receiver had the corresponding key or password to unlock the true meaning of the message. With the key sheet in hand, the receiver proceeded in reverse steps, using his Enigma machine to decrypt the message and reveal its meaning in plain German text.[14]

To pry into an Enigma-enciphered message, cryptographers had to establish the machine's configuration, then which three of the eight wheels were in use, the clip position of the rings, and the setting of the three-letter key. Once that was done, they had to figure out the configuration of the plug board. Complicating this task was the fact that each service possessed its own keys and constantly introduced more keys and networks after every victory in Europe or every security scare. In 1940, for instance, the Kriegsmarine employed one basic key for Home Waters traffic, which it called *Heimisch*, or later *Hydra*, and which the British code-named *Dolphin*. After the German invasion of Western Europe, the navy branched out into more keys. By mid-1941 it had separate keys to denote Norwegian, Baltic and Mediterranean traffic. Eventually the U-boat fleet had its own unique key, code-named *Triton* by the Germans and *Shark* by the British, along with two special derivative keys that officers and staff (*Offizier* and *Stab*) used for highly sensitive messages. To complicate matters still more, each key could have further security precautions attached: there might be special instructions for different internal settings for the staff, in contrast to operational command, or even separate plug-board settings for individual commands or commanders.

Physically, the machine and its rotor wheels usually remained under the tightest security, with the operator given specific instructions to destroy the components if capture seemed imminent. The key sheets and code books, sometimes printed and stored for a month or even a year in advance, required special precautions. At sea, where capture and compromise could occur at any time, ships stored the requisite setting sheets for a limited period, such as thirty to ninety days. They were heavily guarded, either in the captain's safe or squirrelled away in his footlocker or the panelled wall of his cabin, or hidden in other parts of the vessel. On land, the shore-based facilities, depending on their function and position in the communications chain, could stock six or twelve months' worth of sheets and code books, likely in the commanding officer's safe. The German navy, like most of its counterparts, printed cipher materials in water-soluble ink so the writing would vanish if they were tossed into the sea by the crew.

On land or at sea, there were standard operating procedures calling for the destruction of the machine and its parts in the event of imminent capture: first, remove and dispose of the rotors; then pull out the plug-board cables; finally, destroy the machine completely or partially by physically smashing its components or by disposing of it in a way that would render recovery impossible. In some German shore-based facilities, such as in the heavily defended town of Dieppe, the Kriegsmarine trained special units to prepare for an attack: they would quickly gather all the machines, along with the code and cipher materials, and destroy them.

Given all these precautions, it is not surprising that the German high command placed such great faith in Enigma. Even if the Allies got a break, it would be limited in time and scope and therefore temporary in nature, meaning the Germans could simply let the current material expire, without going to the enormous expense of overhauling their entire signals system. Because of the time and energy required to wade through the data and decipher messages, they believed that any captured materials would yield vastly outdated information. According to the pre-war estimate, one Enigma machine could produce 10.5 quadrillion possible keys for each message, meaning it would take a thousand enemy cryptographers working with four captured or copied keys close to 1.8 billion years to test them all.[15]

However, the Nazi high command, despite some brilliant and maverick minds at work in their own code-breaking organization, Beobachtungsdienst, or B-Dienst for short, suffered from an institutionalized anti-intellectualism and arrogance that gave the British the time and space needed to conquer Enigma. The British harnessed their greatest intellectual resources right from the outbreak of war in 1939 and put them to work at Bletchley Park. They challenged these people to overcome the staggering odds and take the science of cryptography to levels never before imagined. To make an analogy, they stood the same chance of defeating the three-rotor naval Enigma in 1939 as an individual would have in winning a national lottery once a day, every day, for nearly one hundred years. Nevertheless, by mid-1941, the cryptographic team—led by the legendary Alan Turing, Peter Twinn and Dilly Knox, among many other stellar minds—had done just that. The journey to this great accomplishment was anything but smooth, however, and when Turing first took on the project with his team in Hut 8—the Bletchley hut devoted to cracking the naval Enigma ciphers—he did so under a cloud of pessimism.[16]

Fortunately, help for the Bletchley Park cryptographers came in several forms. First, they received tremendous aid from the work of exiled Polish cryptographers, who had pioneered the cryptographic assault on an earlier version of the German army Enigma in 1932 and who turned their work over to the British and French just before Germany invaded their country in 1939. The Poles invented the original Bombe, a high-speed electromechanical device designed specifically to attack Enigma encryption. It in turn was improved upon by Turing, who created the first machine able to decipher the German

encryption—something that Fleming would have appreciated, given his fascination with Charles Babbage's pioneering work in computers and cryptography.[17]

There were fundamental differences between the two designs. Unlike the Polish Bombe, which relied strictly on mathematical principles, Turing's Bombe was based on "cribs," or "cheats"—a system similar to possessing answers to one or more questions on the *Times* crossword which also hint at the solutions to other questions. In essence, the Bombe sifted through all the possible configurations of the three Enigma wheels, searching for a pattern of keyboard-to-lamp-board connections that would turn the encrypted letters into plain German.[18] Although the Bombe worked in mathematical terms at superhuman speed, reducing the man-hours needed to a mere fraction of what the human brain alone would have required, in real time during a war it simply wasn't fast enough. Each Bombe took days or even weeks to crack an out-of-date message from an Enigma key. Turing tried using one of his Polish-inspired inventions, "Banburismus"—a cryptographic process that in theory could speed up the machines by enabling code-breakers to narrow down the number of wheels that could have been in place when a message was

---

OPPOSITE: "The Prof": Dr. Alan Mathison Turing was a wild and eccentric genius among code-breakers. Often called the 'father of modern computing," he was a brilliant mathematician and logician who developed the idea of the modern computer and artificial intelligence. Turing's work helped develop the Bombe, an electromechanical device used to decrypt Enigma-encrypted messages, and later the world's first computer—the Colossus. His tragic death, whether suicide, accident or murder, has never been satisfactorily explained, although urban legend claims his death is reflected in the Apple logo: after being convicted of an illegal sexual relationship with a man a few years after the war, he was sentenced to chemical castration by hormone injection. In June 1954 he was found dead, after having allegedly bitten into an apple dipped in cyanide.

sent. Still, without any bigram tables to consult, he had no matching pieces of German and English text to help him reduce the odds.

Then a most fortuitous pinch of material in Norway provided just what Turing required to solve the problem.

On April 26, 1940, the German armed trawler *Schiff 26*, disguised to resemble the Norwegian vessel *Polaris*, which was taking mines and torpedoes to German forces in Narvik, crossed paths with the British destroyers HMS *Griffin* and HMS *Acheron*. The destroyers quickly disabled the trawler and captured her crew before they could destroy their cryptographic documents. The haul, delivered promptly to Bletchley Park, was a godsend for Turing: it revealed the precise form of the indicating system, the plug-board connections, and the starting positions of the three rotors for a twenty-four-hour period. In addition, the operators' log contained a significant stretch of plain text and enciphered material for the cryptographers to analyze.

These documents were the "cheat" they needed. Feeding the results of the Banburismus into the nascent Bombe, the result demonstrated, despite the out-of-date and essentially useless immediate results, that their overall deciphering approach had merit. Banburismus in itself was not a stellar leap forward, but it was still significant. As one veteran of Hut 8 recalled, it was "not easy enough to be trivial, but not difficult enough to cause a nervous breakdown."[19] Soon, however, the joy and relief felt within the sparse confines of Hut 8 turned into despair when the Germans changed their bigram tables just weeks later, in June of that year.

Ideally, the solution lay in building more Bombes that could work together, harnessing their collective might to break into intercepted Enigma messages. But each Bombe was extremely expensive and difficult to produce, and the cryptographers in Hut 8 did not have time on their side. Additional Bombes would take months or years to arrive, leaving pinched material the only alternative to enable the British to attack German naval codes and ciphers.

Thus, with the stark reality of defeat facing them in 1940, the various sections that made up British intelligence, and specifically naval intelligence, knew they had to get what they needed by any means at their disposal—and as quickly as possible. For the great mathematicians at Bletchley, Alan Turing and Peter Twinn, even a small pinch would again meet their immediate requirements. However, "if the whole bag of tricks was pinched," Frank Birch informed Fleming, "there'd be no delay at all."[20] "Ideally," he said, "those on board should not have been able to destroy anything," or have time to get rid of "papers on their persons, or to throw anything overboard."[21] Birch,

---

OVERLEAF, LEFT: Alan Turing's Bombe. In mathematical terms, it worked at "superhuman" speed. The Poles designed the original Bombe just before the Germans invaded Poland—a high-speed electromechanical solving device for Enigma. It in turn was improved upon by Turing, who created the first Bombe able to decipher the German encryption. As Jack Copeland describes in his book *Turing: Pioneer of the Information Age*: "The bombes were special-purpose electromechanical computers. At superhuman speed, a bombe searched through different possible configurations of the Enigma's wheels, looking for a pattern of keyboard-to-lampboard connections that would turn the coded letters into plain German. At root, though, the machinery depended entirely on human instinct: in order to set the process going, a carefully chosen crib was required."

TOP RIGHT: A close-up view of the Bombe. Each row contains thirty-six rotating drums that simulate the action of the rotor wheels on the Enigma machine, effectively functioning like twelve Enigma machines. It took hours to set up and required great care in handling as it contained live electrical wires that could electrocute a careless operator.

BOTTOM RIGHT: Members of the Women's Royal Naval Service, known as Wrens, skilfully operated the Bombe machines, which worked to speed up the code-breaking process. Allegedly, during a visit to Bletchley Park, Churchill thanked its hard-working, uncomplaining residents for "laying the golden eggs without cackling."

isolated at the Naval Section in Bletchley Park from the hub of the war effort in London, argued that alternative methods of capturing the essential materials should be examined and the concept of pinching continuously maintained. The Germans, he said, could "muck their machine about" at any moment, which would right away require another pinch. He demanded to know if there was "anything in the wind," because "there ought to be."[22]

The superficial treatment of Operation Ruthless in most past accounts portrays it as a lone-wolf operation, lacking in context or a sound basis, conceived by the impetuous Fleming and launched in cavalier style without any regard for its consequences. Recently declassified files clearly show that this interpretation needs overhauling. Once the Germans changed their bigram tables in June 1940, the Naval Intelligence Division, with Fleming in the lead, began a methodical and well-reasoned search for pinch targets within arm's reach of English shores. Researchers began tapping into the wireless frequency and plain-language traffic of German salvage ships operating in the Channel, and before long they had established a "hit list" of vessels that possessed Enigma machines and related material or other codes that could be used as temporary solutions to the problem. The list focused on four types of vessels: S-boats (patrol boats) or German motor torpedo boats known popularly as E-boats; German torpedo boats that resembled mini-destroyers; aircraft security boats specifically dedicated to the rescue of downed flyers and aircraft; and minesweeping craft such as R-boats, M-boats and minesweepers that occasionally carried out rescues at seas.

By early September, all this research was collected in a special report on the "Activities of German Naval Units in the Channel."[23] Without doubt, it made an impression on Fleming. The report analyzed the strengths and weaknesses of each potential target. The habits of S-boats and E-boats were difficult to read because, generally, they were night predators, attacking British coastal convoys before returning to friendly ports by first light. They had no specific routine or patrol area, so the chances of intercepting them were slim. The larger torpedo boats had arrived in the Channel only recently, so little was known yet about how they would use Enigma. Aircraft security boats, which operated from the Dutch, Belgian and French coasts and engaged in daily rescues of Luftwaffe airmen, remained too close to the German-occupied coast unless they could be drawn out into mid-Channel and away from the view of potential witnesses to a pinch. In addition, evidence suggested they did not carry Enigma at all, but rather a minor salvage code known as *Seenot*, which was not yet readable by Bletchley. That left the minesweepers as the most promising prey. They generally hugged the coast and operated daily off Boulogne and Calais, carrying out their sweeping duties unless interrupted by a distress call from a downed plane in mid-Channel.[24] Again, because they had no regular positions, intercepting them depended on a surprise attack—if they could be lured farther from the coast.

"Is it too fantastic to suggest," wrote Frank Birch in response to the report, "that efforts should be made to capture one of these in circumstances which would prevent the destruction of the Enigma Machine, attachments and papers?" He could not think how to attempt such a daring exploit himself, so turned it over to NID and the imaginative Ian Fleming. "We are incompetent to suggest the means," he admitted, "but the elements would seem to be surprise, shrapnel and boarding."[25] The result was Operation Ruthless, six weeks later.

In December, Birch, who was still wrestling with Enigma, put forward another proposal along similar lines. "Though operation Ruthless has been postponed on practical grounds," he wrote, "the reason which caused it to be proposed has lost none of its force."[26] That month new information obtained from traffic analysis surfaced to suggest that aircraft security vessels, once believed Enigma-free, now carried both naval and air force Enigma materials, along with lower-level material corresponding to the German naval air code and the *Seenot* code. Immediately they became prime targets for a pinch.

Birch and his colleagues in the Naval Section at Bletchley Park suggested a plan that same month that was almost a carbon copy of Operation Ruthless, except that this time it would be carried out by ships instead of aircraft. In this case French *chasseurs*, or patrol boats, in the employ of the Free French Vichy would carry the commando strike force to its target. The first victim decided on was the *Bernhard Von Tschirschky*, an 880-ton seaplane tender operated by the Luftwaffe. Travelling under cover of darkness or in the obscurity of last light, the *chasseur* would approach the *Von Tschirschky* using the appropriate signal to announce that it had wounded on board in need of immediate attention. Having learned the commander's name from an intercepted lower-level signal, the organizers in Naval Section suggested that the boarding party should shout out to him in perfect French or German as they approached, to gain the confidence of their intended victims. Once close enough, the raiders would open fire with their submachine and deck guns in an effort to panic and scatter the crew, followed by a tear-gas attack to incapacitate all aboard and prevent "destruction of the books and alteration of the settings of the Enigma machines." The planners placed great emphasis on this aspect of the mission, directing that the plug settings, locked in position by the commander, be left in place.[27]

In the end, the suggested operation against the *Von Tschirschky* was shelved, just as Ruthless had been. In a series of terse letters, the furious Frank Birch urged the head of Bletchley Park, Commander Alastair Denniston, to act aggressively towards the naval Enigma problem, telling him, "The present position is a nightmare . . . and it is wearing the life out of me . . . Not enough is being done to break German naval ciphers."[28] Birch's frustration boiled over to include shots at the Admiralty too, which he accused of foot-dragging, even though

Fleming and his section had provided clear evidence of the type of material to be pinched and where it could be found: "The long and short of it is that the Navy is not getting a fair dose."[29] Birch's solution went straight to the heart of the problem. He chided:

> Cryptographers at their present rate of advance . . . will trundle
> along, getting out odd days, but at ever increasing intervals from
> the present unless they are given either a pinch or a very large
> number of bombs [sic] . . . Well, the issue is a simple one. Tot up
> the cost and the difficulties and balance them against the value
> to the nation of being able to read current Enigma. The value of
> the latter has been put at 1,000,000 a day. Could the cost of any
> number of machines, plus the difficulties of making and run-
> ning them, exceed that value? . . . I have never been in favour of
> the very melodramatic Operation Ruthless, but there are many
> ways of trying to pinch a small craft intact—it was done in this
> last war, so why not in this? It certainly is not a forlorn hope, it
> only needs perseverance.[30]

Despite this bitter disappointment for the cryptographers at Bletchley Park at the end of 1940, it seems from the *Von Tschirschky* file that Ian Fleming and the Naval Intelligence Division did learn something of significance from contemplating the attempt. While tracking the movements of this seaplane tender, they came to realize that all ships at sea using Enigma needed to communicate with shore-based facilities strung along the Channel coast, which made these ports, with their naval headquarters and signals equipment, prime targets for a pinch as well. They also saw that vessels like the *Von Tschirschky*, as well as other types of hotly desired ships, maintained an operational course that started at Brest and made a pit stop in Cherbourg, before pushing on to their terminal in Dieppe.

FOUR

ANNUS MIRABILIS

The Atlantic is the vital area[,] as it is in
that ocean and that alone in which we can lose
the war at sea.

—Admiral Dudley Pound, First Sea Lord,
August 28, 1941

Annus mirabilis was the only phrase John Godfrey felt accurately
described the flood of captured material that transformed the complexion of the cryptographic war in 1941. And not only Godfrey—
many in the Naval Intelligence Division and at Bletchley Park rejoiced
in this "year of miracles," especially as the year had got off to a very
rocky start.[1] The frustration and impotence of the cryptographers in
those early weeks had mirrored the miserable collective experience of
the British people. Yet, in the vicissitudes of war, fortunes continuously
change, and as we shall see, the so-called miracle of 1941 would in
turn give way again to despair in 1942—and the pressing need for ever
more "pinch" missions on Bletchley Park's behalf.

For several weeks following the late summer of 1940, while nightly
bombings rocked London and other cities during the Blitz, the English

had faced the even greater threat of a German invasion from across the Channel. Mounting attacks by German U-boats reinforced the sense of smothering claustrophobia, as the submarines tightened their grip around the British Isles with each passing day. Admiral Karl Dönitz, the brilliant fifty-year-old commander of the submarine fleet, had convinced Hitler that his nimble underwater vessels, working together via radio communications in the "wolf pack" tactic he had devised, could locate, stalk and destroy the convoys and thereby starve Britain and its war economy into defeat.[2] Before long, the successes scored by the U-boats in this "Happy Time" transformed Germany's top-scoring aces—Otto Kretschmer, Fritz-Julius Lemp, Günther Prien and Joachim Schepke—into media darlings rivalling the famed German fighter aces of the First World War. In just six months between June and December 1940, U-boat attacks sank nearly 350 ships and claimed almost 3,000 lives in just 180 days, while only nine of these seemingly invincible submarines were lost. A distraught Churchill lamented, "Without ships, we cannot live, and without them we cannot conquer."[3]

It was staggering: in the first twenty-eight months of the war, U-boats claimed some 5.3 million tons of British and neutral shipping, or 1,124 ships—a loss rate five times greater than the number of ships currently under construction in British shipyards.[4] Planners projected there would be a seven-million-ton deficit in raw materials, including two million tons of food. But what really alarmed them was the 300,000-ton deficit in the crucial imports of oil that fuelled the British war machine. As imports fell to half their normal levels, strict rationing policies for food, petrol and other essential items in the United Kingdom had to be imposed, threatening to drain the already limited British morale and restrict the nation's ability to maintain, never mind expand, its power. And more bad news was about to come.

Although Hitler had neglected the U-boat fleet in the run-up to the war—a curious oversight given that German submarines had

almost crippled England during the First World War—these early successes soon translated into a crash building program that would see a fourfold increase in the number of U-boats threatening the vital Atlantic lifeline. By the end of 1941, eighty-eight U-boats (up from twenty-eight earlier in the war) were on patrol, even though twenty had already been sunk or captured. Beginning in July 1940, Hitler promised Admiral Dönitz twenty-five new submarines a month—meaning a grand total of three hundred within the year. Although it was questionable that Hitler would reach this target, Churchill, the chiefs of staff, the Admiralty and the NID were nonetheless all deeply worried.

Submarines, however, were not the only problem. The Germans also possessed a small but potent surface raiding fleet that posed a major threat to Great Britain's Atlantic trading routes, even though it was not yet large enough to rival the Royal Navy ship for ship. Admiral Erich Raeder, the head of the Kriegsmarine, was no fool: he had nothing like the Kaiser's Grand Fleet of the earlier war, but he knew that simply maintaining a "fleet in being" to make periodic convoy raids would do more to tie down British resources than actually engaging in a traditional Götterdämmerung-style showdown with the Royal Navy. In many ways the war at sea was a war of innuendo and perception—not about what your opponent will do but what he could do. However, Hitler grew tired of this chess-like waiting game being played at sea and, in the spring of 1941, ordered his surface raiders, including the super-battleship Bismarck, to launch attacks on British convoys to supplement the

---

OPPOSITE: Admiral Karl Dönitz, head of the German U-boat fleet and one of the very few in the Nazi high command to suspect the British of breaking Germany's Enigma-enciphered messages. He ordered the change from the three- to the four-rotor Enigma machine, which for nearly a year imperilled the Allied war effort.

deadly work of the U-boats. It appeared that Germany was about to attempt a knockout blow.

Then, seemingly in an instant, the course of the war at sea began to change.

As the dismal winter gave way to spring, a series of incredible events started to unfold that would continue until the end of the year. In the last few days of March, having broken the Italian naval version of Enigma, a less complex but still daunting version of the German machine, Bletchley Park provided Admiral Sir Andrew Browne Cunningham (nicknamed ABC), the commander-in-chief of the Royal Navy's Mediterranean Fleet, with an early warning that an Italian naval "task force" had sortied to intercept and destroy highly vulnerable British convoys bringing troops from the Egyptian city of Alexandria to Greece. Swiftly, Cunningham devised a plan to outfox and ambush his Italian adversary, Admiral Angelo Iachino.[5] First, he sent reconnaissance aircraft out to "discover" the task force, so as not to betray the source of the intelligence—a requisite for any action based solely on Ultra. Second, he found a way to keep his own movements secret as he made a surprise attack—the key to victory at sea. Cunningham—again through the good graces of Ultra—knew that the Japanese consul general in Alexandria maintained a vigil on his whereabouts, figuring that if Cunningham remained in Alexandria, so too did the Mediterranean Fleet.[6] The clever British admiral realized, therefore, that he must delude the consul general.

On this occasion, while the fleet prepared for battle, Cunningham arranged for a false story to circulate in the local golf club about a grand ball aboard his flagship that night. When he arrived in the afternoon for his habitual round of golf, he had his dress uniform in his bag and made his presence felt. That evening, nothing appeared in Bletchley Park intercepts to suggest the Japanese consul general suspected subterfuge, even though by then Cunningham had slipped out the back door of the club, jumped into a waiting car and sped to Alexandria harbour to catch up to his own fleet moments before it sailed for its historic confrontation with the Italian fleet. The only warning Iachino received of an approaching British strike force came from the roar of shot and shell crashing into the decks of his ships.

Two days of heavy fighting ensued, which left three Italian cruisers and two destroyers at the bottom of the sea, while the pride of the Italian navy, the battleship *Vittorio Veneto*, limped back into the port of Taranto heavily damaged; it would never see battle again. It was, as Churchill later claimed, the "tearing up of the paper fleet of Italy."[7] In forty-eight hours Cunningham had inflicted the greatest defeat in Italian naval history. It not only secured the sea lanes to North Africa for the British but kept the Italian fleet wed to its ports. When the ships emerged two years later, en masse, it was to surrender to the Allies.

Great Britain had scored an outstanding victory at the bleakest of times, one that Churchill suggested rivalled Horatio Nelson's legendary triumph at the Battle of Trafalgar nearly a century and a half earlier. It also clearly demonstrated to John Godfrey in Room 39 at the Admiralty the full weight and power of what Bletchley Park's Naval Section could deliver: not only had it defined the Italian fleet's intentions and location, but it had also ensured that the intelligence source and the subsequent ruse remained undiscovered. So impressed with the fruits of Ultra was Cunningham that, on his return to England, he made a priority visit to Bletchley Park to thank the cryptographers in person for providing the critical intelligence required for the victory in the Mediterranean—once again Churchill's "golden eggs" had proved priceless.

In addition to the U-boat worries, the British also had to concern themselves with periodic breakouts into the Atlantic by the deadly

German surface raiders, which presented a constant threat to the vital convoys. Between October 1940 and March 1941, the pocket battleship *Admiral Scheer* sank sixteen merchant ships, accounting for nearly 100,000 tons. In the first three months of 1941, the battle cruisers *Scharnhorst* and *Gneisenau* took down another twenty-two ships comprising over 115,000 tons, while the heavy cruiser *Admiral Hipper* sank slightly more than 40,000 tons during its two raiding cruises.[8] However, just two months after the Ultra-inspired victory over the Italian fleet, the cryptographers at Bletchley would contribute in no small fashion to sinking the pride of Hitler's fleet, the super-battleship *Bismarck*, after she broke out of the Denmark Strait into the North Sea with the battle cruiser *Prinz Eugen*, intending to prey on the Allies' convoy traffic in the Atlantic.

The Royal Navy's legendary hunt for the *Bismarck* that followed revealed just how potent an intelligence weapon Godfrey's NID had become by the late spring of 1941, with signals intelligence (cryptography, direction finding, radio finger printing, traffic analysis), naval attachés' reports and aerial photography all combining to help the Admiralty carry out Churchill's instruction to "Sink the *Bismarck*." Together, they allowed the Admiralty to maintain an almost constant vigil over the movements of the behemoth battleship and gain insights into the intentions and decision making of Admiral Günther Lütjens, the German task force commander, who joined the *Bismarck*'s Captain Otto Ernst Lindemann on her bridge for the operation.

This remarkable story began on May 18, when Ultra reports indicated that German aerial reconnaissance had suddenly increased in the area between Jan Mayen, a Norwegian island in the Arctic Ocean, and Greenland. Although the intelligence did not reveal the exact nature of the German interest, it was clear that something was afoot.

That night, unknown to British intelligence, the *Bismarck* moved quietly from her anchorage in Gdynia, in German-occupied Poland, and the following afternoon entered Kiel, Germany's traditional home port for its navy, where she joined the *Prinz Eugen* and a group of destroyers. The next night, they quietly and secretly sailed out through the Great Belt, a strait that divides Denmark in two. It wasn't until late on May 20 that the Admiralty received a report through its naval attaché in Stockholm that neutral Swedish vessels had spotted "two large warships escorted by three destroyers" making for the northwest.[9] The report did not immediately set off alarm bells in the Operational Intelligence Centre in London, though it raised suspicions requiring further investigation. Aerial reconnaissance flights eventually spotted the *Bismarck* and *Prinz Eugen* off Bergen, on the southern coast of Norway, but the NID viewed the ships' movements at this point as nothing more than an administrative reorganization or a training run. Just as the picture was building, bad weather prevented further reconnaissance flights, leaving the OIC in the dark for the next twenty-nine hours—until Bletchley Park came to the rescue. The cryptanalysts had dug up a series of out-of-date decrypts from April, and although the first messages did not reveal anything overt, on May 21 Bletchley Park sent the following message to the OIC: "*Bismarck* embarked five prize crews with necessary charts at end of April and been carrying out practices in the Baltic with *Prinz Eugen*."[10]

The Operational Intelligence Centre responded immediately: "prize crews" used for manning captured merchant ships plus requests for charts of the North Atlantic could mean only one thing. It informed Admiral John Tovey, the commander-in-chief of the Home Fleet, that "it is evident that these ships intend to carry out a raid on trade routes."[11] With the original message so far in the past, Tovey initially regarded the OIC's interpretation with some suspicion, thinking that the *Bismarck* might be sortieing for a "winner take all" showdown with the British ships. However, based on the accumulating evidence, Tovey accepted the OIC's breakout theory. Now he was faced with another decision that Ultra could not answer: what route would the beast take?

Intelligence is seldom complete or 100 percent certain; it generally requires a highly educated weighing of the odds. Tovey knew that Lütjens had several routes to choose from: he could cruise through the English Channel, or between the Faeroe Islands and either Scotland or Iceland, or through the Denmark Strait. Although the odds heavily favoured a dash through the Denmark Strait, Tovey took no chances and spread his force out to intercept the Bismarck no matter what course she chose. In the process he spread his line too thin, leaving the battle cruiser HMS Hood and the battleship HMS Prince of Wales, along with a collection of cruisers, at the mercy of the Bismarck's long-range fifteen-inch guns in the Denmark Strait. In less than ten minutes, the first round was over: the Hood disappeared in a giant explosion following a salvo from the Bismarck, taking the lives of all but three members of her crew of 1,418. The Prince of Wales, severely mauled, pulled back outside the range of the big guns. Immediately the Royal Navy ordered all battleships in the area to join the pursuit—and the race to sink the Bismarck began.

For more than a week, the Royal Navy's Home Fleet chased the pride of Hitler's fleet from the North Sea to the Bay of Biscay and hounded her back again towards the coast of France, using direction-finding (DF) apparatus to pick up a constant stream of radio messages from the hunted ship. The British had a real-time picture of where she was, but not of what she intended to do. The DF apparatus was at the mercy of the ionosphere, and for a whole day the pursuing fleet floundered along amid complete radio silence. Fortunately, the Bismarck resumed regular transmissions, which eventually betrayed her position again to the Operational Intelligence Centre. To identify the transmissions, the OIC called on its radio finger printing and traffic analysis experts. The finger-printing group used a "photograph" of the intercepted radio transmission to distinguish a unique pattern in radio waves produced not only by each transmitter but also specifically by each radio operator—a pattern as recognizable and unique as a human fingerprint. The traffic analysis group examined the characteristics of the method in which the wireless messages appeared. When both concluded that the messages indeed came from the Bismarck, plans went ahead to attack the great German warship with torpedo bombers.

The strike damaged the Bismarck badly enough to force her to forgo her raiding mission and head to port for repairs. But the Operational Intelligence Centre was not privy to the extent of her damage, so had no idea what she would do next. Three courses of action seemed possible: Admiral Lütjens could steam to the west, hoping to fix the problem at sea; turn tail and head back through the Denmark Strait, making for a German port; or move southeast towards the French port of Brest or, better yet, St-Nazaire—the only dry dock big enough to properly repair the ship. Soon, new direction-finding bearings indicated that the Bismarck was making for Brest. However, the signals quickly died as Lütjens shut down the wireless sets, leaving Admiral Tovey working from well-reasoned guesses until Bletchley intercepted a series of messages on the Bismarck's predicament from land and air sources. They revealed preparations for her arrival and repair at St-Nazaire.[12] Within minutes the OIC informed Tovey: "Information received graded A1 that intention of Bismarck is to make for west coat of France."[13]

With his hunch confirmed, Tovey confidently proceeded, using a combination of direction finding, traffic analysis, radio finger printing and Ultra intelligence to move in for the kill. After a small but inconclusive encounter that allowed the Prinz Eugen to slip away ahead of the Bismarck and make for Brest, it took almost two full days to catch up with the giant battleship. Finally, on May 27, with the Prinz Eugen already in Brest for repairs, the Royal Navy put more than four hundred shells and several torpedoes into the Bismarck.[14] Only when the ship had become a burning hulk did the order to abandon ship sound, followed by orders to scuttle the vessel. Quickly the battleship slipped beneath the surface with Lütjens, Lindemann and more than 2,000 of her 2,200 crew.[15]

The victory over the supposedly invincible Bismarck was a great relief to the Admiralty—one that also provided a massive and desperately needed propaganda coup to inject life back into the sagging morale of the British people. In the space of the following two months, the war at sea took a drastic turn in the Allies' favour as the Royal Navy's Home Fleet turned its attention to the battleship's many support vessels. During the month of May, Bletchley Park provided the OIC with accurate locations for the twenty-one tankers, trawlers and ships that had been tasked with providing fuel, supplies and weather reports to the Bismarck and Prinz Eugen. That information allowed the British to attack the vessels in piecemeal fashion into the second week of July—and by the eleventh they had sunk or captured fifteen of them. Unfortunately, popular history has focused exclusively on the dramatic hunt for the Bismarck and ignored this important epilogue to the battle.[16]

In the North Atlantic, the "Happy Time" for the U-boats also came to an abrupt end that spring, with the four top U-boat aces captured or killed in action. Until June 1941, with the exception of a slight lull in early winter, the German submarines had continued the deadly pace they had set the previous year. In May alone, U-boats had claimed sixty-six ships or 324,000 tons of British shipping in just one month, followed by another sixty-five and over 300,000 tons in June. But then their success dropped dramatically, to twenty-one ships and 61,000 tons in July and thirty-two ships totalling 81,000 tons in August. By the end of June, despite the rising numbers of U-boats operating in the Atlantic sea lanes, the submarines' proficiency in locating convoys suddenly vanished, with ships slipping past their patrol lines to arrive unmolested in British ports. More alarming for Admiral Karl Dönitz was the fact that only forty-nine British ships during July and August fell victim to his crews. Meanwhile, by the autumn, sinkings of his own craft had risen at an alarming rate, with thirty-five U-boats gone by the end of the year, ten in December alone.

The change in fortune was in large part directly attributable to the new-found ability of the Operational Intelligence Centre to locate U-boats at sea and redirect vulnerable convoys away from potentially disastrous collisions—a move that saved more than three hundred merchant vessels from the clutches of these deadly underwater predators.[17] It also provided the Admiralty with the "tremendous advantage" of knowing "continuously and in minute detail" how German naval authorities were reacting to the various anti-submarine weapons and operational tactics the British were trying out.[18] All these developments had a huge impact on Dönitz, eventually forcing him to pull his U-boat fleet out of the Atlantic to regroup.[19] Although the inexperience of his new crews and the growing demands of other theatres of battle such as the Baltic and the highly charged Mediterranean played a role, his decision to withdraw stemmed largely from his crews' inability to find and sink merchant vessels.

The turnaround in British fortunes was stunning. It was explained in part by the sheer guts, determination and skill of the commanders and crews of Royal Navy and Royal Canadian Navy ships and aircraft. In practical terms, the success was the cumulative result of superior strategy and doctrine, sound convoy organization, increased air support, and a greater number of escort forces, including destroyers and corvettes. Added to this mix were the development and improvement of new and existing anti-submarine technologies such as ASDIC (sonar), radar, and high-frequency direction finding (HF/DF or "Huff Duff"), all of which were used to track U-boats at close range above or below the surface.

Most significant of all, Special Intelligence had now exploded onto the scene. The cryptographic abilities of Bletchley Park, buttressed by the other forms of signals intelligence and by the deft work of the staff of the Operational Intelligence Centre in translating all this information into focused activity, had led to unparalleled success on the high

seas by the middle of 1941—something that Ian Fleming and John
Godfrey in NID, not to mention Alan Turing, Peter Twinn and Frank
Birch at Bletchley Park, could only dream of after the postponement of
Operation Ruthless in October 1940.

The cryptanalysts at Bletchley Park recognized that the dramatic
success they were enjoying did not result, at this point, from any
major technological breakthrough. Rather, it stemmed directly from
the concerted efforts by the NID and Bletchley's Naval Section, backed
by the Admiralty, to implement a uniform and systematic approach
to pinching.

By the end of 1940, the British had acknowledged the crucial importance of pinched material to cryptographic breakthroughs. Theoretically,
there was no limit to the complexity possible in cryptography: with
every alteration, tweak or fundamental change in the messaging systems, the cryptographers' difficulties increased, and their chances of
breaking into the codes by analytical means dropped further. The only
way they could make progress was through a steady supply of pinched
Enigma machines or parts and the supporting code books and setting
sheets. Fortunately, because the German navy relied heavily on radio
communications to coordinate its actions, equipment of all kinds was
widely distributed on shore and to U-boats and ships of all kinds at
sea, making it vulnerable to seizure and exploitation so long as it could
be stolen without the Germans catching on.[20]

For years after the war, the only information historians had about
pinch raids came from anecdotal evidence or from the limited number
of after-action reports written by a few participants in pinch operations.
Documents related to the pinch policy and doctrine—the framework or
"playbook" for carrying out these operations—remained classified until
2013, when GCHQ agreed to release a set of Ultra Secret documents
to me that established just how the British planned to carry out these

operations. What I soon discovered was that, following the "tentative and crude" attempts in 1940, a clear and distinct pinch policy began to emerge early in 1941, which, as the year wore on, proved "well-informed and practical." Thereafter the British spared no effort in developing techniques they could use whenever the opportunity for pinching arose.[21]

Pinch operations, I learned from these released documents, were loosely divided into categories—by chance, by opportunity and by design—reflecting a more mature and systematic approach than previously suggested. The first type, "pinch by chance," involved the incidental capture of enemy intelligence material during the course of an unrelated action. As the Admiralty gained more experience with these opportunities, it published a series of general advisories in the form of a Confidential Admiralty Fleet Order (CAFO), laying out the ground rules for British crews, whether boarding parties or raiders, to follow so they could exploit chance discoveries as they arose and cover their accomplishments with plausible excuses or security measures.

These advisories had two objectives: to create a general awareness among the crews of the importance of this material within the context of the overall war effort, and to make clear the vital need for crews not only to capture the materials but to bring them safely home, protecting them from overzealous boarding parties bent on looting or ransacking vessels (as had occurred on one ship, the *Polaris*, in early 1940). These orders included detailed photographs and diagrams to assist boarding parties in their tasks, with suggestions about possible locations where they might find what they were after on a particular vessel. The orders also gave strict instructions for the safe delivery of the Enigma machine, if one was captured, and its ancillary code books and setting sheets into British hands. The Enigma machine "should be carefully packed and forwarded to the Director of Naval Intelligence [John Godfrey, in London] . . . by the quickest possible route" under officer guard and "should not be touched or disturbed in any way, except as necessary for its removal and packing."[22]

The second category, "pinch by opportunity," called for quick planning when a particularly attractive target or set of targets came into reach as the result of a planned operation on sea or land. Usually that meant piggybacking the pinch onto an existing operation or one in embryo, allowing the size and scope of the planned operation to provide both the convenient delivery vehicle and the security cover for the pinch.

In the third category, "pinch by design," the pinch itself formed the imperative or main driver for the entire mission. In other words, the pinch was not the caboose or passenger car hitched to the locomotive for the ride—it was either one of the locomotives or the only locomotive pulling the train. In this case, to ensure surprise and cover, a much larger operation was built up around the pinch to conceal the truth.

The essential precursors to any successful pinch operation, whether by opportunity or by design, lay in surprise, shock and security. As soon as the first contact was made, the clock began to tick in a race against time between the force attempting to pinch the material and the defenders bent on destroying whatever sensitive equipment and paperwork they possessed. To reduce the German defenders' chances of success, the British plans instructed the raiders to appear suddenly, seemingly out of nowhere, to close in at top speed, and to employ heavy firepower either to kill the defenders or to create enough confusion so they could be overwhelmed before they destroyed anything of value. In this respect, the British hoped to exploit what they interpreted as the "cultural characteristics" of their German enemy. As one observer noted: "Theirs is the normal occidental attitude, personal safety first. Hence, under surprise attack, only a certain amount of classified material is destroyed, only as much as can be accomplished without endangering the individual responsible."[23]

For reasons of security, the raiders had to cover both the true intent of the mission and any success they might achieve. The Germans must

never be able to discern what they had been after or if they had succeeded in capturing any vital materials. So John Godfrey's Naval
Intelligence Division in the Admiralty designed operations that provided elaborate covers for the pinch—an approach akin to using a
steamhammer to crack a nut. They surrounded the pinch with dispro-
portionate force, to give the appearance that anything they stole had
simply come by chance or that their objective was something much
larger or more orthodox in nature. In theory, this reasoning was sound:
no enemy would ever suspect that the allocation of such large amounts
of resources was merely a cover for a different purpose. And that disbelief was exactly what the British were counting on.

Because of the sensitive nature of all these pinch operations,
responsibility remained firmly in the hands of Godfrey and his well-
organized Naval Intelligence Division in London. But Bletchley Park's
highly secret Naval Section, housed in Huts 4 and 8, was designated
to receive the captured enemy naval documents immediately after
they arrived in England so the code-breakers there could put them to
use. In some cases Frank Birch, the director of the Naval Section, and
members of his staff drafted and revised the Confidential Admiralty
Fleet Orders or suggested possible targets for pinches.[24] One of the
most gifted of the highly accomplished experts in the Naval Section
was the young Cambridge history undergraduate Harry Hinsley,
whose skills in interpreting decrypts and the other fruits of signals
intelligence were unrivalled, as was his ability to sense that something
was afoot from an accumulation of tiny clues.

In general, though, Godfrey and the NID controlled the drawstrings
for any pinch operation, and input from Bletchley's Naval Section was
secondary and responsive in nature. Other than noting what the
experts in the Naval Section required, the NID was under no obligation
to act on the methods suggested by Frank Birch to obtain the desired
material. Together with Ian Fleming, who had a firm understanding of
cryptography and a key role in Section 17 "to co-ordinate intelligence"

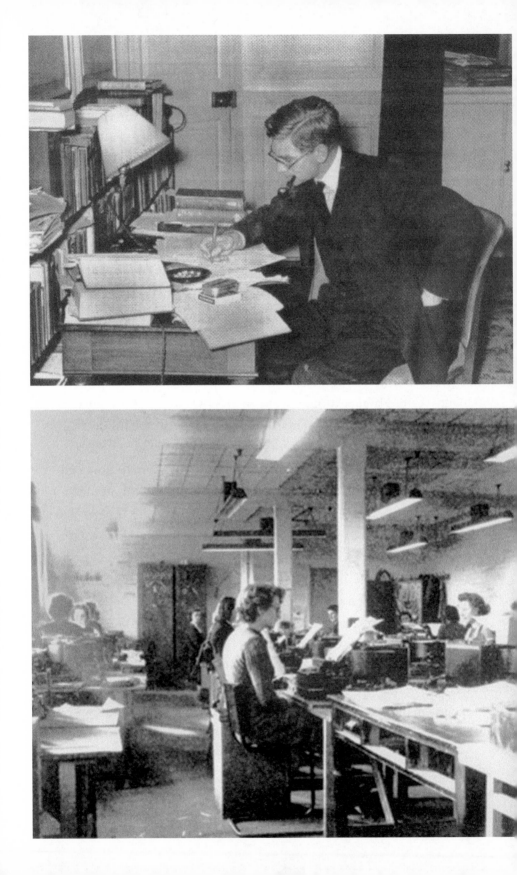

and liaise between the NID and the other intelligence bodies, Godfrey could move ahead confidently to organize and launch pinch operations without the knowledge of the Naval Section.[25] In an effort to maintain that authority and channel Birch's increasing demands, Godfrey created an official liaison position with Bletchley Park to reinforce the direct link already handled by Fleming, who visited there regularly. Early in 1941 Godfrey posted several representatives from his NID to Bletchley; they were expected to find out precisely what the Naval Section and the cryptographers needed for their work, help plan the pinch operation, and physically go into action with the attacking forces and bring the critical stolen material home.

Very few people have heard of, let alone ventured to, the Lofoten Islands—a tiny snow-swept archipelago just inside the Arctic Circle off the coast of northern Norway. On March 4, 1941, five hundred of the newly formed British commandos, supported by fifty-two Norwegian Marines and a section of Royal Engineers, swept ashore from Royal

---

OPPOSITE TOP: Harry Hinsley (later Sir Harry) at his desk in Cambridge, where he was a history undergraduate before being recruited to Bletchley Park at the age of twenty-one. His skills in interpreting decrypts and analyzing enemy wireless traffic patterns were unrivalled, and he had an uncanny ability to sense that something was afoot.

BOTTOM: Code-breakers using modified British Typex cipher machines in Hut 6. On September 6, 1941, Winston Churchill made a rare visit to Bletchley, visiting Huts 3 and 6. As Anne Hamilton-Grace would write in her diary: "In came the PM himself, smoking the proverbial cigar and looking very well and pleased with life," and after reviewing their work he announced, "Well, if we don't win the war with information like that I don't know how we shall win it!" She reported him saying in his speech outside the main house that day: "It is amazing that a place that looks so simple can really be so sinister."

Navy landing ships as part of Operation Claymore. In a matter of hours they had captured more than two hundred German prisoners and destroyed fifteen fisheries-related factories as well as a bunker crude-storage facility. In the process, they also sank ten German trawlers and captured one, the *Krebs*. Not only were these results good for public relations, they also provided the Naval Section with a landmark pinch—the first since it had put the Operation Ruthless and the *Bernhard Von Tschirschky* pinches on permanent hold.

The Lofoten Islands presented a chance for Combined Operations Headquarters—another Churchill creation—to conduct its first sizable amphibious raid of the war. Established in the summer of 1940 during the final days of the war in France, Combined Operations had yet to make much of a splash, having engaged so far in only a few pin-prick raids of little or no consequence on the French Channel coast. Exasperated with this lack of aggressiveness on the part of its original commander, General Alan Bourne, a career Royal Marine, Churchill pressed for larger and bolder attacks. He replaced the cynical Bourne with Admiral Sir Roger Keyes, the hero of the daring Zeebrugge Raid in 1918 during the First World War. Keyes appeared to be the man Churchill was looking for—someone who could establish a thoroughly aggressive raiding program that would not only signal Britain's will to fight on alone but placate in a responsible fashion what John Godfrey later called Churchill's appetite for "wildcat" operations—such as the Gallipoli landings in the last war.[26] The opportunistic Godfrey seized the chance to wed his pinch requirements to this enticing vehicle for raiding.

Under Keyes's command, Churchill ordered the creation of a "band of brothers," as he called them, a highly trained but lightly armed elite force designed for raiding enemy shore facilities in amphibious operations. They were known as commandos—a name he pilfered from the Boer raiders he had witnessed during his time in South Africa at the turn of the century. Drawn at this point from army volunteers, the commandos—forerunners of today's Special Operations and other elite units—planned to make their combat debut at Lofoten.

The squadron of five destroyers and two landing ships crowded with commandos managed to sail the roughly eight hundred miles from Scapa Flow in the Orkney Islands undetected by the Germans. Code-named "Rebel," this task force arrived at its destination at dawn on March 4 in a surprise attack. Quickly, both commando units were able to land and take their objectives with little or no enemy resistance, grabbing prisoners with ease. At sea, the *Krebs*, a German trawler outfitted for harbour defence, put up a short fight, but the Tribal-class destroyer HMS *Somali* knocked her out, running her aground and killing her captain in the process. When the boarding party arrived, however, they discovered that the captain had tossed the Enigma machine overboard seconds before his death—but had left other "valuable cypher material" in place, which was seized by the commandos.[27]

It was this haul of pinched material that allowed Bletchley Park, after almost a year in the dark, to read Enigma-enciphered messages on the *Dolphin* key (the principal Kriegsmarine naval key used by all vessels other than U-boats) for the months of February and April. And the information Turing gleaned from the material enabled him to reconstruct the current bigram tables—a breakthrough that eventually helped Bletchley Park unlock the naval Enigma code.[28]

Right from the start, the planners of Operation Claymore made the capture of seemingly innocent German trawlers their prime objective, simply because the evidence collected through traffic analysis and radio finger printing indicated that these vessels either used the Enigma machine in their work or maintained other material that Bletchley could use for cribs in its efforts to crack the codes.[29] On that basis, although Claymore was "planned with this end in view," with Churchill fully aware of the pinch imperative, other objectives naturally found a seat on the Combined Operations train that provided the necessary cover.[30]

Fires burning in the small town of Stamsund on the Norwegian Lofoten Islands, as British commandos leave following the first of two pinch raids on March 4, 1941.

For instance, two of Churchill's other pet projects were both part of Ian Fleming's liaison portfolio in NID and made their debuts in Operation Claymore. The first project, the highly secretive Special Operations Executive (SOE), which was sometimes called Churchill's Secret Army or the Ministry of Ungentlemanly Warfare, had been formed in July 1940 by amalgamating various sections from the Foreign Office, the War Office and the Secret Intelligence Service. It was established specifically to coordinate subversion and sabotage against the enemy in Europe and in countries occupied by Germany. The express purpose of the second project, the clandestine Political Warfare Executive (PWE), established in August 1941 and reporting to the Foreign Office, was to attack the economic heart of Nazi Germany by direct means or by radio or print propaganda designed to lower morale. Because the Lofoten Islands had several small fisheries and large oil-storage tanks for fish oils and bunker crude, they naturally caught the interest of the PWE. As for the SOE, Lofoten also offered an opportunity to score propaganda points by demonstrating the organization's destructive capabilities in a grand fashion while rounding up quislings (Norwegian collaborators with the German occupiers), providing weapons to the local resistance and fulfilling Churchill's cry to "set Europe ablaze."

The NID also hoped to score a propaganda triumph from the Lofoten raid. Fleming was responsible for public relations too, and once again he had full support from Godfrey—perhaps the only high-ranking Royal Navy officer to grasp the need for a cooperative press. Godfrey, sometimes accompanied by Fleming, called regularly on editors from most of the London papers, just as he had from the time he was appointed Director of Naval Intelligence in early 1939. In addition, he held weekly conferences at the Admiralty for naval correspondents, designed to draw them in as unofficial members of the NID team.[31] According to Godfrey, the newspapers generally "played the game," led along with tidbits of specially fed "off the record" information that they used in formulating their background material. The journalists soon learned not to question too closely what they were told.[32]

With their ability to dictate when and where they would launch these raids, the NID had the luxury of constructing its public relations lines well in advance of any operation—a crucial element not only in striking a blow in the propaganda war but also in covering each pinch. With the ability to "spin" events in their official communiqués following a victory, defeat or any other outcome, Godfrey, Fleming and their cohorts provided carefully crafted versions of events which satisfied the contemporary press and permeated postwar historical accounts as well, ensuring that the documents classified as Ultra Secret remained just that, even decades after the guns fell silent. In the case of Lofoten, the communiqués, reported almost verbatim, featured the military and other intelligence objectives, except for anything to do with the pinch. By offering explicit confirmation of the sinking of all the enemy ships the raiders encountered, they allayed, or at least reduced, German suspicions of the capture and compromise of their precious communications gear.[33]

Although the planners drew many genuine conclusions from the Lofoten operation of March 1941, the main lesson was something that remained hidden to the public for seventy years. Emerging in the aftermath of Claymore was a nascent brand of special operations warfare—a template for properly organized pinch raids that whetted the appetites of both the Naval Intelligence Division and the Naval Section at Bletchley Park for a repeat performance. A series of operations materialized starting in May, just a few weeks before the Bismarck made her fateful breakout into the North Atlantic.

As in the Lofoten raid, trawlers and minor ships became the focus of the next pinch operation, for several reasons. First, from what he could deduce from traffic analysis, the gifted Harry Hinsley noted that the small vessels, particularly weather-reporting ships, did use a series of codes and, at times, the Enigma machine. The odds were therefore extremely high that these lightly armed and thoroughly vulnerable ships could deliver the materials that the experts at Bletchley Park required; moreover, they would be easier to raid. Second, the weather-reporting ships operated alone and in isolated areas of the ocean, far from prying eyes on shore or above—a decided advantage compared with the Lofoten Islands and other harbours where small ships worked as part of a group of vessels or a flotilla.

Because these seemingly insignificant vessels did not present an obvious target, capturing them, at least initially, ran a distinctly lower risk of raising suspicion in Admiral Dönitz's headquarters than an intentional, or even unintentional, capture of one of his U-boats. In an impressive piece of signals intelligence sleuthing drawn from inferences in wireless transmissions and the material captured from the *Krebs*, Hinsley put together a detailed "hit list" of target weather ships, providing both their potential hauls and their suspected operational locations.[34]

The oddly named Operation EB went into effect on May 7, with unprecedented support. To effect the pinch, the Admiralty allocated three cruisers (HMS *Edinburgh*, *Manchester* and *Birmingham*) and four destroyers (HMS *Somali*, *Eskimo*, *Bedouin* and *Nestor*) from Admiral John Tovey's Home Fleet, putting them on hold and ready to move at a week's notice. The scale of this preparation testifies to the utmost importance of the raid, given that these precious assets, particularly the destroyers, were in high demand for anti-submarine patrols with the U-boat war at its most intense. In addition, with Godfrey's formalization of the pipeline between his NID and Bletchley's Naval Section, Captain Jasper Haines, RN, became the first liaison officer to work at Bletchley Park specifically for pinch purposes. A striking figure with movie-star looks and silver hair, Haines stood out in the bleak surroundings of the huts and attracted attention from the

This remarkable photograph shows a "pinch by chance" raid in progress (from later in the war, March 1944). The crew of HMCS *Chilliwack* are about to board after subduing the German U-boat *U-744*. They retrieved valuable code books and intelligence documents, though on this occasion much of the material was lost at sea in the raid.

many young women who worked there. His job was to cull information about specific needs and then go into action with the pinch forces to retrieve what was required and escort it back to London—a risky proposition should he be captured, given his intimate knowledge of Bletchley Park and the cryptographic effort.

Before Operation EB began, Haines briefed the force commanders (cruiser squadron commander Vice Admiral Lancelot Holland and his destroyer captains) on the requirements of the mission—clear proof of the significance of the pinch and the increasing power and influence of Naval Intelligence in such matters. Holland, who would soon lose his life during the battle with the Bismarck, listened intently while Haines explained that he would accompany the raiding force and personally deliver any pinched material directly back to London. He emphasized that "drastic action was important on first sighting to induce the enemy to abandon ship in a panic and . . . fail to destroy as much as they otherwise might."[35] Although the cruisers had float planes for reconnaissance, Haines had them grounded. He knew that the sight of a search plane would give away the presence of the strike force and lead the crew to dispose of the invaluable signals material. Surprise, followed by what we would now call "shock and awe," proved the keys to success.

By 1500 hours on Wednesday, May 7, the ships were on station just inside the Arctic Circle, actively searching for the German weather-reporting ship München. At 1707 they sighted the tiny trawler between the Edinburgh and the Somali. The Somali quickly opened fire at long distance to frighten the crew and then proceeded towards the trawler, along with the Edinburgh carrying Haines on board, at a full thirty knots in "sledgehammer" fashion. The approach partially worked, but the crew still managed to dispose of the Enigma machine and most of its signals material and to fire off a message to their headquarters that they were under attack. By the time Haines arrived on the stricken vessel, the boarding party had seized and bagged what remained of the

code and cipher material and had brought the surviving crew on board as prisoners. Later, in the privacy of a wardroom on the Edinburgh, he found "interesting documents . . . in the spoil"—the Enigma keys for June and the short-signals book (for messages of fewer than twenty-two characters) used by submarines, weather ships and other small vessels in certain circumstances.[36] Immediately he photographed the material and, once he returned to Scapa Flow, had the originals flown straight to Godfrey at the Admiralty, who then sent them on to Birch at Bletchley Park.

To cover the pinch, particularly as the München had got off a signal before she was boarded, Haines sent a Hush Most Secret message to the Admiralty about his imminent return with an "important" document. He suggested that a press announcement be released mentioning that the München, now in tow, had actually been scuttled by her crew and not captured. Promptly, the story appeared, reporting in great detail the sinking of the ship and, to alleviate German suspicion, portraying the action as strictly incidental. The Kriegsmarine seems not to have suspected any compromise of their cipher material, and the München remained hidden in Scapa Flow until the end of the war.[37] Before Haines reached British shores, however, another pinch, this one a classic "pinch by chance," occurred in the North Atlantic—and

----

OPPOSITE TOP: An Enigma machine with German code books, setting sheets and other highly prized material sought by British Naval Intelligence for use by the cryptanalysts at Bletchley. These are mock-ups created for the documentary *Dieppe Uncovered,* based on this book's research.

BOTTOM: A rare photograph from the Bundesarchiv of a German "signaller" at work in a wireless room, identified as March 1941. An Enigma machine lies in its box beside him, the three rotors visible at the top of the machine close to his left hand. In U-boats the wireless room was the communications nerve centre, and in the event of a pinch raid the crews were trained to rapidly destroy the machine and the code books.

it propelled the code-breakers' penetration of the German naval
Enigma to unprecedented levels.

For more than a year, not one scrap of paper bearing on the Enigma
problem had fallen into British hands, yet within days of the seizure
of the München, the British destroyers HMS Bulldog and HMS Broadway,
along with the corvette HMS Aubretia, captured submarine U-110 after
it engaged a convoy off Iceland on May 9.[38] The U-boat, commanded
by Captain-Lieutenant Fritz-Julius Lemp, the ace who had sunk the
Athenia in the opening hours of the war, gave up what Bletchley Park
would come to consider the "richest prize" so far. After three days of
almost constant depth-charge attacks, Lemp ordered the submarine
to surface and its crew to abandon ship.

Fearing that the Germans had set scuttling charges on a timed fuse
and racing against time to reach the submarine before it exploded, a
boarding party led by Sub-Lieutenant David Balme from Bulldog paddled
quickly in a launch under the watchful eye of cameras that caught the
extraordinary events as they unfolded. Once on board, Balme entered
the vessel through its conning tower and slipped into its control room,
"abandoned in great haste," he recalled, "as books and gear were
strewn about the place." The signals room, in contrast to the rest of the
ship, was in "perfect condition," with no signs of destruction. Here he
found signals books, logbooks and correspondence—and, sitting on
the desk, the Enigma machine, still plugged in, as though it had been
in use when abandoned. Quickly, Balme organized a human chain and
took every book, chart and scrap of paper, along with the Enigma
machine, from the vessel, moving it one armful at a time up the con-
ning-tower ladder to the waiting launch. Only when the whole dangerous job was completed did Balme return triumphantly to Bulldog, where
he reported the find while the destroyer took U-110 in tow as a cherished prize.[39]

To cover the capture and pinch, Godfrey decided to sink the damaged sub en route to the Scapa Flow and the NID swiftly issued a Hush Most Secret message instructing the crew to maintain utmost secrecy and to refer to the U-110 and its capture only by the code name "Primrose." From that moment forward, Lemp's submarine ceased to exist, stored away out of sight for the remainder of the war. The British, who were now increasingly co-operating with the still-neutral Americans, did not even inform them of this capture until January of the next year.

When *Bulldog* arrived in England, a Naval Intelligence officer, likely Jasper Haines, met the ship and whisked the pinched machine and documents to the Naval Section at Bletchley Park. The materials stolen from the *München* and the U-110 only days apart provided the answer to Bletchley's prayers. As a result, the cryptologists could now read naval Enigma messages on the *Dolphin* key in real time for the month of June and, even more critical, they possessed a copy of the special *Offizier* codebook—a key to the most secret information circulated to U-boat commanders, such as notifications of upcoming changes in key and encryption systems.

The overwhelming joy unleashed in the Naval Section by the twin pinches and the sinking of the *Bismarck* proved short-lived: on June 15, the Germans changed the bigram tables. Foreseen as a distinct possibility, this development prompted the Naval Intelligence Division to launch a repetition of the *München* pinch.[40] Again Harry Hinsley's trawlers played a starring role, with the *Lauenburg*, one of ten weather trawlers that ploughed the Atlantic in support of the *Bismarck*, the intended victim. In an almost carbon-copy replay of the earlier pinch, a task force of two cruisers and three destroyers was specifically laid on for this operation, briefed by Lieutenant Commander Allon Bacon, who worked with Fleming in Section 17. As handsome as Captain Jasper

Haines, the thirty-eight-year-old Bacon, "rangy, dark-haired, round-faced," who before the war had worked in London's financial sector and for the Foreign Office on signals intelligence assignments, had been recruited into the NID for his intellect and resourcefulness, both of which would be called upon in the upcoming operation.[41]

Once aboard HMS *Jupiter* for the mission, Bacon inspected his boarding party, outfitted like privateers of old with cutlasses and axes, along with their modern submachine guns. The intermittent fog and rain presented perfect conditions, cloaking the progress of the raiding force towards the trawler and maximizing the chance of surprise. After a series of icebergs set off false alarms, the crew finally spotted their quarry in the distance.[42]

Jupiter immediately increased to flank speed and headed straight for the trawler. It opened fire with the main armament, intending to frighten rather than kill the crew.[43] The men quickly abandoned ship without destroying their communications material; the boarding party entered and grabbed what they were looking for, then sank the vessel to cover their tracks.[44] Once again the press played a role in covering the pinch, with a banner headline reading DEPRESSION OFF ICELAND FOR 22 GERMANS. The news report stated that in the course of a "periodical sweep" to the north of Iceland, "our forces sank a German weather reporting trawler, capturing her crew of 22."[45]

This pinch allowed the cryptologists at Bletchley Park to continue to read the naval Enigma traffic after the expiration of the key sheets captured for June and July. In terms of breaking the three-rotor Enigma code, the pinches provided Alan Turing with the "cheats" necessary to mine for the current operational gold and with "cribs" for the increasing number of Bombes being used in the Naval Section's investigations. As the year went on, the experts employed anything that might give Bletchley a break, even through the back door, into Enigma: weather codes, short-signal codes, the restricted *Offizier* and *Stab* ciphers, the German dockyard cipher, a special emergency hand cipher called RHV, and Long-E bars. In fact, the cumulative success of the pinches provided the basis for an almost daily penetration of the Dolphin key for the remainder of the war.

Frank Birch considered the Lauenburg pinch the "masterpiece of cooperation between Naval Section and the Navy."[46] Along with the other operations, it showed just how far the Naval Intelligence Division had progressed in the twelve months since Operation Ruthless—and how integral these operations had become in both the cryptographic war and the war at sea.

The sudden change in British fortune against the deadly U-boats in the summer and fall of 1941 did not go unnoticed in higher quarters. In September, Winston Churchill paid his only visit to Bletchley Park, to survey the inner workings of the "intelligence factory" that provided his golden eggs. He was already thoroughly addicted to Bletchley's end products. Ultra was unique and offered him a direct line to something that nobody else had: a finger on the pulse of the enemy war effort. It was an intoxicating power that the micromanager in him could not resist.

As First Lord of the Admiralty, he had enjoyed access on demand to all the naval Ultra. "Shortly before he became Prime Minister," Godfrey remembered, "I had some piece of information to impart and was asked by his private office to go to Mr. Churchill's bedroom in Admiralty House. He was sitting up, freshly shaved, in an enormous double bed smoking a cigar and surrounded by his morning's correspondence, despatch boxes, papers, breakfast, a bottle of white wine, coffee, cigars."[47] By the time he became prime minister and the highest authority in the land, he received a daily delivery of all forms of Ultra (not just naval) direct from the head of the Secret Intelligence Service, Stewart Menzies—the man called "C"—who was responsible for the overall production of this rare commodity. Each morning a locked red security box, marked "Only to be opened by the Prime Minister," would arrive containing the Ultra that kept Churchill thoroughly engrossed for hours on end. It is not surprising, then, that on his congratulatory visit to Bletchley Park, when he was confronted by demands for additional funding for the projects there, he responded with a "prayer" stamped *Action This Day*. It ordered full and unending financial support for Bletchley and its parent organization, the Government Code and Cypher School (GC&CS).[48]

In stark contrast to Churchill, Admiral Dönitz had no idea of the scope of the British cryptographic effort. Although he recognized that something along those lines did exist, he had no clue just how much current success Bletchley was enjoying. After the sinking of the *Bismarck*, when the majority of her support ships methodically and quickly fell to British action, Dönitz and his staff became suspicious that Enigma had been compromised. Then, in late August, the U-boats suddenly lost their ability to find convoys, which were now routinely rerouted because of the steady flow of Special Intelligence the Operational Intelligence Centre was receiving. Dönitz had always doubted the impenetrability of Enigma, and he now decided to introduce a separate key, apart from *Dolphin*, for his U-boats. *Triton*, as he called it—the British named it *Shark*—came into effect on October 3, 1941.

Because *Triton* remained a key for a three-rotor machine, it did not create much anxiety at Bletchley after an initial delay. Compounding Dönitz's worry, one of his submarines, the U-570, simply disappeared after sending a message that she was under attack by British planes and vessels. On that occasion, when the boarding party entered the submarine, which had been badly damaged from depth-charge attacks and prepared for scuttling by its crew, they found a few Enigma-related items: the remains of a destroyed code book and table, and the lid of the smashed machine. The disappearance of the submarine led Dönitz to suspect the worst, and he demanded an inquiry.

Dönitz's security advisers assured him that, even if the British had managed to break into the cipher, their success would only be temporary: the odds against permanently subverting the machine were astronomical. However, now that they had the ability to penetrate naval Enigma, the British tended to push their luck to the limit, reaffirming Dönitz's suspicions. Although they took strict precautions to limit the distribution of Special Intelligence to a tiny circle of "indoctrinated" officers and ensured that reconnaissance, or some other plausible intelligence source, covered operations spawned by the captured intelligence, there was always a chance that, given the frequency at which they were now enjoying success, something unforeseen could occur. The overwhelming power of this source of information tended to blind British intelligence planners to the fact that overuse or misuse might give the game away. In three separate episodes, evidence emerged that led Dönitz to conclude that the three-rotor Enigma used by his U-boats had sprung a leak.

First, a British submarine attempted to ambush the rendezvous between three U-boats and a supply ship in the Cape Verde Islands. Then a British prisoner of war admitted that, during the sweep of the Bismarck's supply ships in the summer, one of the victims, the Gedania, had yielded signals documents long thought destroyed. Finally, on November 22, another ambush of a supply ship and U-boats off St. Helena occurred.

Dönitz refused to wait any longer. Exactly one week later, he changed the bigram tables and made plans to deploy a new weapon in the cryptographic war, something the British had suspected was in development and feared was close to introduction, particularly after the capture of the U-570. When experts in the Naval Section had examined the lid of the smashed Enigma machine recovered from the submarine, they found the usual brown-washed label on the inside. This one, however, possessed a sinister difference: instead of a stamp bearing the moniker Schlüssel M3 to denote the three-wheel version of the machine, it read *Schlüssel* M4. For months, Bletchley Park had been picking up indications that something new and troubling was afoot—that a machine sporting a fourth rotor existed. Now they had the first concrete evidence that an improved version of the naval Enigma machine not only existed but was about to be issued to the deadly U-boat fleet. It was only a question of time before that would happen.

The four-rotor Enigma machine—really an improved three-rotor machine—was introduced by the German navy for its U-boats operating in the Atlantic on February 1, 1942. For over ten months the new machine left the British dangerously in the dark in terms of their ability to access U-boat communications in the most vital of all theatres in the Second World War, the Atlantic Ocean. That blackout presented an immense, almost insurmountable challenge to the cryptographers working tirelessly in Bletchley to gain a break into the new machine.

FIVE

SWIMMING WITH SHARKS

Of course as far as we are concerned here,
pinching is the best form of cryptography.

—NIGEL DE GREY, ROOM 40 VETERAN
AND DEPUTY DIRECTOR OF BLETCHLEY PARK

News of the four-rotor Enigma machine did not catch the British completely by surprise.[1] In January 1941, John Godfrey had learned from a set of captured instructions that such a version existed, created likely in 1940 or even before the war, but as the Bletchley Park history of Hut 8 notes, "forearmed was not forewarned."[2] The four-rotor's appeal was exactly that—an extra rotor that multiplied the already astounding odds against decryption another twenty-six times, rendering it almost impervious to penetration.[3] The cryptographers swiftly embarked on designing a special Bombe that could attack the four-rotor, but estimates put delivery at spring 1943 at the earliest, and even then it relied on pinched material—the essential code books, ciphers and tables—to operate efficiently.

The Kriegsmarine as a whole had no proof of the systematic British penetration of their three-rotor Enigma machines. They had therefore felt no urgency to implement a costly and time-consuming conversion of their entire encryption system. However, with the swing of the pendulum in the war at sea in the summer of 1941, the ever-vigilant Admiral Karl Dönitz, suspecting that his U-boat communications had been compromised, ordered his U-boats in the Atlantic to implement use of the four-rotor machine beginning on February 1, 1942. It was exactly what Godfrey had been dreading, though the British as yet had no knowledge of this specific order. Meanwhile, the Naval Intelligence Division and Bletchley Park were grappling with a two-part question: How long did they have before this new machine would appear, and how pervasive would it be? The nightmare scenario from Godfrey's perspective would see the device introduced to the entire surface and submarine fleets of the Kriegsmarine, leaving the British, without this crucial and hard-won weapon in the signals intelligence war, entirely in the dark.

After Dönitz discontinued use of the *Dolphin* key for his U-boats in the Atlantic and introduced the new key, *Triton*, Turing and the cryptographic team in Hut 8, fearing the worst, struggled frantically with the problem for several days before they realized that the change stemmed from a separate three-rotor key and not the new four-rotor machine. But the scare rocketed up the chain of command to Churchill, who was by now accustomed to his daily delivery of naval Ultra in the "small red box" direct from Stewart Menzies at the Secret Intelligence Service.

Suddenly deprived of U-boat message traffic, Menzies wrote to Churchill immediately to explain what had happened and to assure him that everything was in hand. "From the beginning of October, our difficulties have been increased by the Germans separating the U. Boat cyphers from the Main Fleet traffic," he told the prime minister. "The latter should present no increased difficulties, but the U. boats present a separate problem which will have to be solved by our machines." When Menzies reported progress a few days later, Churchill responded with a measured and encouraging note: "Give my compliments to those concerned."[4] With the all-clear a few hours later, Churchill simply replied, "Good."[5]

By this time, Bletchley Park had mastered the use of cribs, or cheats, to break into the three-rotor Enigma traffic—an approach Turing hoped would solve the four-rotor challenge should it appear. First, however, his team would require the materials from which to crib. For months the cryptographers relied on the lower-level codes and ciphers to provide what they needed. RHV (short for *Reservehandverfahren*), for example, was an emergency hand cipher used by vessels as a backup for Enigma when it broke down or on vessels not yet outfitted with the machine. E-bars, B-bars and WW (or *Wetterkurzschlüessel*), the weather code, were all "short-signal" ciphers (specially formatted, re-enciphered messages) that gave German U-boats and ships a quick way to send brief but standard messages without staying on the air for long and betraying their position to British direction finding, radio finger printing or traffic analysis.[6]

Other ciphers—such as the *Werftschlüssel*, a dockyard hand cipher, which touched on the activities of all vessels from the lowliest harbour dredger to U-boats to the *Tirpitz* (the *Bismarck*'s sister ship) operating in port—paid huge dividends because this traffic supplemented and rounded out those messages sent via the Enigma machines. The "lesser" messages might be about damage to ships, building progress, and special orders for radio silence on certain occasions, making these ciphers a crucial band-aid solution during Enigma blackout periods.[7] Unfortunately for the cryptanalysts, every so often these codes and ciphers changed too, requiring further pinches. Which is what happened when, at the end of November 1941, the Kriegsmarine introduced the new set of bigram tables.

The great worry for Godfrey and the NID was the double-edged nature of pinches: they helped to solve the problem, but they also piqued German interest in their own security, making it progressively more difficult to maintain that success. The British had no choice but to approach the situation in a more guarded way. In this case, when Combined Operations Headquarters asked Section 1, the geographically organized "country section" in the NID that covered Scandinavia, as well as the Inter-Services Topographical Department for a work-up for a return raid to Norway, Godfrey pounced on the chance to hitch a pinch operation onto this Combined Operations train, now under the command of Lord Louis Mountbatten.

In late October 1941, Churchill had lost patience with Sir Roger Keyes, his Director of Combined Operations, and appointed the youthful captain Lord Louis Mountbatten, a great-grandson of Queen Victoria, to replace him. By this time a growing pessimism had engulfed the indomitable old First World War veteran, who told Mountbatten as he passed the torch that "Britain had lost the will to fight."[8] Keyes was completely frustrated by the lack of co-operation from the land, sea and air service branches. Without any real power, he had been forced to struggle constantly with the chiefs of staff and with Churchill himself to get the precious assets he needed to conduct even pinprick raids along the European coast.

"Dickie" Mountbatten, as he'd been known since childhood, represented the new war. He was bold, vain, diplomatic and highly ambitious, ready to engage with the enemy. Churchill ordered him to take the offensive and develop a programme of commando raids along the Norwegian and Atlantic coastlines that would tie up German resources and help prepare for the Allies' eventual return to Europe. Before long Churchill promoted him to commodore, and in the spring of 1942 he changed his title from Director of Combined Operations to Chief of Combined Operations (CCO)—the same position Keyes had argued for in vain. That distinction allowed Mountbatten to serve as a member of the Chiefs of Staff Committee, despite palpable resentment from the other service chiefs, who viewed his organization as a bastard stepchild and resented his rapid rise in rank. In due time Churchill promoted him to vice admiral in the Royal Navy, bestowing on him simultaneously the honorary ranks of air marshal in the Royal Air Force and lieutenant general in the army, making him the only individual besides the King to hold rank in all three services. It was an extraordinary rise to power, despite his reckless "palace playboy" image.[9]

Mountbatten had entered the Royal Navy as a cadet at thirteen, and at forty-one, after a quarter-century of service aboard battleships, submarines and destroyers, he exhibited a flair for signals and the nascent wireless technology they employed.[10] By 1941 he was commanding destroyers in combat in the English Channel and the Mediterranean—though with dubious results. Six months before his appointment to Combined Operations, his destroyer HMS Kelly was lost while evacuating British troops from Crete, following a direct hit from Stuka dive-bombers—a scene played out heroically in the film In Which We Serve, starring his friend and rumoured lover, Noël Coward.[11] At the time of his appointment he was preparing to take his rising star to the bridge of the aircraft carrier HMS Illustrious. As far as Churchill was concerned, however, Mountbatten was the perfect candidate to handle the new raiding operations he intended to expand in size and scope.

Like Godfrey, Fleming and Churchill, Mountbatten possessed a maverick personality and displayed little fear of doing things in unconventional ways. Later, he would skilfully manoeuvre his way through the treacherous waters of Whitehall by relying on his well-oiled personal "force enhancers"—matinee-idol looks, royal bloodline and innate charm. As Elizabeth Nel, Churchill's secretary, recalled years later: "His was quite the most glamorous personality among our circles; not only was he tall and extremely good-looking, with gold braid flashing on his uniform, but he seemed to exude a special kind of charm which had us all falling over backwards."[12] Critics claim, however, that much of Mountbatten's meteoric rise stemmed from a mix of Churchill's guilt and his notorious penchant for patronage appointments. Churchill had

In October 1941, Winston Churchill appointed the youthful Lord Louis Mountbatten as Chief of Combined Operations. Despite his "palace playboy" image, the bold, ambitious and glamorous "Dickie" Mountbatten, a great-grandson of Queen Victoria, like Ian Fleming clearly understood the paramount importance of intelligence at the dawning of the information age. Here he is photographed by Yousuf Karsh for the cover of *Maclean's* magazine, February 1, 1944.

sacked Dickie's father, Prince Louis of Battenberg, as First Sea Lord at the outbreak of the First World War because of the political optics of his German heritage and name. Now he was ready to make amends and repay the son—with his newly anglicized name, Mountbatten—for his unwavering support during Churchill's own years in the political wilderness, when his repeated warnings about appeasing Mussolini and Hitler had been met with derision.

What has never been appreciated in the standard biographies of Mountbatten is that this upstart royal possessed something that was vitally important both to Churchill and to Britain's pressing needs: an understanding of the fundamental nature and significance of intelligence, along with an intimate knowledge of signals intelligence and cryptography that appealed to the prime minister in a primordial way. "I was born and bred in an atmosphere of Naval Intelligence," Mountbatten wrote. His father, who had served as Assistant Director and then Director of Naval Intelligence at the turn of the century, "continued to talk of the fascination and importance of Intelligence even after he had moved on."[13]

Furthermore, like Ian Fleming, Mountbatten exhibited technocratic zeal and embraced modernity. He developed the signals intelligence capabilities for his station while working as a fleet wireless officer in the Mediterranean, where he raised the standard of signalling to new heights. During a brief stint at the signals school in Portsmouth, he earned a reputation for energy, efficiency and inventiveness and was well respected for his cryptographic foresight. He urged the Royal Navy to adopt the Typex encryption machine as the British equivalent of the German Enigma at a time when few of his colleagues had any faith in this device. Later it was readily adopted.[14]

"I realized I could not expect to achieve any successes without really good Intelligence and a knowledge of how to use it," Mountbatten wrote after the war, attributing many of his achievements as Combined Operations chief and later as supreme Allied commander in South-East

Asia to the fruits of this work.[15] His interest in and devotion to naval intelligence, and in particular to signals intelligence, reveals a long-ignored cornerstone of the Mountbatten–Churchill relationship. Despite his daring and aggressive spirit that bordered at times on the reckless, he recognized the need to foster the intellectual and techno-logical work at Bletchley Park—a process and a product that was increasingly viewed as a new-found natural resource.

The injection of a charismatic and influential character like Mountbatten into the intelligence-gathering world reinvigorated the potential the raiding scene offered to the war effort. For Godfrey, Mountbatten's ascendancy to the crown of Combined Operations not only ensured continued co-operation on pinch matters but amplified the possibilities. The coming twin raids on the Lofoten and Vaagso Islands in the final days of 1941 were proof of that—especially as they turned out to be the most successful pinch raids of all.

Until this point in the war, attacks carried out by Combined Operations had been limited to small hit-and-run raids along the coast or to unopposed landings—as in Lofoten the previous March. The plan to return to the Lofoten area had been on the books since June, when the Ministry of Economic Warfare (MEW), which was responsible for attacking German economic interests, approached the Special Operations Executive (SOE) about conducting a fierce campaign of industrial sabotage throughout Norway. At this point, however, the means for such action was lacking. SOE needed a cata-lyst, a vehicle and a "coalition of the willing" to put any raid into effect. As things turned out, very few missions or operations were carried out for monocausal reasons. Rather, to attract co-operation from the other services, even in a minor way, targets had to offer something that appealed to them all. Originally, under Sir Roger Keyes's direction, Combined Operations had shown little interest in spearheading such raids. When Mountbatten took over, however, the pinch needs of Godfrey's NID meshed well with the evolving strategy of Great Britain's ever-widening war effort.

After Hitler's invasion of Stalin's Soviet Russia on June 22, 1941, the British had entered into a tenuous alliance with their former enemy. Despite his intense hatred of Communism, Churchill had no hesitation in joining forces with the Soviet Union at this time. "If Hitler invaded Hell," he declared, "I would at least make a favourable reference to the Devil in the House of Commons."[16] Simply put, the British and the Western world in general needed the Soviet Union and its most precious natural resource—manpower—to have any hope of defeating Hitler's armies. Yet they remained fearful that the Russians might give up more quickly than the Czarist armies had done in the First World War. In an effort to encourage Stalin to fight on, Churchill needed to demonstrate the value of his alliance in any way possible short of opening a second front by invading Western Europe—an impossible proposition at the time.

So Churchill decided to extend the hand of friendship, arranging for British-made weapons and materials vital to the Soviet war machine to reach the Soviet Union via massive Arctic convoys that would skirt German-occupied Norway and bring the goods to northern Russian ports. In addition, using a series of amphibious raids along the Norwegian coast, he hoped to fix Hitler's attention on that region. If he could convince the Nazi leader that Norway had become the "zone of destiny" where the war in the west would be won or lost, he would draw German air and land forces away from the Russian front.

A return to Norway would not only satisfy these desires but offer a further opportunity to restock the bare shelves at Bletchley Park. If Mountbatten could deliver the crucial pinched material, he would prove the value of Combined Operations under his command.[17] With all these objectives in mind, Churchill and the Chiefs of Staff Committee approved a twin operation—Operation Anklet and Operation

Archery—that Combined Operations would carry out close to the Norwegian coast. Together, these two operations could deliver a one-two punch in the Lofoten Islands (Operation Anklet) and on the island of Vaagso, three hundred miles to the south, between Trondheim and Bergen (Operation Archery). The ostensible purpose of Operation Anklet was to seize and hold the harbour at Reine as an advanced naval base from which the British could prevent German interference with the Arctic convoys, but in fact it would allow the SOE and the MEW the chance to wreak havoc on the local fisheries industry and provide a fertile environment to troll for further Enigma-related material.[18] A strike at Lofoten would also serve as a diversion to draw German attention away from the main raid—Operation Archery—which was designed specifically to fulfill the intelligence-gathering requirements of the NID. In other words, it would be a pinch raid.

With Operation Archery, the age of combined operations truly began. All three services—the British Army, the Royal Navy and the RAF—worked together to plan and execute it. Right from the beginning, each service provided a force commander and staff to integrate its particular contribution into the overall or combined plan to achieve the common goal—a process that is normal now in planning military operations but was startlingly new at the time. Moreover, Archery laid the groundwork for the coming raids at Bruneval and St-Nazaire—and, in August 1942, for Operation Jubilee at Dieppe.

Publicly, the aim of Operation Archery was the destruction of the fisheries on South Vaagso and the tiny island of Maaloy, which guarded the waterway known as the Ulvesund—the sound that separates these beautiful but isolated islands from the Norwegian coast.[19] These fisheries provided minerals that were used to manufacture two essential products for the German navy: vitamin supplements for U-boat crews long deprived of sunlight, and glycerine for the explosive charges in submarine torpedoes. Unlike Operation Anklet farther north in Lofoten, where little resistance was expected,

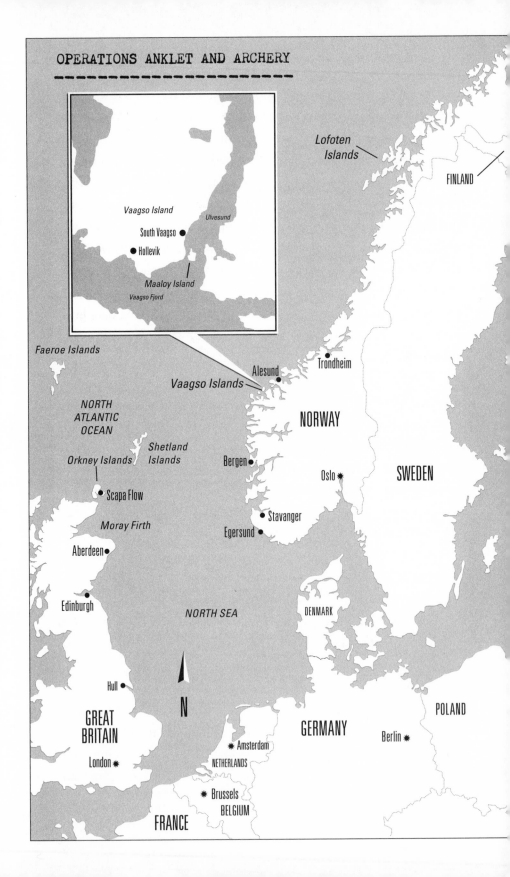

OPERATIONS ANKLET AND ARCHERY
- -

Vaagso Island

Ulvesund

South Vaagso

Hollevik

Maaloy Island

Vaagso Fjord

Lofoten
Islands

FINLAND

Faeroe Islands

Trondheim

Alesund

Vaagso Islands

NORWAY

NORTH
ATLANTIC
OCEAN

Shetland
Islands

Orkney Islands

Bergen

Oslo

SWEDEN

Scapa Flow

Moray Firth

Stavanger

Egersund

Aberdeen

Edinburgh

NORTH SEA

DENMARK

Hull

N

GREAT
BRITAIN

GERMANY

POLAND

Berlin

London

Amsterdam

NETHERLANDS

Brussels

BELGIUM

FRANCE

the Germans had garrisoned the village of Vaagso in respectable numbers, so Mountbatten prepared for a fight—an engagement welcomed by the men of Lieutenant Colonel John Durnford-Slater's veteran No. 3 Commando unit who had participated in the first Lofoten raid and would later be called upon again for Dieppe. According to the plan, the commandos would launch an amphibious raid on four areas to knock out the German gun positions and defences as well as the built-up area in South Vaagso. To support the attack, the Royal Navy sent a cruiser squadron with destroyers, troopships and a submarine. The RAF supplied several squadrons of Blenheim and Beaufighter aircraft, marking the first time it contributed significantly to a Combined Operations plan.

However, the imperative of the operation was the pinch—either during the capture or sinking of German patrol boats, trawlers and merchant vessels or on land, with the commandos targeting a wireless station and the local Kriegsmarine headquarters, each housed in a hotel, in an attempt to scrounge the critical code books and other materials Bletchley Park urgently needed. The operational instructions prepared for Operation Archery included this carefully crafted advisory:

> It is very important that ships, particularly escort ships, armed trawlers, etc., be prevented from destroying or throwing overboard any papers, etc. On boarding, a thorough search is to be made for papers especially those found in the charthouse, wheelhouse or captain's cabin. All papers are to be brought off and great care is to be taken to avoid damaging such documents or moving the keys of typewriters or simply machines as the value of their capture may be reduced thereby. The discovery of any of the above must be reported at once to the rear admiral commanding 10th Cruiser Squadron. It is of the greatest importance that this signal should NOT be made in plain language.[20]

With the pinch net spread, John Godfrey attached a liaison officer from the Naval Section to the raid in an effort to home in on potential targets. On December 18, just days before the twin raids, Lieutenant Commander Allon Bacon, the veteran of the Lauenburg pinch and the officer sent by Godfrey to retrieve the material from U-110, evaluated the potential pinch targets offered by both operations.[21] The resourceful Bacon based his assessment on the intelligence provided by a Norwegian fisherman whose brother worked for the Special Operations Executive. He concluded that both operations offered good pinch opportunities.[22] "In view of this report which provides 4 possible Z targets and greater speed than the Northern Anklet party," he decided that "this party i.e. Archery offers best chances."[23] Most significant, Operation Archery appears to be the first time that military forces took an active part in a pinch alongside their naval counterparts.

Another conspicuous "first" was Mountbatten's decision to attach one of his own staff officers, Royal Navy Lieutenant Commander Ackroyd Norman Palliser de Costobadie, to the raid. Better known as "Dick" to his colleagues, De Costobadie had earned the Distinguished Service Cross for "good judgement and initiative" while he commanded the flat-bottomed Royal Navy river gunboat HMS Locust during the Dunkirk evacuation in 1940.[24] After his investiture by the King at Buckingham Palace at the height of the Battle of Britain, he joined Combined Operations, where he worked on the staff of the naval adviser responsible for the selection of targets and the creation of outline plans for all Mountbatten's operations.[25] His attachment to Operation Archery did not seem curious at the time because the staff at Combined Operations were still learning their trade, and observers were commonplace.

When the day for the mission arrived, Mountbatten tasked De Costobadie with commanding the boarding party slated to protect Bacon while he sought out and pinched the vital material. This move clearly reflected Mountbatten's personal interest in the raid and its crucial importance to Combined Operations—spurred by the potential "political" gain for his organization should the pinched materials provide another triumph.

It was not until he was on board HMS *Onslow* that De Costobadie found that the ad hoc collection of officers and ratings provided from the destroyer's crew seemed to have no training at all as a boarding party.[26] "I was more than worried, I was in fact horrified. They consisted to the best of my recollection of one Sub-Lieutenant, one Midshipman, one Petty Officer, one Leading Seaman, three seamen and two stokers. None of these men appeared trained. They turned up when paraded in any sort of rig, so I roared them up and sent them off to get into proper rig."[27] He was in an invidious situation: he was a guest on the ship, with no knowledge of the men now under his command. He would have much preferred to go into battle with a specially organized and trained pinch unit, but at this eleventh hour he had no choice but to make the best of the situation.[28]

The raid kicked off after a short delay caused by foul winter weather over Scapa Flow and following a brief address from Mountbatten, who reputedly told the troops in his closing remarks: "One last thing. When my ship, the destroyer *Kelly*, went down off Crete earlier this year, the Germans machine-gunned the survivors in the water. There's absolutely no need to treat them gently on my account. Good luck to you all!"[29]

The *Onslow* headed into Vaagso Fjord. It did not have to wait long for a victim. Directly in front of the oncoming destroyer was the German trawler *Fohn*, which on first sighting turned and fled, accompanied by two other vessels, steaming up the inlet and firing at the British aircraft overhead while its crew desperately threw documents over the sides. When the collection of ships reached a bend in the waterway, they turned hard to port and beached themselves, with *Onslow* closing fast. Within minutes, the order "Away All Boarding Parties" bellowed, and both De Costobadie and Bacon stood amidships on the destroyer's

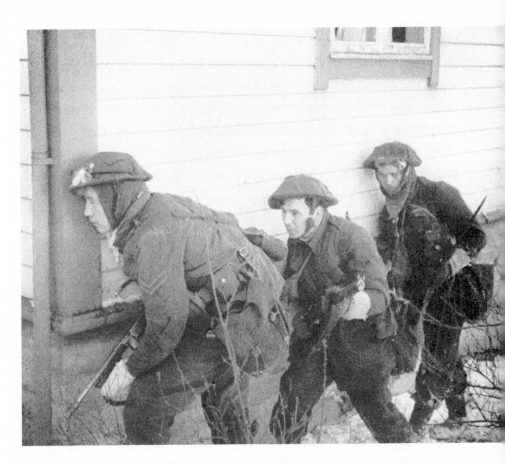

Commandos in action during the pinch raid on Vaagso, Operation Archery, which brought back a "precious haul." Dramatically posed action photos like this were used to promote the commandos and Combined Operations, and build up morale at home, while at the same time helping to deflect attention from the pinch imperative of the raid.

motor launch, steaming for shore.[30] They quickly crossed the three hundred yards to the Fohn with rifles, pistols and bayonets at the ready. By the time they reached the stranded trawler, most of the crew had leapt ashore, positioning themselves across a road from where they sniped at the boarding party. Without a properly trained commando unit, taking over the Fohn proved difficult at first. Eventually the boarding party forced the remaining Germans to flee, and De Costobadie and his band moved on to the next ship while Bacon was left to search the Fohn and execute the pinch.

Stepping over the body of the captain, Bacon entered Fohn's wireless room, which yielded nothing. He proceeded to the captain's cabin, where "the application of a jemmy to the Master's desk produced the highly-prized list of Enigma daily settings."[31] A more detailed search of his wardrobe revealed "the current bigram tables encased in a celluloid container and stowed away amongst his well laundered shirts."[32] Bacon immediately placed the documents, printed in soluble ink, inside a double-skinned, watertight rubber bag specially made for this purpose and moved on to the other ships.[33]

Not as lucky on these vessels, the commando party quickly made their way back to Onslow in time to witness the destroyer's four-inch guns obliterate all the German craft—part of the pre-arranged plan to cover their tracks. On shore, explosions and fires raged in the wake of the simultaneous successful operations by Durnford-Slater's No. 3 Commandos. The scale of the destruction they inflicted shocked the German commander days later when he toured the smouldering ruins in South Vaagso. Everywhere he looked, German barracks, telephone exchanges, gun positions, the wireless station, fish canneries and oil storage tanks all lay in smashed and burnt-out ruins, as did the Hotel Ulvesand, which had housed the German headquarters. But the level of the devastation hid the truly vital thing that had taken place; it gave no indication that a pinch had occurred—or that a "precious haul" had returned to England.

The prized materials—some of them seized from another patrol boat, the Donner, and by another boarding party from HMS Offa, coupled with material from the patrol vessel Geier—made these two operations the most successful pinch raid of the war thus far.[34] At least two complete three-rotor Enigma machines, parts of a third, extra rotors, and a variety of tables, key sheets, RHV emergency and WW weather code books, short signals, and the long-sought-after bigram tables ended up in Alan Turing's hands by New Year's Day 1942.[35] This material paid huge dividends, enabling the cryptographers at Bletchley Park to break the Kriegsmarine Home Waters, Mediterranean, Norwegian and Baltic keys, and the cryptanalysts to gain invaluable insights into German encryption methods and technology. The only black spot was the failure to uncover anything substantial connected to the four-rotor Enigma machine. With fingers still firmly crossed, the British moved on into a new year and a new war.

On December 7, 1941, the Japanese launched their surprise attack on the American Pacific fleet based at Pearl Harbor, Hawaii, and ushered in a new era that took the European conflict worldwide. In the House of Commons that night, Winston Churchill seemed relieved, proclaiming with almost boyish glee what he saw as the course of the eventual Allied victory. "In the past we have had a light which flickered" in the atmosphere, he said; "in the present we have a light which flames, and in the future there will be a light which shines over all the land and sea."[36]

Indeed, the prime minister had reason to be ecstatic. For close to two years he had desperately courted the United States, using every means at his disposal to bring the sleeping giant into a formal, overt alliance. Churchill's campaign of covert subversion, propaganda and diplomatic cajoling had already brought the two nations closer, with President Franklin Roosevelt extending what help he could during the isolationist period by trading much-needed "Destroyers for Bases" and entering into the all-encompassing Lend-Lease agreement. Meanwhile, Godfrey and the Admiralty cozied up to the "neutral" U.S. fleet on convoy and intelligence matters. The sum total of this relationship saw the Americans adopt an increasingly belligerent stance towards Germany and Japan as 1941 wore on. With luck, one of those enemy countries would react with an incident that would sway the isolationist American public opinion to favour a declaration of war. The devastating bombing of Pearl Harbor by Japan was perhaps more than Britain and Roosevelt had bargained for, but it had a galvanizing effect on the Americans. They were now set on war—an attitude reinforced two days later when Hitler joined Japan and declared war on the United States.

But the British still had a long year ahead, during which they would be more or less on their own. The massive U.S. industrial potential was not yet organized for the war effort and could have no immediate impact on the war situation. The British would have to survive on their own all through 1942, until the retooling of the American economy shifted into high gear and the much-anticipated American troops, aircraft and naval vessels reached the United Kingdom. Once there, they would help build up the forces for the eventual liberation of Europe.

For the Admiralty, the widening war immediately brought with it increased responsibilities, which in some cases were impossible to meet. Life was dire in the weeks and months following Pearl Harbor: the garrison of Hong Kong quickly fell to the surging Japanese army, as did the Dutch East Indies with their vital oil and rubber resources. At sea, the pride of the Royal Navy, the battleships HMS *Prince of Wales* and HMS *Repulse*, Godfrey's former flagship, succumbed to Japanese air attacks off Malaysia, leaving little doubt of the vulnerability of surface ships to Japan's air power. Meanwhile, the Japanese fleet launched carrier raids from Hawaii to Australia and into the Indian Ocean at Ceylon (now Sri Lanka). In February, the British bastion at Singapore fell to the Japanese in the most humiliating capitulation in British history.

As a result of all this sudden activity on the other side of the world, the Royal Navy found itself in an exceedingly precarious situation, overstretched in all aspects and with ever-increasing demands worldwide. First and foremost, it had to maintain the vital North Atlantic convoy routes, deliver convoys through the treacherous Arctic Ocean to Russia, and keep lines of communication open and supplies flowing to its armies in the field in Gibraltar, Persia, Iraq and India, and in West Africa, East Africa and North Africa. With the fall of the Dutch East Indies to the Japanese, the vital Middle East and Persian Gulf oil reserves became more vulnerable to submarine attacks. An already overburdened anti-submarine force now had to reinforce the Arabian Sea and the Persian Gulf area, where any blows against tankers and the loss of their precious supplies were likely to produce a paralyzing effect on the Allies. The answer in part was to increase the number of escort vessels and long-range aircraft covering the convoys' routes and to keep up pressure on the U-boats.

Unlike modern submarines that operate fully submerged, the Second World War version was in fact a submersible vessel. When not involved in direct combat, it had to sail on the surface in order to operate its diesel engines, maintain a decent speed, and provide fresh air for the crew and its batteries. Although aircraft anti-submarine armaments were not yet as lethal as they would become later in the war, the simple appearance of a warplane overhead was enough to force a submarine to dive. Once underwater, a U-boat's speed declined by half or two-thirds, meaning that the ships in the convoy the U-boat was stalking could escape, even as the U-boat used up its precious fresh-air supply and battery power. Eventually it would have to surface, where it would be at the mercy of any aircraft or surface ships in the area.

The convoys' escort vessels, including destroyers and corvettes, were the most effective protection against U-boats, particularly given the constantly improving British anti-submarine weapons: depth charges, short-range shipboard radar and direction-finding "Huff Duff" instruments. But supplies of these escort ships were limited, leaving convoys hopelessly exposed to organized groups of U-boat wolf packs unless air power could pick up the slack. Unfortunately, there was not enough of anything to go around, and the growing demand for aircraft brought the Admiralty into direct conflict with the RAF, which required the same type of long-range, heavy-payload planes for the nascent bombing campaign over Germany.

Part of Churchill's relief over the recent pinches stemmed from the fact that, thanks to the resumed flow of Ultra, he no longer had to divert his attention and scarce resources away from his most recent panacea— the strategic bombing of Germany. Ultra offered him a tool he could wield to manage his strategic assets more effectively and to engage in operations and policies based on calculated rather than blind risks.

The tremendous intelligence and pinch successes of 1941, capped off by the Lofoten and Vaagso raids, ushered in a new era the following year for both the Naval Intelligence Division and Bletchley Park. Not only had the Bletchley boffins broken into Germany's Enigma via the crib-fed Bombes, but lesser codes, the ones originally used to get in the back door, began to contribute intelligence dividends themselves. This payoff forced Godfrey to revamp his pinch priorities. Over the year, his NID, working in conjunction with Frank Birch at the Naval Section, had created a simple rubric to denote their vital needs. Using a letter-and-number method, the letters A to G represented the level of importance of the particular code and cipher, while the number marked the veracity of the actual information obtained. In this scheme, *A* represented the most secret codes and ciphers; B, small-ship ciphers; C, naval air codes; D, merchant navy codes; E, meteorological codes; F, miscellaneous; and G, Armistice Commission codes.[37] Intelligence derived from naval Enigma remained, as it had been since the beginning of the war, as *A1*, but now, with the ascendancy of the "lower-level" codes in the cryptographic realm, RHV—the emergency hand cipher used when Enigma broke down, and which changed very rarely—appeared as *A2*; short-signal codes (E-bars, B-bars and the WW weather codes) as *A3*; Kriegsmarine general cipher as *A4*; and the *Werftschlussel* dockyard cipher as B1.[38] Each one of these codes and ciphers could now be tapped to provide cribs for the Bombes or for their own intrinsic value.

The cumulative results of all this pinching and decoding during the previous twelve months proved staggering: by year's end in 1941, almost every area of the Kriegsmarine's operations was under British surveillance to one degree or another. Godfrey refused to push his luck any further. On January 20, 1942, he convened a meeting with his senior staff and with Frank Birch, where he laid out a pivotal change in pinch policy.[39] It was an extremely difficult time, despite the recent success at Lofoten and Vaagso, because ominous warnings about the imminent introduction of the four-rotor Enigma machine continued to surface. A new series of "four-rotor duds"—setting mistakes by German operators using the new machine as though it were a three-rotor—confirmed the suspicion that some U-boats stationed in the Atlantic already carried the machine.[40] Then, just a week before the meeting, an intercepted message indicated that some surface vessels too were using the machine.[41]

Godfrey refused to be discouraged. Both he and Birch knew they faced a sticky dilemma. Currently, penetration of German message traffic enciphered on the three-rotor naval Enigma was both fruitful and free-flowing, and the last thing either of them wanted was to tip off the Germans to their success by continuing to pinch material from individual vessels at sea. They quite rightly feared that further pinches would eventually alert the Germans and accelerate the introduction of the four-rotor machine.

Part of this decision sprang from the discovery five months earlier of the four-rotor lid from U-570, mentioned at the end of chapter 4.

Cross-checking the serial number with existing three-rotor machines, Naval Section had calculated that too few four-rotor machines existed to outfit the entire Kriegsmarine immediately and thus they still had some breathing room before a wide-scale replacement would be introduced.[42] They rationalized that as long as the Germans continued to cling to their delusion that the three-rotor was impenetrable, the Kriegsmarine had no immediate reason to incur the huge cost and effort of introducing the new machines en masse. With all that in mind, Godfrey decided to suspend pinch raids for the time being but to set out clear provisions for renewing them when Donitz changed the bigram tables as he did periodically. Birch added, "If the U-Boats were put on basically different keys to surface craft or began to use a fourth wheel, a pinch would be the only hope."[43]

In his new policy, Godfrey tried to balance current and potential needs with security. The recent operations in Norway had demonstrated the potential for cloaking the pinch within the framework of a larger raid on a port or other shore-based facility.[44] Given that surprise and speed were paramount in any effort to obtain the desired material before the Germans could destroy it, it seemed more promising to attack ships in a confined area in order to overwhelm them quickly and prevent a chase or even their escape. Inland waterways or ports offered enticing possibilities, particularly with the ships berthed in tight groups along the docks and quays, either lightly guarded by skeleton crews or even unguarded in some cases, rendering them relatively easy targets for pillage.

In addition, ports offered other tantalizing features—signals facilities, such as wireless stations, and storage depots—which, along with the local naval headquarters, made up a target-rich environment for pinches.[45] At Vaagso the Germans had proved adept at moving their signals stations on short notice, but a naval headquarters, fixed in a particular location, would remain in operation almost to the bitter end of the fight, giving the raiders a better chance of capturing vital material.[46] There, stockpiles of signals-related material for the current period and, even more important, for months into the future would be found tucked into files and desks or in the safe, most likely in the commandant's office or quarters. It was the job of the German harbour headquarters to maintain wireless contact with all types of vessels at sea, as well as with other headquarters in the wireless chain. Regardless of size or location, these headquarters would have to possess various forms of the Enigma machine, along with the associated code books, tables and setting sheets, not to mention copies of RHV, short-signal code books, weather codes and dockyard ciphers—all of critical importance to Bletchley Park.[47] As an added bonus, other materials—such as plans, charts, technical documents, lists of commanders and the order of battle, and the key for nomenclature of German naval operations and procedures—were generally held in the naval headquarters. It was one thing to read the enemy's mail, but quite another to understand the technical terminology that resisted normal linguistic translation.[48]

From the perspective of security, pinch raids on headquarters under the cloak of larger operations were also ideal for several salient reasons. First, because most of the desired target locations were housed close to the shoreline, they could be overrun quickly and effectively during amphibious operations. Second, the ransacked facility could then be destroyed, leaving the Germans unaware of what, if any, material had been pilfered.[49] And third, as earlier operations had established, a veil of secrecy could easily be drawn by cloaking the pinch mission under the cover of a larger raid offering up other legitimate, but nonetheless secondary, objectives, thereby deflecting any suspicion from the prime target. In short, from the pinch perspective, taking these raids to shore offered the British a form of "one-stop shopping."

With the new shore-based policy accepted, Frank Birch created a card index of probable targets, with a description of all the German communications and headquarters establishments likely to contain the desired material. The index was based on information from all possible sources—Ultra, captured documents, photographic reconnaissance, agent reports and prisoner-of-war interrogations.[50] Eventually, he built up a network of all enemy communications facilities, the type of traffic they handled and the codes that might be pinched from them.[51] This information was posted on a large wall chart in the Naval Section at Bletchley, with pins of various colours and shapes indicating the different codes and ciphers held at each location. One glance at the chart indicated what a raiding force could expect to capture at any given shore establishment.[52]

But the discussions between Godfrey and Birch over this issue also marked the beginning of a dramatic change in their relationship. In the weeks and months following the January 1942 meeting, Frank Birch's Naval Section would play an ever-decreasing role in the planning and execution of pinch raids. As before, it could offer up potential targets, relay needs and even suggest methods to obtain the material, but it no longer had any representative attached to the Section who actively participated in the raids. Instead, by the spring of 1942, Godfrey preferred to keep this role "in-house," joining forces with the delivery vehicle provided by Mountbatten's Combined Operations Headquarters—a budding collaboration cemented during the wildly successful raids at Vaagso, and later at Bruneval and St-Nazaire. "You will be interested to know," Godfrey told Mountbatten, "that you are the first person, occupying any position of importance, who has given the NID such unstinted and unsolicited praise."[53] Ever quick to seize a chance to charm, Mountbatten replied, "I am amazed at your statement . . . because I thought it was commonly accepted that NID was far and away the best Intelligence department and running better now than at any time since the famous Blinker Hall's days."[54]

The intense courtship between the two organizations grew, leaving the Naval Section to play the role of jilted lover. Birch complained loudly about their exclusion from the pinch-raid process, claiming that, if they had possessed advance knowledge of a raid or its specific objectives, he and his staff could have enhanced the overall success.[55] But no argument from Bletchley Park penetrated the thick walls of Godfrey's and Fleming's Room 39 in the Old Admiralty Building. Birch was fobbed off with practical reasons for his exclusion: first, to meet security concerns, the number of those in the know about upcoming raids had to be limited; second, because most raids never moved past the planning stage, it would be a waste of time and effort to generate unnecessary interest; third, there was little that Frank Birch and his Naval Section could bring to the table that Godfrey's NID did not already know about naval cryptography.[56] The cryptographic knowledge that Ian Fleming and others possessed, the expertise with pinch raids gained by Allon Bacon and by Jasper Haines as the liaison officer between the NID and Bletchley Park, and the close association that the NID was developing with Combined Operations had all made Godfrey more comfortable in proceeding without the need for consultations with Birch and Bletchley.

It is not surprising, then, that the first serious indication of a projected raid on the port of Dieppe appeared just twenty-four hours after the Godfrey-inspired change in pinch policy.[57]

On January 21, 1942, Combined Operations' target search committee, led by Captain John "Jock" Hughes-Hallett (who would eventually become the naval force commander for the Dieppe Raid), began to make plans to fulfill Churchill's wish for a raiding programme along the German-held coast of France. Mountbatten's selection of Hughes-Hallett to pilot this committee, to recommend potential targets, and to oversee the creation of outline plans for upcoming operations was indicative of a new direction for his Combined Operations organization. A career Royal Navy officer who had gained brief combat experience at the end of the First World War, Hughes-Hallett had been educated at Dartmouth Naval College and at Cambridge before serving as a torpedo officer in 1918. In the interwar period, he became a torpedo specialist on the aircraft carrier HMS *Courageous* and gained praise for his ingenuity with torpedoes, mines and shipboard electronics before rising to executive office. During the Norwegian campaign in 1940, he was mentioned in dispatches for his role in whisking the Norwegian royal family to safety in the midst of the full-blown Nazi invasion of the country.

Following his short stint at sea, which never included a command appointment, Jock Hughes-Hallett had spent the next year and a half as the navy's lead planner for various schemes to defend British ports and beaches against German invasion. He had developed an intimate knowledge of and expertise in this field. His course and career progression reports were outstanding, marking him as "an officer with a brilliant and original mind." He had "intellectual capacity of a very high order and is full of ideas. He has great energy and drive and pushes through schemes to their conclusions, undeterred and unperturbed by practical difficulties. A strong personality with great confidence in himself, he expresses himself clearly and decisively both in speech and in writing."[58]

Although he had talent and demonstrated a "clear brain," Hughes-Hallett was not "the money of some naval officers."[59] An overtly "ambitious type," he offended many who found him "insufferable."[60] "He is considered, and I think with reason, as too loud-voiced, overbearing, and too cocksure of himself without adequate reason," recalled Rear Admiral H.T. Baillie-Grohman, the man who preceded him as naval commander for the Dieppe Raid.[61] Mountbatten concurred with this assessment but cited professional jealousy as the reason. "It is just because he is right 99% of the time that he does annoy so many people," he replied, praising Hughes-Hallett as "one of the most brilliant and outstanding officers in the service" who had "more than fulfilled expectations." Later in his personnel file he noted that

Captain John "Jock" Hughes-Hallett, who was the architect, lead planner and naval force commander for the Dieppe Raid. With his intimate knowledge of port defences, his specific responsibility was to search for raiding targets and to draw up the plans for all of Mountbatten's Combined Operations.

Hughes-Hallett "is perhaps a little fond of laying down the law (his friends call him Hughes-Hitler)."[62]

In December 1941, after Jock Hughes-Hallett had caught Winston Churchill's eye for his work preparing to repel the expected German invasion of England, Mountbatten recruited him to Combined Operations to act as his naval adviser. Given Churchill's increasing desire to take the fight to the enemy, coupled with the new policy of launching pinch raids at enemy ports and naval facilities, who better to call upon than the man responsible for defending British ports from attacks by the Germans? Hughes-Hallett's intimate knowledge of port defences and the tactics used to breach or subvert them was likely to be priceless. Having joined Mountbatten's head-quarters just before the last round of Norwegian pinches, where his subordinate Dick de Costobadie would play a key role, Hughes-Hallett set about creating a raiding programme for the following six months.[63] "Our urgent task," he recalled on his arrival at Combined Operations Headquarters on Richmond Terrace in Whitehall, "was to select targets for raids on France and Norway," something "every-one agreed . . . must fall to the Navy . . . [because] it was no use suggesting places which could not be reached by appropriate land-ing craft or other vessels."[64]

Despite the "combined" nature of Mountbatten's headquarters, the Royal Navy's interests were often front and centre. The air adviser was little more than a liaison officer who sought co-operation from the RAF squadrons in covering and supporting a raid, while the military adviser provided the land-force elements, such as the army comman-dos, and helped to create the detailed military portion of the com-bined plan. This division of responsibilities left the genesis of any raid—the creation of the vital outline plan, including the original objectives and intent—firmly in the hands of the naval adviser. He in turn kept both the Admiralty and the Joint Planning Committee informed of what was going on at Combined Operations Headquarter.[65]

The sudden appearance of Dieppe as a proposed target could not be coincidence, particularly given the men who assisted Jock Hughes-Hallett in making the decision and the timing, just one day after the change in pinch policy. Along with Lieutenant Commander Dick de Costobadie came Commander David Luce, fresh from a year as the head of the Admiralty's Plans Division and now recruited by Mountbatten to be Hughes-Hallett's main adviser on raid planning.[66] Hughes-Hallett would recall in his memoirs, "David Luce, Costabadie [sic] and I sat down to make tentative proposals for one raid every month up to and including August," but "were not so much concerned at this stage with the intrinsic value of objectives on a particular raid, but rather with the feasibility of reaching the place undetected."[67]

With his hands often tied by logistical concerns—such as a limited amount of specialized landing craft at his disposal—Hughes-Hallett planned to start small, with an attack on the coastal radar station at Bruneval in late February, followed by another on a Luftwaffe hospital in the Ostend area in early March.[68] As the logistical capabilities increased, he envisioned proportionately larger and bolder raids, including a daring and almost suicidal attack on the large dry dock situated at the German U-boat base at St-Nazaire for March, followed days later by another Vaagso-style attack on the port of Bayonne in southwestern France.[69] For May he suggested the seizure of Alderney, to cut the supply route for U-boats, and in June and July back-to-back raids on the same target—the port of Dieppe. He offered no particular purpose for these two raids in his carefully measured memoirs, written long before the official release of any information about Ultra.[70]

In the background, larger schemes such as the opening of a limited second front on the Cherbourg peninsula (Operation Sledgehammer), the invasion of Madagascar (Operation Ironclad) or the potential seizure of the Canary Islands (Operation Puma) were all in the works. But they were quite different operations, with strategic implications involving other elements outside the direct command of Mountbatten's COHQ.

The interesting point about each one of Hughes-Hallett's proposed operations is that it met two objectives: it had an overt strategic purpose, as the earlier raids in Norway had demonstrated, but it also contained provisions for a "pinch"—either by opportunity or by design. Because these requirements were not mutually exclusive, this symbiotic relationship offered the perfect natural cover: on the one hand, the operation could legitimately satisfy strategic demands, while on the other, it could capture vital material to inject into the intelligence infrastructure in a way that no other arm of service could deliver at that time. On paper, these proposals seemed the perfect plan to serve as the blueprint for a unique "brand" of warfare that both Godfrey and Mountbatten were anxious to parlay into political currency. Churchill was Ultra's greatest devotee, and the ambitious Mountbatten in particular wanted to position his organization to deliver the precious goods and justify its existence to both the all-powerful prime minister and the skeptical chiefs of staff.[71]

On January 23, just days after Godfrey announced the change in pinch policy, Mountbatten gave permission for Hughes-Hallett to draw up a rough plan for what they coined Operation Rutter—the first incarnation of the raid on Dieppe.[72]

SIX

FADE TO BLACK

The first of all our dangers is the U-Boat peril.
That is a very great danger. Our food, our means of
making war, our life, all depend upon the passage
of ships across the sea. The whole power of the
United States to manifest itself in this war
depends upon the power to move ships across the
sea . . . what a terrible waste it is to think of
all these great ships that are sunk.

—WINSTON CHURCHILL, OCTOBER 31, 1942

0330 hours, February 1, 1942, 250 miles off the New Jersey shoreline

From the bridge of the surfaced U-109, Captain-Lieutenant Heinrich
Bleichrodt peered through the targeting binoculars at the silhouette
of an 8,000-ton British merchant steamer cutting across his bow
less than two thousand yards in the distance. The thirty-two-year-old
Bleichrodt, nicknamed "Ajax" after the Greek hero from the Trojan
War, was one of Germany's leading U-boat aces, sinking twenty-five
ships and 150,000 tons of shipping in just eight war patrols—a feat
that warranted the highest award for valour in Nazi Germany, the

Knight's Cross with Oak Leaves. Following a curt series of commands, three torpedoes in quick succession lurched out from the submarine's bow tubes and streamed towards the unsuspecting *Tacoma Star*, which was zigzagging unescorted through the darkness.

On the same day that Combined Operations had raided Lofoten and Vaagso, U-109 slipped out of her berth in the giant concrete U-boat pen at Lorient, France, for the month-long journey to reach the Eastern Seaboard of North America and participate in Admiral Karl Dönitz's new submarine offensive, Operation Paukenschlag (Operation Drumbeat). Suspecting that North American waters might provide a healthy killing ground, Dönitz had shifted his U-boats from the mid-Atlantic and unleashed them on merchant vessels carrying troops, passengers, and essential food and war supplies. The submarines had a wide swath of ocean to cover, as the ships travelled from the Caribbean and the Gulf of Mexico to critical points along the Eastern Seaboard of the United States and Canada, penetrating at times the Gulf of St. Lawrence.

In the last two years of the Great War the British had learned that the most efficient way of moving vast quantities of supplies and manpower through U-boat-infested waters was to form their merchant vessels into protective convoys, numbering anywhere between thirty and seventy vessels, and then sail them across the ocean at almost a snail's pace, zigzagging or rerouting as needed to avoid enemy submarines. The upside was increased security for these vessels: packed together and sailing with a naval escort of destroyers and corvettes (later joined by aircraft and aircraft carriers), there was safety in numbers. If warned in advance, the entire complement of ships could avoid a single U-boat (or a group of submarines working together as a wolf pack) or, in some cases, prepare for a fight. The downside was lost time—not only the slow passage but the wait to form the convoy, unload all the ships once they reached their destination, and regroup them for the return voyage. The convoy system certainly reduced the number of trips each ship could make in a year, but the British were willing to pay that price.

The Americans, however, stubbornly chose to send ships individually and without escort, leaving them at the mercy of roving U-boats and with little means of defence. Stifled by their own antiquated strategy, the United States Navy had initially rejected the convoy system, opting for speed rather than safety. Compounding this vulnerability, the Americans lacked sufficient air cover along the U.S. coast and were still lax about implementing the basic precaution of blacking out bright lights in cities and seaside communities along the Atlantic coast, making it easy for seasoned hunters like Bleichrodt to pick out their victims as they steamed past the shore, perfectly silhouetted. As Dönitz would later boast:

> The U-boats found that conditions there were almost exactly those of normal peacetime. The coast was not blacked-out, and the towns were a blaze of bright lights . . . The lights, both in lighthouses and on buoys, shone forth, though perhaps a little less brightly than usual. Shipping followed the normal peacetime routes and carried the normal lights. Although five weeks had passed since the declaration of war, very few anti-submarine measures appeared to have been introduced. There were, admittedly, anti-submarine patrols, but they were wholly lacking in experience. Single destroyers, for example, sailed up and down the traffic lanes with such regularity that the U-boats were quickly able to work out the time-table being followed.[1]

It was a painful beginning to the war at sea for the Americans, while the German U-boat crews called it their "Second Happy Time." But even harder times lay ahead after the Allies experienced that new kind of blackout they had been dreading: the silence that followed the introduction of the four-rotor naval Enigma to the Atlantic U-boat fleet on February 1, 1942.

Blissfully unaware of the submarine only 1,300 yards to starboard, Master Robert George, the captain of the *Tacoma Star*, believed that his ship led a semi-charmed life.[2] Already sunk once in Liverpool harbour by a German bomb during the Blitz in 1940, she had lived to fight another day after being raised, repaired and relaunched.[3] Now, as she steamed towards Liverpool on her way home from Buenos Aires with her cargo holds full and ninety-three souls on board, her legendary luck ran out. In just under three minutes, two of U-109's three torpedoes fired from essentially point-blank range struck the forward hold and the engine room amidships, engulfing her in a giant detonation cloud that smothered the vessel for a long time. When she finally emerged, the mortally wounded vessel turned hard to starboard and settled fast by the bow.[4] Sinking in less than four minutes, the steamer had the dubious honour of becoming the first of nearly one thousand Allied merchant vessels, totalling an unprecedented 7.1 million tons of vital shipping, sunk during the four-rotor blackout that lasted from February to December 1942.[5]

According to the report from U-109, the captain and his crew made it to their lifeboats, but in the panic before they abandoned ship they sent the wrong coordinates in their frantic distress call. Never seen again, the ninety-three souls on board the *Tacoma Star* joined close to ten thousand others whose names appear in the sombre lists of the missing and dead from the Battle of the Atlantic.

To boast of his success and arrange a rendezvous to restock dwindling fuel supplies, Bleichrodt sent a triumphant message to Ernst Kals, the captain of the nearby U-130, which, if Bletchley Park had been able to decipher it, would have provided near-perfect intelligence. "Just sank *Tacoma Star*," he reported. "Please meet me earlier in CB 4965 at 0900 hours." Kals quickly replied, "Can't reach rendezvous point before 1500 hours."[6]

Only twenty-four hours earlier, when the three-rotor Enigma was still in use on Dönitz's submarines, the contents of these messages would have been gold for the Submarine Tracking Room. Located in the basement of the Admiralty Citadel, the brown fortress-style bunker attached to the Old Admiralty Building in London, the tracking room formed one annex of the Operational Intelligence Centre. There, women from the Royal Naval Service, the Wrens, placed coloured markers tracking the location of each German U-boat and every Allied ship or convoy at sea on giant wall-mounted map boards showing the world's sea lanes. If they had been privy to the positions of U-109 and U-130, these U-boats would have appeared on the wall as well. Immediately, the analysts there would have sent messages to Western Approaches Command in Liverpool, and the alarm would have been repeated to tracking rooms in Canada and the United States. Other vessels could be rerouted or an "incidental" ambush by anti-submarine forces orchestrated, turning the hunters into the hunted.[7] But without the intelligence, nothing happened.

In hindsight, the failure to take immediate and direct action against the potential threat posed by the four-rotor naval Enigma is likely the greatest miscalculation made by both John Godfrey's NID at the Admiralty in London and Frank Birch's Naval Section at Bletchley Park during the entire war. The combined effects of wishful thinking and a "wait and see" approach—something Godfrey railed against in others—led to a near catastrophe on the seas that rivalled, at least in material terms, the massive land battles of attrition on the western front during the First World War. The U-boats exacted a bloody toll on merchant shipping in much the same way that the machine gun and heavy artillery shattered the flesh and bones of infantrymen caught in a no-man's land between trench lines. With high casualties incurred (and for what appeared to be little reciprocal gain in sunken U-boats), this stage of the Battle of the Atlantic stirred up the ghost from the brutal charnel-house land battles of Verdun, the Somme and Passchendaele a generation before.

Looking back on the struggle after the war, Winston Churchill noted: "I am sure that no one knows so much about dealing with U-Boats . . . as the British Admiralty, not because we are cleverer or braver than others but because, in two wars, our existence has depended upon overcoming these perils [and] when you live for years on end with mortal danger at your throat, you learn in a hard school."[8] The learning curve was steep. One week after the changeover from the three- to the four-rotor Enigma, few if any of the colourful submarine-shaped markers used to denote the position of individual U-boats on the map board in the Submarine Tracking Room remained. One by one, the Wrens returned them to their cabinet drawers alongside the Special Intelligence dockets marked *Shark*, which were no longer stuffed and sagging. Dönitz's submarines had begun to fade from sight in the most vital of all theatres—the Atlantic Ocean.

Godfrey would later write: "The tracking of U-Boats is perhaps the most important of NID's functions." The demanding job of the talented analysts toiling in the dungeon-like atmosphere of the tracking room was to stay on top of current events and predict the future. Their ability to "foresee, day, week, month or even longer ahead" was their sole purpose.[9] In addition, they had to know what was happening with their own warships, convoys, aircraft and enemy U-boats. Their work relied on piecing together countless clues and scraps of information to create a background of knowledge against which to judge and weigh probabilities. When available, Special Intelligence served them well, and indeed it had quickly formed the backbone of their work. Now, with the four-rotor naval Enigma in place, the analysts had little current intelligence to draw from, which left them gravely disheartened, particularly when the sombre distress signal from a stricken Allied tanker, troopship or merchant ship, such as the *Tacoma Star*, became their only source material.[10]

The four-rotor was not the only problem facing Alan Turing and the cryptanalysts at Bletchley Park. The Germans had also introduced a new weather code book just days before the four-rotor appeared, and they followed that up all through February with new editions of other codes and ciphers as well. Cumulatively, these new versions of the lesser codes blocked Bletchley's "backdoor approach" and, for the time being, effectively shut them out of cribs. From this point onward, there was a steady fade to black. It began with a "grey-out" in February, darkened quickly, and spread like a cancer, leaving the Submarine Tracking Room, the Operational Intelligence Centre and the Naval Intelligence Division to rely on an "estimate and guess" approach— or, in the term Godfrey coined, a "Working Fiction"—rather than the solid base provided by Special Intelligence that had served the English so well.[11]

During this "depressing period," as the future head of Hut 8, A.P. Mahon, wrote, any message enciphered by the Germans on the new four-rotor device withstood the intellectual and electromechanical probes from the cryptanalysts at Bletchley Park.[12] Nothing, at least in the immediate future it seemed, could fix the problem. Lamenting the situation, Mahon recorded, "Clearly we had lost the most valuable part of the traffic, and no form of cryptographic attack was available to us."[13] Shaun Wylie, who worked with Alan Turing in the hut as a crib specialist, recalled:

> We knew it was coming. But it was a grim time. We were very much frustrated; the things that we'd hoped to use went bad on us. We realised that our work meant lives and it ceased to be fun. We did what we could, of course, and we got on with what there was, but we kept an eye out for any possibility on Shark [the new key introduced for the U-boat fleet] that might present itself. There was a lot of pressure and we were trying all we could but we didn't have many opportunities. We had to get Dolphin [the

principal key used by naval Enigma] out, but Shark was the prime target, the focus of our interest.[14]

When Rolf Noskwith, a German Jew who had escaped from Nazi Germany a decade earlier and a fellow crib specialist, was asked years later if the relative impotence and the resulting loss of life created a sense of guilt among the cryptanalysts, he soberly recalled:

> While we knew the seriousness of the situation, I cannot say that we felt guilty. First, we genuinely felt that, without more captured material, there was no short-term solution. Secondly, we knew that there was a long-term solution because of plans, in collaboration with the Americans, to build more powerful Bombes capable of breaking the four-wheel machines. Thirdly, we were still regularly breaking Dolphin.[15]

With the exception of a few odd days in March, when Bletchley took advantage of cribs supplied by an operator's mistake to decrypt already stale traffic (ironically, a message announcing Dönitz's promotion to full admiral), *Shark* would remain impenetrable until a heroic chance pinch of material from the U-559 in the last days of October 1942.

Through that warm and unusually dry summer, the Bletchley Park cryptanalysts worked literally round the clock to break the four-rotor Enigma in the same way they had succeeded with earlier versions of the machine, but with no success. Although they attempted to solve their dilemma with the less-sophisticated three-wheeled Bombes they had in their arsenal, these proved much too slow to outwit the four-rotor Enigma. Even when the German operators' occasional transmission mistake provided Bletchley with a few cribs, it took six of the three-wheeled Bombes working together for seventeen straight days to decrypt the settings for just one day of traffic, providing messages more than a month out of date. This usage was a nonsensical waste of valuable resources for little, if any, gain; the few precious three-wheeled machines were desperately needed to decipher message traffic encrypted on three-rotor Enigma machines from other theatres of war (at this point, the German high command had put the four-rotor machine into operation only in the Atlantic), so it made no sense to devote their time to a task that offered little chance of success.

The only solution was to race against time to build a four-rotor Bombe. But even then, until the British could pinch the new code books for the four-rotor machine and regain a flow of cribs, the four-rotor Bombes would be of little use against Shark.[16]

The reaction from Godfrey at the Admiralty, from Bletchley Park and from the Operational Intelligence Centre in London in the short term was to fall back on the still-breakable German home waters key (Dolphin) and on lower-level codes and ciphers. As the history of the OIC records, Special Intelligence may have been "by far the most important information received," but at least for now experts there maintained the ability "to read German local signals relating to local moves or tugs, escorts, minesweepers, repair and supply facilities . . . [and] had knowledge of new construction, completions and exercises in the Baltic."[17] However, they knew that, as use of the four-rotor Enigma machine spread more widely throughout the German navy, these lower-level codes and ciphers would likely disappear incrementally in the intelligence equation. To meet that possibility, the OIC attempted to rely on other sources to fill in the blanks—aerial reconnaissance, for example, and other signals intelligence technologies and techniques the English were fast developing.

The most promising sources in lieu of cryptography for the Operational Intelligence Centre were high-frequency direction finding (HF/DF or Huff Duff) and very high frequency direction finding (VHF/DF) technologies, in either their shore- or ship-based forms.

These technologies could detect the general location of a vessel by intercepting its radio signals, but they could not pinpoint the specific location. Unfortunately, because the Germans suspected that the Allies employed such measures, they drastically restricted their radio time on air to the absolute minimum to limit the chances of being found. Even if they were located, the information would quickly grow stale unless Allied ships or aircraft were in the immediate area to take action, and after a few hours it likely became useless. In addition, the radio intercepts could not establish the direction in which the vessel was travelling; only if the Allies picked up subsequent transmissions could they confirm that they came from the same vessel and thereby know the direction of travel. All this sleuthing was more art than science—and to round out and properly interpret the findings, the cryptanalysts required a consistent corpus of evidence to draw on as needed.[18]

Bletchley Park also enjoyed limited success with the techniques of radio finger printing (RFP, where they identified specific transmitters by photographing the particular wave form) and TINA (where they analyzed the characteristics of the radio operator himself). On their own, as Godfrey noted, these techniques were "without operational value as far as the U-Boat war was concerned," but they paid dividends with regard to large surface vessels such as cruisers and battleships.[19] Combining these two sources of SIGINT—signals intelligence— offered a much better chance of identifying a particular boat and inferring from its movements its possible intentions, though again, Godfrey complained, "neither RFP or TINA was precise."[20] Moreover, all these methods lay at the mercy of ionospheric conditions and were further crippled by the fact that U-boats generally maintained radio silence. They used their radios only when they were near Allied ships or convoys, meaning that by the time the British picked up a signal, it was far too late for the hunted vessels to implement the avoidance strategies that had been so successful in the latter half of 1941.[21]

The other promising cryptographic weapon was something the British called "Tunny"—a dual code name given to the deciphered message traffic passed by non-Morse teleprinters called *Hellschreiber* and *Geheimeschreiber* and to the first analogue device developed in an attempt to decipher the encryption machines. Unlike the Enigma, which was widely distributed throughout the German army, navy and air force, these teleprinters were rare and provided a direct and "secure" link for only the most sensitive strategic material passed between Hitler's headquarters and his diplomats and commanders in the field, such as Dönitz.[22] Eventually, Bletchley Park, much to Ian Fleming's delight no doubt, would take the analogue machine light years ahead and develop the world's first programmable computer, a monstrosity code-named Colossus. Used to break into various Tunny channels, Colossus and its forerunners produced what Bletchley called "Fish" traffic, which on certain levels was cryptographic and intelligence gold that surpassed even Enigma and played a pivotal role in the Allied successes from 1943 onwards. However, in the late spring of 1942, when the blackout was hitting its peak, Tunny was still in the developmental stage, leaving Godfrey, who was at the cutting edge of SIGINT development, to lament that "the bulk of the traffic is non-naval."[23]

Potent as all these alternative sources would become later in the war, in the spring and summer of 1942 they had yet to reach maturity as consistent intelligence weapons. Meanwhile, the three-rotor *Dolphin* key, combined with the lower-level dockyard cipher, continued to produce a limited amount of intelligence. Reports of ship movements in home waters, the Baltic training grounds and Norway, along with details of the inner workings of U-boat bases on the west coast of France, allowed the Operational Intelligence Centre to track the comings and goings of U-boats from their ports. Using a combination of methods, it could glean intelligence regarding the commissioning of new craft and their trial runs, the names of their commanders, their new armaments, and even their departure from and return to port through the Bay of Biscay. Crucially, however, the OIC remained in the dark as to the location of submarines while at sea. As the Submarine Tracking Room reported, "Little can be said with any confidence in estimating the present and future movement of the U-boats."[24]

By the end of February 1942, the direct effects of the blackout on shipping were already setting off alarm bells within the Admiralty. The worry snowballed rapidly and became a full-blown crisis by the summer and fall. In January an "acceptable" 440,000 tons of merchant shipping had been lost in the opening of the new U-boat offensive off the American coast—a regrettable number, but not too serious as long as the rate of sinkings did not rise and continue unabated.[25] In February, sinkings dramatically increased, claiming 615,000 tons and leaving the Admiralty worried about future possibilities. Its concerns were recorded in a policy draft prepared for Admiral Sir Dudley Pound, the First Sea Lord and, in 1917, the officer who had been appointed to lead the first Plans Division in the Admiralty after it was established: "So far our naval operations . . . have been successful in maintaining our essential imports and war supplies, and bringing safely to this country large Dominion military forces. But the losses have been severe, and during January and February . . . have again risen to dangerous figures."[26]

If the first two months of the year could be classified as "dangerous" and "severe," the peak months of March and April, respectively with 723,000 and 760,000 tons lost, brought near panic. So did the enormous monthly average of 685,000 tons lost in the remainder of the year.[27] This figure was almost twice the crisis level from 1941, forcing Pound's staff to warn by the fall:

> We are now approaching a crisis in the war and we must face the facts. We have lost control of the sea communications over a very wide area, and wherever we have lost this control we have also

lost all that depends upon it. Every day the enemy is extending his challenge to new areas and is increasing in strength . . . our merchant losses are immense; the tanker situation is grave, and the supplies reaching this country are less than we require.[28]

At least half the losses were British or Dominion vessels. Although help from the American merchant fleet was able to offset this hemorrhage to some degree, the losses placed an enormous strain on all aspects of an already overtaxed British war economy. Told to expect replacements for the lost vessels in 1943 through either the British or the American shipbuilding programmes now gearing up, the Admiralty's trade division, headed by the son of the renowned Blinker Hall, viewed the overall "acceptable" loss rate for the entire year at 4.5 million tons of shipping.[29] By July, losses had eclipsed that level, and by year's end they were almost double.[30]

Even more alarming were the types of ships suffering at the hands of the U-boats. In the first two months of Operation Drumbeat, the Admiralty calculated that it could absorb a 20 percent loss rate for merchant vessels and a 13 percent loss rate for the tankers that brought oil—the very lifeblood of the modern war machine—across the seas to British ports.[31] By March the rate of merchant ship sinkings held, but the tanker toll skyrocketed to a staggering 24 percent—meaning that one-quarter of the vital oil heading to Great Britain was lost and, even more important, so were these specialized vessels and their crews.[32] In one short period in May, six U-boats alone took down more than thirty tankers in the Gulf of Mexico. That led to extraordinary temporary measures such as the suspension of oil shipments and the wide-scale rerouting of convoys.[33] By the end of the year, tanker losses would amount to over 1.5 million tons, with only a little over 200,000 tons set to be replaced by the current shipbuilding programme—indicators that pointed to a near-crippling chokepoint for the Allied war machine if the situation was not dealt with quickly and effectively.

The United States Navy training manual attempted to put all these losses into perspective:

> If a submarine sinks two 6,000 ton ships and one 3,000 ton tanker, here is a typical account of what we totally lost: 42 tanks, 8 six-inch Howitzers, 88 twenty-five pound guns, 40 two pound guns, 24 armored cars, 50 Bren Gun Carriers, 5,210 tons of ammunition, 600 rifles, 428 tons of tank supplies, 2,000 tons of stores and 1,000 tanks of gasoline . . . In order to knock out the same amount of equipment by bombing . . . the enemy would have to make three thousand successful bombing sorties.[34]

As if all these losses weren't discouraging enough, the problem was exacerbated by the blind and evasive rerouting of convoys away from suspected rather than known U-boat positions and hunting grounds. Such defensive manoeuvres began to extend trips by thousands of miles. They also elongated the convoy cycle—the time at sea—meaning that without the Germans even firing a shot, the mere threat of running into a wolf pack without warning during this period contributed to a dangerous drop in Britain's oil quotas, which averaged 30,000 tons a month. By June, only 75 percent of required petroleum products were reaching the United Kingdom because of actual and threatened U-boat attacks, compared with more than 85 percent the year before.[35] The United States may have been able to out-produce the world's oil supply twenty times over, but that potential was useless if the oil could not leave home shores or wound up floating in one of the many slicks that now dotted the oceans. It became clear, on a global scale, that without oil, entire war economies faltered—factories ceased production, trucks and ships did not move, tanks could not fight, and aircraft could not fly—and that meant severe restrictions on the power Great Britain could wield on the world stage. Power, position and prestige were at stake.

A showdown with the Kriegsmarine was building on the high seas. When the war began, the situation for the British was relatively simple in naval terms: the German navy was small in comparison with the Royal Navy and, though it possessed a handful of U-boats and a small surface fleet, it was bottled up in home waters that were vulnerable to blockade. Two and a half years later, close to three hundred U-boats streamed unharmed out of bases on the western coast of France, in Germany and in Norway to raid shipping at will in the Atlantic, the Arctic and, as of the new year, the Mediterranean as well. Most of the key German surface vessels, including their battleships and cruisers, now called the Norwegian fjords home, standing ready to pounce on the vital Arctic convoys to Russia at any moment. The Italian fleet, despite its mauling at Cape Matapan a year earlier, remained a potential regional threat in the Mediterranean, while the French fleet, under the control of the collaborationist Vichy regime, formed a wild card that needed constant monitoring. In the Pacific, the Japanese navy proved more than a match for the American fleet in the opening rounds of their fight. That left the United States no longer capable, at least in the short term, of honouring in full its pre-war naval commitments for the Atlantic theatre; for the time being, the British had to shoulder the major responsibility there as well.

The great worry permeating the Admiralty, given the mounting success of the U-boats against Allied shipping, along with the active German naval building programme, was that Germany was slowly winning the war at sea through attrition, reducing British naval and merchant capacity while their own side remained untouched or, at least, did not suffer proportional losses.[36] As early as February, based on the estimates supplied by Godfrey's NID, the Admiralty's incisive Plans Division sounded the alarm bell:

> All this points to the expectation[,] and intelligence tends to confirm this, that in the Atlantic the German navy will during

the spring and summer of this year [1942] make an all-out effort to break down our sea power, and bring the war to an end. For us it is vital to win this battle by providing the adequate counter to the anticipated German naval and air measures.[37]

The proposed remedy was "early intelligence" coupled with "persistent attack on enemy submarines" and "adequate air cover."[38]

And what of the future? It looked grim. The estimates Ian Fleming brought to Godfrey's attention at their weekly meetings in Room 39 concluded that Dönitz's fleet now had ninety of its nearly three hundred submarines working in the Atlantic, with that overall number, based on current projections of German construction, set to increase by 60 percent the following year.[39] In June, Sir Dudley Pound reflected the growing alarm. He warned his political master, A.V. Alexander, the First Lord of the Admiralty: "If we do not do something to stop the sinkings we should, as an alternative, immediately introduce most drastic steps in civilian consumption and the use of raw materials."[40] Attempts to placate Pound with assurances that the new shipbuilding programme would make good the losses did nothing to convince the wily old sailor, a lifelong and ever-loyal naval officer. There were just too many "ifs" in the equation—if the shipbuilding programmes lived up to expectations and if the sinkings did not increase. "We cannot be certain of either of these things," Pound told Alexander. "For instance, we do not know what toll will be taken on our shipping when the German U-Boats number 500 as they will in July 1943."[41]

The rate of U-boat construction far outpaced the Allies' ability to destroy the submarines—a feat exponentially harder now that the British had lost their ability to hunt them down effectively. In fact, in early 1942 only 20 percent of the fleet had been sunk, leaving 160 of them in operation, with 115 training for battle in the Baltic. Every month, an additional twenty-two submarines were delivered fresh from German factories, far outpacing the measly five to seven U-boats sunk or lost to other causes each month.[42]

All indicators pointed to a mounting crisis. Pound sensed an oncoming confrontation with both the enemy on the high seas and the Air Ministry at home. In part to make up for the void left by the loss of Special Intelligence in the Atlantic, the Admiralty was demanding a portion of the heavy bombers that the RAF was presently using to bomb German cities—the only practical support, apart from the Arctic convoys, being tendered to the hard-pressed Soviets on the eastern front. The Admiralty wanted a chunk of this precious air commodity to maintain a constant vigil over stretches of the Atlantic and the Bay of Biscay, where the bombers would attack U-boats departing for or arriving from their bases in western France. In addition, it argued that Bomber Command should target assembly plants—or U-boat "hatching" areas, as Churchill called them—or even take a shot at U-boats inside their impregnable pens. On this last point, the Admiralty now had strong support from the United States president Franklin Roosevelt.[43]

There is no doubt that Churchill was fully alive to the situation. In the annex close to his flat, he kept his own map room—as he had during his time as First Lord. The room was run by a tall Irishman, Captain Richard Pim—a civilian, like Ian Fleming, commissioned into the RNVR—who marked the maps with pins showing the positions of British (now Allied) forces and, where known, of enemy forces. There he also recorded naval engagements, air attacks, ships, convoys, shipping losses and, now infrequently, U-boat locations. The pins' positions were constantly updated, so the prime minister was never out of touch. As Elizabeth Nel, Churchill's personal secretary, recalled:

> Each morning while we were in London a Map Room officer would present himself soon after Mr. Churchill waked, to give the latest news; and at all hours of the day or night somebody was on duty to report anything new or to investigate any inquiry

we might wish to make. From the time of Casablanca onwards Mr. Churchill never travelled without a detachment from his Map Room, which always included Captain Pim, complete with maps, dividers and other trappings, so that wherever the Prime Minister was, even aboard ship, a Map Room could immediately be set up.[44]

Knowing Churchill's keen interest in the navy and that his steady diet of U-boat Special Intelligence had ceased, Dudley Pound suggested a course of action that shrewdly took account of the strategic situation, of the Admirality's needs and of the prime minister's very demanding idiosyncrasies. With Churchill doubling as minister of defence, his influence within the War Cabinet was decisive when it came to the allocation of resources. Pound therefore made sure, in his bid to gain the aircraft he needed to solve the pressing crisis at sea, to include a prioritized list of the glaring issues that he felt coincided with Churchill's personal interests—intelligence, the *Tirpitz* (the *Bismarck's* sister ship) and the defeat of the U-boats topped the list.[45] This list was the opening shot in what Pound later dubbed the Battle of the Air—the fight over allocation of air resources for the Admiralty and the Air Ministry and, ultimately, over the direction of British grand strategy.[46]

But Pound's tactic with Churchill backfired: he had miscalculated the prime minister's approach to the issue. Although Churchill in no way dismissed the urgent and pressing needs faced by the Royal Navy and the British merchant fleet, he viewed the war at sea and the Battle of the Atlantic as purely defensive in nature. Strategic bombing, in contrast, gave him an immediate *force de frappe*—the only offensive weapon capable of bringing the war directly to the German people while hammering away at their morale and their crucial industrial infrastructure. With mounting air raids, sometimes in excess of a thousand bombers over a given city on one night, strategic bombing was for Churchill "better than doing nothing and a formidable method of injuring the enemy."[47] Also important, it provided substantial propaganda value and aid in lieu of a second front for Stalin's Soviet Union. Unfortunately for John Godfrey and Dudley Pound, the bombing denied what the Royal Navy desperately needed to offset the results of the intelligence blackout.

So far as the Admiralty was concerned, this refusal of its request appeared to show that Churchill, in his quest to bring maximum pressure to bear on Germany, was willing to trade heavy shipping losses at sea for his own priority—strategic bombing. Indeed, in July 1942 Churchill wrote a memo that included these telling words: "It might be true to say that the issue of the war depends on whether Hitler's U-boat attack on Allied tonnage, or the increase and application of Allied Air power, reach their full fruition first."[48]

Although Pound brokered a limited agreement for the transfer of four squadrons of long-range aircraft in mid-April, they were still not enough to fill the void left by the loss of Special Intelligence. By June the frustration within the Admiralty had reached crisis point. Admiral John Tovey, the commander-in-chief of Home Fleet and the officer who not only had led the final charge against the Bismarck but was responsible for protecting the Arctic convoys to Russia, told Pound:

> It was difficult to believe that the population of Cologne
> [Germany] would notice much difference between a raid of
> 1,000 bombers and one by 750.
>
> I informed Their Lordships that in my opinion the situation at
> sea was now so grave that the time had come for a stand to be
> made, even if this led to Their Lordships taking the extreme step
> of resignation. I was supported in my contentions by Admiral of
> the Fleet Sir Charles Forbes and Admiral Sir Andrew Cunningham.[49]

To these men, it clearly appeared that Churchill had abandoned the Royal Navy at its darkest moment. However, the likely scenario is that, wisely or unwisely, he maintained faith in the eventual resumption of the flow of Special Intelligence. Certainly John Godfrey did, and why not? After all, the bold and increasingly systematic approach to pinch raids the previous year had paid handsomely when the problem with the three-rotor Enigma was equally dark and daunting. With Mountbatten's Combined Operations in place—an exciting and virile delivery vehicle—optimism made sense. Already it was basking in the results of its Norwegian escapades and a set of spectacular raids on the French coast in February and March 1942 (exploits we will explore in more detail in chapter 7).

Mountbatten's nascent brand of Combined Operations offered a relatively cost-effective approach to accomplish several essential goals simultaneously: in the wake of recent defeats in Asia and North Africa, to demonstrate Britain's continued will to fight and raise morale; to assist the hard-pressed Soviet Union; to develop the amphibious capabilities for an eventual second front; and to work in covert fashion to maintain, or in this case re-establish, the cryptographic success and break the blackout with a major pinch.

Britain had yet another reason to fear the four-rotor Enigma and Shark, the key used by Dönitz's U-boats in the Atlantic. Ultra, or Special Intelligence, was not only a remarkable British breakthrough but, arguably, one of the last natural resources that Great Britain possessed. The technology and processes developed in Bletchley Park's code-breaking huts to exploit both the Enigma machine and, a year later, to build Colossus, the world's first programmable computer, in order to break Tunny, were undeclared national treasures that remained wrapped in a cloak of secrecy for decades following the war. The fruits of the collective intellectual labour at Bletchley Park were expected, first, to help defeat the Allies' enemies on the field of battle and, later, to give Great Britain a rare commodity for the future.

With the sun setting on the Empire, monopolization of crypto-graphic technology gave the British the ability to stand toe to toe with the rising Americans, who would soon eclipse them as a superpower on the world stage. Right from the beginning of the war, the British jealously guarded their cryptographic abilities. They went to great lengths to control and protect this source, not only from their enemies but in certain respects from their allies as well—unless circumstances dictated otherwise.

In the summer of 1940, while Ian Fleming was devising Operation Ruthless, Churchill, spurred on by his country's dire predicament and the need to protect vital interests in the Atlantic, had approached President Roosevelt with an offer to establish a limited signals intelligence partnership built around the basic premise of "spheres of influence." By this time the Americans were already engaged in their own cryptographic pursuits, largely centred on message traffic from Asia and the Pacific. Churchill's proposal called for a division of labour in which the Americans maintained their Far Eastern focus while Great Britain dominated the production of signals intelligence in Europe.[50] Part of this approach stemmed from the sober realization that the aggressive rise of Japan in Asia and Nazi Germany in Europe would likely draw the United States into the war sooner rather than later. However, as Churchill knew full well, the entry of the Americans was a double-edged sword. On the one hand, this new ally brought unprecedented economic and industrial might that would likely guarantee ultimate victory. On the other hand, if left unchecked, this power threatened to bleed proportionately into the realm of cryptography, leaving Britain as a bystander rather than the lead actor in both a new world order and the dawning of the information age.

Several additional factors cast shadows over the proposed special relationship between Britain and the United States. The British harboured a justified fear of the cavalier, indiscreet way in which the Americans treated the fragile nature of cryptographic security. For example, at the height of the Great Depression and in desperate need of money, Herbert Yardley, the former head of the American cryptographic bureau who had worked with the British and the French during the last years of the First World War and into the interwar period, published *The American Black Chamber*.[51] The book was based on his personal experiences and exposed the work not only of the U.S. bureau but also of his allies, particularly the reading of Japanese envoy messages during the Washington Naval Conference in 1920–21. As expected, the book was an instant bestseller on three continents. It succeeded in pulling the bon vivant and rumoured serial womanizer out of his financial bind but left him a pariah. Immediately, it set off a firestorm of controversy and bitterness, with the British in particular feeling betrayed.

In British eyes, Yardley exemplified a careless American brashness that should be avoided at all costs in an industry where discretion and security were paramount. Eventually, he resurrected his career, offering his talents in mercenary fashion first to Chiang Kai-shek's Nationalist party in China in the late thirties and then to the Canadian government, which in 1940 seemed bent on joining the exclusive signals intelligence club. His tenure was short-lived: once the British got wind of his employment, the Government Code and Cypher School refused to continue its support for the novice Canadian signals intelligence community as long as Yardley remained on staff. And so he was fired—the day before the Japanese attack on Pearl Harbor—and replaced by Oliver Strachey, a legendary Bletchley Park cryptanalyst, whose work on breaking German agent traffic led to the ISOS process being named after him: Intelligence Service Oliver Strachey.

This British fear was entirely genuine and legitimate. The Americans had not experienced the same level of cryptographic success that the British had already enjoyed for decades—first during the Blinker Hall days in the Great War and later in the early years of the new war. As such, cryptography, at least at first, did not maintain the same pedestal position as it did with the British, who viewed the Americans as essentially loose cannons when it came to security. The British knew that American codes and ciphers were notoriously porous and that even the State Department cipher had been penetrated by friend and foe alike. In England, Bletchley Park and cryptographic work in general came under the control of the Foreign Office and the Secret Intelligence Service, while in the United States the navy, the army, the FBI and the State Department all delved into signals intelligence and cryptography independently for their own, at times competing, purposes. Protecting their fiefdoms became their main focus, and the lack of a central coordinating body left the British fearful that one jealous, ignorant or otherwise malicious dispute could jeopardize their whole mission.

Despite this mistrust, when events in the Atlantic seriously heated up, the British were forced to approach the Americans about becoming active participants and intelligence partners in the war at sea—even if, ideally, they would keep them as limited intelligence partners. That meant that the issues surrounding Germany's Enigma machine became the major points for discussion in most of their intelligence dealings.

Neither side at first rushed into the other's arms, but despite British promises of full disclosure, it was the Americans who extended the first hand in late 1940, when they gave Bletchley Park a reproduction of the "Purple" machine that the Japanese used to encipher diplomatic messages. That allowed Britain's Far East Combined Bureau in Singapore to attack Japanese ciphers.[52] Following on the heels of this historic exchange, Churchill permitted representatives from the Government Code and Cypher School to discuss Bletchley's breakthroughs into all forms of the Enigma, but then, despite earlier promises, he pulled up short of authorizing a full exchange of technologies. Although the Americans demanded a physical specimen of a captured Enigma for their cryptanalysts to work with, the mission team they sent to Bletchley Park for two months late in 1940 came away with only a paper copy of the inner workings of the machine. Citing security concerns and a potential redundancy of work, the British guarded their precious commodity tightly. In addition, the Americans were not permitted to take notes about anything related to the Enigma, nor could they view documents or other material about its solution.[53]

The sudden change in the British approach to sharing intelligence with the Americans was a curious development that warrants clarification. On February 13, 1996, a little over two years before he passed away, I met with the recently knighted Sir Harry Hinsley, who, fresh from his valuable analytical work in Hut 8 in the early years of the war, had gone on to be the GC&CS representative for naval cryptographic negotiations with the Americans for the remainder of the war and for some time after. He then returned to St. John's College, Cambridge, where he enjoyed a stellar academic career as an international relations historian and, in particular, as the author of the voluminous official history of British intelligence in the Second World War.

And so it happened that, five decades later, when I arrived in Cambridge after an overnight flight from Montreal for our scheduled meeting, I was told at the college that both Sir Harry and Lady Hinsley were at home ill, but that I should phone him at once. In his legendary enthusiastic way, Hinsley refused my offer to come back on another day. "My dear boy," he said, "you have come a long way across the ocean to see me—and you shall." For Sir Harry, "all the way across the ocean" conjured up a two-week journey on an ocean liner that had to ply U-boat-infested waters. He insisted that I come to his flat near the university. By this time in his late seventies and rather gnomish in stature, he greeted me with a wide smile and an outstretched hand, withered and malformed by rheumatoid arthritis. For the next few hours we sat and discussed signals intelligence, Ultra and intelligence-sharing with the Americans. On that point he confided, "control of the technological know-how was the overriding theory in guiding GC&CS relations with the U.S."[54]

Harry Hinsley made it clear to me that, from the start, the British were adamant about agreeing to a partnership only after "it became obvious that another power was on its way to create the technology necessary to discontinue reliance on GC&CS."[55] If confronted with this scenario, they would "provide . . . any information they required from this type of technology, partially to protect the source, but primarily to protect their monopoly."[56] In other words, it was one thing to open the taps to the pipeline and allow the Americans as much of the product as they required, but under no circumstances should they help the Americans find and develop their own deposits, let alone gain the knowledge to create their own refinery and pipeline system. They were adamant that control must remain in British hands, and only if met with an inevitable takeover or duplication would they move quickly to establish a full working partnership.

When the British achieved the first breaks into the three-rotor naval Enigma in early 1941, they were more than happy to offer the products of their findings to OP-20-G, the acronym used to denote the "Office of Chief of Naval Operations (OPNAV), 20th Division of the Office of Naval Communications, G Section / Communications Security"— the Washington-based version of the Operational Intelligence Centre. The British needed material co-operation from the U.S. Navy to protect their shipping in American waters, and the provision of Special Intelligence seemed a small price to pay for American assistance during this period of neutrality.

By June, a regular delivery of Special Intelligence passed from England to the United States, either through an Ultra Secret radio relay link known as Hydra (at a specially built facility known as Camp X located just outside Toronto on the shores of Lake Ontario) or via cable and diplomatic pouch direct to the offices of the British Security Coordination in the Rockefeller Center in New York.[57] In

August, the Government Code and Cypher School posted a liaison officer to OP-20-G to handle Special Intelligence. By the time Pearl Harbor was bombed on December 7, the United States and Great Britain had been limited partners for almost a year.

But the relationship was tense that December and, according to Godfrey, quickly developed into a "very prickly subject."[58] Less than a week before Pearl Harbor, complaints from the United States Navy put a strain on the special relationship. Having waited for more than a year for a reciprocal delivery of the naval Enigma machine they had requested earlier, the U.S. Navy now accused the British of holding back on Enigma-related material. It threatened to withhold further information on the Pacific unless it received full reciprocal information on European work. In response, the GC&CS representative in Washington warned: "There is a grave unrest and dissatisfaction in free exchange of Special Intelligence . . . You will appreciate the importance of this matter as United States are developing rapidly. The question should be faced and settled with the least delay or our relations will deteriorate and lost ground will be hard to recover."[59]

Up to this point, the Operational Intelligence Centre had been providing the Americans with daily reports listing U-boat dispositions as known through Special Intelligence. However, when the wolf packs shifted to American shores and, soon after, the four-rotor Enigma appeared, that service was quickly snuffed out; an already tense relationship was left near the breaking point.[60]

Faced with legitimate demands from the Americans for help in curbing the German U-boat feeding frenzy off the American coast inflamed by the blackout, the British found themselves in an awkward situation. At first, not realizing that the Americans were planning to embark on their own design for a Bombe, they explained that they had neither the time nor the machines to solve the issue—an honest response but, nonetheless, a grave miscalculation. The Americans, who had been content at first to take a back seat and play a supporting role in the signals intelligence effort in the Atlantic, were no longer prepared to sit idly by, given their own skyrocketing shipping losses and the failure of the British to produce the cryptographic goods promised. The United States had genuine operational concerns. By June 1942 the head of the U.S. Army, General George C. Marshall, told Admiral Ernest King, the head of the United States Navy, that "losses by submarines off our Atlantic seaboard and in the Caribbean now threaten our entire war effort . . . I am fearful that another month or two of this will so cripple our means of transport that we will be unable to bring sufficient men and planes to bear against the enemy."[61]

If the losses continued, operational issues would turn into political issues as well. Soon enough the press would begin to ask even more difficult questions about the mounting number of sinkings and the loss of life, and the lack of offensive action would lead to public demands for answers. The congressional or Senate investigation that would inevitably follow would force President Roosevelt to pressure the Navy to adopt corrective measures. And those measures in turn could well mean that the Americans, with their deep coffers, would press ahead on the naval Enigma issue, leaving the British behind if necessary.

In the early spring of 1942, the British learned that the Americans were indeed taking the first of several huge steps in that direction. Tucked away in an obscure structure innocuously named Building 26 on the grounds of the National Cash Register Company in Dayton, Ohio, the Americans had assembled an impressive array of intellectual talent and embarked on their own Bombe-building scheme, which was given equal priority and funding with the Manhattan Project—the attempt to build the world's first atomic bomb.[62] How long it would take to achieve results was anyone's guess, but it was clear that the Americans were embarking on a parallel approach to the problem. This overt industrialization of the American cryptographic mission, backed by millions of dollars (trillions by today's standards), meant that the clock was indeed ticking on British efforts at Bletchley Park.

In response, the Government Code and Cypher School sent a team of cryptographic liaison officers across the Atlantic to exercise damage control. It was led by Lieutenant Colonel John Tiltman, or "the Brig" as he was later affectionately known in intelligence circles (he became a brigadier in 1944), one of Bletchley Park's finest cryptanalysts on non-machine systems. Tiltman had been an early and eager advocate for British co-operation with the Americans in cryptology, and his task now was to buy time for the British to solve the four-rotor riddle by direct or indirect methods. His précis on Enigma policy, written in 1942, confirms what Hinsley referred to during my interview with him. Operating under clear instructions from both Stewart Menzies, the head of the Secret Intelligence Service, and the "gruff, rough and burly" Edward Travis, the loved and respected successor to Alastair Denniston at GC&CS, Tiltman was asked to "point out that we did not wish to hide from the services in Washington the details of our successes, but that we wished to discourage them from attempting any exploitation until it became essential."[63] Failing that, he was to channel or quarantine American angst and determination so as to minimize any damage to Britain's own programme either through competition or security leaks.

When Tiltman arrived in the United States, tension was running high, and tempers among American cryptanalysts were shattered and thin. Greeted at his first meeting with open derision by some American cryptanalysts, the thoroughly professional Tiltman kept his equilibrium, recording only that it was "clear that the [U.S.] Navy Department were extremely disturbed over the German U-Boats situation."[64]

Despite the rough beginning, the British mission produced encouraging results. First, Tiltman smoothed ruffled feathers by candidly revealing the problems Bletchley Park faced with the Germans' recent introduction of a four-rotor machine—a move that apparently thawed the tense atmosphere after the Americans, who had received no previous confirmation of the existence of this new machine, realized that the value of their initial work on the three-rotor Enigma was now moot.[65] Despite the current critical situation, he downplayed the need for the United States to develop its own Bombe, assuring the Americans that the British had one in the works that would crack the machine in the near future. Finally, he promised to open up the stingy lines of communication and share more information on naval Enigma. He even invited the U.S. Navy to send a team of experts to Bletchley Park to see everything they were doing to solve the crisis.[66] The Americans now realized that "thefts, German errors, and cryptanalytic craftsmanship had been, and would be, the only ways into naval Enigma."[67]

Before long, Tiltman won the Americans over, essentially through his honesty and in part thanks to his disarming nature, which they viewed as the embodiment of British eccentric brilliance and quite unlike the intellectual and cultural condescension they had expected. They warmed to his relaxed style, devoid of deference for uniform or tradition, along with his paternalistic but never patronizing use of "old boy" with everyone he encountered.

Reporting back to Commander Travis, Tiltman explained that he had reached agreement with the United States Navy that the solution and exploitation of Enigma could best be carried out by Bletchley Park.[68] He warned, however, that certain considerations must be taken into account. "In view of the fact that they [the Americans] are now at War and have a vital interest in Submarine traffic," he wrote, "they are entitled to results or a detailed statement as to why this traffic cannot be read at present and what are the prospects for the future." The fact that this compromise was only a band-aid solution was not lost on Tiltman. He warned Travis that "unless a rapid and satisfactory solution is found[,] the High Command will insist on their naval Cryptanalysts attempting to duplicate our work on E."[69]

It was clear that Tiltman's visit had achieved the desired effect of calming the Americans, at least in the short term, but it was equally certain that the clock was ticking. At some point, likely in the near future, the U.S. Navy was bound to become an undeniable force with an insatiable appetite in the world of British-dominated cryptography. In *realpolitik* terms, this realization meant that the British could either attempt to solve the issue immediately or, in the face of futility, admit as much to the American Navy and bring them on board as full rather than limited partners. Full co-operation with the Americans on the four-rotor Bombe could be viewed as an "acceptable" loss—in fact, as the cost of retaining the rest of their slowly collapsing cryptographic monopoly.

With all these complexities in mind, the best course of action for the British was to hedge their bets by acting on both fronts simultaneously: they would move ahead full throttle on their own development but, when necessary, co-operate with the United States. Either way, even if both sides could develop an operational four-rotor Bombe in 1942, they would still require pinched material for it to work efficiently. Another successful pinch was therefore of the utmost urgency.

SEVEN

KICK AT THE DARKNESS

We must not lose our faculty to dare,
particularly in dark days.

—WINSTON CHURCHILL, MARCH 24, 1942

I f pinch raids offered the only viable short-term option to feed
Bletchley Park's voracious appetite for German code and cipher
materials during the four-rotor blackout, Mountbatten's Combined
Operations provided the ideal vehicle to carry out the raids. Dickie
Mountbatten, who had built his reputation in part on his work in signals intelligence, understood what was at stake when at the end of
1941 he hired Jock Hughes-Hallett specifically to create a raiding programme on several targets along the coast of France.

By the new year, outline plans were shaping up for raids on
Bruneval, St-Nazaire, Bayonne and Dieppe, among other targets. And
here John Godfrey came in too. Early in the war, he had recognized
that, in a raid, detailed knowledge of the terrain ashore was crucial to
the success of any amphibious operation, so in the summer of 1940
he had established the innocuously named Inter-Services Topographical
Department (ISTD)[1] to create intelligence work-ups on selected areas.

Each of these reports was first class for its time, containing impressively thick planning dossiers and maps, photos and diagrams, local postcards, and even family holiday snapshots submitted by the general public of both the natural and urban environments. In any military operation, a fundamental understanding of the terrain is essential to success, and the creation of the ISTD showed Godfrey at his professional best. The Topographical Department rapidly became his pet project—and ultimately his crowning glory during the war.

Almost every Wednesday morning, John Godfrey climbed into his chauffeured staff car with briefcase in hand and headed north to Bletchley. The trip that began in the rubble-strewn and, at times, smoke-filled streets of London ended roughly ninety minutes later in the splendour of the Oxfordshire countryside. The journey provided the Director of Naval Intelligence with a rare opportunity to engage in uninterrupted study and peaceful reflection as well as a short visit with his wife, Margaret, and their eldest daughter, Katherine.

In the best nepotistic traditions of the intelligence world, Godfrey had placed first his wife and then his daughter in support positions at Bletchley Park, as had his RAF counterpart on the Joint Intelligence Committee, Air Marshal Charles Medhurst, whose daughter Rozanne worked alongside Kate and the "boffins" in the huts. In his other roles as a member of the Joint Intelligence Committee and of the Y Committee, which set policy for signals intelligence, Godfrey found that these regular visits to Bletchley allowed him to keep abreast of the latest developments in both the Naval Section and Hut 8, where he liaised with Frank Birch, Alan Turing and others involved in cryptanalysis. Just days before he announced his January 1942 change in pinch policy, Godfrey could rightly boast to Bletchley's overlord, Stewart Menzies, "I have seen more of the workings of B.P. than any other Director of Intelligence and probably more than any outside authority."[2]

The secret home of British cryptography was just the first stop on his Wednesday route. Later in the day, Godfrey would drive the forty miles into Oxford to visit the Inter-Services Topographical Department, where he kept an office with a direct link to Room 39 in the Old Admiralty Building in London. Godfrey transferred Margaret, after her brief tenure at Bletchley Park, to the ISTD, and there she very ably played much the same role for her husband as Ian Fleming did in the Naval Intelligence Division.[3]

The role of the Topographical Department was to act as a central collecting, collating and compilation department for all the topographical knowledge bearing on a proposed site for amphibious assault.[4] The concept stemmed from yet another of Blinker Hall's First World War ideas, where he recruited civilians from the universities to create a series of geographical handbooks. Godfrey's Second World War version occupied several buildings in the Schools of Geography in Manchester and Mansfield colleges and in the Bodleian Library. For Godfrey, the location was key: first, he needed to tap into the brightest minds that Oxford and Cambridge had to offer, much in the same way that the Government Code and Cypher School had stocked Bletchley Park's cryptographic endeavours; and second, it gave him full access to the machinery of Oxford University Press, which printed, among other highly sensitive documents, the Most Secret Royal Navy signals code books. By 1942, the ISTD accounted for more than two-thirds of all the material published by the university press, including a series of pamphlets known as the Inter-Services Information Series (ISIS) and special topographical intelligence work-ups on potential landing areas, which were used in the planning for amphibious operations.[5]

Ironically, it was Winston Churchill's return to the Admiralty as First Lord on the opening day of the war that had set the wheels in motion for the creation of Godfrey's Topographical Department. The signal sent by the Admiralty board announcing emphatically and defiantly that "Winston is back!" came as both a blessing and a curse. Not all members of the Royal Navy interpreted the magisterial pronouncement as a "second coming." Churchill's return put the Royal

Navy on its toes and drove some members, such as Dudley Pound, the First Sea Lord, and John Godfrey, to look for ways to harness or at least channel Churchill's notorious proclivity for incessant meddling and "wildcat operations."[6] They could only double their efforts when, in May of the following year, he was also appointed prime minister.

Godfrey had initially created the Inter-Services Topographical Department—with ample backing from the chiefs of staff—in the wake of the British debacle during the German invasion of Norway. The specific goal was to prevent another Gallipoli, the 1915 tragedy in which Allied troops were massacred partly because of their profound ignorance of the Turkish terrain, defences and enemy forces.[7] As he would later write:

> Every year between 1919 and 1939 the staff college spent a month or six weeks examining every aspect of combined operations and opposed landings. We knew in 1939 how to conduct an amphibious operation, what preparations were needed, and what to avoid, but at Gallipoli we were ignorant of [the] nature of the country over which we were to fight, of the condition of the defences we were called upon to assault, and of the morale, equipment and order of battle of the Turkish Army.[8]

He records in his unpublished memoir that the chiefs of staff, the Joint Planning Staff, the Joint Intelligence Committee and the Joint Intelligence Staff all "carefully curbed . . . Churchill's appetite for diversionary operations . . . but not until the ISTD . . . had put in a great deal of hard preparatory work."[9] Ironically—and happily for Godfrey—it was precisely Churchill's interest in these "diversionary operations and landings on hostile shores" that accelerated the growth of his new organization.[10]

Godfrey's vision for the ISTD was for it to act as a combined intelligence body, or as a clearing house that would cut across the partisan rivalries that had plagued operational planning and execution during the First World War, and provide the essential intelligence needed to carry out successful amphibious combined operations.[11] He hoped that, when the chiefs of staff and the joint planners could not effectively dissuade or contain Churchill in one of his ill-conceived schemes, they could at least satisfy his orders and filter the idea through a proper planning process—one founded on solid intelligence provided by all three services and coordinated under one roof. "Total War deserved Total Intelligence," Godfrey believed, and the Topographical Department gave him the machine for serving up information on unusual topics at very short notice—a valuable commodity with Churchill at the helm.[12] At the same time, Godfrey knew he was crossing a Rubicon of sorts by delving into this domain: the work, while decidedly military in character, came under naval direction and could easily "ricochet on the DNI and Admiralty if anything [went] wrong."[13]

From its inception, the beaches, the landing areas and, above all, the ports along the Channel coast were the "cardinal interest" for the Topographical Department.[14] Yet when Dudley Pound requested a full work-up on the French coastline to prepare for the Dunkirk evacuation in late May 1940, Godfrey discovered that his Naval Intelligence Division had no information to share; nothing in advance of this historic moment had required intelligence on an area they expected would remain in Allied hands. Immediately, he called on several captains from a British shipping firm that regularly plied the Channel for their expertise and dispatched two reconnaissance teams to scour the coastline for the much-needed intelligence.[15] With the German armies advancing towards them, one team covered the area from Le Havre to Dieppe while the other raced from Dieppe to Cherbourg.[16] Given the circumstances, both reports were crude, hasty endeavours, with photographs of the terrain pasted onto folio-sized brown paper and linked by a simple text. "It was I think inadequate and shabbily dressed compared with the elaborate productions used later," Godfrey recalled, "but at least it was a start."

Meanwhile, Godfrey sent Ian Fleming to France as well, though not to do scouting along the coast. Even as the German invaders advanced towards Paris, Fleming was in the capital trying to maintain links with the French navy and to ascertain Admiral François Darlan's intentions with regard to the disposition of his fleet in the event that France fell to the enemy. Arriving to find that Darlan had moved his headquarters to Tours, on the west coast of France, Fleming removed the Royal Navy's Top Secret teleprinter from the British embassy and the cash contents from the Secret Intelligence Service safe in the city and beat a hasty retreat towards Bordeaux, keeping Godfrey informed on the rapidly unfolding events via wireless. The man who travelled with him and helped him signal Godfrey was Patrick Beesly, Godfrey's future biographer.[17]

Initially, the Inter-Services Topographical Department had been greeted with apathy in wartime Britain. But with Churchill's increasing demands for operations of all sorts and the creation of Combined Operations to carry them out, the unit swelled from its first seventeen members after it was set up on June 12, 1940, to seventy-two by the end of 1941 and eventually to 541 by 1944. It became, as Godfrey remembered, "an inter-service monster" that, as his biographer notes, signalled a bid for "empire building on a grand scale."[18] From June 1940 onwards, "no single Commando, hardly an agent of SOE and certainly no major Allied force set foot on German or Italian held territory without the benefit of detailed information about the terrain and its natural and man-made features and characteristics supplied by ISTD."[19] By the time 1942 rolled around, the monster had taken on several heads and was "continually bombarded with requests for topographical data about possible landings and enterprises, many of them emanating from the Prime Minister's fertile mind."[20] Churchill was not the only suitor: all three services, along with the SIS, the Special Operations Executive and the Joint Planning Staff, made regular use of the information it provided, as did its greatest client, Mountbatten's Combined Operations Headquarters.

The association with Combined Operations predated Mountbatten's tenure; it had started immediately after the organization was established. At first, Combined Operations had been inclined to produce its own topographical data, but Godfrey soon persuaded Admiral Sir Roger Keyes, the first director, to attach one of his staff to work in Oxford—a move that paid immediate dividends.[21] Very quickly, close co-operation developed between the two organizations as they worked in conjunction to gather intelligence for a large number of raids and an even larger number of plans—some of which never went into effect.[22] Originally, the requests were small, supporting pinprick raids along the French coast in 1940. Within a year, however, the ISTD had produced the report that would be the basis for the very successful raids on the Lofoten Islands and Vaagso.[23] By May 1942, Mountbatten had come to rely so heavily on the work of the Topographical Department that Godfrey felt compelled to issue a memo, circulated inside the Combined Operations intelligence section, to stop sending requests for a short period "as the ISTD staff are working 24 hours a day and it is feared some may collapse."[24]

Godfrey's caution was not without foundation: during a ninety-day period between October 1941 and January 1942, the ISTD created more than thirty "special reports" in response to urgent requests from both Mountbatten's staff and the Joint Planning Staff. Among the requests that topped the lists were work-ups on the areas of St-Nazaire, Bayonne and Dieppe.

The raid on St-Nazaire has been dubbed the "Greatest Raid of All," with scores of articles, books, a feature film and a recent BBC documentary canonizing the bravado, courage and sheer audacity that brought about spectacular results.[25] It was not by any means as large an operation as Dieppe—but it was successful. And it still remains a show-case for what Lord Louis Mountbatten's Combined Operations could accomplish. The daring idea of attacking Hitler's heavily defended *Festung* (Fortress) St-Nazaire at the mouth of the Loire River on the Biscay coast first arose in the weeks following the successful hunt for the *Bismarck* in 1941. In the summer, the Admiralty had learned through Ultra that her sister ship, the *Tirpitz*, an equally daunting and powerful adversary, had just finished sea trials in the Baltic before heading into position to blockade the Soviet fleet near Leningrad. So far, there were no indications that she would venture out to wreak havoc on the Atlantic trade, but preparations had to be made for that eventuality.

Within the NID, the French part of Section 1 was responsible for intelligence concerning the Channel coastline and the rest of France. It was headed by retired Royal Navy commander George Edmund Gonin, a British businessman who lived in Antwerp and had a special interest in ports. With Godfrey's blessing, Gonin, who represented NID at the first meeting following the formation of Combined Operations in 1940, approached Keyes's staff in the hope of gaining their support for a cunning plan. The approach did not come out of left field given the close association that had already developed between the NID and Combined Operations Headquarters, with the former providing intelligence and advice in the selection of raiding targets.

The idea Gonin proposed was straightforward: because Ultra had clearly revealed that the *Bismarck*, when she was attacked and sunk, was making for the Normandie dry dock in St-Nazaire—the only facility in western France with a dry dock capable of housing the 42,000-ton vessel for repairs—why not launch a commando raid on that port itself, which also housed one of the largest U-boat bases?[26] With one bold move, the British could achieve two major goals. Destroying the lock gates or disabling the pumping mechanisms used to control the flow of water into and out of the dry dock would render the port "tidal," flooding the dry dock and denying the Tirpitz a repair facility. That act alone would dramatically reduce, if not eliminate, the chances of the giant battleship venturing into the Atlantic. At the same time, the attack offered a chance to destroy or disable a few of Dönitz's deadly submarines while at anchor and, although not stated, pinch vital material in the process.

Unsure of whether their current operational capabilities would permit such a daring raid, Keyes initially balked at the idea, leaving it in limbo for months, until the Admiralty's Plans Division, thoroughly prompted and backed by Godfrey, decided to push ahead with the scheme, generating a planning docket that included intelligence gathered by both his ISTD and the wily Gonin.[27]

Having discovered through his myriad contacts that the engineering firm which helped construct the locks was based in London, Gonin had obtained a model of the lock gates along with detailed reports and air photographs, and then consulted the Special Operations Executive on where best to place the explosive charges. The resulting plan was desperate, bold—and close to suicidal. It involved taking a group of highly trained commandos and placing them on board a collection of motor torpedo boats (MTBs) and an obsolete and therefore expendable destroyer, HMS Campbeltown, which would be disguised as a German vessel. With the destroyer's bow lower decks primed with a timed explosive charge, the entire force would then sail into St-Nazaire harbour at night, the Campbeltown would ram headlong into the lock gates, and the commandos would storm ashore to knock out the pumping stations and other targets while waiting for the destroyer to explode. Once the mission was accomplished, the commandos would essentially be on their own. The lucky ones would make it back to the MTBs for departure or, more probably, would try to find their own way through southwestern France and across the Pyrenees into neutral Spain before setting out to return to England.[28]

On September 14, Gonin met with the Plans Division, which had originally hoped to deliver the attack on Trafalgar Day, October 21, as a public relations nod to the great victory of the British fleet over Napoleon's navy in 1805. Unfortunately, environmental conditions reduced the likelihood of surprise, and the plan was shelved for the time being.

And so it remained until January 1942, when Ultra from Bletchley revealed that the Tirpitz was on the move: she had left the Leningrad blockade and sailed first to the port of Wilhelmshaven in northern Germany and then on to Norway, suggesting she might break out into the Atlantic and follow in the Bismarck's path. The Operational Intelligence Centre, tracking her every move through the German Home Waters key and then the Norwegian key, was relieved at first to report to Churchill and the Admiralty that her immediate objective was the fjords rather than the Atlantic sea lanes. But once she had made the move to Norway, the battleship was clearly positioned within easy striking distance of both the North Atlantic and the vital convoys bound for Russia. Churchill feared it was only a matter of time before she made her move for open water. As he related melodramatically in his memoir *Hinge of Fate*, he informed Major General Hastings "Pug" Ismay, his shrewd and loyal personal liaison with the chiefs of staff, just days before the four-rotor Enigma machine went into action on February 1 on Dönitz's U-boats in the Atlantic, that "the destruction or even the crippling" of the Tirpitz was, in his estimation, "the greatest event at sea at the present time. No other target is comparable to it."[29]

Previously, in November, when Mountbatten had first taken over the reins of Combined Operations, his headquarters had begun, as Godfrey relates, "a keen search for targets" that revived Gonin's "hope for his neglected child."[30] After Churchill sounded the alarm in late January, Gonin's daring but relatively low-cost strategy to cripple the Tirpitz before she could position herself in the Atlantic became an imperative. Suddenly, the raid was back on the table. When Gonin approached Combined Operations with the idea, the result, according to Godfrey, "was magical." Instantly, Dickie Mountbatten latched on to the idea, and he put his naval advisory team onto detailed planning for the mission. In late February, Operation Chariot was born—a commando raid that would prove to be one of the greatest acts of heroism and self-sacrifice of the entire Second World War.

What is not commonly known is that the St-Nazaire Raid also doubled as an elaborate pinch operation. Restricted by the Official Secrets Act, which for years prevented any whisper of Ultra or the four-rotor crisis, Churchill properly made no direct mention of this side of the story in his carefully crafted memoirs, although there are vague and veiled references to "other sources." Nor did he dare touch upon the second half of the St-Nazaire saga: its long-forgotten twin operation called Myrmidon, which took place in April 1942 some 260 miles to the south at Bayonne, France.

As with Vaagso and Lofoten, the plan was to launch twin attacks—Operations Chariot and Myrmidon—within twenty-four hours of each other in an effort to deliver on the two imperatives of the day, the Tirpitz and the four-rotor-derived intelligence blackout. On February 25, Mountbatten presented both outline plans, drawn up by Jock Hughes-Hallett, David Luce and Vaagso pinch veteran Dick de Costobadie, to the chiefs of staff and the prime minister for approval, admitting that both operations were "somewhat hazardous" but "the prize was considerable."[31] While the primary goal of Chariot was the destruction of the Normandie dry dock, the secondary target was the destruction of all the U-boats and shipping gathered there for repairs. The plan made no particular mention of pinch provisions, but the operation obviously did offer the potential for "chance" pinches.

The stated objective of Operation Myrmidon at Bayonne—"to clear the French Coast of the enemy troops in the areas between the River Adour and the Spanish Frontier" by landing three thousand soldiers to disrupt rail and road transport in that area—appears at first so

Mountbatten addresses the troops as they embark for Operation Myrmidon, April 1942. He seized upon and amplified the role of pinch raids in an effort to help "brand" his daring form of Combined Operations.

vague as to be suspect.[32] Working from my understanding of the doctrine of pinch raids and the types of targets they sought, however, I undertook more fine-tuned research into the details of the planning papers, which reveal that Myrmidon was a pinch by design. In this case, a naval task force with No. 1 and No. 6 Commando units, carried in assault landing craft (ALC) and destroyers, would sail up the Bayonne estuary to the harbour, where it would strike shore-based strategic facilities, including explosives and petrochemical plants, an unspecified headquarters (likely naval) and a Luftwaffe airfield. Meanwhile, special boarding parties would capture shipping in the tight confines of the estuary and the harbour specifically in search of "code and cipher material."[33]

After trolling through both outline plans, the chiefs of staff and Churchill "fully approved" the proposals, with the prime minister stating for the record that in his opinion both "raids were justified." Signalling his direct interest in the pinch operation, he requested to "hear further details of Op Myrmidon in due course."[34] It is not recorded whether or to what degree Churchill made himself intimately aware of the details of Operation Myrmidon. But if he did flip through the various detailed orders, he would certainly have seen that the main purpose of the operation was clear:

> Enemy armed trawlers are to be attacked with the utmost ruthlessness at short range with pom pom and small arms weapons, the object being to kill or panic the crew but to leave the ship relatively undamaged in order that search may be made for codes cyphers etc. If this search is successful it is essential that there should be no survivors other than prisoners, and that the ship should be sunk as soon as possible.[35]

Later, the plan reiterated this imperative, stating that crews from any ship, enemy or neutral, should be overpowered and that any resistance should be dealt with ruthlessly. It continued: "If German, they are better dead, though a Naval Officer would be of value as a prisoner for interrogation."[36]

Operation Myrmidon was scheduled to take place within twenty-four hours of the St-Nazaire Raid, but it was dogged by problems. Weather conditions delayed it, and the records are unclear whether it was then pushed back or the St-Nazaire Raid was pushed forward. In the end, the raids were separated by one week, with Myrmidon following Chariot. Even then, although the raiding force reached the mouth of the Ardour River, leading to the Bayonne estuary, a shifting sandbar—of which the ISTD had made Combined Operations Headquarters fully aware—prevented it from entering. The raid was aborted without the Germans catching on to what had been planned. Given the spectacular success at St-Nazaire on March 28, 1942, the failure at Bayonne proved easy to gloss over, but it nevertheless came as a great disappointment.

Although it is now clear from the declassified records that a pinch was the driving force behind Myrmidon, the main idea in Operation Chariot was essentially preventative in nature: to destroy St-Nazaire's giant dry dock and prevent the Kriegsmarine from unleashing the *Tirpitz* on the already beleaguered merchant fleet in the Atlantic. The word "daring" does not sufficiently describe the plan.

The strategy drew heavily on the legendary Zeebrugge Raid, which had garnered much-needed positive propaganda in the dark days of the spring of 1918. Like it, Operation Chariot required complete surprise: the raiding force, led by the disguised *Campbeltown*, would have to sail unobserved past the coast of Brittany and down the French west coast through U-boat-infested waters dotted with French and Spanish fishing trawlers. Mountbatten issued strict instructions that, if the element of surprise was lost, the raid should be aborted, the ships returned to

English ports, and the mission remounted on the same target once the frenzy had abated. However, if the surprise held, the raiding force would capitalize on the detailed report the Inter-Services Topographical Department had issued, which revealed that an unusually high spring tide would permit a "one time only" chance for a light ship to pass over the shallow water close to shore and avoid the big German guns dominating the approaches to the port. Once the convoy had got past the guns, the Campbeltown, disguised as a German destroyer, would create heavy diversionary fire designed to suppress or otherwise occupy the gunners, just as the raiding force closed on the port entrance at the mouth of the Loire.

The final plan followed Gonin's original scheme quite closely. To take full advantage of the confusion, Robert Edward Dudley "Red" Ryder, the naval force commander, riding in a motor torpedo boat (MTB), would use a captured low-level German code book to send a series of deceptive messages to the port to hold fire, passing the force off as a German coastal convoy in need of emergency shelter. Once they breached the harbour defences, one of the MTBs would blast the gates leading to the U-boat pens, the commandos on the other boats would land on the harbourfront and destroy the four lock gates leading to the old dock, and Campbeltown would deliver the *coup de grâce*. With its bow packed with high explosives rigged up by the experts at the Special Operations Executive and set on a timed fuse, the old destroyer would ram headlong into the main lock gate of the Normandie dry dock. Once lodged, the commandos riding her "back," or main deck, would jump off and attack the pumping stations and lock mechanisms that controlled the dry dock. In that way, there was an inherent redundancy built into the planning to achieve the major objective: even if the Campbeltown failed to explode on time, three hours after it struck, the commandos would at least disable the dock temporarily.

In the end, the raid turned out to be as effective as it was daring and deadly. It began badly: the plan was nearly scuttled when the convoy encountered a German submarine, which was chased off, and then two French trawlers, which Ryder boarded and sank. Nothing in the available documents indicates whether he did so for pinch purposes or strictly for security reasons, but his unpublished memoir shows that in the process he did seize lower-level French and Spanish material. This bold and courageous commander then pushed on with the mission because none of the Germans on shore had yet raised an alarm. When the diversionary bombers arrived, however, surprise was no longer possible, and at that moment the commandos hoped the German gunners would be more interested in taking on the bombers than their quickly approaching raiding force. At that time in the war, a Cabinet order forbade the blind bombing of French towns, and with the skies overcast, the airmen's view of the target below was obscured. All the bombers managed to do was fly around above St-Nazaire, putting the gunners on full alert rather than drawing their fire or making them run for cover. As a result, although the raiding force succeeded in reaching the mouth of the Loire and the harbour in good shape, the captured-code ruse worked for only a short time before the Germans responded with full force.

Immediately, searchlight beams and heavy fire bathed the raiding force, hitting a few of the torpedo boats while the others made a dash for their targets on shore. As planned, the *Campbeltown* rammed into the target lock gate at full speed, crumpling her hull in the process. Her commandos leapt off the decks and hit the majority of their targets on shore. The others following in their MTBs were not as successful, but the thirty-seven-year-old commander of No. 2 Commando, Lieutenant Colonel Augustus Charles Newman, or "Colonel Charles" to his men, managed to seize and establish his headquarters in the German harbour commandant's office.[37] From there he organized the attack on shore. They met heavy and increasing German resistance from the start, including from an armed trawler he tried unsuccessfully to subdue.

Initially, it appeared that the main objective of the raid had failed: the explosive charge, carefully welded shut into the bow of the *Campbeltown*, did not blow up on schedule. But the next day, when the ship was crowded with German soldiers, sailors and a few captured commandos and surrounded by French bystanders, it suddenly exploded, knocking out the gate, flooding the dry dock and leaving a grisly scene strewn with the body parts of those on board and nearby.

Only 228 of the original 622 commandos and Royal Navy personnel were able to return to Britain over the next few days, with the total casualty lists recording 169 dead and 215 in German hands. This list included "Colonel Charles" and his small band, who heroically attempted to fight their way out of the port. Newman was awarded the Victoria Cross for his conspicuous bravery and valour, but because he was captured, whatever code and cipher material he may have been able to seize—and it is possible he jettisoned it in advance of being taken—went for naught. Not surprisingly, given the long-classified Ultra Secret nature of such information and of these kinds of materials, nothing has surfaced in the years since in any in-house histories of the Government Code and Cypher School or in other files relating to pinches that failed outright or missed their mark.

Despite the heavy cost, the St-Nazaire Raid can be considered a success because it achieved several of its intended objectives—and some that were unintended too. On the tactical and operational levels, the destruction of the lock gates rendered the dry dock tidal and successfully denied the *Tirpitz* a maintenance or repair facility on the Atlantic coast, thereby ensuring it would remain in its Norwegian home for the foreseeable future. Although the raiders did not succeed in knocking out the other three lock gates and flooding the inner port where the U-boats berthed, the brief capture of the port commandant's office forced the Germans to move all headquarters off the shoreline and into safer but less accessible locations slightly inland.

On the strategic level, the raid—which Churchill called a "brilliant and heroic exploit" and "a deed of glory intimately involved in high strategy"—demonstrated that Great Britain could strike offensively and remain steadfast during this very bleak period in the war. The success also impressed the Americans, who were looking for signs of life from a war-weary Britain.[38] Glowing headlines spoke of the tremendous daring and supreme sacrifice of the raiders—a feat that instantly captured imaginations not only in Britain but around the Allied world. The *New York Times* ran the banner headline BRITISH RAID ST. NAZAIRE U-BOAT BASE, RAM DOCK WITH EXPLODING DESTROYER, and the *Boston Globe* likened the event to the celebrated Zeebrugge Raid. For the first time in the dismal opening months of 1942, positive news of daring offensive action greeted readers who were becoming stoically accustomed to stories of Allied reverses.

On the German side, the raid forced the adoption of a defensive mindset in the west. Hitler slackened his intense focus eastward towards the Soviet Union somewhat and allocated extra *matériel* and personnel to the French coast, mostly slave labour, to speed up and improve defences all along his Atlantic wall.

For Godfrey, St-Nazaire clearly demonstrated that the targeting information provided by Gonin's French sub-section of NID and by his own ISTD had proven its worth. The triumph also further solidified his working relationship with Mountbatten's rapidly rising Combined Operations Headquarters.[39]

The grand success of St-Nazaire invigorated Mountbatten and his staff at Combined Operations and led to a major escalation in operational planning there. The mission seemed to vindicate Mountbatten's sudden and dramatic rise to prominence under Churchill's patronage. Just weeks before the raid, the prime minister had promoted Mountbatten three levels to vice admiral and widened his official powers, elevating him from "adviser" to "Chief" of Combined Operations. Initially, the now-ailing Dudley Pound interpreted this unprecedented rise as Churchill's bid to put Mountbatten in Pound's own seat as First

Lord of the Admiralty; but it was more likely a recognition of the growing importance of Combined Operations Headquarters in the armed
services framework, as well as evidence of the prime minister's desire
to inject younger blood into the British leadership. At forty-two, the
charismatic Lord Louis Mountbatten was the youngest vice admiral in
the long history of the Royal Navy, surpassing even the hero of the
Battle of Trafalgar, Lord Horatio Nelson.

But within Mountbatten's own headquarters, this meteoric ascent
had a sharp trickle-down effect on the staff that led quickly to a dangerous overconfidence. In the afterglow of St-Nazaire, Jock Hughes-
Hallett could not contain his excitement over "Dickie's" promotion
and its promise for the future. "My own reaction," he recalled, "was
one of exhilaration, almost exultation. At one stride, our organization
had penetrated to the very centre and citadel of power. We were now
to work for a man with access to all the secrets, and for one who
could, and would, be an advocate at top level for any plan."[40] Indeed,
along with this sense of validation and vindication came a new-found
arrogance and hubris. Yet St-Nazaire, followed by the aborted
Myrmidon, had done nothing to alleviate the most pressing issue of
all: the four-rotor blackout.

Immediately after the abandoned Operation Myrmidon pinch raid
at Bayonne, Mountbatten had dismissed charges from an army interrogator with experience in several raids (including Vaagso) of poor
and hasty operational planning as well as an almost criminal neglect
of intelligence. In a confidential report penned for Combined
Operations Headquarters (COHQ), this officer noted serious over-
sights, including incomplete briefings and operational orders devoid
of basic information about the enemy. He had been shocked to find
crucial items—such as the location of the enemy in relation to key
targets, and an assessment of the enemy's air and naval situation—
absent from both the operational orders and the commander's briefing. He also noted other potentially critical mistakes: the wrong set of

aerial photos had been issued for Myrmidon, along with a suspect demolition programme that, if carried out as planned, was bound to inflict more harm to friend than foe.[41] These kinds of mistakes were indicative of what Admiral Bertram Ramsay, the man in charge of the Dover area of operations, including the protection of cross-Channel military traffic, later called "inexperienced enthusiasts."[42] In response, a thoroughly irate Mountbatten complained to Major General F.H.N. Davidson, the Director of Military Intelligence, about the critical report, but the officer behind it remained unrepentant. In Mountbatten's words, he left the impression that if "Combined Operations had been a public company the shareholders would have been within their rights to call a meeting to investigate the way in which the show was being run."[43]

These complaints were serious and valid. But they went unheeded within the walls of Mountbatten's headquarters in Whitehall, still basking in the afterglow of St-Nazaire. A mounting level of "victory disease" began to dismiss any intelligence relating to enemy forces that might be unsettling or inconvenient: any information that could dampen enthusiasm for a raid was ignored. As Arthur Marshall, the British raconteur who worked as a security officer for Mountbatten, quipped years later, the motto for COHQ should have been "Regardless"—meaning "regardless of effort, regardless of risk, and regardless of cost."[44] But nothing at this moment, save an inglorious and costly defeat, could have shaken the headquarters out of its dangerously triumphant mindset.

The excitement over the St-Nazaire Raid was particularly intense because it came at a very dark moment, following the fall of Singapore and amidst General Erwin Rommel's mounting victories for Germany in the North African desert. To ramp up the public relations level into overdrive, maximum press coverage was given when thirty-eight decorations were awarded for merit and bravery, including four additional Victoria Crosses (besides Newman's), to members of the raiding force.

The classic hero: Robert Edward Dudley "Red" Ryder with his wife, entering Buckingham Place to receive his Victoria Cross. Ryder had commanded the naval force in the St-Nazaire raid and would go on to command the "Cutting Out Force," which included Ian Fleming's Intelligence Assault Unit, in the Dieppe Raid. His "brilliant attack" on St-Nazaire was, as Mountbatten described it, "carried out at night, under a vicious enemy fire, by a mere handful of men, who achieved, with certainty and precision, what the heaviest bombing raid or naval bombardment might well have failed to do."

Red Ryder, who would later play a pivotal role in the Dieppe operation, was one of this select group.[45]

Robert Ryder was a rare character in the annals of military and naval history, the almost perfect classic hero. He was as resolute, determined and courageous in battle as he was reserved, humble and self-effacing in its afterglow. Uncomfortable with small talk and ceremony, he remained, as his biographer put it, "a reluctant hero." On the occasion of his investiture at Buckingham Palace to receive his Victoria Cross, he chose to sneak out afterwards through a side door rather than deal with the throngs of reporters who waited to shower him with adoration and praise.[46]

Born in 1908 in Dehra Dun, India, where his father, Colonel Charles Henry Ryder, held the prestigious post of surveyor general for that subcontinent, Robert, or "Bob" as he was known to family and close friends, was the youngest of six children. Unlike his father and older brothers Lisle and Ernle, who held commissions in the army, he chose to buck family tradition and join the Royal Navy, driven by his love of sailing and his penchant for adventure. After he won the King's Dirk as the outstanding cadet in his final year, he went on to a spectacular career that led eventually to his command of the raiding force for St-Nazaire—as well as the "Cutting Out Force" for Dieppe and, eventually, Ian Fleming's creation, 30 Assault Unit, his Intelligence Assault Unit.

First Sea Lord Sir Dudley Pound was one of Ryder's biggest fans, though Ryder initially was unaware of the old admiral's regard. Pound appears to have marvelled at the exploits of his young subordinate as far back as 1934, when "Red" Ryder successfully piloted a Royal Navy yacht on a wild, year-long journey from Kowloon harbour in Hong Kong to Dartmouth, England. Ryder then signed on for a twelve-month stint with the famous British Graham Land Expedition, which explored Antarctica for three years, before finally crossing paths with Pound on HMS *Warspite* just before the outbreak of the war. Among his many hobbies were painting, writing and intelligence work—and this last interest was about to become very useful indeed.

During the First World War, the Germans had developed the concept of the Q-ship, which the British readily adopted, where a tramp steamer outfitted to carry concealed weapons and disguised to resemble a merchant vessel was used to lure submarines and their crews to their fate. Early in 1940, Ryder was given command of his own vessel, the Special Services ship HMS *Edgehill* (X-39), and he personally designed its camouflage to include two pigs roaming the decks for full effect. In February he set out on the high seas in search of prey. To succeed, he first had to put his ship in harm's way, even absorbing a torpedo hit if necessary to bring the U-boat to the surface. Once the submarine was above the waterline, Ryder intended to unleash his nine concealed four-inch guns on his enemy in a torrent of fire designed to sink the vessel. Nothing, however, went according to plan when the *Edgehill* met its first U-boat off the coast of Ireland in June 1940. Instead, Ernst-Günther Heinicke, the wily captain of U-51, sent Ryder's ship to the bottom, leaving the captain alone in the water for four harrowing days until a passing ship rescued him from certain death.

From there, Ryder was given command of HMS *Prince Philippe*, a large landing craft of the type later employed at Dieppe. She too was lost, in 1941 off Scotland, when, in the dead of night and thick fog, another vessel rammed her amidships and nearly cut her in half, despite Ryder's best attempts to avoid collision. Much to his dismay, Ryder ended up in a shore posting, until he was offered the opportunity to command the seemingly impossible St-Nazaire Raid. Notwithstanding his string of bad luck, nothing had tarnished his reputation with the First Sea Lord, who seems personally to have chosen him to command the naval force for St-Nazaire. By all accounts, Pound was not disappointed by the results.

The success of this raid made Ryder a reluctant media star, but it also established him within the Combined Operations framework as a heavy hitter—the "go-to guy" for tough raids of extreme importance. If a raid required the utmost in leadership, skill and intrepid courage amid the risk of heavy cost, Ryder was the man. As such, his inclusion in any operation warrants close scrutiny.

The St-Nazaire raid firmly planted a series of lessons learned—and perhaps mislearned—in the minds of the Combined Operations planners which directly shaped the developing concept for Dieppe, and in particular Ryder's role in the raid. The very success of St-Nazaire validated the brand that Mountbatten brought to the table, leaving the Chief of Combined Operations glowing in his assessment:

> I know of no other case in naval or military annals of such effective damage being inflicted so swiftly with such economy of force . . . This brilliant attack was carried out at night, under a vicious enemy fire, by a mere handful of men, who achieved, with certainty and precision, what the heaviest bombing raid or naval bombardment might well have failed to do.[47]

With raiding and pinching concepts still emerging, however, this was the critical time for Mountbatten and his planners to draw the right lessons from Operations Chariot and Myrmidon. Unfortunately, with Myrmidon aborted at the eleventh hour, Combined Operations learned precious little that challenged or qualified the concept of storming into an enemy port with commandos and boarding parties ready to strike targets and pinch vital material. At St-Nazaire, David slew Goliath, but instead of recognizing it for what it was— an outlier—the Combined Operations planners adopted it as the norm, embracing a daring and adventurous attitude without reservation or qualification. And at this crucial point, this opinion was supported by both Prime Minister Winston Churchill and the chiefs of staff.

Unfortunately, with Mountbatten's Combined Operations relying increasingly on daring "mission impossible" operations to offset their limited assets, they were neglecting the very basics of strategy—the balance between firepower and manoeuvre—as they tried to reach their goals. From this point forward, deception, boldness and fighting spirit underpinned by surprise *supplanted* rather than *enhanced* the basics. The earlier operations in Norway and more recently at St-Nazaire had shown how much could be achieved with few resources when, and if, all elements came together like clockwork. Now they were poised to rely far too much on the elusive element of luck and the overwhelming need for surprise, particularly in pinch raids. If these elements worked at St-Nazaire, they reasoned, and would presumably have worked at Bayonne, why would they not be effective for other, larger operations?

EIGHT

"AUTHORIZED LOOTERS"

Speaking on behalf of the Admiralty, Commander
Fleming stated that there was an urgent
requirement for personnel who could be
intensively trained to carry out special naval
intelligence duties . . . Commander Fleming went
on to say that the Admiralty had pointed out the
urgency of this requirement as long ago as March,
and he emphasised the now increasingly urgent
need for a permanent body to which this type of
naval intelligence work could be entrusted.

—MINUTES OF A MEETING AT COHQ TO DISCUSS THE
FORMATION OF SPECIAL INTELLIGENCE UNITS, JULY 22, 1942[1]

In the daring and costly raid at St-Nazaire, the army commandos
had once again proven their worth in spades, as they had during
several small amphibious assaults stretching from Norway to the
Mediterranean. At this darkest point of the war, they were highly
sought after, and it was difficult for any commander to get them
without friction, delay and even cancellation of future operations.

For Mountbatten, it was frustrating not to have them directly under his control; like many of the forces employed by Combined Operations Headquarters, the commandos had been seconded from the army's Special Service Brigade.[2] The confident Dickie Mountbatten refused to be dependent on other branches of the armed services, and he determined to create his own force to carry out his objectives.

Already, at the end of 1941, he had tasked Jock Hughes-Hallett with planning a series of raids along the northwestern coast of France for strategic and intelligence purposes. Now he pressed the Admiralty to create a well-trained and cohesive group of "naval" commandos to carry out these amphibious raids. By January 1942 he had succeeded. And where better to find the men for this top unit—the first Royal Marine Commando, designated A Commando—than in Mountbatten's own beloved Royal Marine Division.[3]

The Royal Marines had grown slowly but surely in stature over three centuries, acting as the assault force for the Royal Navy. They were legendary. Tracing their origins back to the Second Anglo-Dutch War in 1685–87, they had played a dual role on His Majesty's ships: ensuring discipline among the crew and leading boarding attacks on enemy ships or raiding shore facilities. Fighting in all major Royal Navy engagements, their long and stellar history included chapters in the Seven Years' War, the American War of Independence, the War of 1812 (where they carried out raids along the Virginia and Maryland coasts) and the Crimean War. As sail power passed to steam and oil, the Marines added another duty to their list: manning the aft (rear) turrets on Royal Navy cruisers.

During the First World War they were transformed into the Royal Naval Division—which Winston Churchill observed in action as they defended Antwerp from German attack in 1914—and later played vital roles in both the Gallipoli campaign and the Zeebrugge Raid; all told, five of their men earned the Victoria Cross. Not long after, however, scandal hit, when one battalion mutinied in Murmansk while serving in the tumultuous Russian Civil War, until finally, during the interwar retrenchment years, the Marines succumbed to the budgetary axe, which left them with fewer than ten thousand men—down from nearly sixty thousand during the Great War. In 1939 they reformed into the Royal Marine Division but had no real role in the Royal Navy's order of battle, and instead of keeping together as a unit, their battalions spread around the globe in "penny packets" fighting independently in Asia, North Africa, Norway and on the island of Crete. Despite proving themselves on the field of battle, this once-proud division seemed destined to be broken up and used only to reinforce other units.

Hoping to stave off their dissolution, Roger Keyes, Lord Louis Mountbatten's predecessor at Combined Operations, had already suggested converting the Royal Marines into a series of battalion-sized commando units, each roughly five hundred strong, for use in raiding operations. Mountbatten now took up the torch, arguing that the Royal Marines were Britain's natural amphibious commando force, one that could and should be equal to the army commandos.[4]

Right from the formation of this new force, the "commando concept" transformed the face of the Royal Marines into the elite unit they are today. Initially there was tension within the unit itself: some of the officers refused to lower themselves and undergo the same gruelling regimen as their men in the "rough fun and games" of commando-style training.[5] Other officers pushed convention aside and saw merit in combining the commando role with the ethos of the Royal Marines. "The commandos are tough," their own journal, the *Globe and Laurel*, proclaimed. "Vaagso is proof of that. The Marines are tough. Crete and Norway—where they fought two hopeless Thermopylaes*—are the

---

* Thermopylae refers to the ancient battle for the small mountain-pass town in Greece in 480 BC, when a vastly outnumbered force of soldiers from the Athenian city-states—in particular Sparta—held off, with self-sacrificing courage, an advancing Persian juggernaut that vastly outnumbered it.

proof of that. Wait till they mill together."[6] For Mountbatten, however, a commando unit from a naval bloodline not only provided a tangible role for the Royal Marines—a goal he had championed for months—but also gave Combined Operations and the Admiralty their own private army of sorts, to be used as they saw fit.*

Training for the three hundred men of the first Royal Marine Commando started in early February in Deal, on the Channel coast near Dover. To pay tribute to their naval heritage, the commando unit was divided into three fighting companies entitled A, B and X—corresponding to the turrets on His Majesty's cruisers—and one "headquarters company" (comprising the commander, his staff, communications and heavy weapons). Each of the fighting companies was further broken down into three platoons of thirty officers and men, numbered 1 to 3 for A, 7 to 9 for B, and 10 to 12 for X.[7]

These platoons became the homes—the surrogate families—for the fresh-faced recruits, mostly aged between eighteen and twenty-one (some weren't even shaving yet), who flowed in from commands throughout England. They volunteered to come, attracted by the adventure, the challenge of hazardous duty and a modest raise in pay. Greeted by an officer review board, the tone was set immediately with one sobering question: "What makes a young lad like you tired of living?"[8]

Once through the initial interview, the men paraded before the commanding officer, the diminutive thirty-two-year-old Lieutenant

---

* There is nothing in the Admiralty's intelligence files to suggest that the creation of the Royal Marine Commando in February 1942 stemmed either from the change in pinch policy in January towards operations on shore rather than at sea or from the need to solve the looming four-rotor crisis. The reason seems to have been the mundane need to save the division from the bureaucratic chopping block. The timing, however, could not have been more fortunate for all concerned.

Colonel Joseph Picton-Phillips, rumoured to be a descendant of Wellington's General Picton, who had been shot through the temple by a musket ball at the Battle of Waterloo in 1815.[9] A career Royal Marine officer with a high-pitched voice, pencil-thin moustache and fiery temperament, he was always immaculately dressed. When he arrived on the back of a white stallion to inspect the men, he only reinforced the new recruits' belief that he suffered from a "small man's complex." He was a "sight to behold and his mannerisms, to many of us they were hilarious," recalled one Marine. "We knew then that we had someone very different."[10]

In one of his many attempts to inculcate his version of Spartan-like discipline and initiative among the men, Picton-Phillips forbade the use of the main gate, forcing them to scale an eight-foot wall every time they entered or exited the barracks. Later he dispatched them into the wilderness for a three-day survival exercise, simply stating, "Fend for yourselves."[11] Soon his antics became the stuff of comic legend, forever ensconced in Royal Marine "dits"—those cautionary tales told to while away the off-hours.* Within the first few months, recruits who survived their initial training without being returned to unit, or RTU'd—the ultimate disgrace—became accustomed to maintaining an almost twenty-four-hour vigil for their tightly wound commander, "Tiger" as they called him, who habitually prowled the grounds at night, hoping to catch an unwary sentry off guard. At one point the overzealous Picton-Phillips's bizarre actions nearly got the better of him when a startled sentry unloaded the full weight of his rifle butt on the colonel's collarbone, leaving him to cry out in pain, "It's your commanding officer. Carry on!" The next day, when summoned to Picton-Phillips's office, the young Marine expected revenge but emerged minutes later with a promotion to lance corporal—the

---

* "Dits" were Royal Marine tales, repeated in the barracks or the mess, that conveyed essential lessons learned through a less than formal manner.

reward for his ruthless vigilance.[12] Picton-Phillips may have appeared "daft as a half-penny," but at least there was some method to his legendary madness.[13]

Idiosyncratic or not, "a general hardening up" started immediately, designed to weed out those considered physically, spiritually or psychologically unfit. "It rained all the time, so we were never dry, and then there were the speed marches, six or seven miles in an hour for hour after hour, in full kit with platoon weapons," recalled one recruit; "many would have fallen out, but were helped on by their mates."[14] Another hallmark of commando training, in addition to the near-death forced marches with sixty-five-pound packs, called for the use of live ammunition in exercises to simulate conditions on the battlefield—a policy that sometimes claimed "friendly fire" casualties but reinforced in the most powerful fashion the violent nature of the business at hand. "Climbing cliffs, crawling through bogs, under barbed wire, while the staff shot over us with Brens, or chucked grenades about" was all part of the daily routine for the prospective commandos.[15] Today, "precise application of will" rather than mere violence defines the ethos of a Royal Marine commando, but this modification developed during the peacekeeping era. For the Marine commandos in 1942, the violent application of will was front and centre.

By the end of the first week of training, nearly 20 percent of the recruits voluntarily returned to unit—a rate of attrition that held throughout the formation period. One did not simply join the Royal Marine Commando; one became a Royal Marine Commando. The extremely hazardous nature of the job, particularly with men so young, required full immersion in the new elite ethos that demanded high standards, unity, fortitude, humility, adaptability, and the wry and at times irreverent sense of humour essential for psychological survival in this stressful environment.[16] As the training regime increased in intensity and realism, the basic instruction in the handling of small arms, mortars and hand grenades evolved into advanced subjects such as the recognition and disarmament of enemy land mines and booby traps, and then to the use of Hawkins grenades or "sticky bombs" designed to disable enemy tanks. The recruits also took courses in demolition and counter-demolition, learning how to use timed and untimed explosive charges to destroy a multitude of targets.[17]

In the end, the result was a tight-knit cohort at the platoon level ready to take on all comers. The very nature of commando-style special operations called for the platoon to be prepared to operate independantly during a raid. Of necessity they had to work together as a well-oiled machine, the senior commanders continually warning that "there will come a day when you will depend on each other."[18] The Royal Marine Commandos wisely permitted the platoon commander and his sergeant to have the final say on whether a man made it as a commando or not. If they, or the group, lacked full confidence in an individual or felt that his attitude was not right, they immediately cut him loose with no reason offered besides one simple comment: "Unsuitable."[19]

By Easter Sunday, the same day that Operation Myrmidon was planned for Bayonne, the first cadre of Royal Marine A Commandos, who had survived six weeks of indoctrination at Deal, moved on for further gruelling training to the Combined Operations training centre at Acharacle in Argyll, Scotland, known as HMS *Dorlin*. This isolated former naval base now became the elaborate training ground for Mountbatten's Combined Operations Headquarters. Despite its name, it was not a ship; the *Dorlin* estate included six luxurious houses and offered the commandos a half-dozen demanding assault courses over a seventeen-mile radius, pitting them against natural and artificial obstructions and challenging them to hone their tactical skills, particularly their street-fighting smarts, which were expected to be a key part of their deadly raiding repertoire on shore. In addition, the landing craft, cutters and drifters, as well as a former French fishery

protection vessel at the base, gave ample opportunity for the commandos to practise assault landings, boarding of enemy ships and simulated pinch operations.

Once this portion of the training was complete, the recruits moved on to the basic intelligence-training phase, where they learned to recognize enemy vehicles, uniforms, documents and equipment; to conduct searches of premises to recover sensitive material; and to interrogate prisoners—and endure interrogation themselves should they fall into enemy hands. They then went on to advanced intelligence work—in chemical warfare and the interpretation of aerial photos. They received demonstrations of enemy electronics, wireless sets and radar, and learned how to photograph documents on the spot. Some of them specialized in map reading, topography and hydrography, and a few allegedly went off to Scotland Yard for an "intensive three-day crash course in safe blowing and other such arts."[20]

In late May, the Marines moved to the Isle of Wight, where, unknown to them at the time, the training regimen was shaped specially to prepare them for their first major role—in the small French coastal town of Dieppe. There, on that island off the south coast of England, one of the platoons, No. 10, would become the prototype

---

OPPOSITE TOP: Dorlin House at Acharacle in Argyll, Scotland, was originally known as the No. 3 Combined Training Centre. It was used by the Royal Navy as early as 1940 but was commissioned as HMS *Dorlin* in 1942 following the British Naval tradition of christening shore-based establishments with the names of ships. The HMS *Dorlin* was the site of several assault courses and a specialized boat training centre operated by Mountbatten's Combined Operations which allowed the commandos to train for pinch operations.

BOTTOM: Commandos in the type of landing craft used during the raid, seen here during a training exercise in Scotland, February 28, 1942.

for Ian Fleming's latest brainchild—a naval intelligence commando unit for pinch purposes, or, as he would call it, his Intelligence Assault Unit, or IAU.

On March 20, 1942, Fleming approached his boss John Godfrey with an intriguing proposition. His memo, entitled "Proposal for Naval Intelligence Commando Unit" and signed with his famous "F" scrawled at the bottom, went straight to the heart of the four-rotor crisis.[21] He conceded that he had poached the concept directly from the Germans, and that he intended to draw the original cadre for his IAU from the No. 10 Platoon of the Royal Marine Commando's X Company. (After Dieppe, the platoon would evolve into the nucleus of the illustrious 30 Assault Unit, whose motto would be "Attain by Surprise.")[22]

"These 'commandos,'" he wrote in his proposal, would "accompany the forward troops when a port or naval installation is being attacked and, if the attack is successful, their duty is to capture documents, cyphers etc., before these can be destroyed by the defenders."[23] Their first duty, before any operation, would be to assemble a list of the types of materials required by all sections in the Naval Intelligence Division and then to ferret out every scrap of information they could about possible locations where these pieces might be found in a given port. Once the target had been established, the unit would be inserted into a combined operation to train with the assaulting force. It would "proceed with 2nd or 3rd wave of attack into the port, and make straight for the various buildings etc., where the booty is expected to be found, capture it, and return."[24] Undoubtedly incorporating the lessons from the pinch raids on Lofoten and Vaagso, Fleming's proposal for the NID to create its own intelligence-gathering commando unit stemmed straight from the four-rotor crisis and the desperate need to pull in German intelligence materials. At first, Fleming envisioned that his small elite unit would comprise a platoon's worth of hand-picked men, specifically trained to conduct pinch raids ashore under the cover of larger operations.

Fleming's proposal did not come at Godfrey out of left field. In early December, a month before the pinch policy shift that abandoned targeting lone ships at sea in favour of pinching material onshore, the Secret Intelligence Service, headed by Stewart Menzies—known to all as "C"—had warned the NID that German naval intelligence had successfully employed a commando unit of its own—the *Marine Einsatzkommando*, or MARES for short.[25]* Members of this unit would accompany the assault waves of advancing forces and seize "documents, charts and naval stores," perform "counter-demolition missions in captured harbours," provide "operational intelligence concerning the harbour," and interrogate "POWs [and] civilians" while conducting "counter-espionage work"—even going so far as to work in plain clothes during the invasion of Russia so their capture of documents would not be traced back to Germany.[26] The report highlighted the great successes of the German commandos in Greece, Crete and Yugoslavia, where they had captured not only top secret British material but the entire staff of the Yugoslav army's North West Command, along with a complete set of their papers.[27]

For Godfrey, the notion of "a force of armed and expert authorized looters" made a great deal of sense, for several reasons.[28] First, instead of relying on ad hoc boarding parties as had happened in the Norway raids, his Naval Intelligence Division would be able to select and rigorously train its own "private army" with intimate knowledge of its

---

* Although the report did not mention it, Fleming had escaped the clutches of MARES in 1940 when he was cleaning out the SIS safe in Paris ahead of the advancing Germans. In 1943 MARES carried out the highly successful raid on Grand Sasso, where the rescued Mussolini failed miserably later that year in trying to capture Marshal Tito, the Communist partisan leader in Yugoslavia.

MOST SECRET

PROPOSAL FOR NAVAL INTELLIGENCE COMMANDO UNIT

One of the most outstanding innovations in German Intelligence is the creation by the German N.I.D. of special intelligence "Commandos".

2.   These "Commandos" accompany the forward troops when a port or naval installation is being attacked and, if the attack is successful, their duty is to capture documents, cyphers etc. before these can be destroyed by the defenders.

3.   They have various other intelligence duties which are described in the attached memorandum.

4.   I submit that we would do well to consider organising such a "Commando" within the N.I.D., for use when we reassume the offensive on the Continent, in Norway or elsewhere.   The unit would be modelled on the same lines as its German counterpart and would be placed under the command of C.C.O. perhaps a month before a specific objective is attacked.

5.   Its duties would be

(i)   to find out all N.I.D. Sections' requirements from the port attacked, e.g. cyphers, specimens of material (including enemy oil fuel and food, for instance) charts, enemy fleet orders, mines, R.D.F. gear, photographs etc. etc.

(ii)   obtain all intelligence available as to where in the particular port these things would be found.

(iii)   train with the raiding force.

(iv)   proceed with 2nd or 3rd wave of attack into the port, and make straight for the various buildings etc. where the booty is expected to be found, capture it and return.

6.   Operation "SLEDGEHAMMER" is a typical example of an objective which might yield valuable fruit if tackled by such a unit.

7.   Propose:

(i)   I should submit the plan in greater detail with suggestions for organisation and personnel.

(ii)   The principle be ~~submitted to~~ C.C.O. ~~for his~~ worked out w aikaul in collabn ~~covering approval.~~

Yes
more
decidedly;
but we want
"submit"

F.

N.I.D.(17)
20.3.42.

special requirements—and, by extension, of Bletchley Park's too. Armed with the appropriate firepower, the commandos would be able to overtake the local defences, prevent the last-minute destruction of the Enigma machines and their supporting code and cipher books, and get out undetected.

Second, having a trained commando unit at the ready would give the NID a consistent and dedicated tool for pinching. In a sense, such a development was a natural extension of the process Godfrey had been building up over the previous year, and it offered, if successful, a chance not only to solve the four-rotor problem but to re-establish and maintain a constant flow of the vital materials needed to feed the Bletchley beast.

Third, the NID would no longer have to risk sending Ultra-indoctrinated officers, as it had done in Norway with Captain Jasper Haines and Lieutenant Commander Allon Bacon, to execute the pinch, which had created the possibility of precious secrets being compromised should these officers be captured and interrogated. The employment of a fully armed commando unit trained specifically for this hit-and-run work would greatly limit that unwanted prospect. Their knowledge would be confined to these particular missions and specific target requirements; and although the commando unit's officers and senior non-commissioned officers would know what to look for and where, they would remain ignorant of why it was needed, and even of the very existence of Bletchley Park and its secret work.

OPPOSITE: Ian Fleming's MOST SECRET proposal for the creation of a Naval Intelligence commando unit to carry out raids specifically to "capture documents, cyphers etc . . . to make straight for the main buildings etc. where the booty is expected to be found" and bring it home. His "F" is scrawled at the bottom. Also visible, scribbled in the lower left margin, is Admiral John Godfrey's enthusiastic support, "Yes, most decidedly," and his next directive, "but we won't <u>submit</u>"—to Mountbatten, since Godfrey preferred to push the idea of working in collaboration.

Fourth, now that the NID was working closely with Combined Operations, it had the physical means—the vehicle—with which to deliver a commando unit effectively to an onshore target and to cover the commandos' existence by blending them seamlessly into a larger raiding operation.

That was the young Commander Ian Fleming's ostensibly simple but game-changing suggestion. He also proposed that the unit should come directly under the command of the new director of Combined Operations, Louis Mountbatten, about one month before it took part in any raid, so it could train with the general assault forces.[29] "Nothing but good could come of an organization which would enable our intimate knowledge of the port to be constantly at the disposal of the attacking force," commented one of the section heads examining the proposal at NID.[30]

The whole idea had a swashbuckling flair to it, well in line with the prevailing tone that Mountbatten sought for Combined Operations and that Churchill adored. Sweeping down on the target in lightning-quick fashion, overcoming the enemy, and scooping up Ultra Secret material that could help win the war or re-inject life into a now sagging empire had a romantic allure for officers who were hopelessly desk-bound in Room 39. After the war, Fleming reflected flippantly on his various plots to outfox the enemy, calling them "nonsense" and chalking them up to "those romantic Red Indian daydreams so many of us indulged in at the beginning of the war."[31] In truth, however, many were deadly serious—a matter of life and death for those involved, with enormous potential in their results—and more calculated than he was willing or able to admit publicly given the restrictions of the Official Secrets Act, even in the postwar period.

Stripped of their swagger, these schemes reflected a sober reality that was consistent with Fleming's Machiavellian nature. Essentially, he and Godfrey deemed the unit expendable in those operations designed to pinch what they listed as "A-1 targets"—the code and cipher material. The history of 30 Assault Unit lays out the lethal intent underlining this target grading with cold aplomb, defining it as "material and documents of the highest operational priority, the importance of which is sufficient to justify the mounting of special operations and the incurring of heavy casualties on the part of 30 assault unit."[32] Taken in isolation, this passage is remarkable, but given the context of the times and what was at stake, it is not surprising. Neither, perhaps, is the fact that Godfrey secured a positive nod for the creation of the unit from his fellow heads of intelligence on the Joint Intelligence Committee, who filtered intelligence schemes for the chiefs of staff. In due course the chiefs too gave their sanction to Fleming's commando unit.

With the raid at St-Nazaire and the pinch attempt at Myrmidon less than two weeks away, Fleming suspected that a new operation currently in development, and loosely scheduled to take place in August or September 1942, would provide the earliest opportunity to get his assault unit into action. Operation Sledgehammer was essentially a strategic operation with political overtones, designed to postpone demands from the Soviet Union for the Allies to open a second front in Western Europe. It called for the landing of British and American (mostly British) divisions to capture either Brest in Brittany or the Cherbourg peninsula in Normandy. The plan, pushed largely by the Americans and generating little enthusiasm among the British chiefs of staff, was designed to draw German land and air forces into a giant battle of attrition, luring units away from the eastern front and Stalin's hard-pressed Soviet Red Army. For Fleming, the idea of slipping his newly minted Intelligence Assault Unit into the larger operation made perfect sense: the big German naval bases at Brest and Cherbourg had long been considered prime pinch targets.

In late March, and with Godfrey's blessing, Fleming sent the proposal to Louis Mountbatten's flamboyant Combined Operations intelligence officer, Wing Commander Marquis de Casa Maury. "Bobby" de

Casa Maury, a Cuban-born playboy, was a controversial figure who attracted open scorn and ridicule from the established set in Whitehall. Although he had flown for the Royal Flying Corps in the First World War and, during the interwar period, had held a commission in the air force reserves, he was rumoured to have been promoted far above his ceiling. With no obvious background for the job—his main claims to fame were revitalizing Bentley Motors and establishing the Curzon and Paris cinemas in London as art house theatres—his personal connection as a former admirer of Mountbatten's wife, Edwina, appeared to be his main qualification for the job.[33] On April 1, De Casa Maury returned Fleming's docket with an encouraging note attached: "CCO [Mountbatten] likes the idea and suggests a conference should be called at this Headquarters under his chairmanship to discuss the matter fully."[34]

But the covetous tone of Mountbatten's request made John Godfrey balk. Realizing the immense potential of Fleming's concept, he ordered that the IAU remain firmly in the hands of the Admiralty—or, more particularly, of his own NID:

> On further consideration I think it would be a mistake to turn over the working out of an "advanced Intelligence unit" to the CCO. CCO's main function is chiefly of an operational nature, and an Intelligence set-up similar to what has been proposed is bound to get low priority. Moreover, to turn it over to him is an admission that he and his Intelligence staff are better able to work out such an arrangement than DNI, DDNI and Section 17. I should therefore like the matter to be tackled by Cdr Drake and Cdr Fleming under the supervision of the DDNI, who is requested to treat the matter as one of primary importance.[35]

Part of Godfrey's opposition stemmed from his genuine desire to ensure the commando unit's proper organization, training and development and its potential for solving the crisis. At the same time, his memo clearly demonstrates an increasing tendency within the Naval Intelligence Division to go it alone—and especially for Godfrey to add yet another resource to his ever-widening empire.

Operation Sledgehammer would soon be pushed to the back burner and eventually shelved permanently, much to the relief of the British chiefs of staff. Instead, they decided to embark that fall on Operation Torch—the invasion of North Africa. The cancellation did not deter Godfrey and Fleming from pressing ahead: with the failure of Operation Chariot at St-Nazaire to produce any German intelligence materials, and with the abortion of Operation Myrmidon at Bayonne before it had even begun, Dieppe suddenly loomed large on their radar screens.

NINE

DARKNESS TO DAYLIGHT

Dieppe was a small seaport and it would be interesting to capture it for a time and then withdraw. It had no particular military significance but was about the right size for a divisional attack.

—Captain John Hughes-Hallett, unpublished memoir

August 19, 1942, did not mark the first enemy attack on the seaside resort of Dieppe and its inhabitants, *les Dieppois*. Over its thousand-year existence, its geographic location, less than seventy miles from England and not far from the Dover Straits, the narrowest part of the English Channel, had led to both fortune and suffering. Vikings, foreign navies, marauders, pirates and privateers had all paid the old settlement costly visits, the most recent being just two years before, when the Germans invaded France and unceremoniously evicted the British Expeditionary Force from the continent at Dunkirk. The British had held on to Dieppe, the closest port to Paris and one of the six principal deepwater ports in France, until the last possible moment, then quickly tried to destroy its facilities to deny their use to the Germans. The combination of German attack and British sabotage inflicted some damage, but the port remained operative even though several "block ships" had deliberately been sunk just outside the harbour mole, or breakwater. Although the submerged wrecks did not cut off access completely, they prevented large ships from accessing the port and made navigation treacherous for smaller inbound vessels as well.

Located at the mouth of the river Arques in a break in the cliff-lined coast, Dieppe sits squarely between two formidable three-hundred-foot headlands that stretch a mile and a half in opposite directions to the tiny seaside villages of Puys and Pourville. In between the two headlands lies the chert-rock beachfront, "the poor man's Monte Carlo," beloved of British summertime visitors. For more than half a century, British tourists had arrived in Dieppe's sheltered port on ferries from Dover, Newhaven and Portsmouth, anxious to walk along its beaches, picnic in its fields, paint its stellar vistas or lounge in its seaside or port-side cafés before a stroll on the grassy promenade or a game of chance in its famous beachfront casino. Dieppe was a convenient draw for military and naval officers, writers, painters and socialites—*la colonie* of temporary émigrés who leased or purchased property by the sea. Among them was the beautiful Clementine Hozier, Churchill's future wife, who called Dieppe her home for a year at the turn of the century.

Tucked away just a few hundred yards behind the line of hotels on the beachfront lay the town proper, including the port, its entrance guarded by the eastern headland known in English as Pollet Cliff (the Dieppois call it *le Pollet*). Crowned by a large church, Notre Dame de Bonsecours, this vantage point provided a spectacular view out to sea for visitors—and for defenders too. Anyone standing atop the cliff could see halfway across the Channel, glance over the beach to the fourteenth-century castle on the western headland, or gaze straight down into the inner channel that led to the port behind this promontory—to the interlocking basins of its outer and inner harbours.

DIEPPE

Approaching from the N.N.W.

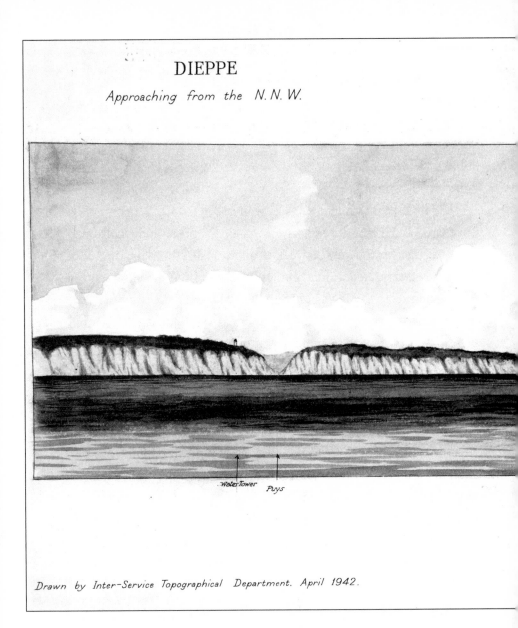

Water Tower   Puys

Drawn by Inter-Service Topographical Department. April 1942.

Signal Station
Power Station
Tobacco Factory
Hotel Metropole
Cathedral
Hotel Royal
St. Remy Church
Casino
Old Castle
Chateau

otre
ame
s bon
rcours

An artist's representation of the cliffs and beaches at Dieppe, part of the topographical report on Dieppe prepared by Godfrey's Inter-Services Topographical Department, which supplied the information required for amphibious operations. One of the many specialties of the ISTD was zero-elevation aerial photography, usually taken close to the water's surface to simulate the view of an incoming ship; the photos were then pasted together into horizontal strips. It also scavenged for and called up old magazine photographs, postcards and family holiday snapshots to get clear pictures of the different German-occupied areas.

At the base of the same eastern headland lay the harbour mole, a massive stone breakwater protected by two jetties that protruded like giant, welcoming arms for scores of vacationers arriving by ferry as well as the small fleet of cargo and fishing vessels returning from a day's work along the coast. But getting into the port, particularly after the events of 1940, was a complicated affair. Before a ship could reach either of the harbours, it had first to slip past the block ships and squeeze through a slim 330-foot gap in the mole, with the chalk bluff of Pollet Cliff rising above on its east, or left, side and some of Dieppe's buildings and shops on the right, to the west. Then it entered the inner channel, a claustrophobic funnel that, depending on the tide and the frequency of dredging, forced any vessel to remain arrow straight for nearly five hundred yards or risk running aground. Once the ship got through this narrow passage, the outer harbour appeared to the right while, directly in front, another channel opened up that led to the inner harbour, which connected to the Bassin Duquesne and the Bassin du Canada, named before the war to honour a group of colonists who sailed to New France from Dieppe in 1632.

The outer harbour was the centre of action in Dieppe. Fishing boats, pleasure craft, ferries, steamers, dredgers and barges all jockeyed for berths alongside one of the three quays that ringed its sides. On the right as ships entered stood the small port railway station, the Gare Maritime on Quai Henri IV, which catered to people travelling by train to or from Paris.[1] Directly across the outer harbour to the left was "the island," an artificial construct roughly 500 by 300 yards in size that housed a small dry dock, a ship-repair facility, and a fish-curing factory on the Quai du Carénage where the fishing fleet offloaded the daily catch for sorting. Connected to each side of the port by a series of swing bridges, the island controlled all the traffic in the port for pedestrians and vehicles, along with the shipping accessing the inner harbour and the two large basins that connected to the customs

Taken from a report on Dieppe created before the raid, this photo shows the daunting route HMS *Locust* and the rest of Ryder's Cutting Out Force were to take to reach the inner harbour and the pinch targets. In the foreground is the harbour mole, with two jetties extending like welcoming arms under the watchful gaze of the eastern headland known as Pollet Cliff, crowned by the Notre Dame de Bonsecours church. In the middle lies the inner channel, flanked on one side by the cliffs and on the other by the town. In front of the buildings lies Red Beach, where the Essex Scottish would land. Behind the buildings is the Quai Henri IV, where the trawlers were berthed, and, to the far right, the island where *Locust* was supposed to bring the Royal Marines. The photo cuts off just short of where the Hôtel Moderne is located to the right.

house, rail yards and several warehouses stocked with coal and timber. Straight ahead lay the Quai Duquesne, where the fish market once drew crowds that congregated in front of the hotels and cafés that "arcaded" the outer harbour. There the port control office guarded a small drawbridge that connected to the island and the Quai de Carénage. Quai Duquesne was also the main route linking the port to the beachfront, running past an oddly placed tobacco factory that sat sandwiched between the hotels, schools and cafés lining the boulevard de Verdun. From there, pedestrians could stroll across the grassy promenade to the boulevard Maréchal Foch, which connected to Dieppe's main beach. Traditionally, Dieppe was a lively, thriving place, save for the dark years of German occupation.[2]

The German army's 302nd Infantry Division was responsible for defending the area around Dieppe, along with units from the Kriegsmarine, which controlled the port defences, coast guard stations and a few coastal artillery batteries. As part of their defensive doctrine for foiling raids, the Germans focused on firepower, fortifications and obstacles such as roadblocks and barbed wire in order to maximize their manpower. Given the topography at Dieppe, they did not need to man every inch of the beachfront with infantry. As long as they had machine guns, artillery, anti-aircraft guns and mortars that could cover the area and dominate the ground, they could bring down punishing fire on any invader at short notice, buying time to bring in reinforcements to drive the enemy back into the sea.

In the eighteen months leading up to the Dieppe Raid in August 1942, the Germans progressively laid out a series of fortified zones along the coast which could extend their range miles out into the Channel. One such zone covered the sea approaches to Dieppe and all the beaches in the area. The defences included concrete pillboxes and bunkers, weapons pits, abandoned seafront buildings turned into fortified positions, and the numerous natural caves clawed deep into the chalk headlands that now housed machine guns, anti-tank guns and

An aerial reconnaissance photo of Dieppe harbour from a previously classified
intelligence report, taken in the spring of 1942. Note the trawlers and other small
craft to the right of the outer harbour, berthed along the Quai Henri IV: these were
the main targets, along with the Hôtel Moderne marked at the top, for the Royal
Marine Commandos that included the No. 10 Platoon (Fleming's carefully gathered
Intelligence Assault Unit). In the Bassin Duquesne, to the upper left of the "island"
in the middle where the Royal Marines were to land, are the German invasion barges
whose capture was to be a part of the cover for the pinch raid.

artillery pieces. Together, these carefully crafted killing zones would expose any raiding force to a torrent of bullets and shellfire. The Germans marked each zone on a special gridded battle map as an easily recognizable two-digit location reference, rather than the six- or eight-digit indicators traditionally used on military maps, to provide the defenders with a quick way of communicating and calling in additional firepower during the heat of battle. Having been in the area for two years by 1942, the Germans also enjoyed the home-field advantage of knowing every crack and crevice, every bottleneck, and they pre-sighted their weapons accordingly and held regular drills to rehearse their reaction to every situation that might suddenly confront them.

Five potent artillery batteries ringed Dieppe; later, Jock Hughes-Hallett, the lead planner and naval force commander for the Dieppe Raid, would code-name them Hitler, Rommel, Goering, Goebbels and Hess. In theory, these batteries were designed to work together to destroy a raiding fleet as soon as it approached any beach in the area—particularly the main beach. Two of the bigger batteries, Hess and Goebbels, were of the larger coastal type that belonged to the navy and straddled Dieppe on its extreme flanks about five miles out on either side of the town. To the east, around the hamlet of Berneval, stood the six 150-millimetre guns of Goebbels battery, which could sling a salvo of six 113-pound shells a distance of thirteen miles once every minute. On the opposite flank, just outside the little town of Varengeville, lay Hess battery, with seven guns, three of the 170-millimetre type that could deliver a walloping punch to any exposed ships preparing for or supporting a landing. The other batteries held smaller guns but were located closer to the city—Rommel behind Puys, Hitler south of Dieppe on the high ground next to the river Arques, and Goering to the southwest.

Closer to Dieppe, in and around the flanking towns of Puys and Pourville, German defensive works sprouted up on the hills and cliffs overlooking the beachfronts. At Puys, situated in a narrow bowl with two great bluffs on either side, three bunkers stood poised on the eastern side to pour heavy fire down on invaders as they rushed up from the waterline. A fourth, farther down on the heights overlooking the seawall, covered one of only two obvious ways to get off the beach and head inland—a narrow staircase built into the seawall—while a fifth stood guard high atop the cliff that led to the eastern headland. But dense barbed wire entanglements clogged the stairs and lined the base of the bluffs, protecting the bunkers and slit trenches manned by the German defenders.

To the west, the seaside village of Pourville sat in the valley of the tiny river Scie. The surrounding terrain was more open than in Puys, and the Germans, considering it the natural landing spot for any raiding force attempting to capture Dieppe, went to considerable lengths to defend the area. They placed bunkers and pillboxes in the town overlooking the beach, and others along the valley walls farther inland. These defences were to catch raiders in fully exposed enfiladed fire as they attempted to work up the river valley towards the Luftwaffe airfield on the southwestern outskirts of Dieppe a few kilometres in the distance, or along the rolling hills that led to the western headland overlooking Dieppe's main beach.

On this commanding point, in the shadow of the old castle, the Germans used the cliff caves that ran just under the bluff's crown to place artillery that could cover the far end of the main beach and hit invading boats a few thousand yards out into the Channel. On the beach lay the decrepit hulk of the formerly whitewashed casino, now camouflaged with greenish-brown and yellow paint. The Germans maintained a modest barrack in the casino and positioned small-calibre anti-tank guns on each side of the building and a few machine guns within the walls. Snipers could perch on the casino's roof and its tall twin towers, as well as on the headlands and in the buildings facing the water.

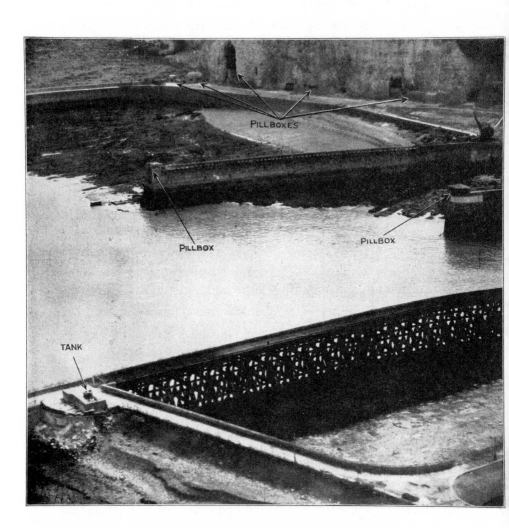

An RAF aerial photograph showing the German pillboxes housing machine guns, anti-tank guns or artillery pieces, as well as a dug-in captured French tank doubling as a pillbox on the Dieppe harbour mole, defending the entrance to the inner channel at the base of Pollet Cliff. These were the first of the formidable German defences that would be faced by the men on the ships when they ran the gauntlet through the inner channel into Dieppe harbour.

This reconnaissance photo shows a further part of the gauntlet that the raiders would have to run to reach their targets: the Hôtel Moderne and the trawlers in the harbour. The plan was for the Essex Scottish, after storming ashore on Red Beach, to first take control of the buildings (bottom of the picture) and then fire into the caves across the channel, while the Royal Regiment of Canada, landing on Blue Beach, would capture the German positions on the cliff top above. The Canadians' task was to create a secure corridor to allow unfettered entry and exit from Dieppe. If they failed, the raiders would run the gauntlet anyway with all guns blazing; if their ship was sunk or ran aground in the narrow passage, the men were to jump ship, swim to the ladders lining the harbour walls and fight on.

Looking ahead over to Pollet Cliff, the defenders could see the hotels, the grassy promenade and the beach, the tobacco factory, the left arm of the jetty and the harbour mole. The long, narrow beach, devoid of sand but covered with pieces of chert rock the size of a man's fist, is one and a half miles long but stretches only about a hundred yards deep from the waterline to the seawall. At this point in the war, the Germans had yet to sow the beach with land mines, but they had erected underwater obstacles designed to rip the hull out of any vessel attempting to land troops onshore during high tide. The beach itself changes with every tide, with parts of it sometimes left in either a steep or a gentle rise, creating small rolling valleys whose dips provide the only cover, or "dead ground," a man might find between the sea and the seawall. And from that barrier wall the Germans erected a sizable barbed wire entanglement stretching out for fifteen feet towards the beach. It was designed to slow or stop any invaders, allowing the defenders to subject them to murderous fire.

On the other side of the seawall lay the three-hundred-yard-wide grassy promenade between the boulevard Maréchal Foch on the town side and the now-vacated hotels, schools and cafés on the waterfront boulevard de Verdun. Here the Germans dug a series of slit trenches and strategically placed machine-gun pits and pillboxes, protected by a smattering of barbed wire and backed up by machine-gun and sniper positions in several reinforced rooms in the hotels behind. On the tiny streets that ran perpendicular to the boulevard de Verdun and led to the port, they built ten-foot-high concrete barricades to prevent raiding tanks or vehicles from penetrating the town and the port beyond. If these defences withstood destruction, enemy vehicles would remain trapped on the main beach, open to fire from the town and from the headlands on either side.

In the port, however, the Germans placed few fixed defences—only a pillbox and a long string of barbed wire that ran along the western bank of the inner channel, through the Quai Henry IV and then down the Quai Duquesne. They did, however, keep a Kriegsmarine security force in the town, which in the event of a raid was tasked with destroying the pumping stations, swing bridges, and any classified material that was housed in the port commandant's headquarters and other facilities. Otherwise, they placed their faith in the defences along the east headland.

Pollet Cliff formed the other arm in the horseshoe that overlooked the main beach. Like the west headland, the caves on the sides and at its base provided excellent natural positions in which to place weapons designed to hit the main beach or control access to the port. On top of the cliff, the Germans built an observation bunker and set up a battery of anti-aircraft guns near the port's signals station. In the cliff itself they positioned artillery pieces that faced the harbour mole and the beach. In the caves at the base overlooking the inner channel, they fixed anti-tank and machine guns to shoot up any vessel daring enough to attempt to breach the harbour and run the deadly gauntlet of fire.

By the summer of 1942, the once-peaceful seaside resort of Dieppe had become a strongly fortified area designed to stop raiders dead in their tracks with all the will the defenders could muster. And in the spring and early summer of that year, Lord Louis Mountbatten's Combined Operations Headquarters was intent on making bold plans that would test that resolve.

I have yet to uncover any evidence that explicitly states when the original idea for the Dieppe Raid materialized. Although Jock Hughes-Hallett stated many years after the fact that the concept for a raid on Dieppe germinated during his January 1942 brainstorming session with his advisers David Luce and Dick de Costobadie the day after Godfrey introduced the new pinch policy, there is no record of any serious planning or intelligence collection at that time to definitively support his statement.

As one digs deeper into the Combined Operations files, Dieppe does register in a cursory way in the summer and fall of 1941, when Godfrey's Naval Intelligence Division and General Sir Bernard Paget's GHQ Home Forces—the British army headquarters that held jurisdictional responsibility over military operations in the Channel—both provided sporadic and limited intelligence about the port. In addition, because Dieppe lay so close to the English coast, standard operating procedure called for a constant watch on the port, and very brief mentions routinely appeared in reports. Even in the two months following Hughes-Hallett's group session, there is no sign of any active interest in Dieppe, probably because of the trio's preoccupation with the planning for Operation Chariot at St-Nazaire, Operation Myrmidon at Bayonne and Operation Sledgehammer at Cherbourg. Everything seems to have remained relatively quiet on the Dieppe front. Then, suddenly, in the week-long period between St-Nazaire on March 28 and the launch of Myrmidon in early April, the collection of intelligence and operational planning for what would become Operation Rutter—the direct predecessor to the Dieppe Raid—went secretly into overdrive.

On April 3, the previous trickle of intelligence turned into a flood. The GHQ Home Forces produced a report on the defences and terrain in the Dieppe area; the Ministry of Economic Warfare provided a list of potential industrial targets in the town; two days later, on Easter Sunday—the same day that the commando forces involved in Operation Myrmidon failed to pinch material—the Inter-Services Topographical Department delivered a special report on "Dieppe and the Beaches Five Miles to Each Side" in response to a direct request marked a "matter of urgency" from Hughes-Hallett's planning group.[3] This report, according to Godfrey, represented "a first class indication that the operation had got really hot."[4] At close to eighty pages, it displayed the best that the ISTD had to offer, supplying detailed terrain and potential targeting information that not only laid out the broad outline for the raid but clearly indicated that, right from this formative stage, the NID was working hand in glove with Mountbatten's headquarters to produce two possible plans for the Dieppe Raid.

The first plan called for an indirect three-prong pincer attack: the infantry or commandos would land on both sides of Dieppe at the little towns of Puys and Pourville while tanks and infantry landed farther west, down the coast at Quiberville, before rushing overland to envelop the town and port as rapidly as possible. On paper, this plan seemed the less risky option because it avoided a direct frontal assault on the town; this was the one to adopt if the objective was simply to test the ability of the various service arms to work together in an amphibious raid, score a quick propaganda victory, or attempt to draw the Luftwaffe into a battle of attrition.

The second option was a much riskier and more complicated proposition—a 1942 version of "shock and awe." In addition to the flanking attacks, it called for a direct assault in a crablike fashion over the main beach. Under the cover of darkness, infantry would land from the sea at Puys and Pourville, then push on towards the port while airborne units would drop from the skies to attack the coastal gun batteries at Varengeville and Berneval. That would be followed sixty minutes later by the frontal assault, led by tanks, infantry and engineers, which would storm the main beach in Dieppe after a bomber strike and naval bombardment had obliterated the hotels and other structures that lined the waterfront, separating it from the port tucked a few hundred yards behind. Using a carefully synchronized formula in which surprise was paramount, the assaulting forces would employ speed and a dual thunderclap of aerial bombing and naval bombardment to bewilder the defenders, allowing the raiders to close quickly on their positions, seize the dominating headlands and penetrate over the main beach into the town to capture the port.

While the main landing unfolded, an additional infantry battalion would land at Pourville and, with help from some of the tanks that had landed on the main beach, push southwest to capture the Luftwaffe airfield on the outskirts of Dieppe and the German army headquarters located in Arques-la-Bataille. An interesting feature of this plan, one worthy of Horatio Hornblower, called for a Cutting Out Force of Royal Navy vessels, with commandos riding on their decks, to storm into the port in the best "privateering" tradition and snatch as many German barges as they could to take back to England as "prizes." As one critic later wrote, this was "a classic example of a planning officer dreaming up a task for the lack of finding anything better since there was no possibility of these craft being of any use to the British."[5] Or so it seemed.

Operation Rutter, as the plan was code-named, would be a race against time. Unlike an invasion attempt, where assaulting forces storm ashore to capture and hold ground, build up their strength and expand the bridgehead, then break out into enemy-held territory—as happened in Normandy in 1944—the Dieppe Raid from the start was planned as a one-day "return ticket" or "butcher and bolt" raid designed to last no more than seventeen hours. That meant the raiders had to cross the English Channel undetected to maintain surprise, get ashore and quickly overwhelm the defenders, seize their objectives, wreak havoc in the port area, and withdraw under cover of darkness before substantial German reinforcements could arrive to obliterate them.

At this point, although the planning process clearly laid down the two options available when it came to method, nothing specifically revealed the exact goal for the raid. Obviously, the objective involved the capture of the port, even by frontal assault if necessary. But what was so important about gaining the port in the first place, let alone in such a direct and perhaps costly way?

Technically, Jock Hughes-Hallett was correct when he said that Dieppe had "no particular military significance." Bound by the provisions of the Official Secrets Act, he chose his words carefully while penning his unpublished memoirs, "Before I Forget," long before the secret of Ultra was released to the public. Much of the truth behind his account of Dieppe has been left in the shadows, replaced by convenient excuses, omissions or redirections of sensitive issues that make no mention of any pinch, captured documents, or special operations that were planned to obtain these materials. When he employed the term "military" in this context, the shrewd naval officer was using it in its proper sense. For most laymen, the word is synonymous with all branches of the armed services. Within the confines of the defence establishment, however, it was, and still is, applied only to issues involving the army or air force, and never the navy, which always used the term "naval." In this case, although Dieppe may not have offered Hughes-Hallett and his planning team a tantalizing "military" target, it certainly loomed large for "naval" concerns.

By the first week of February 1942, the NID and the Naval Section at Bletchley knew that Admiral Karl Dönitz's U-boats operating in the Atlantic had begun to use the four-rotor Enigma machine to encrypt their top-secret messages. As frightening and potentially cataclysmic as this development certainly was, a more disturbing prospect had appeared just weeks before, when Bletchley learned that a small number of German destroyers bound for operations in Norwegian waters had been outfitted with the machine as well. So far as the NID could tell, these destroyers had yet to begin operations with the new machine, and the extent of its use seemed limited, but the potential implications were clear. Godfrey went into overdrive to monitor the situation and actively pursue remedies, one of which involved Fleming's proposed Intelligence Assault Unit.

First, however, Godfrey had to locate the right target—one that would house the desired material for the pinch but not be so obvious

Until the recent release of classified Ultra Secret documents that reveal the importance of the codebooks and encrypting sheets that were contained in trawlers like these stationed in Dieppe harbour, the significance of their capture, detailed in the original raid plans, made little sense. Rather, it seemed to paint a picture of gross incompetence on the part of the planners.

as a heavily defended submarine base or an isolated U-boat or trawler at sea. As Godfrey had already laid out in January in his new pinch policy, port headquarters, naval wireless stations and other shore-based facilities were prime targets; the fluid nature of naval warfare meant that all these sites, regardless of location, had to possess the latest cipher machines and materials in order to maintain a link in the elaborate Kriegsmarine net. In April, when the Naval Section discovered that "some ships in the [English] channel were provided with the new machine," the information simply confirmed Godfrey and Fleming's suspicion that the Channel offered a lucrative environment, just as it had earlier when they planned Operation Ruthless. The small resort town of Dieppe, which was well within the reach of RAF air cover, offered a potential pinch gold mine. [6]

By early April, the combined efforts of the Operational Intelligence Centre in London and the Naval Section at Bletchley had firmly established through Ultra, TINA, aerial photographs and agent reports that Dieppe regularly handled a collection of vessels that most likely carried the desperately needed materials.[7] Armed trawlers, E-boats, R-boats, MTBs, destroyers, patrol boats, and auxiliary craft that engaged in coastal convoy escort, mine laying, dredging of accesses to ports and anti-submarine missions all at various times called Dieppe home. Among this collection of vessels—especially the trawlers—they could find material for the naval Enigma as well as the cribs that were ideal back-door cheats: RHV, short signals, E-bars, Z-bars, weather and dockyard ciphers, a Kriegsmarine general cipher, and books containing naval nomenclature. Although there was no guarantee that these vessels would be in the harbour on the morning of an attack, the odds were definitely in the raiders' favour that at least some of them would be berthed along the quays in the outer harbour, and probably with only skeleton crews to defend them. If not, Godfrey had another—fail-safe—plan.

Because of its geographical location, Dieppe had to be prepared to handle communications with all types of craft at a moment's notice, as had occurred in February when the Prinz Eugen had joined with the battleships Scharnhorst and Gneisenau in a mad "Channel dash" from Brest to the German home waters. With Dieppe forming a key link in the Kriegsmarine signals chain in France, Godfrey suspected that the port would house the latest cipher equipment and material. Given the fact that the port also served as a naval supply base for this part of the Channel, the German navy in Dieppe would have to maintain code books and cipher materials not only for the current period but for months into the future, ready for eventual issue. With the recent distribution of the four-rotor to surface vessels operating in the area, the odds were extremely high that the British could find the four-rotor material there. In short, Dieppe was, in modern parlance, a "target-rich environment."

And so, on April 6, less than twenty-four hours after the abandonment of Operation Myrmidon and its failure to pinch material at Bayonne, the possible location of a German naval headquarters in Dieppe suddenly appeared as an urgent addendum to the report of Godfrey's ISTD. It included a "New Objectives List," and was joined later by a request from the NID for the capture of various types of craft in the harbour. The pinch was very much in the forefront before the operational planning actually began and Mountbatten's headquarters officially adopted Dieppe as its next target.[8]

Two days later, in a move that clearly indicates great urgency, Godfrey, or perhaps more likely Fleming working on his behalf, challenged an intelligence report about a small hotel called the Moderne, apparently located at 21 rue Vauquelin on the corner with the Quai Duquesne, overlooking the inner harbour. Usually these matters were left to lower-ranking officers to deal with, so the personal interest of these top men in the target search, let alone the challenge to the veracity of the report, indicates the vital importance of this target. For Godfrey and Fleming, the detailed description of the hotel cast doubt on whether a structure as small as the Moderne was indeed used by the Kriegsmarine, which traditionally preferred seaside villas and other grandiose buildings:

> This hotel is situated on the RUE VAUQUELIN on the corner of the street nearest the harbour. The hotel is almost certainly on the north side of the street but a possibility exists that it is on the south side. The full address is 21, RUE VAUQUELIN.
>
> The hotel is a small one consisting of a restaurant with a few rooms upstairs. The main entrance is on the quay and is in the centre of the building. This leads into the Restaurant. To the north of this is a second entrance leading upstairs. It is believed that there is a third entrance on the RUE VAUQUELIN. The quay at this point is arcaded so that the entrances open onto the Arcade.
>
> Since this hotel is so small, it does not seem likely that it is being used as Headquarters and considerable doubt is therefore thrown on the original report. Special enquiries are being made and it is hoped to give further information shortly.[9]

There are no indications in the documents as to what inquiries were made, and I was unable to uncover any paper trail to establish exactly what changed their minds, but six weeks later, in the second week of June, neither Fleming nor Godfrey had further concerns. Without any explanation, there is a simple note in the file to say that the Hôtel Moderne "is now considered by NID to be Naval Headquarters."[10]

From a historical perspective, whether the hotel actually housed a German naval headquarters or some other naval facility is still open to debate, but the point is of secondary importance to this story; what is crucial is what the planners thought at the time. Although they did not know it, the first location at 21 rue Vauquelin was incorrect: it housed the Hôtel Les Arcades, which had been there from the turn of the century and, in 1942, still hosted German soldiers and sailors and the occasional civilian to lunch or dinner in its lobby restaurant. That ruled it out as a functioning naval headquarters.[*]

The secondary target, located across the street, was in fact the Hôtel Moderne; it fit the physical description that the NID originally balked at, but no record has surfaced to show what was happening there during the occupation. Some photographs from the wartime period clearly show one naval headquarters facility on the boulevard de Verdun located in an old school not far from the casino, while others show a similar facility near the end of Quai Henri IV, where it meets the inner channel. Although existing German documents do not reveal a specific location in the port, a preliminary report drawn

---

[*] While on location filming *Dieppe Uncovered* for History Television, my filmmaking partner, producer/director Wayne Abbott, and I spent a day talking to some of the local inhabitants, including Karine and Mathieu Leducq, the present owners of Les Arcades hotel, which is still there. As Mathieu pointed out to us, with photographic evidence in hand, his hotel had been in the same location for over fifty years before the raid. He confirmed that there used to be a hotel/restaurant called Le Moderne across the street in the alternative target location, until approximately 1973. Wayne and I then checked in a phone book from 1939 in the local Dieppe archives, and it confirmed Mathieu's story, although we could not discover what became of the hotel during the occupation. We did, however, have with us an account from the diary of Georges Guibon, a Dieppe resident, who chronicled his experiences wandering through the town on the morning of the raid. Quite incidentally, he mentions the death of the owner of Les Arcades—a man by the name of Verel—who, after being hit by a stray bullet from Pollet Cliff, crawled into the tiny elevator and died. This account was confirmed by Mathieu, who then called the archives and had them produce a copy of Verel's death certificate. It was witnessed by one of his waitresses, meaning that his hotel and restaurant were in operation on the day of the raid. Obviously, then, the Hôtel Les Arcades did not host a German headquarters.

up by the German naval commander in the Channel area provides a list of the German naval formations on duty in the town. They include close to 360 men in total, with 152 attached to the "harbour commandant's headquarters," 44 with an "Army signals transmission station," 11 with a "naval signals station," 4 with a teletype detachment, 4 with a "wireless deception sender," 44 with the "6th Flotilla Base unit," and roughly 100 with the "port protection flotilla."[11] In the same file, another report makes mention of a special security unit tasked with destroying vital objectives such as pumping stations and lock gates, but, even more important, classified signals material located in the port should they be faced with capture.

Although this information does not confirm that the Hôtel Moderne was the correct target, it certainly shows that British intelligence was in the ballpark and that at least one site containing the desired material did exist somewhere in the tiny confines of the outer harbour, well within reach of any raider landing over the eastern half of the main beach or storming into the port to land along one of the quays.[12]

Exact location aside, the significance resides in the personal involvement of Godfrey and Fleming: their nitpicking leaves little doubt of the importance and nature of the target. No other objective received so much attention. It also shows that the NID took an overriding interest in locating a rich source of pinch material—a factor that was in play right from the beginning of the planning process for the raid, even before Mountbatten, the chiefs of staff and Churchill approved the mission.[13]

More significant still, the evidence reveals a new and potentially game-changing aspect of the raid that has never before been raised, let alone considered, in the Dieppe story—a saga of critical importance to Canada's role in the Second World War.

HOTEL MODERNE, DIEPPE.

This hotel is situated on the RUE VAUQUELIN at the corner of the street nearest the harbour. The hotel is almost certainly on the north side of the street but a possibility exists that it is on the south side. The full address is 21, RUE VAUQUELIN.

The hotel is a small one consisting of a Restaurant with a few rooms upstairs. The main entrance is on the quay and is in the centre of the building. This leads into the Restaurant. To the north of this is a second entrance leading upstairs. It is believed that there is a third entrance on the RUE VAUQUELIN. The quay at this point is arcaded so that the entrances open onto the Arcade.

Since this hotel is so small, it does not seem likely that it is being used as Headquarters and considerable doubt is therefore thrown on the original report. Special enquiries are being made and it is hoped to give further information shortly.

On April 14, just over a week after the aborted Operation Myrmidon failed as a pinch mission, Jock Hughes-Hallett, the head of Mountbatten's target search committee, convened the first recorded meeting to discuss a raid under the code name Rutter at Dieppe.

Brigadier Charles Haydon, the vice chief of Combined Operations and the man who had not only commanded the military force but organized the army commandos during the Lofoten pinch raids, presided that day. Hughes-Hallett opened the meeting with a brief pitch about Dieppe as a prospective target, and the group readily agreed that it seemed "attractive and worthwhile," an idea definitely worth pursuing.[14] Over the next five days, the planning syndicate laid out a set of objectives, with the capture of the invasion (or landing) barges and a series of German army headquarters in and around the town topping the list. Conspicuous by its absence was the Hôtel Moderne—probably because of its unconfirmed status as a German naval headquarters at that time.[15] The dicey frontal assault option was also agreed upon, with the proviso that the raid be preceded by a heavy air bombardment and that the two batteries east and west of Dieppe be taken out before the landing by airborne troops. On hearing that condition, Hughes-Hallett remarked, "Though . . . hazardous, it was perfectly feasible so far as the Navy was concerned."[16]

On April 25, Lord Louis Mountbatten chaired his first meeting on Operation Rutter, at Combined Operations Headquarters on Richmond

---

OPPOSITE : Brought to light here for the first time in the history of the Dieppe Raid, this is a detailed report on the Hôtel Moderne, located in the harbour at 21 rue Vauquelin, which Naval Intelligence suspected housed the German Naval HQ. Godfrey first questioned the suitability of this facility to house the Headquarters they were trying to find, but by June 12, six weeks later, Naval Intelligence was convinced, and the hotel along with the trawlers became the target for Fleming's IAU. Along with the trawlers, the Hôtel Moderne, which no longer exists, has become the centrepiece of the Dieppe discussion.

Terrace in Whitehall. There the planning group adopted the outline plan and confirmed the method of direct assault.[17] At first Mountbatten was taken aback by the prospect of this daring frontal raid, but he quickly came on side once the arguments were laid out before him. With surprise and shock essential for success, the planners argued, it made no sense to land tanks far out on the flanks where, even under good conditions, they would need considerable time to reach the port. Each group would first have to cross a small river, and if the Germans reacted quickly and destroyed the bridges, the tanks would be delayed even more. Moreover, the latest intelligence assessment of Dieppe's defences indicated that only 1,400 low-category troops held the town and that reinforcements would be slow to arrive, bringing the total at most to 2,500 men in the first four hours after the attack.[18] Mountbatten was assured that the bombing would be of "maximum intensity," delivered in a combination of high- and low-altitude attacks to confuse and disorient the defenders—first by heavy bombers hitting the general area, followed quickly by low-level runs with fighter bombers that would strike specific beach targets during the landings. Suitably impressed, Mountbatten signed off on the outline plan for Operation Rutter, allowing it to proceed to the Chiefs of Staff Committee for their approval.

By the time the outline plan reached the chiefs of staff for their consideration on May 10, the target and the objective list had grown substantially. Now, in addition to the earlier goals, German E-boats and motor launches had joined the list, along with food stores, the town hall, the post office, the railway marshalling yards, the beach-front casino, and the coastguard station on the cliff at Puys, as well as the capture of prisoners and of secret documents from the divisional headquarters. The stakes were growing.

When the chiefs of staff actually met to discuss the proposed operation three days later, Mountbatten sought permission to move ahead with the outline plan so he could provide the various force commanders, who had yet to be appointed although they had already been named, with some guidelines to help them shape their detailed planning. At this point, the outline plan for Rutter envisioned it taking place over two tidal periods lasting roughly seventeen hours, giving the raiding force the maximum time on target before it had to withdraw. The date was set for the night of June 20–21 or any day thereafter up to June 26. It would be the largest raiding force yet put to sea. From the naval perspective alone, Jock Hughes-Hallett's plan called for a 250-ship armada that included six Royal Navy destroyers, seven infantry assault ships, twenty-four tank landing craft, fifty R-crafts for transporting troops to shore, and a collection of motor gunboats, torpedo boats and motor launches, including HMS *Locust*—a flat-bottomed river gunboat formerly captained by Dick de Costobadie. This ship would carry the newly formed Royal Marine Commando, including Ian Fleming's Intelligence Assault Unit, into battle.[19]

If the proposed naval force was indeed impressive, the turnout in the skies in support of the operation was stellar. With more than 800 aircraft taking part, including 150 heavy bombers, eight squadrons of low-level attack aircraft, and more than 500 fighters providing an air umbrella above, it promised to be the greatest display of air power since the Battle of Britain.

As for the military contribution, the plan required almost a full infantry division—roughly four thousand men. There was also a battalion of tanks containing three squadrons of the latest Churchill tanks, supported by a battalion of about five hundred airborne troops that included paratroop and glider forces.

The executive responsibility for launching, postponing or cancelling the raid came under the Commander-in-Chief, Portsmouth, Admiral Sir William James, one of Blinker Hall's veterans from Room 40 in the Admiralty. He would be responsible for giving the order to commence the operation. But once the forces left the harbours in southern England, they would be in the hands of the naval force commander, who would shepherd them across the Channel to their

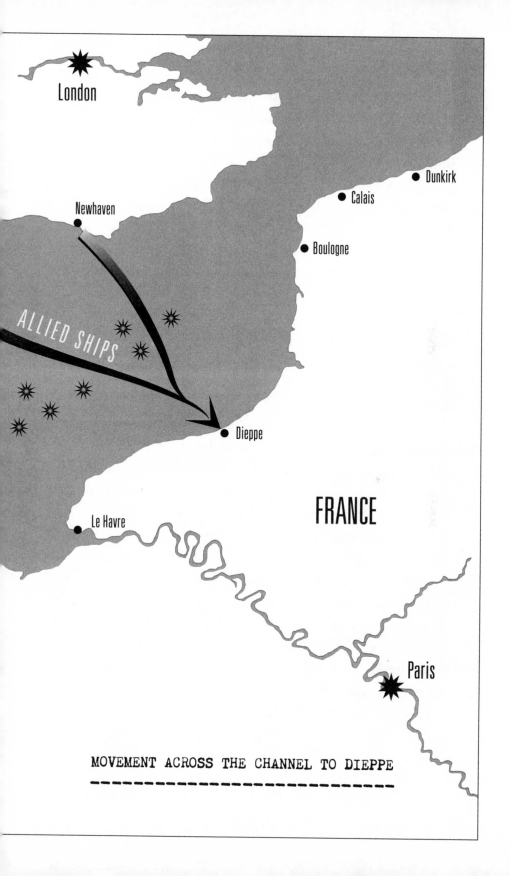

London

Newhaven

Dunkirk

Calais

Boulogne

ALLIED SHIPS

Dieppe

FRANCE

Le Havre

Paris

MOVEMENT ACROSS THE CHANNEL TO DIEPPE

landing sites and deliver them to shore. From there, the military commander would take over once they landed and until they re-embarked for their return to England at the raid's end. The air force commander would conduct the air battle throughout from his base at home.

Officially, Operation Rutter steamed ahead without a clearly specified goal: following direct orders from Churchill, the minutes of the meetings could not include anything that was classified as Ultra Secret.[20] It is this ambiguity has led to many misconceptions over the years—for example, that the raid was launched to placate calls by Stalin and the Americans for a second front; or that the objective was to prove the strategic impossibility of a second front at the time; or that the raid was put on simply to draw the Luftwaffe into a battle of attrition. But none of these goals are credible as the main reason or the driving force for the raid, as a brief review of the other operations planned for the months ahead reveals.

Operation Sledgehammer, scheduled for the fall, would placate calls for a limited second front and also serve to draw German land and air forces from the eastern front; when the British chiefs of staff nixed the idea in the spring, replacing it with Operation Gymnast— the invasion of North Africa, later known as Operation Torch—even Stalin, Britain's most demanding critic, was satisfied with that relocated second front.[21] In addition, the Royal Air Force firmly believed that Operation Imperator, the proposed landing of two to four divisions on both sides of Boulogne, designed specifically to entice the Luftwaffe into a potentially fierce battle lasting from two to four weeks, went much further towards achieving this goal than Operation Rutter's seventeen-hour duration.[22] On that same note, the RAF also began to consider using feints and fake raids, such as Operation Coleman, to draw the Luftwaffe out over the Channel rather than risk the commitment of land forces ashore to achieve that objective.[23]

Most important, the intelligence blackout and the failure of Operations Chariot and Myrmidon to produce the materials Bletchley needed strip away any notion of the Dieppe Raid being organized strictly for the sake of raiding or designed specifically to fail. In fact, just one day after the Dieppe Raid, Frank Birch at Bletchley's Naval Section called for "a special operation or cutting out expedition" to be launched against ships in the harbour and German shore facilities at Derna in Libya, in Marsa Matruh in Egypt or on the island of Crete.[24]

Meanwhile, at home, both Godfrey and Mountbatten knew that if Combined Operations Headquarters, supported by the NID, could pull off a pinch at this darkest of times and end the silence brought on by the four-rotor Enigma, that feat would also enhance their own reputations and deliver "political currency" far exceeding its weight in gold within the closed Whitehall establishment—and, of course, with Ultra's number one consumer, Churchill.

The evidence from the early planning in April and May 1942 points to Operation Rutter being a unique stand-alone mission of an intentionally ambiguous nature, which, because of its limited size, scope and duration, could not achieve, let alone replace, the strategic objectives called for in the other operations. Why, then, was it planned and approved, particularly without a hint of opposition from the chiefs of staff? The elements of surprise and shock, the novel use of tanks, and the capture of the port, the airfield and various German headquarters were considered essential features right from the start. But only if we bring those points together within the context of the evidence now emerging—the vital role of intelligence in the war effort, the critical importance of pinch raids to the cryptographic efforts, the urgent need to solve the four-rotor Enigma blackout, the preferred form for pinch raids and the desire to conduct them ashore—does the Dieppe Raid start to make sense.

Although Lord Louis Mountbatten and Jock Hughes-Hallett would cry foul after the actual Dieppe Raid, Operation Jubilee, on August 19, 1942, they, just like Churchill and the chiefs of staff, expressed no hesitation at all in the lead-up to the same plan in Operation Rutter in the spring. Even the obdurate Alan Brooke—the newly promoted Chief of the Imperial General Staff who kept Churchill's penchant for wildcat operations in check and, while applauding Mountbatten's enthusiasm, dismissed his martial ability—voiced nothing but support throughout the planning process. In fact, Brooke had in pre-war days spent his summers in Dieppe and, after hearing about the proposed raid for the first time, noted emotionally in his diary: "Little did I ever think in my journeys of Newhaven–Dieppe that I should have been planning as I was this morning!"[25] It was only after the disastrous results that these men attempted to distance themselves from the fallout. At any point during the planning process, they had the opportunity and the obligation to shut the whole project down or to force a fundamental change if they felt they should. Yet they saw merit in this risky direct assault—even though, without inside knowledge, it seemed to make no sense at all.

TEN

ALL THE KING'S MEN

We just wanted to get at them.

—Private Ron Beal to David O'Keefe

Since the fall of France in 1940, Canadian Army divisions had been idling their time in camps along England's Sussex coast. Originally they had the important task of standing guard against the threat of a German invasion, but by the spring of 1942 it was clear that Hitler's focus and forces had moved east, to the Soviet Union. Restless in this role, the men had begun to show the first signs of sagging morale the year before, when the repetitive training and pointless defensive exercises started to take their toll. Unproven in battle in this new war, the Canadians in their own estimation had a great legacy from the Great War to uphold.

By the end of the First World War, the Canadian Corps was renowned as the "Shock Army of the British Empire," ready, willing and able to take on the toughest, dirtiest and costliest jobs. Stunning victories at Vimy, Hill 70 and Amiens, to name but a few, had all made significant contributions to the Allied war effort. This new generation of Canadian soldiers now demanded a chance to have their own crack at the enemy.[1] "We just wanted to get at them," Private Ron Beal of Toronto's

Royal Regiment of Canada told me—a simple but common refrain among the nearly fifty thousand Canadian troops cooling their heels in England while other Commonwealth nations engaged Axis forces around the globe. That February, with no signs of battle on the horizon, the crusty and uncompromising technocrat General Andrew McNaughton, the senior Canadian Army commander in England, began to agitate for action.

To alleviate the growing tension among the soldiers, the Canadian units had for over half a year been engaged in commando-like training for small-scale amphibious operations, hoping at least to participate in a series of hit-and-run raids along the French and Norwegian coasts. Up to this point, the Spitsbergen raid in Norway in August 1941, which had included some five hundred Canadian soldiers, had been the highlight, along with limited involvement in a few other pinprick attacks. That left the vast majority of the Canadian officers and men without any experience in large-scale operations of any kind. At home, Canadians were getting as restless for real action as the soldiers waiting around in England. Fearing, somewhat naively, that the war would be over before the Canadians could take part in any substantial fighting, Canadian prime minister William Lyon Mackenzie King added his voice to his general's complaints. Suddenly, from early 1942 onward, the pressure from Canadian authorities to engage in active operations increased dramatically.

Meanwhile, Lieutenant General Harry Crerar, General McNaughton's highly ambitious subordinate, was pulling out all the stops to get the Canadians into action. Ready, if necessary, to use his personal relationship with his old friend and First World War compatriot General Sir Alan Brooke, Crerar got the nod from McNaughton to approach General Sir Bernard Paget at GHQ Home Forces, as well as the chiefs of staff. In a move that one historian has called a clear case of "misplaced nationalism,"[2] the crafty and determined Crerar managed to obtain full support from Paget's headquarters and, eventually, from

General Brooke and the chiefs of staff. That left the Canadian high command, unknowingly at first, muscling in on the embryonic Operation Rutter—thereby hitching itself to the Combined Operations train bound for Dieppe.[3]

The Canadians, however, were not Louis Mountbatten's first choice to take part in the Dieppe Raid, nor had he seriously considered them for the operation until the political realities of coalition warfare forced his hand. His original preference was his favourite, the Royal Marine Division, the infantry arm of the Royal Navy. "I was anxious to use troops that had amphibious knowledge," he wrote years later, "and had some actual active services experience. There were enough of the Royal Marines and certainly in the Commandos to qualify them for such a description."[4] But the chiefs of staff saw no reason to keep the Royal Marines around as a division-sized unit; it was only the decision to break them down into commando-sized units that saved this storied branch of the armed services. At that point, Mountbatten still held out the hope that they would be the preferred commando unit to handle pinch operations in his expanding empire, particularly at Dieppe.

"I remember going on and on at Brookie [Alan Brooke]," he wrote years later, "and asking not to have to take the Canadians. However he said that Crerar was absolutely adamant that they should be used and that the P.M. was prepared to accept them. I was thus overridden."[5] His reluctance likely stemmed in part from the starring role he had in mind for his Royal Marines, but also—and perhaps this was more important—from the secret pinch imperative in Operation Rutter. In a carefully crafted, vague recollection of events penned years before the public revelation of Ultra, Mountbatten stated:

> Brookie spoke to me personally about the desire of the Canadians to be brought into a raiding operation as soon as possible. My recollection is that I protested strongly because Dieppe was such a large scale and uncertain operation. We were still trying to find

out things and even if successful in all our aims there would be nothing much to show for it to the outside world and we were bound to have heavy casualties.[6]

Certainly, Mountbatten's professed regard for Canadian casualties, or any casualties in this context, is strictly designed to distance himself from the disastrous results, just as the vague mention of "trying to find out things" is a euphemistic cover for the pinch.

Although Mountbatten likely didn't know it at the time, Canada was an emerging SIGINT partner. A handful of Canadians, including Prime Minister Mackenzie King, the Canadian Chief of the Naval Staff, Vice Admiral Percy Nelles, and his Director of Naval Intelligence, Commander Herbert Little, were aware of Ultra, with the latter two actively using the intelligence supplied by the Naval Section at Bletchley Park to help fight the convoy battle in the Atlantic. Both were all too aware of the terrible problems being caused by the current blackout but most likely knew nothing about the pinch. In addition, the Canadians had made inroads of their own into cryptography with the establishment of the Examination Unit in Ottawa and a network of intercept stations across the country, which were providing intelligence to assist in both the European and Pacific theatres of the war. Perhaps more important, Churchill's British Security Co-ordination, a covert organization established in May 1940 by the British Secret Intelligence Service (or MI6, as it was coming to be called at the time) for intelligence and propaganda purposes in the Americas, was run from its Rockefeller Center offices in New York City by William Stephenson, a Canadian multi-millionaire industrialist who, by the end of the war, would be a close friend of Ian Fleming. Stephenson handled the main relay station for Ultra traffic in North America, code-named Hydra and located at a Top Secret base in Whitby, Ontario, known famously as Camp X.

Although members of the Canadian high command in England were not yet fully "indoctrinated" into or apprised of Ultra (with the exception of Lieutenant General Kenneth Stuart, the Chief of the Canadian General Staff), there was nothing to prevent them from being partially let in on the secret. But in the carefully stovepiped world of intelligence and the military, which operated on a "need to know" basis, all they were told was the main objective for the raid, its general significance to the war effort and the fact that it was worth risking everything to obtain. In other words, they had generally the same limited information as the men in Ian Fleming's Intelligence Assault Unit.

At that time, cultural and nationalist lines between Canada and Great Britain were much more blurred than they are today, so it is not surprising that the British high command viewed Canada's contribution to the war as part of the Empire or Commonwealth effort. In their thinking, Canadian troops were to play their role as part of the imperial team, not as a stand-alone national force like the United States Army. The Canadian servicemen stationed in Sussex were thus under the Home Forces command of the British general Sir Bernard Paget, who was responsible for all military contributions to operations in the Channel area. Once persuaded by Crerar, it was easy for Paget to acquiesce to Canadian demands for action, even in an operation like Rutter with an Ultra Secret core.

On April 27, just two days after Mountbatten had signed off on the outline plan for Operation Rutter, Lieutenant General Bernard Law Montgomery, who under Paget commanded the South-Eastern Army, called Harry Crerar to a meeting at his headquarters. Monty, as he was fondly called, was about to head off to North Africa—and legendary fame as the hero of El Alamein. Never one to suffer fools gladly or deviate from his precise approach to military professionalism, he told the eager Canadian commander that a raid on an unidentified port was in the offing and asked whether the Canadians wanted to be part of the operation.

"You bet," came the reply.

And with this quick utterance, the fate of thousands of Canadians was sealed.[7]

Now began the internal battle for command. The mixture of military and naval minds, talents and temperaments was what Combined Operations was all about, with all three services putting aside their partisan differences for the common good under the overall leadership of Dickie Mountbatten—or so the theory went. Through late April, the three armed services had been selecting the men they wanted to nominate as force commanders for Operation Rutter, although the appointments would not be made official until after the chiefs of staff had met on May 13. The raid, like other combined operations, would come under joint command, meaning that, on the day, each of the force commanders from the land, sea and air elements would have his own job to do, but there was no single head responsible for overall planning or execution. The RAF put forward Air Vice-Marshal Trafford Leigh-Mallory, who, as commander of No. 11 Group from Fighter Command, was responsible for the air defence of southern England, including London. The Royal Navy chose Rear Admiral Tom Baillie-Grohman, who was currently on active duty in the Mediterranean and would join the triumvirate after their first meeting in June. For the land force commander, General Paget's headquarters selected Major General Hamilton "Ham" Roberts, the commander of the Second Canadian Infantry Division.

The fifty-year-old Trafford Leigh-Mallory came from the Cheshire countryside and had studied history at Magdalene College, Cambridge, before becoming a barrister in the years leading up to the First World War. He had survived two gruelling years of front-line fighting in the trenches as an infantryman, including the first poison-gas attack in history at the second battle of Ypres, before transferring to the Royal

Flying Corps, where he won the Distinguished Service Order for commanding aerial reconnaissance squadrons. In the interwar years it was his older brother, the celebrated mountaineer George Mallory, who stole the headlines as he attempted to become the first man to reach the summit of Mount Everest, only to disappear on her slopes in 1924 not far from the peak.[8] By the time the Battle of Britain began in the skies over England in the summer of 1940, Trafford Leigh-Mallory had risen to command No. 12 Group, which defended central England, with fifteen squadrons containing nearly two hundred Spitfire and Hurricane fighters under his command. He then moved on to No. 11 Group, which had already borne the brunt of the fighting on the south coast of England. Leigh-Mallory was as aggressive as he was ambitious, pioneering the "Big Wing" theory of air warfare in the RAF: he advocated decisive battles with the Germans, using large groups of fighters in a pack, rather than the piecemeal, hit-and-run attacks currently employed. He wanted to try out this strategy in the skies over Dieppe.

Harold "Tom" Baillie-Grohman is a minor figure in the Dieppe saga. Born in British Columbia to a British father and a Canadian mother, the fifty-four-year-old rear admiral had, like John Godfrey, made the Royal Navy his home for nearly forty years. Having served extensively in the Mediterranean and the Far East, he had then been captain of minesweepers in the Channel before taking command of the battleship HMS *Ramillies*. At one point he had even been Mountbatten's commanding officer. First Sea Lord Dudley Pound and Admiral Cunningham both thought highly of him as a consummate naval professional with valuable experience in combined operations in the Mediterranean. He had participated in the fight to save the besieged island of Malta and, earlier in 1941, had commanded the naval end of the brilliant raid on Rhodes, where he earned the Distinguished Service Order for his part in evacuating nearly fifty-five thousand British troops from Greece—the same action that claimed Mountbatten's HMS *Kelly*. However, both Mountbatten and Jock Hughes-Hallett, his lead planner for Operation Rutter, regarded

Baillie-Grohman with deep suspicion—and Baillie-Grohman in turn was no fan of Mountbatten's mounting hubris or his style of combined operations. The common feeling around Mountbatten's headquarters was that Pound had inserted Baillie-Grohman, a stickler for tradition and procedure, into the operation to act as the Admiralty's inside man, keeping watch on his one-time subordinate, who displayed a penchant for operating outside normal channels. More likely, it was Baillie-Grohman's strong personality and forceful character, coupled with his highly influential voice and excellent leadership, that Pound wanted to counterbalance the maverick tendencies displayed by Mountbatten and his hand-picked staff of "inexperienced enthusiasts." Whatever Pound's intentions, the Chief and his naval commander were ill matched. Baillie-Grohman, as his personnel file reveals, was "obstinate, tenacious of his own opinions and inclined to be intolerant of the opinions of others. A good man to have behind you in a tight corner, provided he agrees with your reasons for getting into it."[9] Mountbatten never succeeded in drawing him fully into the spirit of the operation, nor was he ever likely to be, as Mountbatten later said, "one of us."[10]

When Baillie-Grohman arrived in England from the Mediterranean in early June, after the chiefs of staff had accepted the outline plan and Mountbatten's staff had begun working on the detailed plan for Rutter, he was immediately skeptical about the potential for the operation and in constant opposition to the over-optimistic planning and unchecked enthusiasm surrounding the mission. He noted significant problems with Jock Hughes-Hallett and his planners, informing Mountbatten that he did not "trust the ambitious type."[11] He complained about the staff's general lack of experience—that half of them, for instance, had no idea of the capabilities of the naval craft they were about to employ.

Baillie-Grohman also questioned the role of a mysterious Royal Naval Reserve lieutenant commander who worked as a special liaison to Mountbatten's headquarters and "was allowed to go on leave on several occasions and visit exercises," meaning he was not available to handle the constant stream of requests.[12] Given that Section 17 in the Naval Intelligence Division handled that portfolio, it is highly likely that the man he was referring to was Ian Fleming—who did hold a Rutter card, giving him the essential security clearance to take part in the planning for the operation.

Baillie-Grohman's most serious complaint, however, was about the absence of a "joint appreciation"—something that is standard procedure in any operational plan. A joint appreciation shows how all the service arms are to work together, ensures that commanders are indeed on the same page, and serves as the litmus test for the plan, reaffirming strengths, exposing potential weaknesses and allowing for amendments—or, in some cases, even the cancellation of the mission. Although Baillie-Grohman admitted that each service might have an appreciation of its own specific role in the mission, there was nothing to test the operational soundness of Rutter as a whole.

In contrast to the dour Baillie-Grohman, the third man, the military force commander, fifty-two-year-old Canadian major general Hamilton Roberts, was exactly the type Mountbatten wanted: eager and ambitious, just like Jock Hughes-Hallett and Trafford Leigh-Mallory. Responsible for providing the detailed military portion of the outline plan for Rutter under the watchful eye of General Montgomery, Roberts, from Pipestone in southern Manitoba, would ultimately become the officer who carried the blame for the Dieppe fiasco, forever vilified for his actions on that one fateful day in August. A "gunner," or artillery officer, by training, like most of the Canadian high command, Roberts had graduated from the Royal Military College in Kingston in 1914 and had gone straight into action in the trenches during the First World War. There he displayed conspicuous gallantry and determination, winning the Military Cross during the horrific slaughter at the Somme in 1916 and finishing the war in a training establishment after being wounded in 1918.

Fifty-two-year-old Canadian Major General Hamilton "Ham" Roberts, commander of the Second Canadian Infantry Division, had earned the Military Cross in the mud and slaughter of the Battle of the Somme. He was given the responsibility of Military Force Commander for the Dieppe Raid, being described as "the best division commander in the Corps." But although he garnered a commendation for his actions on the day in August, in the fingerpointing aftermath he would be vilified by his military colleagues, and then in history, for the failure of the operation and the unnecessarily high casualties incurred. He spent the remainder of the war commanding a training unit before retiring to the Channel Islands, where he remained relatively silent about Dieppe, allegedly vowing that one day history would vindicate him.

Between the wars, Ham Roberts continued his career in the tiny Canadian Army Permanent Force, and by 1940 he was in command of the 1st Field Regiment of the Royal Canadian Horse Artillery, briefly committed to the fighting in France. During the hurried evacuation at Dunkirk, his enthusiastic "can-do" attitude and iron will to see a task through to the end caught the attention of his Canadian and British superiors alike. Imperilled by the quick German advance, he managed to extricate his two dozen guns to a waiting ship while under fire and, with that done, carried on and loaded several more precious British artillery pieces from the beach.

Within two years, he had risen to the rank of major general and, in April 1942, to the command of the Second Canadian Infantry Division—not long before it was selected to make its combat debut at Dieppe. In the interim, he eliminated what he considered weak links in the division by implementing a series of rigorous physical training schemes and intensified commando-style training. Apparently this attention to detail and training is what originally caught Montgomery's attention. Ruthlessly efficient like Roberts himself, particularly when it came to his commanders, Montgomery considered Roberts the "best divisional commander in the Canadian Corps"—an appraisal that might appear glowing but was actually faint praise.[13] In Montgomery's true opinion, Roberts was "very sound, but . . . not in any way brilliant."[14] Still, the Second Canadian Division commander seemed impressive in person, particularly to Admiral Sir William James, the Room 40 veteran who was now Commander-in-Chief, Portsmouth: in one of his letters from the time, he noted that Roberts was "powerfully built" and "looks like a real thruster."[15]

Years after the raid, Jock Hughes-Hallett attempted to distance himself from Roberts, now the pariah. In his memoirs he recorded that the division commander's enthusiasm had bordered on the "over confident" leading up to the raid, that he was "eager for action at all costs" and giving "the impression of being prepared to take anything on."[16]

At the time, however, that was exactly what Hughes-Hallett and Mountbatten had wanted and expected from their military force commander. In an earlier proposed raid on Alderney in the Channel Islands, Hughes-Hallett had criticized the military commander for his reluctance to "chance his arm" or to subject his troops to the hazards that are inevitable in raiding operations—the very same exploits he and Mountbatten now expected Roberts to undertake at Dieppe.[17]

In any event, by the time the three force commanders came on board for Operation Rutter, its overall form, tone and objectives had been set by Jock Hughes-Hallett's planning syndicate and approved by the chiefs of staff, leaving little room for any fundamental changes to the scheme. The job now facing the commanders was not to reason why, but to flesh out the plan and put it into effect. Although responsible for the detailed planning and conduct of the raid, their hands were, in fact, already firmly tied.

Before the Dieppe Raid, Lord Louis Mountbatten's Combined Operations Headquarters had suffered no serious setback on the battlefield and certainly no disaster to check the mounting enthusiasm and hubris that would plague the planning of Operation Rutter and, on August 19, play out in tragic fashion as Operation Jubilee. The year before, the successful raids at the Lofoten and Vaagso islands had generated significant results for the cryptanalysts at Bletchley Park and clearly positioned Combined Operations as the major vehicle for signals intelligence pinch raids. Although criticism had flared up over the planning of the aborted Operation Myrmidon, especially from General Charles Haydon, Mountbatten's chief of staff, the publicity surrounding the simultaneous brilliant raid at St-Nazaire had produced an intoxicating and irresistible confidence within the COHQ on Richmond Terrace. Even smaller raids, such as the one at Bruneval, outside Le Havre, had elevated the profile of Mountbatten's headquarters still further among the British and American publics, with headline stories about surreptitiously snatching a top-secret radar set from the German defenders. The United States, now a major Allied partner, sought co-operation and guidance from Britain on intelligence and combined operations techniques—and Mountbatten was ready to oblige.

On June 5, Montgomery called the three Dieppe force command-ers—Trafford Leigh-Mallory, Tom Baillie-Grohman and Ham Roberts—together for a planning session in his headquarters building. General Charles Haydon represented Mountbatten, who was away in the United States showcasing his wares for President Roosevelt and the American navy. The commanders reached a set of decisions that reinforced the frontal-assault option augmented by air support. Mountbatten would later claim that the disastrous frontal assault was strictly Monty's brain-child and that it appeared for the first time during this session. However, the reference to the formulation of two plans in the special report on Dieppe that Mountbatten requested from Admiral John Godfrey's Inter-Services Topographical Department at the end of March, along with the later outline plan, makes it clear that the fron-tal-assault plan was already a fait accompli by the time of the meeting at COHQ.

At first, the planners had considered launching the flanking and frontal assaults simultaneously, but Jock Hughes-Hallett dismissed that idea for logistical reasons: there was simply not enough sea room off Dieppe to accommodate 250 ships simultaneously delivering troops ashore and providing covering fire. More importantly, he decided, given the differing speeds of the ships in the assault force, it would be impossible to coordinate them all, from the moment they left various ports in southern England and the Isle of Wight, and deliver them all together on time and on target at Dieppe in one fell swoop under the cover of darkness.[18]

The one great negative of the direct assault option was already obvious: by attacking the enemy frontally, the strategy courted disaster if the carefully crafted plan and all its elements did not come off like clockwork. Mountbatten's planners knew that but intentionally disregarded it. They believed that, with the novel use of tanks rolling ashore in the first wave alongside the infantry (something that the British had tried during a raid on Bardia in North Africa the year before), the chances of pulling off such an audacious raid looked promising. That idea initially left Brigadier Churchill Mann, Ham Roberts's efficient chief of staff and deputy military force commander, shaking his head in disbelief and then with a sense of wonderment. "Such a plan, on the face of it," he wrote, "is almost a fantastic conception."[19] But in the gung-ho spirit of the times, he remained open-minded and receptive, finally viewing it as the "outstanding feature of the plan."[20]

He saw many positives in the direct assault, particularly given the force provided by sixty Churchill tanks from the 14th Canadian Tank Regiment—the Calgary Tanks. First, surprise and shock: the sight of successive waves of thirty-eight-ton tanks pouring out of landing craft and rolling towards them would no doubt have a "terrific morale effect" on the enemy. Second, the plan seemed feasible logistically: recent training exercises on chert rock beaches in England had proven most encouraging; the fist-sized boulders occasionally clogged sprocket wheels and immobilized some of the giant machines, but they did not impede their ability to roll off the beaches in sizable numbers. Third, the tanks were not alone. Aided by specially trained teams of Canadian combat engineers who would clear paths over the seawall, the tanks would proceed across the grassy promenade, where the engineers would destroy the anti-tank barriers in the tiny streets leading to the port. With that accomplished, the tanks would then rumble past the tobacco factory, down the short span of the Quai Duquesne and into the port with all guns blazing. Fourth, and most important of all, the tanks, if successful, would be "in easy striking distance of the most appropriate objectives for their employment"—delivering their massed fire-power to subdue the trawlers and any other German resistance in the outer port in the vicinity of the Hôtel Moderne.[21]

Air support was the other area of controversy. Originally, the planners had agreed to the frontal assault when they understood that the buildings overlooking the main beach would be pulverized by an attack from the heavy bombers of the RAF's Bomber Command two and a half hours before the raid began. Although Churchill and the Cabinet had agreed to lift the restriction on the blind bombing of French towns—a rule that had nearly led to disaster at St-Nazaire—Leigh-Mallory now proposed that they should cancel the heavy bombardment and replace it with concentric bombing and strafing attacks by his fighters immediately before the commencement of the raid. He argued that the time lag between the heavy bombing attack and the landings was just too long and would allow the German defenders, by then fully alert, to mount a spirited defence. Ham Roberts agreed.

Leigh-Mallory further argued that the lack of precision in heavy bombing raids—with 150 planes dropping their bombs from seven thousand feet at night—would likely result in the bombs being scattered about rather than hitting their intended targets: the headlands and the beachfront hotels. All told, he feared the result would be uncontrollable fires and rubble-choked streets. Ham Roberts in turn foresaw the debris creating anti-tank obstacles that the engineers would not be able to handle in time. So instead, Leigh-Mallory proposed a series of timed attacks on the headlands and the beachfront by attack aircraft and cannon-firing Hurricane fighters from his command, just as the first assault boats approached the beaches.[22] The surprise and shock would then be reserved to the last possible moment, and the synchronized attack would overwhelm any defender with its intense ferocity.

If the raid itself was to achieve surprise, the force commanders would have to move the largest armada so far assembled by the Allies across the English Channel in the middle of the night without the Germans catching on—or at least without them figuring out its final destination until it was too late. To confuse the German radar, Leigh-Mallory arranged to bomb the nearby airfields at Abbeville–Drucat and Crécy and to strike both sides of the city of Boulogne.* At the same time, Baillie-Grohman would put on a naval operation designed to simulate an impending raid on the giant port at Boulogne, even as the raiding forces were creeping unannounced towards Dieppe, farther down the coast.[23]

In the days following the June 5 meeting, the planning staff and the force commanders rushed to complete a highly detailed two-hundred-page plan for Operation Rutter (which would later become the bible for Operation Jubilee). The mission was set for later that month. The plan demonstrated how everything should come together if all went according to plan. In many ways, Rutter was the amphibious version of

---

* By June 29, Leigh-Mallory was worrying that his pilots, locked into the intricate Combined Operations plan for Dieppe, lacked the operational freedom they needed. He wrote to Air Vice-Marshal Sir William Sholto Douglas, his superior, that his No. 11 Group could expect to lose "60 to 70 pilots, and 120 aircraft." The next day Douglas shot back: "Thank you for your letter of 29th June, about the casualties you anticipate you may suffer during Operation 'Rutter.' I do not know however quite what you expect me to do about it. I certainly do not propose to call the operation off. If I may say so, I think that you are worrying too much about these possible casualties. Unfortunately, one cannot often win a battle without considerable casualties, however much one would like to do so." Leigh-Mallory proved to be remarkably prescient: in the final tally for Dieppe, 70 pilots were killed or missing, and 106 aircraft were shot down. (Sholto Douglas to Leigh-Mallory, 30 June 1942, TNA AIR 16/760; Trafford Leigh-Mallory, "Air Operations at Dieppe: An After-Action Report," *Canadian Military History* 12, no. 4 (2003) : app. C.)

a First World War–style "trench raid": the English coast formed one line, the German-occupied coast the other, with the Channel as the "no man's land." Stealth, surprise, speed and split-second synchronization were critical to success.

In theory, everything was contained within the pages of this highly complex document, from the composition of the raiding forces and their objectives to the sequence of events laid out in a timed play-by-play account—with numerous graphs, tables, matrices and maps to show the dispositions of troops from the approach across the Channel to the landings and re-embarkation. Tacked on at the end, more than a dozen appendices covered in great detail the tasks of the infantry and airborne battalions, the tanks, the engineers, the naval and air bombardments, and the demolitions programmes as well as the re-embarkation schedules for the ride back home to friendly shores.

In the initial plan, Rutter was to begin on the night of June 20–21— or on any of the six nights following should bad weather or any other event prevent its launch. Late in the afternoon on June 20, close to five thousand Canadian infantrymen, including six battalions of Ham Roberts's Second Canadian Division, accompanied by sixty tanks from the Calgary Tank Regiment and teams of Canadian combat engineers, would board more than 250 ships and boats for the journey to Dieppe. It was to be one of the largest task forces yet seen in the Second World War, and it would comprise a vast assortment of vessels, including destroyers, troop transports, torpedo boats, converted Channel steamers, rescue craft, tugs, anti-aircraft vessels (Eagle ships), anti-submarine trawlers, minesweepers, gunboats, and a collection of new tank-landing craft each hauling three Churchill tanks. Two specially refitted Hunt-class destroyer escorts—HMS *Calpe* and HMS *Fernie*— would serve as headquarters ships for the operation.

On board the *Calpe*, Ham Roberts, Tom Baillie-Grohman and Air Commodore Adrian Cole, the air liaison officer (who came from the Royal Australian Air Force), would work from the bridge and from the wardroom to ensure the safe arrival, landing and then re-embarkation of the raiding force. Meanwhile, Trafford Leigh-Mallory would monitor the air battle from his headquarters in Uxbridge, a specially constructed bunker on the Hillingdon estate west of London, with Dickie Mountbatten and Harry Crerar as his special guests for the show. On the coast, in Portsmouth, deep inside his Fort Southwick command bunker, Admiral Sir William James would give the order to go, or if necessary to scrub the mission, and once it was under way he would monitor naval operations and relay current intelligence to the raiding forces.

In any high-risk operation, redundancy and contingency planning are key, so Mountbatten arranged for an alternative set of "backup" commanders under the control of Brigadier Churchill Mann, Ham Roberts's chief of staff, to be on board and work from *Fernie* in case *Calpe* succumbed to enemy fire or any other unforeseen event. Mountbatten, with full technocratic zeal, equipped both command ships, bristling with antennae, with nearly four times the normal allotment of transmitters and receivers, thereby linking the force commanders with the aircraft above, the vessels at sea and the troops ashore.

Once at the mid-Channel rendezvous point, the ships would form up into at least a dozen smaller assault groups. Together, they would follow British minesweepers on a predetermined course through a German minefield and head towards the four landing beaches in and around Dieppe—code-named Blue, Green, White and Red.

In the skies above, the air plan called for the largest and most sophisticated display of aerial warfare seen on the western front since the desperate days of the Battle of Britain two years earlier, when a vastly outnumbered RAF fought Hitler's Luftwaffe to a standstill. More than eight hundred aircraft, mostly fighters drawn from seventy-four squadrons, would maintain revolving air patrols over the landing zones throughout the morning. Most of them would come from British squadrons, with a smattering of Canadian, American, Czech, Polish, Belgian and Free French as well. Their job on the day was complex: to provide

close air support for the troops on the ground, to locate German reinforcements and prevent them from reaching the port area by land or
sea, to lay smokescreens to obscure the view of the German defenders,
and to compose an impenetrable "air umbrella" above Dieppe to fend
off Luftwaffe aircraft attempting to strike the vulnerable ships below.

According to the air plan, just after midnight on the day of the raid,
ground crews that had been working all day and evening would rush to
top up fuel tanks, conduct weapons checks and load cannon shells for
the Hurricane, Typhoon and Spitfire fighters or to rack sticks of 250-
and 500-pound high-explosive bombs and smoke shells onto Blenheim
and Boston bombers. Soon after, the firing of engines would shake the
dew from cowlings as pilots adjusted flaps, goggles and throat micro-
phones, making a quick check of the maps taped to their upper thighs
while throttling up for takeoff. Once aloft, the planes would form up
for about thirty minutes before setting course for their targets along
the French coast and above Dieppe, less than half an hour away.
Meanwhile, a battalion of the British 1st Airborne Brigade, including
some veterans of the Bruneval raid, would squeeze into Wellington
bombers or pack tightly into towed gliders for their journey to the
landing zones on either side of Dieppe, carefully skirting the raiding
force below to maintain surprise.

At exactly 0415 hours, all the various preparations would come
together. As long as weather conditions co-operated, the paratroopers
and glider-borne infantry would float to earth onto predetermined
landing zones and launch their assaults on both the Hess and Goebbels
coastal batteries at the same moment that two Canadian infantry battalions exploded onto the beaches of Puys and Pourville—Blue Beach
and Green Beach.

The battalion landing on Green Beach would come from the South
Saskatchewan Regiment, under the command of Lieutenant Colonel
Cecil Merritt—who would go on to earn the Victoria Cross for his
heroic actions on August 19. His "prairie men," drawn mostly from

the Estevan, Weyburn, Regina and Moose Jaw areas, would land near the eight-foot-wide river Scie that snaked through Pourville into the English Channel. Here, Merritt's force would move fast to create a semicircular bridgehead stretching from the hills on both sides of the river valley to the western headland at Dieppe, and as deep inland as "la ferme des Quatre Vents" (Four Winds Farm)—a German stronghold. According to the plan, part of the battalion would move up the slope leading from the beach and take the western headland, knocking out German bunkers and a lone radar station en route, while the remaining men held the bridgehead.[24] Once there, they would ferret out defenders on the clifftop positions and neutralize any fire from the Norman castle perched atop the Dieppe skyline, while the others mopped up in Pourville and the hills west of the town, and captured the fortified farm.

One hour later—at the same time as the frontal assault was beginning on the main beach—the Queen's Own Cameron Highlanders of Canada, a Winnipeg regiment, would land and push through this bridgehead to a rendezvous point with one squadron of the Calgary Tanks, which would by then have climbed up from the main beach. In unison, the infantry and the tanks would move roughly three miles inland to capture St-Aubin airfield and provide a shield to fend off any German counterattacks trying to reach Dieppe proper. With this protection in place, the raiding forces in the harbour area would enjoy the maximum opportunity to wreak havoc in the port and other targeted areas before retiring into the harbour area themselves to re-embark.

On Blue Beach in the tiny seaside town of Puys, nearly five hundred men of the Royal Regiment of Canada would land in pre-dawn darkness under the command of Lieutenant Colonel Doug Catto, followed by a company of the Black Watch (Royal Highland Regiment) from Montreal. Their job was crucial to the success of the entire plan, for they had to overrun the entrenched German defenders, seize the clifftops above, and then move fast on foot over nearly a mile of

German-occupied territory to their objective—a German gun battery, code-named Bismarck, on Pollet Cliff, able to shell the harbour mole.

The raid was essentially a race against time. Once the first shot had been fired, the clock would start ticking for both the airborne and infantry units: they had only sixty minutes to reach their targets and achieve their objectives before the frontal assault over the main beach began. Should they fail outright or suffer delay, the troops and tanks bound for the main beach would face murderous fire as soon as the ramp doors dropped and the first boot hit the beach. With little or no cover, they would advance into a horseshoe-shaped cauldron of withering German fire.

For the main-beach landings, the Rutter planners divided the zone into two interconnecting sectors, code-named Red Beach and White Beach—with the tobacco factory at the intersection of the Quai Duquesne and the boulevard de Verdun as the dividing line. There, more than a thousand Canadian infantrymen from two battalions, the Royal Hamilton Light Infantry and the Essex Scottish, supported by teams of Canadian combat engineers and two squadrons from the Calgary Tanks (thirty-six tanks from B and C squadrons), would storm ashore, race up the beach, scale the seawall, cross the promenade, and penetrate the town and port before the bewildered Germans could recover from the shock and awe of the initial attacks.

For the exposed men of the infantry and engineers, once they had touched down on the rocky beach, there was little tangible cover until they reached the boulevard de Verdun and the shadow of its hotels and restaurants and the towering smokestacks of the tobacco factory. To cross this deadly three-hundred-yard expanse, they had to work in close concert with their tanks, moving in leapfrog fashion. First, the tanks would lay down covering fire from their main guns and hull machine guns while the engineers and infantry scrambled to cut gaps in the barbed wire at the seawall with wire cutters or blow through them with long snakelike sticks of TNT known as Bangalore torpedoes.

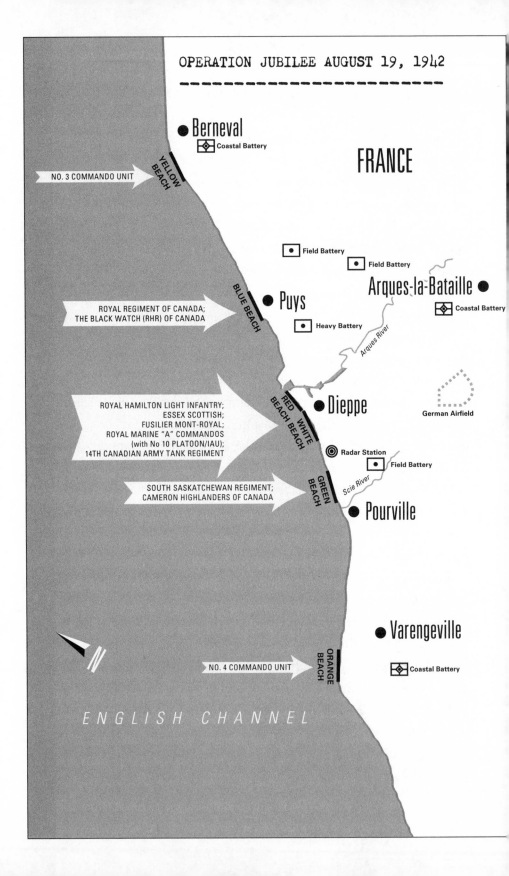

Depending on the course of the tide, the seawall could form a barrier standing anywhere from two to ten feet in height. But the engineers were prepared for whatever conditions they encountered: they would lay belts of chestnut palings across a low-rise tide or use timber crib ramps as needed to allow the tanks to get up and over the wall to the promenade beyond.

Once over this formidable obstacle, the tanks would creep forward with guns blazing in an attempt to kill or suppress any German defenders on the beach or in the buildings or pillboxes ahead. Following them in close order, the surviving infantry and engineers would dash through any remaining belts of wire protecting German slit trenches and machine-gun pits on the promenade, killing or capturing the defenders before they reached the buildings on the boulevard de Verdun.

In the White Beach sector, where the Royal Hamilton Light Infantry and B Squadron from the Calgary Tanks would land, there was one additional hurdle to overcome before they reached the old gates leading to their objectives in the town and the fields beyond: the once-crowded Dieppe casino (the centrepiece, some allege, for Fleming's *Casino Royale*). It was quite possible that the men would have to clear the structure in a bloodcurdling hand-to-hand fight. Once the casino was either cleared or bypassed, however, the four rifle companies would infiltrate the town and fan out, linking up with the South Saskatchewan Regiment on the west headland and at Quatre Vents farm, as well as the Essex Scottish coming in off Red Beach.

In the Red Beach sector, which ran from the tobacco factory to the quay lining the west side of the harbour mole, there was no such obstacle or cover for either the Essex Scottish or the engineers once they landed. Their job was to advance into the town and port accompanied by eighteen Churchill tanks from the Calgary Tank Regiment's C Squadron. Should everything come together, they would quickly breach the seawall, cross the promenade and make it to the boulevard de Verdun in relatively good order. Then the four Essex Scottish companies would penetrate the town on foot via a series of tiny streets and approach the outer harbour, while the engineers cleared a route for the tanks by destroying the concrete anti-tank obstacles near the tobacco factory or, if that route remained blocked, on the streets farther to the east.

With the assault wave ashore, the brigade headquarters of the 4th and the 6th Canadian Infantry Brigade—led respectively by Brigadier Sherwood Lett, a Rhodes Scholar lawyer from Vancouver, and Brigadier William Southam, president and CEO of Southam Press, working directly under Ham Roberts and monitoring the battle from wireless sets aboard their landing craft offshore—would move in and establish their headquarters near the tobacco factory. Their job was to control the general flow of the battle on land and to oversee the search and demolition plans as well. Given the intricate nature of the operation, Mountbatten issued explicit written orders for each brigade headquarters to bring a set of the detailed operational instructions ashore, into what he expected would be a relatively secure area by the time they landed.

If everything unfolded according to plan, the force commanders had two cards left to play once the bridgehead was secured. The first was the "floating reserve," containing a battalion of infantry from the Fusiliers Mont-Royal from Montreal under Lieutenant Colonel Dollard Ménard and roughly thirty Churchill tanks from the remaining squadron of the Calgary Tanks waiting offshore for their cue to join the fray. The FMR and the tanks would land over the main beach at Ham Roberts's discretion and create an inner defensive shield within the town, forming a buffer for the assault troops to fall back on during reembarkation at the end of the raid. If anything had gone awry in the previous phases of the plan, this floating reserve could be used anywhere in support, whether that meant reinforcing a breakthrough or bolstering a wavering part of the line.

The second card—and the one critical to the raid's "pinch" objective—was Red Ryder's Cutting Out Force, whose stated mission seems ripped from the pages of a C.S. Forester novel.

The role of the Cutting Out Force has been the most misunderstood aspect of the entire Dieppe operation, and it is also the most revealing. In some historical accounts, Ryder's force is just another part of the floating reserve—ignored by Dieppe chroniclers who have understandably, given what was known until recently, focused on the dramatic events of the raid itself rather than on what was supposed to have happened if all went according to plan. As things turned out, the commitment of Ryder's group to reinforce the Canadian infantry on the main beach has obscured the Cutting Out Force's real purpose, just as do the carefully crafted portions of Ryder's unpublished memoirs. But as his biographer would later point out, Ryder was a "model of self-censorship."[25]

According to what Ryder recorded for posterity, his job was "to train a special body of artificers, stokers and mechanics etc. as well as a marine detachment to act as a covering force" that would swoop into Dieppe harbour, once safely in Allied hands, and snatch German barges to tow them back to England as "prize" captures.[26] Although the mission "opened up exciting possibilities," he did not have faith in their ability to operate the "complicated bridges and locks" while "possibly under fire" and preferred to sink the barges instead. Given the spirit of the times, Ryder felt strongly that the job was "worth trying" and that "the Royal Navy should be ready to take on anything."[27] This explanation makes no sense at all: wasting the talents of one of the few Royal Navy commanders with significant operational experience—and a recently minted VC winner as well—in an attack on an enemy-held port for a mere "publicity stunt" was by any measure a gross misallocation of preciously scarce resources.[28]

But for the very few in the know, the Cutting Out Force led by Captain Red Ryder had, in fact, a very different duty to perform that day.

ELEVEN

DIEPPE BY DESIGN

Thanks to their geographical position, it is the British who were responsible for the capture of most of the German material which has been important for communications intelligence in the German War. They, in the Mediterranean and off the coasts of France and Norway, have been fighting close to shore . . . It is actions of this character . . . which produce the richest hauls. Knowing this, the British have spared no effort in developing techniques that will enable them to make the most of their chances for pinching.

—UNITED STATES NAVY, ULTRA SECRET REPORT ON
BRITISH PROCEDURES FOR CAPTURING
AND EXPLOITING ENEMY NAVAL DOCUMENTS, 1944

As planning for Operation Rutter unfolded, Ian Fleming was totally engaged in establishing the naval Intelligence Assault Unit he had proposed to his boss, Admiral John Godfrey—the new group specifically dedicated to pinching the critical naval intelligence materials that Bletchley Park urgently needed. It was a daunting task to create an unusual unit of this kind, and the major challenge at this stage was to get around the numerous administrative obstacles that blocked its way in Whitehall. Working in the best traditions of Blinker Hall, Fleming and Godfrey pushed hard to obtain official sanction for their Assault Unit, even as Combined Operations Headquarters feverishly embarked on the detailed planning for Rutter. Putting Fleming "on point" for the job, Godfrey gave high praise to his talents: "For such a novel enterprise," he said, "it is essential to have an officer with drive and imagination of the highest order." It needed "rapid transit," and Fleming was just the man to steer the new unit through government departments, dodging the red tape to ensure it got into action—fast.[1]

Fleming's initial idea had been to have his IAU make its debut in Operation Sledgehammer, set for that autumn, with the German naval headquarters in Cherbourg as its first target. There, Godfrey explained, "naval cyphers held by the authorities of the port concerned" would top the list of materials to be pinched by the new unit, whose job would then be to ensure "that it reached the reception committee at a specified rendezvous with the least possible delay."[2] By mid-May, however, with Operation Sledgehammer on the verge of cancellation and the four-rotor crisis gaining momentum day by day, Fleming suggested moving the Assault Unit's debut forward by four months so it could take part in the embryonic Operation Rutter.[3]

At the coastal town of Dieppe, the Hôtel Moderne and the trawlers in the port offered the perfect targets.[4] Right from the start, the planners knew that Dieppe had good pinch potential, and Fleming now latched on to it as the perfect opportunity for his naval commando unit to make its mark. With that in mind, Godfrey approached the Joint Intelligence Committee, hoping to gain official authorization to raise Fleming's small commando as the nucleus of a larger inter-service intelligence commando. Perhaps not surprisingly in the partisan world of Whitehall, where the three forces—army, navy and air force—jockeyed for position and power, the response was initially lukewarm at best: the RAF already had its own shadowy pinch units, and the army viewed incursions into what it considered its domain—fighting ashore—with suspicion and jealousy.[5] In addition, intelligence collection on land traditionally fell to the army's field security forces, in conjunction with other duties such as interrogating prisoners and the prevention of looting. These security forces were quite prickly about their domain, particularly after they had been assigned this task for Operation Rutter.

The prevailing attitude in Whitehall at this time eschewed "private armies." Fleming and Godfrey realized that official authorization for a unit like the one they proposed would take time and a good deal of bureaucratic manoeuvring, cajoling and arm-twisting to achieve. To speed up the process, they chose to adopt Blinker Hall's long-standing advice to act first and seek sanction later. In the past (as in the adventures of Dick de Costobadie and Allon Bacon in Vaagso), boarding parties drawn from ships' crews had provided ad hoc protection forces for the pinch personnel—a quick and easy solution, but not a viable alternative to a standing unit devoted to pinching. The new naval Intelligence Assault Unit, in contrast, would require cutting-edge training year-round. The obvious place for Fleming to turn was the newly created Royal Marine Commando, the amphibious fighting arm of the Royal Navy that Mountbatten had tried to protect.[6] This idea instantly met with the approval of Godfrey and, not surprisingly, Mountbatten. They agreed to start small, carving out one platoon, or thirty men, from the almost three hundred commanded by Lieutenant Colonel Joseph Picton-Phillips.

In late May, the Royal Marine commandos had moved to the Isle of Wight to begin training for their intended role in Operation Rutter as part of Red Ryder's Cutting Out Force. There, the IAU conducted a series of exercises in Portsmouth harbour "in conjunction with special Naval Parties"; their "main object" was to remove "important cargo vessels" and "carry out certain other special tasks"—a euphemistic reference to the role played by Fleming's fledgling Assault Unit.[7] Tucked away in the Royal Marine Commando War Diary is a copy of a training scheme performed in this harbour in the last week of June. Its significance has never been considered in the Dieppe story before, yet it indicates what Jock Hughes-Hallett had in mind for Ryder's Cutting Out Force in Rutter.[8]

This scenario called for the Royal Marine commandos to leave their billets near Cowes on the Isle of Wight and load onto HMS *Locust* (a flat-bottomed river gunboat designed for colonial policing on the Yangtze River) for a forty-five-minute journey to Portsmouth harbour.[9] Once at the harbour mouth, the "main task" in the training scheme involved the *Locust* rushing into the dockyard area to berth at a specified quay, followed by the Royal Marine commandos swooping down from her decks onto the quayside to surprise the startled dockyard workers and sailors. While the majority of the platoons would spread out to destroy swing bridges and lock gates and capture vessels in the port, one platoon, known as No. 10 Platoon, would take advantage of the confusion in the dockyard area to carry out its own "special task to be detailed later."[10]

It was this one platoon—No. 10—that became Fleming's Intelligence Assault Unit. And that "special task," according to the recently declassified Ultra Secret history of 30 Assault Unit, involved "a special section of No. 40 Royal Marine Commando, led by Lieutenant Huntington-Whiteley, R.M. . . . specially briefed on behalf of DNI [Godfrey, the Director of Naval Intelligence] to attempt the capture of a certain German headquarters in Dieppe."[11] The history does not shed any more light on why Fleming chose this particular unit or why he tapped the twenty-two-year-old Huntington-Whiteley to command the first naval IAU.

Throughout the hundreds of thousands of documents currently in the public domain and the scores of books and articles written about the Dieppe Raid, the name of Peter Huntington-Whiteley rarely appears. Any mention of the young man from Fareham, Hampshire, usually focuses on his later exploits leading the Royal Marine detachment of 30 Assault Unit in North Africa, Sicily and later Normandy and concludes, in a sad irony, with his death at the age of twenty-four outside Le Havre, just over a week after the Allied liberation of Dieppe in 1944.*

With little more to go on than the mention of his name as the leader of the IAU, I reached out to the Royal Navy's Historical Branch in Portsmouth for help. After searching through their files, to little avail, I laid out my research for the historians there—subjecting it to the ultimate litmus test. Within a few minutes the Royal Marine historian, a former lieutenant colonel who had served on active operations during the Cold War, said, "I think you may be on to something," and disappeared into another room. He reappeared minutes later with a sheet of paper on which he had written a name and phone number. "Here, you might want to give this man a call," he said with a big smile. "He's the last living member of Fleming's IAU who fought at Dieppe."

A few days later I was on a plane bound for Edinburgh to meet Paul McGrath, a former corporal with No. 10 Platoon who had gone on to fight with 30 Assault Unit for the remainder of the war. In a small seaside town outside the Scottish capital, McGrath's flat overlooked two of his many passions—the Firth of Forth and a wild golf course on which,

---

* According to Paul McGrath, who discovered Huntington-Whiteley's body in a gutter a day later, the young Royal Marine officer was killed as he accepted the surrender of German prisoners on the outskirts of Le Havre. Apparently, while the surrender was in progress, another German unit, annoyed at their brethren's attempts to capitulate, opened fire on the entire group, killing friend and foe alike, including Huntington-Whiteley. (Interview with Paul McGrath for *Dieppe Uncovered*.)

in his late eighties, he still played. On the mantel were pictures of his elegantly beautiful wife, now passed on.

Conducting historical interviews is extremely difficult. Even at the best of times, not to mention seven decades later, memory is notoriously unreliable and must be cross-referenced with textual documents or other evidence. Still, oral history gives something documents cannot provide: impressions of tone, feeling and atmosphere that can bring historical research to life. And that is exactly what my interview with McGrath offered. No sooner had I knocked on his door than the famous wry, dry wit of the Royal Marines came through. As I squeezed my six-foot-five, 250-pound frame through his doorway, the six-foot, wiry octogenarian looked up and said, "Oh my! You are a big one. Okay, I'll come quietly!"* When we sat down to talk, McGrath apologized that his memory was not what it used to be. With that, I simply asked him to describe what his role had been with the Royal Marines and the IAU. Without missing a beat, his jovial demeanour turned sombre, his intense ice-blue eyes clouded, and he said softly, "Well, old boy, I was

---

* McGrath's sense of humour was again on display during the seventieth anniversary of the raid, when Wayne Abbott and I, with the generous help of History Television and Veterans Affairs Canada, hosted the world premiere of *Dieppe Uncovered* in a local theatre in Dieppe, less than a hundred yards from the Hôtel Moderne. After the showing, the group, which included two young executives from History Television, went for dinner at Les Arcades across from what used to be the Moderne. Not having met either of these young men before, McGrath was in top form, drawing one of the star-struck executives close to him as he sat down at the dinner table. He broke the ice with a question: "You know what the trouble with humans is?" Suitably intrigued by the man who had not only worked behind enemy lines on Ultra intelligence missions but possessed a wealth of worldly experience, my colleague listened intently, expecting the very secret of life to be revealed. "There are too many of them," came the quick reply. "Now," he continued with sly smile, "what's on the menu?"

May 1942 Sandown I of W. No 10 Platoon 'X' Company RM 'A' Commando. Myself middle rank 2nd from R. Platoon CO Lt. Huntington-Whiteley.

A cheerful photograph of the men of No. 10 Platoon of X Company taken during training at Sandown, on the Isle of Wight, in May 1942, just before the Dieppe Raid. These thirty commandos were Fleming's highly trained Intelligence Assault Unit, made up mostly of teenagers aged eighteen and nineteen, and led by their twenty-two-year-old commander Lieutenant Herbert Oliver "Peter" Huntington-Whiteley. Their job was to pinch "material and documents of the highest operational priority, the importance of which is sufficient to justify the mounting of special operations and the incurring of heavy casualties . . ."—meaning they were deemed expendable in achieving that goal. Jock Farmer, middle rank, 7th from left; Ginger Northern, rear, 2nd from left; John Kruthoffer, seated, 5th from left; Peter Huntington-Whiteley, seated, middle, with cap on; Ernest Coleman, seated, 1st from left, next to kneeling man; Paul McGrath, middle row, standing with face slightly turned, 2nd from right.

Three months after Dieppe: the surviving No. 10 Platoon veterans from the Dieppe Raid who had formed the first cadre of Ian Fleming's Commandos. Here, in battledress during Operation Torch, the invasion of North Africa: (left to right) Marine Corporal Leslie "Lofty" Wyman, Marine Leslie "Brad" Bradshaw, Marine Ken "Jock" Finlayson, Sergeant John "Krut" Kruthoffer, Marine Corporal Paul "Mac" McGrath and Marine Jack "Spike" Watson.

Paul McGrath (front row, second from right) with part of his section of No. 10 Platoon, c. 1945, taken less than three years after Dieppe. A series of harrowing missions in North Africa, Sicily, Normandy, Belgium and Germany had taken its toll on Fleming's now-seasoned looking veterans, though they were still only in their early twenties.

nineteen—and I was there to kill Germans." He explained further that
he was "simply" a "minder" or "bodyguard" for those making the
pinch, with orders to breach the harbour on the deck of HMS *Locust* and
hit the Hôtel Moderne, leaving nothing and nobody standing in their
wake to tip off the Germans to what had been removed.

McGrath's cold-blooded and sober reply all those years later was
chilling. It reinforced the crucial imperative of the mission and the
characteristic ruthlessness already demonstrated in earlier schemes
inspired by Ian Fleming. Still sensitive to the Ultra Secret nature of his
mission, McGrath seemed to balk when I pressed for further details,
though it may have been his failing memory. I therefore turned the discussion to the mysterious Huntington-Whiteley.

McGrath described Peter Huntington-Whiteley as "softly spoken,
with a languid air, his spare frame reaching a little over six feet high."[12]
He was "well liked and popular with the men," who nicknamed him
"Red" for his fiery head of hair but never dared utter the word in his
presence.[13] He was a good officer, and the men trusted and respected
him. Like his teenage chàrges, he too was young—yet in command of
a platoon of highly trained killers. McGrath suggested that I speak to
Huntington-Whiteley's brother, Miles, who knew little of their exploits
but could fill me in on the family background.

Meeting with Miles in his London flat proved very useful for
me.* The authorities in England have yet to release the personnel

---

* When I sat down to interview Miles Huntington-Whiteley in his living room,
  I noticed the paintings and pictures on the walls and end tables which revealed
  the family's remarkable history, including a rare portrait above the fireplace of a
  very young Queen Victoria. After examining the photos from his side of the
  family, I inquired about the portrait. Miles simply shrugged and said,
  "My wife's relations." Soon after, his stunningly attractive wife appeared and

records of individuals who served in the Second World War, so Miles was able to provide me with information that was otherwise unavailable. He told me that Peter, as the family and close friends called his brother (whose given names were Herbert Oliver), was commissioned into the Royal Marines in 1938 after he failed to attain the required results on his naval entrance exam. Never truly interested in a military or naval career as such, Peter joined out of a sense of duty, as the eldest son in a family with a long tradition of naval, military and public service. Eventually he was attracted by the daring and unique nature of the Royal Marine Commando.[14] With his father and one of his younger brothers away at sea, his failure to pass the naval exam was a blessing because his posting kept him in England, where he maintained a watchful eye on his mother and youngest brother, Miles, who, nine years his junior, idolized the dashing and daring commando.[15]

Like Ian Fleming, Huntington-Whiteley was very much a product of his privileged background and family tradition of Eton and Trinity College, Cambridge, though he never attended the university. Known as a "fine athlete and musician," he mastered both the piano

---

introduced herself. Graciously responding to my question about the origins of the painting, she proudly explained that she was the great-great-granddaughter of Queen Victoria, the great-granddaughter of Kaiser Wilhelm of Germany, and the great-niece of both King George V of England and Czar Nicholas of Russia. Her full name, Viktoria Adelheid Clementine Luise Gräfin zu Castell-Rüdenhausen, evokes her aristocratic lineage, but disarmingly she quipped, "You can call me Vicky." At that point, I realized I was chatting with perhaps the only living person with a direct family connection to the three men who played a central role in bringing the world to war in 1914. She went on to explain that, as a small child during the Second World War in Germany, she used to bounce on Heinrich Himmler's knee when he paid a visit to her grandfather Charles Edward, who served in the Nazi Party. At the end of the war she moved to England, where she met and married Miles Huntington-Whiteley in 1960.

and the trumpet and excelled on the cricket pitch, playing at Lord's for Eton against Harrow and in other big matches. Ever the stickler for formality and social etiquette, he, like many others of his station in the class-conscious Britain of 1942, kept a healthy distance from his men, despite their intense training regimen and the intimate and potentially lethal conditions in which they worked together. Always formal, he addressed the men by their full names or rank and maintained strict standards. On one occasion he threatened to discipline a man for uttering an expletive in the heat of battle.[16]

The central reason for the creation of Fleming's IAU was the need to reduce the security risk associated with sending highly trained, fully indoctrinated intelligence experts who possessed intimate knowledge of the British cryptographic landscape into pinch operations. The danger was too great that if they were captured they might be broken under intense interrogation. But to do their jobs effectively, the commander of the unit and his senior non-commissioned officer would have to know what types of textual material and equipment or technologies the NID needed from the pinch. Even this partial indoctrination and familiarization with the target material produced a mammoth potential security risk, and Fleming naturally sought assurance that they had an individual to command the IAU who was both trustworthy and accountable. By the standards of the time, he found the ideal candidate in Huntington-Whiteley.

The incestuous nature of British intelligence and the closed world of Great Britain's social and political elite probably played a large part in the young officer's selection, as did the tight-knit world of personal connections inside the Royal Navy. Peter Huntington-Whiteley's paternal grandfather, Herbert James Huntington-Whiteley, had served alongside Fleming's father as a Conservative member of Parliament during the First World War. His father, Commander Maurice Huntington-Whiteley, a career Royal Navy officer, succeeded in obtaining a rare baronetcy—a hereditary rank just above that of knight that established the family's status as part of the aristocracy. He crossed paths on numerous occasions before and during the war with Jock Hughes-Hallett. The men held the rare position of torpedo officer on different aircraft carriers in the early 1930s, meaning they would have attended the same courses, conferences and training schemes. Later, during the war, both worked under the same roof at HMS *President*, the "stone frigate" or shore establishment on the banks of the Thames River near Tower Bridge, though in different departments— Huntington-Whiteley in the Admiralty's Trade Division, led by Blinker Hall's son, while Hughes-Hallett toiled in the Local Defence Division before going off to COHQ.

But the greatest endorsement for young Huntington-Whiteley came from his mother's side of the family, which defined the very notion of Establishment in imperial Britain. His maternal grandfather was Stanley Baldwin, the former head of the Conservative Party and three-time prime minister of Great Britain; and his grandmother, Anne Baldwin, was related to the famous painters Sir Edward Burne-Jones and Sir Edward Poynter, both of whom had headed the Royal Academy of Arts, and counted Rudyard Kipling as part of her clan—a legendary writer who expounded the glory of the Empire. Peter was as capable as any Royal Marine Commando platoon officer of taking on the responsibility of an Ultra Secret role, but being the former prime minister's grandson gave him that extra edge: his pedigree communicated a level of trust and accountability of the highest order.

As Huntington-Whiteley and his men prepared for Rutter, they "received a careful and detailed briefing from [the] Naval Intelligence Division in particular requirements which were of extreme urgency at the time," but their indoctrination was only partial, based on a "need to know" basis: the significance of the material they had to pinch or any information related to Bletchley Park remained above their pay grade.[17] They needed only to recognize what was required: the remains of a smashed Enigma machine, samples of its wheels and wooden case, along with specimens of its code books, including damaged publications printed with soluble ink.[18]

In early June, Mountbatten's headquarters sent out a call to the other intelligence agencies, aside from the NID, that might want to benefit from the Combined Operations train leaving for Dieppe in the coming weeks.[19] The Special Operations Executive, which was already helping to locate targets in Dieppe, attached its agents to the raid, as did the Ministry of Economic Warfare and the Secret Intelligence Service.[20] Their targets are listed in Appendix L of the Rutter plan, the "Search Plan," which details the work to be carried out by General Ham Roberts's 2nd Canadian Field Security Section. In conjunction with these intelligence agencies, the field security teams would follow the assault troops ashore to search the various hotels that housed barracks and headquarters, as well as other targets such as the town hall and the post office. The only caveat put on any target in Dieppe was attached to

---

OVERLEAF, LEFT: Described as "softly spoken, with a languid air . . . well liked and popular with the men," an Eton "old boy," a relative of Rudyard Kipling and the grandson of former British prime minister Stanley Baldwin, Captain Peter Huntington-Whiteley, or "Red" as his men called him, led Ian Fleming's Intelligence Assault Unit in the Dieppe Raid at the age of twenty-two. He did not survive the war; he was killed in action two years later on the outskirts of Le Havre, France, in September 1944, just days after taking part in the liberation of Dieppe with Paul McGrath and the rest of his No. 10 Platoon veterans.

RIGHT: Part of Appendix L of NID's search plan for Dieppe, which subsequently fell into German hands. On this page is a clear stipulation that required the Canadian Field Security Section to seek permission and guidance from Lieutenant Huntington-Whiteley before searching the Hôtel Moderne, located at 21 rue Vauquelin, marking the hotel and its contents as a target of prime importance to Naval Intelligence.

Att to:-
H.Q. 4 C.I.B.

R.V.
Tobacco Factory.

Material Required	Remarks
Military Papers	Military H.Q. Party will contact Lieut. Huntington-Whiteley, Royal Marines, and follow his instructions, before searching Hotel Moderne.
Military Papers	May be Offrs Billets.
Papers of interest	

DIEPPE 3
1 F.S.P.
1 F.S.P. } L.C.T. 8.
1 S.C.I.

Serial	Objectives in order of priority	Location	Route	Estimated Time of Starting Search	Material Required	Remarks
TASK I.						
1	Hotel Moderne	21 Rue Vauquelin at North corner of street nearest harbour.	Rue Vauquelin – Quai Duquesne – P.W. Cage. / Rue Duquesne – Rue Vauquelin. / Rue Duquesne – Quai Duquesne – No. 4 Bde H.Q. – P.W. Cage.	Zero plus 1 hr 30.	Military Papers	Military H.Q. Party will contact Lieut. Huntington-Whiteley, Royal Marines, and follow his instructions, before searching Hotel Moderne.
2	Hotel Arcades	229686 Quai Duquesne		Zero plus 2 hrs 30	Military Papers	May be Offrs Billets.
3	Custom House	230683 Quai Duquesne past Rue Dupont opposite Bassin Duquesne		Zero plus 3 hrs	Papers of interest	
TASK II. **DIEPPE 10.**						
4	Main Ry Sta (Gare Principale)	Quai Georges Clemenceau	P.W. Cage – Quai Duquesne / Ry Sta – Quai Georges Clemenceau – Ave. Pasteur.	Zero plus 3 hrs 30	Military Passes R.T.O. papers. Movement control instructions tables etc.	SEE SERIAL 4a. Search this after Serial 4.
DIEPPE 9.						
5	Hospital	Rue des Hospices		Zero plus 5 hrs	Military papers	Search only takes place if hospital is used by military. Ascertain from Odn sentry.
DIEPPE 10.						
4a	Hotel Terminus	Quai du Tonkin east of Main Ry Station		Zero plus 4 hr 30	Military papers	May be billets or offices.

APPENDIX "A" Page 8

the building that Godfrey and Fleming had set their sights on more than two months earlier: the Hôtel Moderne, located at the junction of the rue Vauquelin and the Quai Duquesne on the direct route running from the main beach to the port, and just a hundred yards from the shadow of the beachfront tobacco factory. This proviso forbade the field security teams from entering the building, with strict orders to "contact Lieut. Huntington-Whiteley, Royal Marines, and follow his instructions before searching Hotel Moderne."[21]

This key piece of evidence ties Fleming's IAU to the NID's most desired targets and confirms that a pinch component designed to solve the four-rotor crisis was indeed part of Operation Rutter. Once the raid at St-Nazaire and the aborted raid at Bayonne had failed to produce gold for the cryptographers at Bletchley Park, it became essential for the next sizable raid to contain a pinch element somewhere in its makeup. So the question is straightforward: was the plan for Dieppe a pinch by opportunity or a pinch by design?

As far back as the opening days of 1942, when Jock Hughes-Hallett pointed to the meeting on January 21 as the conception date for the raid—immediately after John Godfrey announced the change in pinch policy and just weeks after the most successful haul of captured material to date at Lofoten and Vaagso—the distinct odour of a pinch was evident. This need intensified when the Germans introduced the four-rotor naval Enigma to U-boats in the Atlantic Ocean on February 1, and it increased rapidly as the dire effects of the blackout hit home, with merchant shipping losses rising to dangerously high levels with each passing month. Soon this gloomy scenario was made even more threatening by news that some vessels in the Channel and in Norway had also been outfitted with the new machine. In May, word reached Bletchley Park that U-boat headquarters in the Mediterranean had adopted the four-rotor, leading Frank Birch to suggest the need for the same sort of pinch operations as the one currently in planning for Dieppe. In the interim, the creation of the Inter-Services Topographical Department report on Dieppe at the behest of Hughes-Hallett, along with Godfrey's sudden and personal urging of the Hôtel Moderne and the trawlers in the harbour as targets for Rutter just the day after the failure of Operation Myrmidon, all helped to sell Mountbatten on Dieppe as an "attractive and worthwhile" location for the next Combined Operations raid.

With the contextual case in hand, the key to determining the seventy-year-old question of intent behind the Dieppe Raid comes down to weighing the relative merits of opportunity and design. In this case, that involves the examination of three particular realms: the detailed military plan for Operation Rutter in June, which, with but a few refinements, was remounted as Operation Jubilee in August; the allocation of resources to carry out the plan; and the inherent redundancy or contingencies built into the plan to get into the trawlers and the Hôtel Moderne.

Originally, Operation Rutter was planned for June 20, or any of the six days following. However, a dress rehearsal for the raid, known as Yukon I, carried out at the behest of Rear Admiral Tom Baillie-Grohman while Lord Louis Mountbatten was touring the United States just ten days before, revealed crucial defects with the Royal Navy's performance—and forced a two-week postponement. "The first rehearsal from the naval point of view was a shocker," wrote Baillie-Grohman. "In a short run in of 6 to 8 miles from a known position, most landing craft failed to land a large number of troops where required, some indeed several miles from their proper beaches." With close synchronization, shock and surprise the crucial factors for success, the rear admiral realized that even a fifteen-minute delay "could mean a disaster." He persuaded Mountbatten to postpone the operation to rectify the problems. Rutter would now go in on July 4 at the earliest.

In the original concept for what Churchill called the "butcher and bolt" raid, Hughes-Hallett afforded a maximum of fifteen hours on shore to accomplish all the many objectives. Even that length of time seemed short, given the huge challenges facing the raiders: dropping airborne forces to silence the coastal gun batteries on the wings and landing two infantry battalions on each side of Dieppe to race and capture the headlands overlooking the harbour and the main beach—all in an hour flat. Following that came the daring frontal attack, with two more infantry battalions landing side by side on the main beach, backed by teams of Canadian combat engineers and two squadrons of Churchill tanks that would storm ashore to capture objectives in the port and beyond, then link up with yet another Canadian infantry battalion driving south from Green Beach to capture the airfield and division headquarters at Arques-la-Bataille, where finally they would form an outer shield to protect the bridgehead from the inevitable German counterattack.

Just after the landings on the main beach came Ryder's Cutting Out Force, which, with nearly half the new Royal Marine Commando aboard the *Locust*, would run the gauntlet into the outer harbour, by then in Canadian hands, and hit the various targets ashore. Twenty minutes later, the rest of the Royal Marines, riding on French *chasseurs* and a collection of tugs, drifters and anti-aircraft barges known as Eagle ships, would enter the harbour and tow out German barges as "prize" captures—in what Red Ryder later dismissed as a mere "publicity stunt," and Hughes-Hallett refused to elaborate on, calling it simply a failed attempt to take the enemy defences from behind. Needless to say, because both men penned their memoirs before the release of Ultra, these passages were deliberate attempts at obfuscation, primarily for security purposes. In truth, the role of the Cutting Out Force was as dramatic as any Hollywood representation or, perhaps more to the point, any James Bond novel.

The delay from the latter part of June to early July forced changes to Operation Rutter because environmental conditions no longer permitted amphibious landings over a two-tide period. Limited now to only one tide, where the landings would take place at the low-water mark and re-embarkation at high water, the raiding force had only six, rather than fifteen, hours to accomplish its objectives, meaning that raid imperatives had to be compressed to only the most urgent and fundamental of all. In this sense, the new time frame spawned a bastardized version of Rutter that few, if any, have heard of—one the planners called Rutter II. In essence, the new plan was a shortened version of the original, with the inland objectives either scrapped or downgraded from "definite" to "contingent." The "aerodrome and division headquarters will be visited and the local game destroyed, but there is only enough time for a cursory search and quick demolitions."[22] Major General Ham Roberts welcomed the change: he had feared that the original time frame gave the Germans ample opportunity to call in reinforcements and launch a coordinated counterattack designed to hit the raiders when they were most vulnerable—during re-embarkation. "The concentration of all effort over a shorter period ought to produce good chances of a success," he said.[23] That left the units landing on the flanks with only thirty minutes to accomplish their objectives before the frontal assault began.

Faced with a number of changes, the commanders convened a meeting of the forces involved with the pinch component of the plan—a meeting that has never entered the Dieppe debate until now, yet one that reveals there was much more to the pinch than simply hitching Fleming's IAU as a caboose to the Dieppe train. On June 28, representatives from the Royal Navy and the Royal Marines, as well as the Calgary Tanks, the Essex Scottish and the Royal Canadian Engineers, met at Roberts's headquarters. In short order the cast of characters involved with the pinch had grown to a significant portion of the entire raiding force and, perhaps more shockingly, it now directly involved the Canadians on par with the Royal Marines. For decades, the explosive record lay tucked away in a Rutter file in Library and Archives Canada marked "General"; it was likely read by other historians over the years but, lacking the contextual knowledge of what was at stake, they would have discarded it as ancillary or even unnecessary. Similarly, across the Atlantic in the British National Archives, another Dieppe file labelled "Miscellaneous" contained a rare set of operational orders for the Royal Marine Commando that detailed their part in both Rutter and later in Jubilee.

Now, for the first time in seven decades, the role of Ryder's Cutting Out Force and the Royal Marine Commando is crystal clear. Their mission, if it had succeeded, would have rivalled St-Nazaire as the stuff of legend.

For all these intervening years, veterans have wondered why the Dieppe Raid was planned the way it was. Why was so much emphasis placed on the elusive element of surprise that underpinned the entire operation? Why were tanks used in the raid, and, moreover, landed on the main beach as part of a highly controversial and seemingly suicidal frontal assault? Why was the heavy bomber raid on the town cancelled and replaced by carefully synchronized air attacks to hit just as the landing force arrived at the beach? And why was neither a battleship nor a cruiser positioned offshore to support the operation? The answers to all these questions can be found in understanding how Hughes-Hallett and his staff designed the pinch and how, with the help of the force commanders, they built up the detailed plans to accomplish this vital mission.

By stitching together the outline plan and the detailed plan along with the record of the June 28 coordinating meeting and the operational orders for the Royal Marine Commando, the plan for the Dieppe Raid unfolds in dramatic form. Broken down into two battle groups, the first, code-named "Tiger Force" after Lieutenant Colonel Joseph Picton-Phillips, contained one company of Royal Marines, including No. 10 Platoon under Lieutenant Peter Huntington-Whiteley, and a

ENGLISH CHANNEL

Puys (BLUE BEACH)

German Guns

WHITE BEACH

RED BEACH

Roadblocks

INNER CHANNEL

LE POLLET

Gare Maritime

Quai Henri IV

Tobacco Factory

Trawlers

Les Arcades Hotel

OUTER HARBOUR

Quai de la Cale

Rue Vauquelin

Quai du Carénage

Hôtel Moderne

Quai de L'Yser

Quai Duquesne

Quai Trudaine

DRY DOCK

INNER HARBOUR

Quai Mal Galliéni

BASSIN
DUQUESNE

Invasion Barges

Dieppe

N

BASSIN
DU
CANADA

05:20. INFANTRY AND TANKS LAND ON BEACHES AND DESTROY ROAD BLOCKS

APPROX. 06:00. HMS LOCUST ENTERS THE INNER CHANNEL (THE "GAUNTLET")

06:10—06:40. ROYAL MARINE COMMANDOS AND I.A.U. OBTAIN INTELLIGENCE BOOTY

06:30—07:00. IAU DEPART DIEPPE WITH INTELLIGENCE BOOTY

demolition team riding on the decks of HMS *Locust*. The second, code-named "Robert Force," under Picton-Phillips's second-in-command, Major Robert "Titch" Houghton, the career Royal Marine who at the age of thirty was considered "the old man" of the Commando, held the remainder of the men, parcelled out in a half-dozen French *chasseurs* grouped with a pack of tugboats, drifters and Eagle ships.

After embarkation from various points on the Isle of Wight, where the commandos had completed their advance training, they would rendezvous with the rest of the raiding force off Portsmouth before proceeding across the English Channel through one of two mine-swept lanes. The *Locust* would arrive off Dieppe in time to take part in the bombardment scheduled for 0515 hours in support of the frontal assault on the main beach. By that time, if everything went according to plan, the Airborne group would have taken out the coastal gun batteries, the South Saskatchewan Regiment would have grabbed the west headland, and the Royal Regiment of Canada would be perched atop Pollet Cliff, with the air and naval bombardment of the main beach about to commence.

As the frontal assault went in, the *Locust* would remain on station just off the entrance to the harbour mole. From there, she would lob shells from her four-inch guns at German positions on Red Beach in support of the Essex Scottish, directed by a forward observation officer who had gone ashore with the battalion. Alternatively, if the Royal Regiment landing at Blue Beach failed to reach its objectives on the heights, the *Locust* would direct the shells towards the German guns on the east headland.

With the raid now a half hour old, the stakes on the main beach would be high, something Hughes-Hallett and Roberts clearly recognized: "It is vital to the success of the operation as a whole," the plan noted, "that White and Red Beaches be in our hands with minimal delay."[24] On the Red Beach sector, given the role that the Essex Scottish, the tanks and the engineers would play in combination with Ryder's Cutting Out Force to effect the pinch, this timing was even more pertinent. Accompanied by C Squadron from the Calgary Tanks, four companies of the Essex Scottish under the command of Lieutenant Colonel Fred Jasperson, a forty-two-year-old lawyer from Windsor, Ontario, were to move forward with the engineers over the beach and the promenade to the boulevard de Verdun before the Germans could gather their senses following the shock of the aerial and naval bombardment.

Once they reached the boulevard de Verdun, the four infantry companies of Jasperson's battalion would fan out and infiltrate the town through the tiny streets, with one company capturing the west bank of the inner channel, overlooking the German positions at the base of Pollet Cliff on the opposite side, while the other three made directly for the outer harbour. As this scene unfolded, combat engineers would go to work on the roadblock near the tobacco factory at the junction of the rue Duquesne, the shortest and most direct route into the outer harbour from the main beach. If the task proved impossible in the time allowed, the engineers had orders to clear the roadblocks from any street running east, to allow the tanks to proceed into the harbour to link up with the Essex Scottish. If the Quai Duquesne route proved feasible, however, the tanks would burst into the outer harbour right onto Quai Henri IV, less than two hundred yards from the trawlers on the left near the Gare Maritime, and less than fifty yards from the Hôtel Moderne to the right—both within easy range of their two-pounder cannon and Besa machine guns.

Once inside the harbour, the tanks and the Essex Scottish had orders to effect the first phase of the pinch operation—to "destroy resistance, capture the trawlers and prevent destruction of their signals books and documents."[25] Nearly a dozen Churchill tanks would provide mobile firepower to bring the trawler crews under a torrent of intense fire and knock out their four-inch guns, which could pose a formidable threat if not neutralized. The same would apply to any German defences in the vicinity of the Hôtel Moderne. As soon as the crews were subdued, one company of the Essex Scottish would storm on board the trawlers to kill or capture the survivors. They had instructions to tie the hands of all prisoners, to prevent them from destroying the code books and other documents. As one company secured the trawlers, the remaining two would knock out any resistance in the area around the Gare Maritime and the Hôtel Moderne; their specific orders were to "capture military and naval headquarters" and to "search for a naval codebook."[26] These orders connect directly to the caveat the planners had earlier placed on that building: no one was to search the premises before he contacted Fleming's IAU and followed Huntington-Whiteley's instructions.

Within the environment of Combined Operations, where boldness and derring-do were prized above strict military convention, the controversial frontal assault now makes perfect sense, despite its immense challenges. First, no other route to the target was as quick or direct—a crucial element in a plan where the raiders had to close with and kill the enemy fast in order to take advantage of the ongoing chaos. Roberts and Hughes-Hallett hoped that their combined force of infantry and tanks, suddenly bursting into the port, would suffice to panic and subdue the German trawler crews—just as the cruisers and destroyers had done in earlier pinch operations against trawlers in the North Atlantic and Norway. Similarly, the planners' decision not to start the raid with heavy bombing now makes sense. Rubble in the streets would prevent the tanks from reaching the harbour and leave the infantry at the mercy of the trawler guns, just as an errant bomb might sink the ships or uncontrolled fires might destroy the Hôtel Moderne—the two main targets for the mission.

Once the area was secured and the German trawler crews or the headquarters defence units were killed or captured, the Essex Scottish were ordered to "leave the vessels and remain in observation in a position protected from fire of HMS Locust[,] which will engage the vessels unless it is clear that they are in [Canadian] hands."[27] Leaving little to chance, Hughes-Hallett then called for two more contingencies, or redundancies, to ensure that the pinch came off.

Regardless of whether the attack on the trawlers succeeded, stalled or failed outright, Commander Red Ryder and the Cutting Out Force would launch their strike thirty minutes after the main assault, after receiving a special signal from the forward observation officer via radio using the code word "trawlers" or from flares fired from any of Jasperson's companies in the outer harbour.[28] A series of green flares rising up in the sky would signify that the trawlers had been captured and German resistance overcome. Red flares would mean that the attack on the trawlers had failed and that the German defences in the harbour were still active.[29] These signals were not to denote "stop" or "go"; rather, they would inform Ryder of what to expect when he and his force entered the harbour—whether he would get a hot or a cold reception from the Germans.

Whatever the colour of the flares, Ryder was to press on with his part of the plan. First, Tiger Force on the *Locust*, and then twenty minutes later Robert Force on the *chasseurs*, would move through what they hoped would be a pacified corridor in the inner channel, with the Royal Regiment of Canada on top of the eastern headland and one company of the Essex Scottish in over-watch positions in the town. Only if heavy artillery fire persisted could Ryder hold off—temporarily. But once through the mole and past the outer defences on the jetties and at the base of the northern face of Pollet Cliff, they would be on their own. Orders called for Tiger Force and the *Locust* to be fully prepared to run the gauntlet of the inner channel, ready to take on any German positions that remained active—rather as Red Ryder had done when he won his VC at St-Nazaire. With orders to swim to their target on shore should their ship be sunk, this mission was certainly no "publicity stunt."

Hoping for the best but planning for the worst, the Royal Marines had trained in Portsmouth harbour for just this scenario. Manning all of the Locust's guns—her four-inch guns fore and aft, her anti-aircraft "pom-pom" gun, her 3.7-inch howitzer amidships, and four specially mounted three-inch mortars welded to her upper deck—the Royal Marines were to lie prone on the deck, Bren guns at the ready, to "assist in subduing enemy fire from flanks and in beating off air attacks."[30]

Once inside the port, the plan called for the Locust to make straight for the island, berthing Tiger Force on the Quai du Carénage, with A Company leaping off first to take on any German units in the immediate area then moving on to seize the swing bridges and the lock gates. Following immediately on their heels, Huntington-Whiteley and the rest of No. 10 Platoon—Fleming's Intelligence Assault Unit—equipped with their own radio set and the code name "Whiteley," would go directly to their first stop, the Hôtel Moderne.[31] Along with the standard complement of Thompson submachine guns, Lee-Enfield rifles, Bren guns and grenades, all the men in the platoon carried extra ammunition in bandoliers slung over their shoulders as well as spare Bren gun magazines and the Hawkins anti-tank grenades they called "sticky bombs." In addition, they each carried a large haversack filled with explosives, smaller waterproof bags to store captured material, and a small fire extinguisher, in case the Germans attempted to destroy the desired material by fire or an errant shell ignited their target.

Depending on the situation when the men arrived at the Hôtel Moderne, they would enter a building either controlled by the Essex Scottish, if all went well, or, if not, still in German hands. In the latter case, they would attempt to breach and clear the Hôtel in the quickest possible manner—meaning that they would start at the bottom of the three-storey structure and move methodically through every room, killing or incapacitating all the occupants before they had time to destroy the targeted material. It would be a nasty business, calling for speed and extreme ruthlessness in close-quarter fighting, with their Thompsons, brass knuckles, commando knives or bare hands finishing off the defenders. Then they would go on to the next room and the one after that, until the entire building was secured. Only then could the planned search begin.

Once inside, the IAU had orders to rifle through desks, filing cabinets, wastepaper baskets, fireplaces, and every nook and cranny of every room, searching for signs of the vital signals material and equipment they were after and stuffing everything useful they could find into their haversacks. If they came across the commandant's safe, where they would likely find code books for future issue and other potentially vital documents, they would try to open it immediately. If they failed, they would call for the "safe cracker" attached to the IAU to blow open the door and reveal its contents. Once the Hôtel Moderne yielded its expected treasures, they would move on to the trawlers seized by the Essex Scottish and the tanks in the original assault. There they would collect what the Essex men had already pinched or, as Allon Bacon had done at Vaagso, conduct a detailed search of the vessels on their own.

If for some reason the Essex and tank attack did not achieve its objectives, Jock Hughes-Hallett had put a third contingency in place. Huntington-Whiteley and his men would proceed to the trawlers, aided by the guns on the *Locust* and later the French *chasseurs* carrying Robert Force. Regardless of the situation, Titch Houghton's men would follow down the narrow channel and into the port, exchanging fire if necessary with German guns in the caves at the bottom of Pollet Cliff, and land at the Quai Henri IV. Ideally, they would support both Tiger Force and the IAU, corralling captured vessels to be towed back to England. However, as yet another layer to ensure the pinch, Houghton received orders that "if Tiger Force has failed to land, or if it is obvious to Commander Robert Force that Tiger is NOT moving on its objectives[,] Robert Force will seize the objectives itself, informing Tiger of its progress."[32] To reinforce the bold and near-suicidal nature of the mission, the orders warned, "Should any vessel be sunk before berthing, all personnel will land at the nearest steps and fight their way to Tiger HQs" located on the island, to regroup and press on to their objectives.[33]

The orders for the Royal Marine Commando also reveal why seizing both sides of the inner channel was crucial to the entire plan. Not only did it create a corridor to get into the harbour, but it also provided the pipeline to get the captured material out. The exit strategy had a distinct James Bond flavour to it all.

In 2007, tucked away in an old, decrepit shed in the little town of Eye, in Suffolk, England, the son-in-law of Royal Marine Commando corporal Ernest "Lofty" Coleman made a fascinating and unexpected discovery: the partially destroyed remains of Lofty's wartime experiences, which he penned in 1995 but never published. Coleman died just before I began my inquiry into Dieppe, but his son-in-law and I made contact when he reached out online to find anyone who might shed light on this remarkable memoir. His family subsequently sent it to me and have allowed me to quote it here, since the vivid quality of this unique first-person account provides revealing and compelling evidence, particularly when cross-referenced with the official documents. According to Coleman, who as an eighteen-year-old served under Huntington-Whiteley first at Chatham and later as part of No. 3 Section of No. 10 Platoon:

> As section leader, I had to have intensive training in the use of explosives and [the] art of demolition, [as] at this point I had no idea what I [had] got myself into. Further training took place at Portsmouth dockyard[;] it was at this time we were told that Portsmouth dockyard was very similar to Dieppe . . . At the briefing which took place prior to the raid I was given a most unusual job which I [was] rather looking forward to[:] the platoon were to make a landing at the Dieppe dockyard and give covering fire

so that two other commandos could assist me in locating a building which was to be entered[;] within this building was a safe
holding some important documents. For this operation[,] instead
of the usual equipment, I was to wear a hiker's type of haversack
to take the explosives in and take the documents out. When I had
the documents in my possession, I was to make my way to the
dockside[,] where a boat would be waiting for me to take [me]
back home. My two colleagues, one a team leader, the other a
crack safe breaker, had to make their way back to the platoon[,]
where they were expected to collect as many invasion barges
together as possible and bring them back to England[;] the rest
were destroyed.

Although writing more than fifty years after the event, Coleman's
recollection is extraordinarily accurate. In the plans and operational
orders for the raid on Dieppe, special instructions warned all commanders taking part of yet one more proviso regarding the IAU: "A
unit of the R.M. Commando may be expected to bring a special report
from Rutter Harbour to the HQ Ship. Any R.M. Officer or NCO giving
the codeword Bullion is to be given priority passage in any R Boat from
Rutter harbour."[34] Although there is no indication of this code word in
either set of the Royal Marine orders—and it may even have been
replaced with another word at the last moment—there are special
provisions in the orders for Huntington-Whiteley and his platoon to
report directly to Houghton on Quai Henri IV after seizing the material. In this case, a special motor launch, specifically laid on for this
purpose, would arrive in the outer harbour to whisk the designated
members of the IAU and their precious haul out of Dieppe. Meanwhile,
the rest of the raid would continue, with the tanks and the Essex
Scottish moving south and east of the port to cover demolition teams
from both the Royal Marine Commando and the Royal Canadian
Engineers, who would systematically destroy targets in the port,

including the Hôtel Moderne, in order to cover their tracks before they re-embarked on the *Locust*.

This crucial new evidence throws a completely different light on the military plan for the Dieppe Raid: the proportion of the forces allocated to the pinch mission establishes it as a "raid imperative," firmly sealing it as a pinch by design rather than a pinch by opportunity. Nearly *half* the entire raiding force was involved with the pinch. Two battalions out of the five landing in the initial wave, one tank squadron, a series of engineer combat teams, Ryder's Cutting Out Force (with the three hundred men of Picton-Phillips's Royal Marine Commando), along with HMS *Locust* and nearly a dozen French *chasseurs*, tugs, drifters and Eagle ships all played a direct role in creating the conditions to ensure that the pinch succeeded. Even the selection of Ryder to lead the Cutting Out Force was a calculated decision: the planners were counting on his knowledge, his experience, and above all his leadership and guts to carry out this crucial mission.

No other aspect of the military portion of the Dieppe Raid required resources approaching this magnitude, nor did any other military forces need the level of co-operation and coordination necessary to achieve this objective. Even the design of the detailed plan features the core principles associated with the developing pinch doctrine: an emphasis on surprise, speed and shock in order to overwhelm bewildered defenders so that the desired material could be seized before it was destroyed. This time the operation would also include a pipeline— to get the Intelligence Assault Unit quickly to its target and out again— a luxury no other intelligence organization taking part in the raid enjoyed. These same hallmarks had been seen in previous pinch operations, though not on the same scale as in the plans for Rutter.

Finally, no other objective for the raid enjoyed the inherent redundancy of the various backup schemes the planners built in for the pinch. In this case, if the Essex Scottish and the Calgary Tanks failed to reach their target, then Tiger Force would prevail. If Tiger Force faltered, then Houghton's Robert Force would take over. And if Robert Force failed, Major General Ham Roberts still had another, a fourth, card to play: his "floating reserve" of the Fusiliers Mont-Royal and the remaining squadron of the Calgary Tanks was waiting offshore, ready if needed.

On June 1, at the inaugural meeting of the force commanders—almost a full week *before* detailed planning began for Operation Rutter with the finalization of the frontal assault and Mountbatten's invitation to the intelligence agencies to hitch their wagon to the raid—the role of the *Locust* and the Intelligence Assault Unit grabbed centre stage. Concerned about the "political aspect" of covering the potential loss of the *Locust* in Dieppe harbour, Mountbatten suggested that they publicly pass off her role in the operation as a block ship—one specifically sunk to render the port unusable.[35] The force commanders immediately pointed out that this explanation would backfire because both this Yangtze River gunboat and the German invasion barges had flat bottoms, making them unsuitable for this purpose. Undaunted, Mountbatten suggested to Admiral Tom Baillie-Grohman, Air Vice-Marshal Trafford Leigh-Mallory and Major General Ham Roberts that, once the *Locust* ran the gauntlet through the narrow channel to the port beyond and the "special party" disembarked, she would then return to the channel to lend fire support to forces in the bridgehead rather than remain at risk in the tight confines of the outer harbour.[36] Clearly, his request denotes not only that he had an intimate knowledge of the pinch but, even more important, that the plan for delivery of the IAU came in advance of the detailed plan. Even at this early stage, the pinch was the central driver for the entire operation.

With the military and naval plans built around the pinch, Ham Roberts, his brigadiers, and certain battalion and company commanders had to be put in "the know" to varying degrees about this key objective for Operation Rutter. Roberts himself appears to have been told what this operation might mean for the overall war effort. On June 27 he held a conference with his brigade commanders and their staffs at his headquarters on the Isle of Wight to go over the essential elements of the "party," as he called it. First on his agenda was the primary importance of security and surprise, and he reiterated the standing orders that no discussion of the operation would be tolerated in the mess or in any unsecured location. Failure to comply with this order would, he emphasized, be met with severe disciplinary action. "If information gets out," he warned his battle-starved subordinates, the "party will be cancelled."[37] Second, he reinforced the point that speed was "very essential" for success and that "all defences" had to be "run over as soon as possible." Indeed, indecision or hesitation would not be tolerated, he stressed, and the "speedier the assault the fewer casualties"—though he quickly assured his men that casualties would be "very few."[38] The mounting hubris within Combined Operations had obviously trickled down and infected the Canadian commander, igniting his enthusiasm. Saving his best salvo for last, Roberts confided to his brigadiers—the men who would coordinate the detailed military operations onshore—"Certain things which we are after may mean an important factor to the outcome of the war."[39]

TWELVE

ALL ESSENTIAL FEATURES

. . . within this building was a safe holding
some important documents . . . When I had [them],
I was to make my way to the dockside, where a
boat would be waiting to take me back home.

—ERNEST COLEMAN, UNPUBLISHED MEMOIR

HMS *Locust* was not designed for speed; she was likely the slowest vessel scheduled to take part in the Dieppe Raid. Part of the *Dragonfly* class of river gunboats designed to project and protect British imperial might half a world away in China, she had been reassigned to duties in Europe immediately after her launch in 1940. Most of her short but charmed life had been spent in operations in the Thames Estuary and occasionally in the English Channel. Known as a "happy ship" but also a lucky one, she survived a pounding from German aircraft during the Dunkirk evacuation, where Dick de Costobadie guided her "in and out of Hell" during the harrowing departure. Two years later, all those who climbed aboard her for the raid on Dieppe hoped her legendary good fortune would continue to flow.

The *Locust* weighed in at a modest 585 tons but measured more than three-quarters the length of a football field. With her flat-bottomed hull drawing a mere five feet, her trio of rudders enabled her to navigate deftly in shallow and swift-running waters but contributed to a pronounced roll when she encountered rough weather in the open sea. She topped out at only seventeen knots—but it wasn't speed that had caught the attention of Captain Jock Hughes-Hallett. Along with her ability to manoeuvre with ease in strong currents and tight bodies of water—a useful quality for navigating the confines of Dieppe's inner harbour—firepower was her strong suit. Equipped with two four-inch guns, one at the front on the bow deck and another at the back on the stern upper platform, a 3.7-inch howitzer positioned amidships, two three-pounder guns on each side, and a multi-barrelled forty-millimetre anti-aircraft cannon known as a "Chicago Piano" at the rear on the aft deck, the Locust packed a wallop.

To give extra firepower for the run into the harbour, the Marines retrofitted the ship, adding four of their three-inch mortars to the upper deck, strengthening an already potent shipboard arsenal. They knew that the Locust's guns would be its only key to success: the ship was so lightly armoured that it offered little tangible protection from German guns at point-blank range. It would be kill or be killed, just as it had been for the commandos at St-Nazaire, meaning that the Locust's gunners had to be quick off the mark and dead on target, laying down a steady stream of fire on German gun positions in the caves to kill, suppress or incapacitate them—anything to prevent or curtail their firing on the ship. Such action required extreme skill and daring: the fifty-one-man crew would have to pull together to support the gunners even as they kept the Locust steady and prevented it from running aground in the narrow channel, all the while dodging German fire from land and perhaps from the air as well.

With Dick de Costobadie now firmly ensconced in Lord Louis Mountbatten's headquarters, the fifty-four-year-old William John Stride took over as ship's captain. A mature veteran of the First World

War, he was capable and popular, having worked his way up from the lower decks to command. Red Ryder became a fan in the few short weeks they trained together, sensing that Stride's "robust" and "unflappable" character made him an "excellent person to have as a kind of 'flag captain.'"[1] In Operation Rutter, the *Locust* would be under the overall command of Ryder, as the Cutting Out Force commander with the final authority and responsibility, but Stride would control the moment-by-moment operations of the ship while in battle.

Anticipating the danger they would face once they breached the harbour mole at Dieppe, Stride took the precaution of boarding up the walls of the bridge with railway ties to provide an added measure of security—an act Ryder later admitted "probably saved our lives."[2] Below deck, the men, such as the nineteen-year-old seaman John Parsons, whose job it was to feed the Chicago Piano with ammunition hoisted on a conveyor, had little idea what they were about to face.[3] Ryder's appearance on the bridge alongside Stride, coupled with the Royal Marine Commando contingent on board with them, reinforced the idea among the crew that they were in for something big. Their initial excitement over having a legendary St-Nazaire hero with them soon gave way to the sober realization that his previous excursion into battle had included one of His Majesty's destroyers specifically rigged as a ticking time bomb. As Parsons wrote to me, "Lower deck rumour had it that he would want to blow us up in Dieppe harbour. Which did not appeal to us much!" The arrival of nearly two hundred "escape kits" for use by the commandos, plus a vast amount of explosives and other specialized stores, did nothing to alleviate their anxiety.[4]

After carrying out one final exercise in Portsmouth harbour, the Royal Marines were confined to the Upper Chine School on the Isle of Wight, while Ryder and No. 10 Platoon (Ian Fleming's Intelligence Assault Unit) sailed across the Solent to Eaglehurst House on the English coast, where they fine-tuned their mission in the same facility where Marconi had once experimented with his wireless communications. By

July 2, they were all back in the town of Shanklin Chine on the island for the final briefing before embarking for the raid.

The following day, 125 men from Major Titch Houghton's Robert Force climbed aboard eight French *chasseurs*—one of them captained by the young Philippe de Gaulle, the only son of the Free French leader, now in exile in England. The remaining 172 officers and men of the Royal Marine Commando Tiger Force boarded a thoroughly crowded *Locust*; with Lieutenant Colonel Joseph Picton-Phillips and his headquarters staff, the Marines of A Company, No. 3 Platoon, No. 10 Platoon under Lieutenant Peter Huntington-Whiteley, and No. 1 Demolition Party, there was little room for the men to "sling their hook" (or hammocks, in Royal Navy slang).[5]

Similar conditions existed on almost every ship and at every airfield now readying for departure. All across southeast England, soldiers, sailors and airmen prepared for the largest raid of the war—the biggest amphibious operation to date. The excitement in the air was palpable.

But it was not to be. Bad weather set in, forcing a postponement of the operation from July 3 to July 7. Then, after a German air raid on July 5 hit several of the raiding ships in port and lessened the chance of surprise, the continuing inclement weather led those in command to cancel the raid. The war diaries for both General Ham Roberts's Second Canadian Division and the Royal Marines noted the men's deep disappointment. This feeling was no doubt shared by the trio of United States Marines who had been sent to take part in the pinch operation— a story that has remained unknown until now.[6] Just how did these Americans come to be involved in the pinch?

As spring moved into summer that year, the pressure on Rear Admiral John Godfrey and his Naval Intelligence Division had begun to mount in many quarters. Whether he knew it explicitly or not, he should have sensed that the clock was now ticking on his tenure as Director of Naval Intelligence. His sometimes abrasive and obstinate attitude, quick temper and blatant attempts at empire building had led to friction and an increasingly frosty relationship with the other heads of intelligence who sat with him on the Joint Intelligence Committee. His overbearing character and patronizing demeanour could be tolerated as long as he continued to provide the goods, but as soon as the four-rotor crisis deepened, his welcome began to wear thin, particularly after the discovery that German naval intelligence had broken the British naval codes—something Section 10 of Godfrey's NID was tasked to protect.

For the previous two years, as Blinker Hall had once urged, Godfrey and his indispensable fixer Ian Fleming had been working tirelessly to cultivate close liaisons with the American embassy in London and the American intelligence services in Washington. Now, finally, the early returns on both fronts looked extremely promising. First, Godfrey had courted Admiral Alan G. Kirk, the enthusiastic anglophile who served as the American naval attaché in London and also enjoyed a direct line to Roosevelt and the White House. Later, when Kirk ran the Office of Naval Intelligence in Washington, Fleming tried to strengthen the bond through constant personal attention. Second, Godfrey and Fleming fostered their growing relationship with Colonel William "Wild Bill" or "Big Bill" Donovan, who would go on to head the oddly named new government agency, the Co-ordinator of Information— later the Office of Strategic Services (OSS) and forerunner of the Central Intelligence Agency (CIA). The increasing power of this institution had been a British imperative for some time. Along with William Stephenson—the Canadian millionaire known as "Little Bill" who looked after British intelligence interests in North America*—Godfrey,

---

* Although widely known as Intrepid after the war, Stephenson was never referred to by that name during the war. His official code name was the less than dramatic 48000.

SIS head Stewart Menzies and many Foreign Office officials all conspired to make Donovan "their man" in Washington.

Donovan, a Medal of Honor winner from the First World War who shared the same maverick personality and aggressive outlook on intelligence as these men, seemed the perfect candidate. He was much more malleable than the anglophobic J. Edgar Hoover, the head of the FBI who was later described as a "cross between a political gangster and a prima donna."[7] Donovan, an Irish Catholic Wall Street lawyer from Buffalo, was at times brilliant, always tough and extremely cocksure. Like Roosevelt, who learned of Blinker Hall's prowess during a visit to London in 1917 while working as the Under Secretary of the Navy, Donovan, too, became enamoured of the dark world of British intelligence.[8]

More than willing to establish close ties with the British during the period of neutrality at the beginning of the war, Roosevelt had twice sent Donovan to England for a series of meetings with Churchill, Menzies, Godfrey and Fleming—in part to gauge the British will to fight on, but also to learn their way of foreign intelligence, a realm in which the Americans had little experience. From that point on, this British team began an intense courtship of Donovan, giving him unprecedented access to many of their trade secrets, including Bletchley Park and Ultra. As Godfrey advised Admiral Sir Andrew Cunningham, the commander-in-chief of the Mediterranean Fleet: "It was Donovan who was responsible for getting us the destroyers, the bombsight and other urgent requirements . . . There is no doubt that we can achieve infinitely more through Donovan than any other individual."[9]

On his return to the United States, Donovan approached Roosevelt with a controversial idea for a civilian intelligence agency that would bring together research, intelligence, propaganda, subversion and commando operations under one roof—rather like a "fourth arm" of the military services—and which would coordinate all foreign intelligence activities for the United States.[10] British intelligence had firmly shaped and supported the plan, and, realizing the precarious nature of the request, Churchill now sent Godfrey, with Fleming in tow, to Washington in May 1941 to meet with Roosevelt and, even more important, persuade him to appoint Donovan as the head of the new agency, where he would act as the American "spymaster." Staying at Donovan's Georgetown flat, Godfrey plotted his strategy for the meeting while Fleming penned a loose set of organizational requirements that Donovan would need to get in place immediately.

The timing was perfect: Roosevelt was increasingly dissatisfied with the patchy quality of the current intelligence community in the United States. Within days of Godfrey's meeting with him, Roosevelt established the new office of the Co-ordinator of Information, or COI, with Donovan as its head, though the public announcement was delayed until July 11. The new organization looked impressive on paper, with its unlimited budget and presidential backing, but the British were disappointed that its mandate was not absolute. Ordered to "collect and analyze all information and data which may bear upon the national security" for the president and those he designated, the COI was given the authority to request data from other agencies and departments, but not allowed to interfere with the duties and responsibilities of the president's military and naval advisers.[11] And that made its position precarious, particularly when the usually competing elements of the navy, army, State Department and FBI came together in a loosely united front to oppose Donovan's sudden rise to "intelligence czar." Regardless, the British still rejoiced in their accomplishment. William Stephenson told Churchill: "I have been attempting to manoeuvre Donovan into the job of coordinating all United States intelligence . . . you can imagine how relieved I am after months of battle and jockeying in Washington that our man is in position."[12]

Mountbatten was also impressed, doubting "whether any one person contributed more to the ultimate victory of the Allies than Bill Donovan."[13] Like Godfrey, Mountbatten also understood the value a U.S. intelligence pipeline such as Donovan's might offer to his

Combined Operations Headquarters. In addition, Roosevelt's son James, a Marine Corps Reserve captain, was Donovan's aide-de-camp at the COI. Mountbatten and Godfrey interpreted that appointment as an opportunity to showcase the British brand of amphibious "commando" operations—the kind based on intelligence provided by the Inter-Services Topographical Department—and eventually to replicate that approach to pinch operations in the United States.

Even before the Japanese attack on Pearl Harbor, Donovan had led the charge for American "commando-styled" operations. Two weeks earlier, he had presented Roosevelt with a one-page memorandum recommending "that there be organized now, in the United States, a guerrilla corps, independent and separate from the Army and Navy, and imbued with the maximum spirit of the offensive. This force should, of course, be created along disciplined military lines, analogous to the British Commando principle."[14] The brief piqued Roosevelt's interest and garnered his support for action.[15] Encouraged, Donovan reached out to both the U.S. Marine Corps and the U.S. Army for help. The Marine Corps created the 1st Special Training Unit in February "for the express purpose of securing clearer insight into the operations, training and methods of the British commando organization," while the army followed, in mid-June 1942, with the creation of the U.S. Rangers.[16]

The road was not yet smooth, however, and obstacles soon appeared. Over the preceding months, Donovan had drawn the ire of the service intelligence departments, and in particular of General George C. Marshall, the army chief of staff, who, next to FDR, was the most powerful man in wartime America. Never a fan of the audacious or the irregular, the coolly impersonal Marshall once said: "You can sometimes win a great victory by a very dashing action . . . But often, or most frequently, the very dashing action exposes you to a very fatal result if it is not successful. And you hazard everything in that way."[17] J. Edgar Hoover also viewed the the COI with suspicion, in part because of Donovan's close association with the British and his willingness to work with their Soviet ally, and also because of the lack of professionalism he perceived in the cadres of COI agents, who he alleged came from the ranks of socialites, toughs and Hollywood stuntmen.

By early 1942, the COI, despite the open purse strings, had yet to make the impact Roosevelt had expected, and jealous rivals within the American intelligence community quickly accused it of organizational impotence. Before long these criticisms spilled over to Donovan himself, with allegations that he had ignored a direct presidential order by running agents in South America, a traditional FBI domain—not to mention a litany of rumours of adulterous indiscretions and other personal slights designed to damage his credibility.

Like Godfrey, as long as Wild Bill Donovan delivered the goods, he remained on solid ground, but by April 1942 Churchill had received alarming news through Major General Hastings Ismay, his liaison on the Chiefs of Staff Committee, that their much-celebrated man in Washington was in trouble, with his status under review at a high level.[18] They had spent years cultivating Donovan as a prime asset in their delicate relationship with American intelligence and a direct back channel to the president, Britain's most powerful ally. With so much invested, they had to support any feasible effort they could to legitimize and enhance Donovan's status and influence—and by extension their own.[19] The problem was clear: if they could not reinforce Donovan's organization, now rechristened the Office of Strategic Services (OSS), all the hard work that Godfrey, Fleming and to a lesser extent Mountbatten had invested in the relationship would be for naught.

From the beginning of March 1942, the U.S. Office of Naval Intelligence had started harrying the British to uphold their end of the intelligence-sharing agreement by giving them a captured naval Enigma machine. With the United States firmly focused on the U-boat menace off its shores and still unaware of the existence of the four-rotor, handing over a three-rotor machine would not solve the issue and would only reveal the Naval Section's current impotent position. Bletchley Park feared that such an admission would in turn encourage the Americans unilaterally to seek their own solution. There is no doubt that, in part, the British hoped Operation Myrmidon at Bayonne or Operation Chariot at St-Nazaire would result in a prize that would restore the flow of naval Ultra and satisfy the Americans. In the meantime, however, the British were forced to shift gears and admit they were in trouble. Still, they hoped to retain the lead in a co-operative arrangement with U.S. Naval Intelligence by introducing them to the pinch strategy in Mountbatten's brand of combined operations. They set out not only to teach the eager Americans about British pinch operations but to involve them in the potential solution to the crisis.

In this particular case, Mountbatten extended the invitation to a small and select group of U.S. Marines, who, as Donovan suggested, would train with the Royal Marine Commando and prepare to ride into battle with Tiger Force on HMS *Locust*. Given all the complexities over the sharing of intelligence between the two countries, what better way to deliver the pinched material than through a commando-style pinch operation involving the Americans? Simultaneously, the British could narrow the gulf between the two sides on the cryptographic issue, display the work of the new IAU and the pinch doctrine, and pump up the vulnerable Donovan. If they could solve these pressing concerns, they would score hefty political points for all concerned. From every angle, it seemed a devilishly clever plan.

So, on June 20, a special contingent of three U.S. Marines, led by Captain Roy T. Batterton Jr., a former assistant naval attaché, was plucked from the second week of their seven-week training programme with the commandos in Scotland and inserted into Tiger Force—to train specifically with the Royal Marines on *Locust*. Although there is no indication of their attachment to No. 10 Platoon, given what is now known from their operational orders about the mission of the Royal Marines, the Americans would have been involved in some capacity. In addition, plans were made for Marine Corps colonel Franklin A. Hart, who had been attached to Mountbatten's command since the fall of 1941 and was actively engaged in the planning of the raid, to join Commander Ian Fleming and a few other "guests" on board one of the headquarters ships offshore to monitor the *Locust's* role in Operation Rutter. A memo from Frank Birch at the Naval Section sheds some light on their role there, for on August 1 an American liaison officer revealed that they had been "organizing a special pinch team" of their own and "would welcome our experiences on this subject."[20]

In addition to the delicate situation with the Americans, the potential spread of the four-rotor Enigma machine and the deepening crisis at sea were preoccupations in the weeks leading up to Operation Rutter. In early June, the British learned that U-boat ciphers encrypted on the four-rotor naval Enigma had been introduced in the Mediterranean. Then, as the Operation Rutter forces sat in southern English ports waiting to launch the raid on Dieppe, another series of events shed dramatic light on the problem. It happened eight hundred miles to the north, not far from the Lofoten Islands, where the North Sea meets the Arctic Ocean.

One of the few ways Great Britain could provide material and political assistance to the Soviet Union in its intense struggle against Nazi Germany was by running a series of giant convoys through the North Sea and into the Arctic Ocean past Norway en route to the Soviet ports of Murmansk and Archangel. For over a year, these convoys had been viewed as essential in keeping the tenuous link with Stalin alive. On June 27, PQ-17, the largest and most expensive convoy to date, left Iceland for its voyage to Murmansk. Comprising thirty-three cargo ships and one tanker, the convoy was escorted by destroyers, with a group of British and American cruisers shadowing her miles behind. Before it could reach the Soviet ports, the convoy would have to run great risks, successfully avoiding attacks by German aircraft, U-boats and large surface vessels such as the battle cruisers *Admiral Scheer*, *Lützow* and *Admiral Hipper* and the super-battleship *Tirpitz*.

The strong suit for the Royal Navy up to this point had been Germany's use of the three-rotor Enigma for home waters and Norwegian message traffic, meaning that the British had an almost crystal-clear picture of any preparations to attack the convoys. In March, Bletchley Park had intercepted a series of messages that confirmed the Kriegsmarine's focus on destroying the convoys as a top priority, followed by the movement of additional aircraft, U-boats and heavy ships to Norway. They also had Dönitz's message to his U-boat captains: "The task for U-Boats is to prejudice delivery of supplies to Murmansk. Sink everything that comes within range of your torpedo tubes; head other U-Boats on to the convoys. Your own attack should have preference, but act according to the situation. The employment of our own naval surface forces or air forces is intended should the opportunity arise."[21]

The Royal Navy, and in particular Admiral Sir Dudley Pound, the First Sea Lord, the man who had final authority over the convoy, knew that the movements of large surface vessels such as the *Tirpitz* were restricted because of the oil shortage. Nevertheless, the Germans' intent to engage the convoy was clear—whenever the chance presented itself. Should it occur, Pound had but few options. If enemy aircraft and U-boats came on the scene, the best option for PQ-17 would be to keep the convoy together with its destroyer escort; if the *Tirpitz* or any of the other large surface raiders appeared, it would be best to scatter the ships in the convoy in the hope of avoiding utter destruction. Once apart, however, the convoy faced the risk of having each individual vessel sunk by roving aircraft and U-boats. Either way, there could be heavy losses. Without their own air support to cover the convoy, the British had no choice but to rely on Ultra and signals intelligence to give warning of German movements and positions.

On the night of July 4, when it seemed that the Tirpitz was at sea and on her way to intercept the convoy, Pound issued the highly controversial order for the convoy to scatter and for the merchant ships to try to reach the Soviet ports on their own. The result was a slaughter of catastrophic proportions; in Churchill's understated words, it was "one of the most melancholy of naval episodes in the whole of the war."[22] Only eleven of the thirty-four ships that left Iceland on June 27 managed to reach the Soviet Union by July 8, with the rest picked off one by one by aircraft and U-boats. More than 130,000 of the original 200,000 tons of valuable cargo was lost, along with the lives of 120 merchant sailors.

For seventy years, Pound's fateful decision appeared rash and defied explanation. Part of the criticism stemmed from the lack of crucial evidence linking the four-rotor crisis to the convoy's demise. Right from the start of the operation, Pound had made it clear that he would not risk his precious battleships in the confines of the Channel either to support the Dieppe operation or to engage in battle with the Tirpitz, except on terms most favourable to the British. In German strategy, the Tirpitz and the high seas fleet were not crucial for the nation's survival in the same way that the Royal Navy and its ships were for Great Britain. Germany had no overseas empire or trade lines to protect, and so it had turned east to Russia to solve its lack of resources.

So long as Pound had the ability to read almost every move by the Kriegsmarine in Norway and its adjacent waters, he maintained a fragile threshold of confidence—until Harry Hinsley, working overtime at the Naval Section on overnight shift, discovered an ominous and disturbing wireless traffic pattern. Early on the morning of July 4, twenty hours before Pound made his decision, news broke that the Tirpitz might be readying to go to sea. But then, suddenly, all traffic relating to her movements defied every attempt at decryption. Whether her target was the convoy or not remained a mystery, but given the circumstances and without the usual means for confirmation, Pound decided that it most likely was. Within a few hours, his worst fears were confirmed when Hinsley concluded that "special settings" called Neptune, using "specially cyphered traffic" between the German Admiralty and the commander-in-chief of the fleet on Tirpitz, had gone into effect using the four-rotor machine.[23] Stymied, all Bletchley Park could do was warn the Admiralty that, from this point onward, this traffic was "undecodable" and "confirms the conjecture that a special cypher is now in force."[24]

For Pound, the hard evidence stared him directly in the face, showing that the dearth of intelligence about the Tirpitz was not a temporary difficulty, to be remedied quickly by other means or by further cryptographic action by the boffins at Bletchley, but a permanent condition. Whether this information prompted him to make his decision to scatter the PQ-17 convoy or whether it simply reinforced in dramatic fashion his preconceived desire to do so remains open for debate. What it does show, however, is that, from an intelligence perspective, the four-rotor crisis was not abating, but rather escalating at an alarming rate.

There is nothing in the Dieppe story more controversial than the allegations brought against Lord Louis Mountbatten long after the war that suggest he circumvented the proper chain of command to remount Operation Rutter after its cancellation in early July 1942. Historian Brian Villa rightly points out in his seminal 1989 work *Unauthorized Action* that no trace of a signed operational order for the remount has ever come to light—and so it continues to be.[25] However, Villa and the other Dieppe historians who attempted to tackle this issue were stymied by the lack of access to key documents that remained classified when they were penning their works. With the recent releases that reveal the pinch imperative driving the raid, Mountbatten's seemingly spurious claim that he "received special instructions from the Chiefs of Staff that only certain individuals were to be informed of the intention to re-mount the operation" can no longer be easily dismissed.[26]

On July 8, after a series of postponements due to the inclement weather and much to everyone's disappointment, Admiral James, Commander-in-Chief, Portsmouth, issued the order to cancel Operation Rutter. Just over a week later, on July 16, a month shy of the Dieppe Raid's new incarnation as Operation Jubilee on August 19, Mountbatten and Major General Ham Roberts paid a visit to the headquarters of General Andrew McNaughton, the Canadian Army commander, to gain his support for the venture, something McNaughton mysteriously referred to at the time as "Operation J_____."[27] During the course of this discussion, Mountbatten revealed that only a select few knew of the remount.* Dickie Mountbatten had managed to use the cancellation to replace the less than enthusiastic Admiral Tom Baillie-Grohman as the naval force commander for the operation with none other than his own favourite, Jock Hughes-Hallett—who from the start was a driving force behind the Dieppe Raid. There is no mention of either John Godfrey or Ian Fleming in the report.[28]

However, a recently released, previously unpublished history of the NID, with the security classification Ultra Secret, shows that John Godfrey and, by extension, Ian Fleming were part of this tight group and certainly knew about these clandestine plans to remount.[29] In the opinion of the unnamed author of this history, the silence

---

* This inner circle included General Sir Alan Brooke, Air Chief Marshal Sir Charles Portal and Admiral Sir Dudley Pound from the Chiefs of Staff Committee; General Hastings Ismay, their liaison to Churchill; Generals Bernard Paget and Bernard Law Montgomery, and their Canadian subordinates Andrew McNaughton, Harry Crerar, and Ham Roberts along with his senior staff officers; Air Vice-Marshal Sir William Sholto Douglas and Air Vice-Marshal Trafford Leigh-Mallory from the RAF; and, among Mountbatten's own staff, Captain Jock Hughes-Hallett, assisted by Marquis "Bobby" de Casa Maury, his intelligence officer.

surrounding the remount was but "an example of [the] extravagant security" for the whole operation.[30] At a routine daily meeting of the NID on August 14, a request from Mountbatten's headquarters for an intelligence work-up for Operation Jubilee crossed the desk of one of Godfrey's staff officers. He had never heard of Jubilee, let alone been informed of the nature of the operation, the date or the target, but he soon discovered that Godfrey had been "told verbally of Jubilee" and indeed had "some vague knowledge of it, but NID had been denied all official knowledge of the plan."[31] Why would Mountbatten invoke such extraordinary measures to indicate that the Dieppe Raid was an improper or unauthorized action? Part of the answer may lie in Mountbatten's love of the double bluff and his paranoia about rampant security leaks and spies crawling out of the woodwork—particularly on the Isle of Wight.

Just before the St-Nazaire operation back in March, Mountbatten had informed the Chiefs of Staff Committee that, if the raid did not come off on the date planned, he would remount it as soon as conditions permitted: the Germans would never expect a raid on the same place once the cat was out of the bag. Seen in this light, Dieppe was in no way unique as a double bluff; rather, it formed part of Mountbatten's standard cloak-and-dagger playbook. His actions during the remount period show that Jubilee retained much more continuity with Rutter than has previously been believed.

First, Mountbatten did not dismiss his force commanders and their staffs following the "cancellation" of Operation Rutter, with the exception of the prickly Rear Admiral Tom Baillie-Grohman, and put them on alert for an eventual remount. There is no better confirmation than the fact that on the night of August 18, just as Jubilee got under way, General Andrew McNaughton sent a cable to the Department of National Defence headquarters in Ottawa referencing his earlier message of July 9—the day after Rutter was cancelled—a copy of which has yet to be found. In the cable, he informs Lieutenant General Kenneth Stuart,

Chief of the General Staff (Canada), that the "special matter of which I advised you [is] now under way."[32] Clearly, the remount was preordained; the date it would happen remained the only question.

Whether it was Operation Rutter or Operation Jubilee, to pull off a pinch raid on this grand scale required an overriding element of surprise. Every aspect of the plan was cloaked in the tightest secrecy, leading in turn to Mountbatten's extraordinary security measures. By mid-1942—certainly after the successful St-Nazaire Raid—the Germans were expecting raids along the French coast, particularly over the summer period at the tail end of the "raiding season," when environmental conditions lent themselves readily to amphibious operations. The Germans launched a programme to strengthen their coastal defences in the west and maintained regular high alerts during times when tidal and wind conditions permitted landings. Although strategically the Allies could not surprise the Germans, there was nothing to prevent them from trying to achieve tactical surprise by confusing them as to where exactly they would land and when. If the planners and the force commanders played their cards right, and secrecy was maintained in almost hermetic fashion, there was no reason, certainly in Mountbatten's mind, why they couldn't pull off a successful raid.

What Mountbatten counted on above all was that German intelligence would discard or downgrade Dieppe as a potential target: remounting a raid on the same target after its cancellation was hardly a textbook operation of war and something only a fool would try. Relying on the conventional to blind his enemy to the unconventional, Mountbatten hoped to use the naval and air diversions off Boulogne, which Baillie-Grohman and Leigh-Mallory had promised, to distract the Germans while the raiding force struck out undetected across the Channel in the darkness for Dieppe.

The ace up Mountbatten's sleeve in the weeks before Operation Jubilee, and on the day itself, was Ultra. Shore facilities and local traffic in the Channel area, although in some cases equipped with the four-rotor Enigma machine in preparation for its eventual introduction, were still using the three-rotor while distribution of the new machine and its materials continued. Bletchley Park could therefore still read the message traffic in the area, so Mountbatten and his staff could monitor German actions, inactions and reactions on land, on the sea and in the air to ensure that surprise was being maintained. Arguably, Mountbatten's whole concept of the double bluff might never have made it off the drawing board without Ultra; otherwise it was just too risky. Through these means Godfrey, along with the planners and the force commanders, kept tabs on any signs of movements or developments by the enemy in the weeks and days leading up to the raid and, of course, on that day in August as well. Ultra could reveal movements of aircraft, infantry, artillery, E-boats and even U-boats into the area, as well as any buildup of special equipment, extra stores, ammunition or defensive works that might interfere with the projected raid. And they knew, of course, that German convoys routinely ran up and down the French coast almost every night.

To ensure that this crucial raid got off the ground as planned in mid-August, Mountbatten removed all non-essential elements that might attract the attention of German intelligence or, in a bureaucratic sense, tie up planning and lead to compromise or cancellation.[33] Knowing that COHQ was somewhat resented by the other service ministries, and even by members of the chiefs of staff, Mountbatten desperately wanted to prove its value. He feared that the potential for friction and for ultimate cancellation increased exponentially with the number of people who knew about the plan. To avoid any possibility of butting heads with an obstinate bureaucratic enemy, he replaced the airborne element in Rutter with two veteran commando units from the Lofoten and Vaagso raids, which would strike by sea against the coastal batteries on the outer flanks of Dieppe. By so doing, he not only removed the need for near-perfect weather conditions, required for delicate airborne operations, but avoided the perils of bargaining for assets not directly under his control. This change in plan also helped to maintain the vital element of surprise, by eliminating waves of troop-carrying aircraft that would light up German radar and ground defences. In addition, it gave Mountbatten wider "pinch" coverage: these two units were experienced in scrounging for anything that looked promising, and with the coastal batteries under Kriegsmarine control, there was always the possibility that they too could strike gold.*

Yet another threat Mountbatten had to consider were the daily runs, weather permitting, of German reconnaissance aircraft over the south coast of England. These flights had discovered the Rutter forces marshalling for the raid in early July, leading to the subsequent German air raid that hit two of the ships. Now, instead of concentrating the strike force in a few select ports as before, Mountbatten spread it out among many ports throughout southern England. He even disguised the troopships as coastal convoy vessels, given that they had to embark in daylight to make their rendezvous in mid-Channel, and eliminated any vessels that did not usually ply the Channel. He did not mind that the Royal Navy refused to risk its battleships and cruisers in the close confines of the Channel: their sudden presence would only raise an alert along the German-held coast of France and provoke a major response from the Luftwaffe and the Kriegsmarine.

The same restrictions applied for the tugs, drifters and Eagle ships originally assigned to Ryder's Cutting Out Force to tow the captured barges out of the port during Rutter. Normally the tugs and drifters were occupied with duties other than raiding, so their inclusion in any task force would alert German intelligence to the impending action.

---

* Another example of the extravagant security was the fact that each of these units was given its own mission with its own code name, and neither one seems to have known that it was taking part in a larger operation called Jubilee aimed at Dieppe. No. 3 Commando's operation was code-named Flodden, while No. 4 Commando's was Cauldron.

So Mountbatten stripped them too from Jubilee. Similarly, the main role of the Eagle ships was anti-aircraft protection in the Thames Estuary, and any move from their usual operating area was bound to draw German interest. Mountbatten knew that if he left them in place during Operation Jubilee, they would create a false sense of "business as usual." To replace the extra firepower these ships would have provided, HMS *Alresford*, a lumbering First World War–vintage minesweeper, joined the French *chasseurs* in Robert Force for the Dieppe Raid.

The corollary effect of Mountbatten's changes was to underscore the primary role of the pinch in Jubilee. No longer were the Royal Marines concerned with towing back the mass collection of German barges as a publicity stunt, as had been called for in Rutter. For Jubilee, this was abandoned, and the Royal Marines were tasked with capturing them now only as a contingency, and told either to "hot wire" the vessels and sail them back to England on their own if the situation presented itself or sink them as Ryder had originally suggested. In addition, the planned attack on the airfield and on German army headquarters was changed from definite to contingent. In short, the only significant objective from Rutter that remained firm for Jubilee was the pinch operation to be carried out by part of the Canadian raiding force and the entire Royal Marine Commando, with Fleming's IAU in the starring role.

"A visit to the Ogre in his den" was how Winston Churchill's wife, Clementine, described her husband's visit to Moscow on August 12, 1942, for the first face-to-face meeting between the British prime minister and the Soviet leader, Joseph Stalin.[34] Long known for his anti-Communist stance, Churchill had been forced, after the German invasion of the Soviet Union a year earlier, to embrace "Uncle Joe" as an ally of convenience and necessity in the fight against Nazi Germany. The urgent trip stemmed from Stalin's overt displeasure over two pressing items that appeared to threaten the fragile alliance. The first was the failure of the Allies to establish a second front in the west, a distraction designed to force the Germans at the height of their current summer offensive to shave off much-needed land and air forces in the east to fight in the west, and so alleviate pressure on the Soviet Union. The second was the suspension, following the PQ-17 disaster, of the vital convoys to Russia.

Much has been made of the second-front issue, but in fact it was not Stalin's major concern that August, despite his initial disappointment over the cancellation of Operation Sledgehammer (the landing of troops in Brest or on the Cherbourg peninsula) for the fall of 1942 and the postponement of any Allied invasion of Europe until at least 1943. Although he had stated "most emphatically" in his cable to Churchill the previous month "that the Soviet Government cannot tolerate the second front in Europe being postponed until 1943," by the time Churchill arrived, other elements had come into play. The official minutes of the meeting describe Stalin's view as "glum" when he was told about the decision to postpone the European second front, but documents that remained classified until 2013 from the files of Alexander Cadogan, the British undersecretary of state, paint a very different version of events. Cadogan reported to his boss, Lord Halifax, that Stalin's tone had changed from the urgency and outrage expressed in his July cable and in the official minutes to something far more conciliatory.

According to Cadogan, after Churchill had spent some time "explaining the impossibility of invading France this year," Stalin never once so much as hinted that "Well, if you can't do more than that, I don't know how much longer we can stand the strain." Cadogan acknowledged that he was relieved and surprised when Stalin repeated several times that he was "astounded at the spirit and determination of his [Russian] people. He didn't know them[;] he had never dreamt that they could show such unity or resolution."[35] Indeed, the Soviet leader had come to the realization that, despite his urgings and American promises, logistically it was not feasible to launch a second front in Europe in 1942. North Africa was, however, a different story. When Churchill mentioned this proposed invasion, the Soviet leader lit up in a way the delegation had not anticipated. Operation Torch "seemed to have caught Stalin's fancy," Cadogan wrote. The Soviet leader stunned all those in attendance by nodding his approval and stating, "May God prosper this enterprise."[36]

But the suspension of the Arctic convoys carrying much-needed supplies to Russia remained a hot topic of dispute. Stalin's July cable had clearly voiced his displeasure at this most crucial moment. He wrote:

> According to our naval experts, the arguments of British naval experts on the necessity of stopping delivery of war supplies to the northern harbours of the U.S.S.R. are untenable. They are convinced that, given goodwill and readiness to honour obligations, steady deliveries could be effected with heavy loss to the Germans . . . Of course, I do not think steady deliveries to northern Soviet ports are possible without risk or loss. But then no major task can be carried out in wartime without risk or losses . . . I never imagined that the British Government would deny us delivery of war materials precisely now, when the Soviet Union is badly in need of them in view of the grave situation on the Soviet-German front.[37]

As the British knew, this grumbling was not just political bluster but an expression of the extreme fragility of the Soviet war economy. Although much has been written about the inferior types of tanks and aircraft manufactured in the United Kingdom for delivery to the Soviet Union, these armaments did in fact play a crucial role in the fighting: most of the cargo that was delivered went right into action once it was unloaded from the boats. The Soviets would eventually develop their own prosperous industrial capabilities and thrive, in part thanks to

American Lend-Lease deliveries later in the war, but the year 1942 proved to be a most vulnerable point for the Soviet Union. Its industrial centre had been based in its western regions, and in the summer and fall of 1941 Stalin had taken the unorthodox step of closing all the factories that lay in the path of the German onslaught and moving them thousands of miles to safety behind the Ural Mountains. This transfer necessitated a complete retooling of Soviet industry, with considerable downtime—right at the worst possible moment.

In these strained circumstances, the arms deliveries from Great Britain were desperately needed to plug the gaps and buy time for the Soviet factories to start producing again. But over and above that, certain machine tools that had been lost to the Germans had to be replaced. There was no point in building a factory in a safe location if the highly specialized machine tools, castings, or vital resources (oil, rubber, aluminum alloy, special steels and aviation fuel) needed to produce and employ weapons of war and other industrial machinery were lacking.[38] And therein lay the true value of the British convoys: a good measure of their cargo was not simply the denigrated tanks and aircraft, but the vital industrial resources needed for the core infrastructure of the Soviet war effort.[39]

Meanwhile, at home, Winston Churchill was also under great pressure. He had just undergone his second no-confidence vote in six months, easily defeating the motion as he had earlier in the year, yet the clock seemed to be ticking against him as the coalition war leader. Calls from the vocal left-wing minority for a "second front now" could for the present be taken in stride, but the cavalier way in which the merchant seamen in the PQ-17 had been sent to their icy graves raised doubts among the industrial labourers who saw the fruits of their heavy work plummet to the bottom of the ocean.

However, the ever-cautious Admiralty was not willing to risk its fleet and re-establish the convoys that August during the four-rotor blackout, when they had no way to follow the movements of the *Tirpitz* and other German vessels. Until the blackout ended or environmental conditions changed to permit rerouting of the convoys to the northern Soviet ports over a less risky, even if still vulnerable, course, the Admiralty remained reluctant to change its decision.

When Churchill in 1950 was reviewing this turbulent period while writing his memoirs of the war, he deliberately tried to distance himself from the disastrous Dieppe Raid, which was about to start as he bade farewell to Stalin for the trip home from Moscow. In a pointed witticism attributed to him years later, Churchill reportedly said, "History will be kind to me—as I intend to write it." And to whitewash his place in history, and to a lesser extent preserve security, he feigned ignorance over the remount of Rutter as Operation Jubilee at Dieppe. Perhaps preoccupied with his own legacy, the calculating prime minister began the process of appearing to know nothing within four months of the mission. Just before Christmas 1942, he queried Pug Ismay, his chief of staff, about the raid: "Although for many reasons everyone was concerned to make this business look as good as possible," he wrote, "the time has now come when I must be informed more precisely about the military plans." Ismay replied that Great Britain's star commander Bernard Law Montgomery, by then the beloved hero of the victory over Rommel at El Alamein, had approved the overall military plan for the Dieppe Raid. Stymied, Churchill then dropped the matter after Mountbatten defiantly suggested that, if pressed, he would demand an official inquiry.

Victory in 1945 did nothing to quell the raw emotion and stigma associated with Dieppe. By then Mountbatten had become the obvious villain, and Churchill attempted to place the responsibility for the remount squarely on his shoulders. Reaching out to Pug Ismay once again, perhaps in an effort to suggest he toe the party line, Churchill demanded to know who had made "the decision to revive the attack after it had been abandoned and Montgomery had cleared out."[40] Churchill wrote:

> What we say about this is a matter for subsequent consideration, but we must at least know ourselves what the facts were—namely: did the Chiefs of Staff, or the Defence Committee or the War Cabinet ever consider the matter of the revival of the operation (a) when I was in England, (b) when I was out of England, or was it all pushed through by Dickie Mountbatten on his own without reference to higher authority?[41]

Knowing full well the details of the raid, including the pinch portion, Pug Ismay must surely have suspected what Churchill was up to and what he wanted from him. Apologizing "for being so inadequate about the Dieppe Raid," he did not take the bait but reminded Churchill that, "in the vital interests of secrecy, nothing was put on paper," thereby confirming Mountbatten's claim.[42] Then he fired the deciding salvo, telling the now former prime minister that he "must have approved the operation in principle," given that he requested urgent information about the remount before he departed from Moscow.[43] This exchange apparently ended the matter because, in the Dieppe passage in his memoirs, Churchill dutifully, if reluctantly, admitted: "I personally went through the plans with the CIGS, Admiral Mountbatten and the Naval Force Commander J. Hughes-Hallett. It was clear that no substantial change between Jubilee and Rutter was suggested, beyond substituting commandos to silence the flank coastal batteries in place of air-borne troops."[44] This affirmation came after the fact, but confirmation appears in a series of messages exchanged between Churchill and Pug Ismay at the end of the Moscow trip.

On August 15, following a contentious round of discussions concerning the suspension of the Arctic convoys, Churchill wired Ismay, asking, "What is position about renewal of Rutter?"[45] Clearly the prime minister, the highest authority in the land, had knowledge of the raid and had given permission to remount it, even if not through the normal channels. Ismay's reply the following day confirms that Churchill was aware not only of the remount but of the Ultra Secret objective behind the raid. He informed the anxious PM, with veiled details attached, that "Jubilee, which is renewed Rutter *in all essential features*, is due to be carried out at first light August 18th. If weather unfavourable 18th August, operation can be launched any subsequent day up to 24th August inclusive."[46] After a one-day delay caused by inclement conditions, Ismay cabled Churchill just after his plane touched down in Cairo on the return leg of his Russian journey: "Weather sufficiently good—Jubilee has started."[47]

THIRTEEN

THE CROSSING

Britannia needs her privateers
Each time she goes to war
Death to all her enemies
Though prizes matter more

—MARK KNOPFLER, "PRIVATEERING"

Late on the afternoon of August 18, a two-car convoy pulled up to Trafalgar Gate, the main access to His Majesty's Naval Base Portsmouth. Commander Ian Fleming, dressed in a navy peacoat, demanded directions from a confused guard to the precise location of the British Hunt-class destroyer HMS *Fernie*, berthed somewhere near Lord Nelson's flagship, HMS *Victory*. Officially listed as an "observer" for the raid, Fleming, accompanied by several American officers, attachés from the U.S. embassy in London, had come to oversee the operational combat debut of his fledgling Intelligence Assault Unit.[1] The most prominent of his visitors, U.S. Army brigadier general Lucian K. Truscott Jr. and Marine Corps colonel Franklin A. Hart, who, as part of Mountbatten's staff, had taken part in the planning for Dieppe, had now come to study British amphibious techniques and to witness firsthand the combat debut of fifty members of the newly created U.S. Army Rangers.[2]*

As Fleming's entourage entered Portsmouth dockyard, the scene they witnessed resembled that in many other ports along the south coast of England. All around them, ships were making final preparations for the raid under a cover plan designed to disguise it as yet one more tedious training exercise. To maintain this "business as usual" appearance and prevent any dockyard speculation stemming from a sudden surge in activity, ammunition and special equipment essential for the mission had been smuggled on board over several nights, and all extra rations had been cancelled. The guard's strange reaction to Fleming's request for directions confirmed that Louis Mountbatten's extreme and almost obsessive attention to secrecy and security had worked. In the days leading up to the raid, Ultra had revealed nothing to suggest that the Germans had caught on to the remount. With

---

* One of the changes to the raid between its origins as Operation Rutter and its implementation as Operation Jubilee had seen the air drop, scheduled to obliterate the coastal batteries at Dieppe, replaced by an amphibious attack carried out by two additional British army commando units, both of which were veterans of pinch operations in Norway. These units, Lieutenant Colonel John Durnford-Slater's No. 3 Commando and Lieutenant Colonel Simon Fraser's (the 15th Lord Lovat's) No. 4 Commando, would now host the U.S. Army Rangers, distributed throughout them in "penny packets." The Rangers had replaced the U.S. Marine Corps, which in Rutter had been assigned to go into battle with the Royal Marine Commando on board the *Locust*. The switch was likely prompted by *Locust*'s sacrificial role in the pinch attempt—the "political" implication that had been in Mountbatten's mind since early June. Still, with the four-rotor crisis looming and pinch opportunities opening up in the Pacific theatre to exploit their work against Japanese codes and ciphers, the Americans, in particular Colonel Hart, were still most eager to monitor the events surrounding Jubilee. (Marine Corps History Division, Reference Branch, Franklin Hart biographical file.)

Captain Jock Hughes-Hallett about to sneak the largest raiding force in history across seventy miles of the English Channel, everything appeared to be going their way.

After Fleming and the Americans had presented their credentials to the guard, they soon found the *Fernie* and her sister ship, HMS *Calpe*, among the myriad destroyers, troop transports, converted Channel steamers, motor launches, anti-submarine trawlers, gunboats and landing craft in Portsmouth harbour. They were welcomed aboard the *Fernie* by first officer Lieutenant Willett—"a young public school entrant in his early 20s," as Fleming described him.[3] Willett explained that his commanding officer, a gregarious sort with immense bravado, had run his motorcycle into an immovable object earlier in the day and would not be able to take *Fernie* into battle. Nevertheless, Willett did, and Fleming later recorded that he won respect and admiration for his handling of the ship by raid's end. Days earlier, both destroyers had undergone a special refit that transformed them from traditional sub-marine-hunting and convoy escort vessels to modern headquarters ships, or floating communications fortresses, for raiding operations.

Fernie and *Calpe* bristled with scores of antennae connected to hyper-sensitive communications and navigational gear whose settings proved so delicate that they prohibited the firing of her main four-inch gun except in emergencies. Clearly impressed by the technological array, Fleming eagerly noted at least four additional wireless teams totalling forty to fifty operators. Positioned on deck, below deck, in wardrooms and the captain's cabin, as well as on the bridge, these wireless opera-tors would perform a variety of communications tasks designed to keep all parts of the raiding force linked together—the two force com-manders on board and those on shore—either by direct voice link or through eavesdropping on the labyrinthine radio net. Forward Observation Officers (FOOs) would control air and naval support to the troops ashore; "Phantom" and "J Service" personnel would moni-tor Allied messages from special liaison officers; and "Headache" teams of German-speaking radio operators would scan the airwaves for German plain-language messages uttered in the heat of battle. The chatter from these wireless sets would establish the backbeat for the drama about to unfold—and once the operation began, would provide Fleming and the other observers with a ringside seat at the raid.

As Chief of Combined Operations, Mountbatten knew that effective command, control and communications formed the potential key to success in this operation, and he was leaving nothing to chance. As he had planned for Operation Rutter, Jock Hughes-Hallett and Major General Ham Roberts would, respectively, call the shots for the sea and land forces from the floating command centre aboard the *Calpe*, but if something went horribly wrong there, the *Fernie* housed a complete backup command team led by Roberts's chief of staff, Brigadier Churchill Mann. Meanwhile, an RAF liaison officer would work from the bridge of *Calpe*, with Air Vice-Marshal Trafford Leigh-Mallory orchestrating the entire air umbrella from his Uxbridge headquarters in London. In Portsmouth, Admiral Sir William James would keep tabs on every aspect of the raid from his newly constructed command bunker under Fort Southwick. Patched into all the networks, his headquarters became the relay hub: he could eavesdrop on the action from across the Channel and send on the latest intelligence provided from the Operational Intelligence Centre, working under John Godfrey's watchful eye in London.

On the Isle of Wight, close to four thousand men from Ham Roberts's Second Canadian Division, along with sixty tanks from the Calgary Tank Regiment and nearly a dozen teams of Royal Canadian Engineers and other ancillary elements, loaded onto troopships and landing craft. Few, if any, suspected that this "preparatory exercise" would in fact be the "real deal." Amid the scores of vehicle convoys heading to the coast were several trucks with tarpaulins drawn, carrying Colonel

Joseph Picton-Phillips's Royal Marine commandos to the port of Cowes. There they would board the *Locust* and the French *chasseurs* anchored offshore.

Despite the intense security and the cover plan, suspicion had begun to grow within the ranks of the Royal Marines that something big was brewing. On August 15, Picton-Phillips and his company commanders received word that Operation Jubilee would take place on any day between August 18 and 23, weather permitting, and that they should draw up their orders for the pinch—an exact replica of Rutter but with new code names. Under strict instructions to keep the men in the dark until the last possible moment—ideally when aboard their assault craft—only the company commanders and platoon officers knew about the remount of the raid. Picton-Phillips had even initiated Operation Inchen, a bogus week-long training scheme designed to conceal the nature of the preparations—particularly if inclement weather forced a day-to-day postponement, as had been the case in Rutter.[4]

However, the natural flurry of pre-raid activity, which called for the Marines to prime grenades, fill Bren gun magazines and oil weapons, only fuelled rumour and conjecture. "The explanation given," recalled Jock Farmer, "was that we were going on an exercise! Even the dimmest amongst us wasn't going to buy that."[5] By the afternoon of August 18, Picton-Phillips received word that the tanks had embarked—a sure sign that the raid was on—and he held an Orders Group that night with his officers and NCOs to go over the exact details of their mission. Following the meeting, the Royal Marine Commando jumped in the trucks bound for Cowes, and by five o'clock that afternoon all were safely aboard the *Locust* and the *chasseurs* en route to Portsmouth, where they would link up with the raiding force.

For the men of Robert Force, commanded by Major Robert Houghton, speculation hit fever pitch while they waited aboard the *chasseurs*. "After a while no one was allowed on deck and all the NCOs were summoned for a briefing," wrote the intrigued eighteen-year-old

Bob McAlister. The anticipation rose after Commander Red Ryder arrived to discuss "special duties" and the men were issued with ammunition, special tools and emergency rations, along with escape instructions.[6] McAlister recalled:

> We were shown aerial 3D photographs of Dieppe and areas along the coast for two or three miles, and inland too. We were told this was the real thing. A thrill ran through everyone. This was what the lads wanted. Everyone was thrilled and excited . . . the fact that we soon [would] be in action brought us closer to each other and dependent on each other. Our attitudes changed, little differences forgotten. We were brothers in arms and ready for anything.[7]

The same sentiment prevailed among the Royal Marines of Tiger Force and the IAU aboard the Locust. After they squeezed below deck, they were issued with French currency, which immediately told them that this time the raid was on. According to Jock Farmer, "It was so crowded that anybody who had hand grenades hanging from their pouches were told to fuck off, as we did not want any accidents amongst ourselves."[8] Their orders remained the same as in Rutter, reported Corporal Paul McGrath: "driving into the harbour, attacking and capturing the German Naval headquarters based in a dockside hotel and extracting specified contents therefrom, and removing a number of German invasion barges for towing back to England."[9] However, as eager and optimistic as the Royal Marine commandos were about the mission, Jock Farmer recalled that they remained quite sober, realizing that they could be embarking on a one-way ride:

> Locust was designed to ram any obstacle in its way, it was obvious it was not coming back. Somebody tentatively asked "How do we get back?" It was a question that should not have been asked and

Assault landing craft on the one-day crossing of the English Channel, carrying Canadian soldiers towards the beaches in and around Dieppe during Operation Jubilee, as the Allies' raid was code-named. By nightfall, Operation Jubilee would become the deadliest amphibious raid in recorded history.

there was just a stony silence. Later it was suggested in a jocular tone, "Why don't we raise one of the boats we just sunk, dry it out, find out from the Germans where they kept the diesel and fill up?" That too, was greeted by a stony silence.[10]

Capping off the day in grand style, a motor launch approached the *Locust*, bringing Mountbatten for a visit before the raiding fleet sailed. "We were all up on deck," recalled Douglas Bevan, "the whole ship's company, all the Royal Marine Commandos, and, typical of Mountbatten in those days, he jumped up on one of the cap stands at the front of the ship. He stood up and told one of the ship's officers to stand us at ease."[11] Up front with No. 10 Platoon, Paul McGrath was impressed too, noting that the Chief "cut a splendid figure, in the admiral's uniform" as he gave a quick pep talk, then "dashed off to give repeat performances on other ships."[12] Mountbatten's visit had the desired effect: it left everyone with the distinct impression that this "was the real McCoy, it was on definitely"—a welcome relief after the disappointment of Rutter six weeks earlier.[13]

Sergeant John Kruthoffer, the usually tough-minded, twenty-one-year-old second-in-command to Lieutenant Peter Huntington-Whiteley,

---

OPPOSITE TOP: The British escort destroyer HMS *Fernie*, which, along with HMS *Calpe*, was specially fitted to act as a headquarters ship for Operation Jubilee. On board the *Calpe*, Ham Roberts and Jock Hughes-Hallett would command the sea and land portions of the raid, while a backup set of commanders would stand by ready to take over in an emergency situation on the *Fernie*, where Ian Fleming also waited for the intelligence booty obtained by his IAU.

BOTTOM: Long obscured in the history of the Dieppe Raid, the Ultra Secret role of the heavily armed gunboat HMS *Locust* was to breach the harbour and deliver roughly two hundred men—the "Tiger Force" of the Royal Marine A Commandos that included Fleming's No. 10 Platoon (his Intelligence Assault Unit) —to their targets.

found these expectations intensely moving. He wrote later that "the unit was in prime condition—very well trained—handpicked really keen types . . . with a genuine desire and anxiety to prove ourselves."[14] August 19, 1942, would provide that chance in spades. As Paul McGrath recalled in his memoir, "On that awesome day, we were baptised in the blood and thunder of war, and those who survived the carnage will never forget it as long as they live."[15]

On August 17, Jock Hughes-Hallett and Commander David Luce, two parts of the planning syndicate that had conceived the idea for a raid on Dieppe eight months earlier, reviewed the plans and orders "very carefully" and "went over the whole operation in our minds trying to imagine and anticipate all the contingencies that might arise."[16] That night the raid was postponed briefly because of inclement weather, but Hughes-Hallett would not give up. After an intense three-hour meeting with Mountbatten, Admiral James and the force commanders in which he, along with Mountbatten, pressed hard for the raid to go ahead. The Admiralty and the Air Ministry meteorologist were "every bit as gloomy as Old Testament Prophets," Hughes-Hallett wrote, but a local weather expert dismissed their predictions, stating that a pocket of fine weather would cover Dieppe on the morrow. With this encouraging news, Admiral James agreed to launch the raid.[17] At 1715 hours, a warning order, followed minutes later by the code word Tulip, officially signalled the start of Operation Jubilee. General Andrew McNaughton quickly relayed the message to Ottawa, just as Major General Hastings Ismay sent it on to Churchill as he was returning from his visit to Stalin in Moscow.

By 1800 hours, Jock Hughes-Hallett and Ham Roberts, aboard the Calpe, had sailed out of Portsmouth harbour, stopping only at the "gate through the Spithead anti-submarine room to watch as the whole force passed through, eastward bound, in perfect formation." To

Jock Hughes-Hallett, the new Dieppe naval force commander who had replaced Tom Baillie-Grohman—with Mountbatten's ecstatic approval—it had "a certain dream-like quality."[18]

Over the previous few hours, nearly 250 ships had crept out from bases in southern England and the Isle of Wight and formed into thirteen assault groups bound for Dieppe. First, though, they had to navigate through a dangerous mid-Channel minefield. Led by a few minesweepers, each group would maintain its course through carefully cleared lanes marked by dimly lit dan buoys. Ploughing through at close to twenty knots in order to reach Dieppe under cover of darkness, there was little room for error. Although they were aided by advanced navigational gear, some borrowed from the RAF's Bomber Command, Hughes-Hallett's orders called for immediate cancellation if one of the large mother ships ferrying the infantry and their landing craft to the drop-off point, ten miles off the coast of Dieppe, succumbed to a German mine or any other enemy action. The men on the crowded ships donned Mae West life preservers and collectively held their breath as each group took its place in the queue to slip through the danger zone.

Almost miraculously, everything went better than Hughes-Hallett had expected, and almost all of his ships navigated the lanes on time and on target. The major exception was the Locust: with a top speed of only seventeen knots, compared with the brisk eighteen-to-twenty-knot pace for the rest of the raiding force, the river gunboat had apparently been given special permission to trail behind. Following it came Motor Launch 291 (ML291), which most likely was the designated craft that would whisk the pinched material out of Dieppe harbour. As Hughes-Hallett recorded in his official report: "After passing Nab Tower, Locust was unable to maintain speed of Group 4[,] proceeded independently . . ."[19] Ryder's memoirs concur: "Proceeding along the Sussex coast we finally lost all contact with the main body off Beachy Head. Between Rye and Dungeness[,] neither of which were visible in the dark, we had to alter course in a South Easterly direction through a swept channel across a mine field."[20] Except for the ML219, Ryder and Captain William John Stride found themselves alone, behind schedule and on the edge of what they hoped was one of the two channels through the minefield. As Ryder recalled:

> This was to have been marked by a lighted Dan buoy but we could see no sign of it. "Well Skipper" I remember saying to Stride "What do we do now?" "It's awfully best to take them at right angles Sir" he replied calmly . . . we took his sound advice and plunged boldly through the minefield, breathing rather more freely when by dead reckoning we thought we were across.[21]

Whether sheer luck, the shallow draft or a combination of both saved the ship from certain destruction remains unknown, but the Locust was now significantly behind time for its rendezvous off the main beach, where it was expected to provide fire support for the Essex Scottish as they began their landing at 0510 hours. That delay, however, was minor compared with the calamity that was about to unfold.

Despite the scores of post-battle rumours on both sides of the line that the Germans knew in advance about the Dieppe Raid, nothing in any file currently in the public domain suggests that the Germans were aware of it. Through Ultra, the British knew that ever since the raid at St-Nazaire, the Germans had been expecting more raids somewhere along the French coast or in Norway, particularly before the raiding season came to an end in the late fall. The Combined Operations planners expected to encounter a heightened state of alert along the entire coast of France.

Even if the Germans did know about the raid and Allied intelligence had missed that fact, there is no evidence in the available German records that they made any preparations to counter it. No U-boats or German patrol boats suddenly appeared; no extra bombers reinforced Luftwaffe squadrons; no additional army units arrived to augment the German division defending Dieppe. Everything was proceeding normally, including the welcome news gleaned through Ultra that a small convoy of trawler-type vessels, scheduled to arrive on August 17, was delayed until the following morning but should be in port when the raid began.[22] These types of trawlers were expected to house the targeted signals materials, and the message confirmed that, when the raiding fleet arrived in Dieppe, their "prizes" would indeed be ready for the taking.

At 0127 hours, however, just as the last ships cleared the minefield, a series of messages decrypted by Frank Birch's Naval Section at Bletchley Park, sent to Admiral James's headquarters in Portsmouth and then relayed to the raiding fleet, indicated that Hughes-Hallett's luck was about to run out. The first warned that at 0100 hours a collection of "small craft" was on patrol off Treport, just over fifteen miles up the coast from Dieppe.[23] There was nothing to indicate that these craft would enter the operational area, but less than an hour later "fresh reports showed that this was very possible."[24]

Between 0212 and 0244 hours, further intercepts clearly revealed that a German coastal convoy was indeed bound for Dieppe and set to cross paths with Group 5 on the far left wing of the raiding force. At 0216 hours, another Ultra message confirmed that a German coastal convoy, consisting of a small number of armed trawlers, had left Boulogne at 2100 hours on August 18 and was set to arrive in Dieppe around the same time that the landings were slated to begin. A quick navigational calculation by all the ships in the fleet that received the message confirmed that this convoy was on a collision course and would wander into Group 5 about sixty minutes before H-hour, at 0450.[25]

On board *Fernie*, Ian Fleming was busy carrying out Hughes-Hallett's instructions to deposit all personal papers and identification in a sandbag that would be kept in the captain's safe. That done, he climbed into an armchair in the wardroom for a pre-game nap, wondering what kind of prize that bag would make for the Germans should the *Fernie* be sunk and salvaged.[26] On the *Locust*, meanwhile, the Royal Marines made their final checks for battle, reviewing their maps and memorizing their code words and contingency plans in case things went wrong. On the reinforced bridge, Ryder and Stride destroyed "all secret documents related to the operation" by fire, except for map tracings, photographs and communications orders.[27]

At 0347 hours, Fleming and his American comrades were rudely awakened by the noise of distant gunfire echoing off the thin walls of *Fernie*. Moving swiftly up onto the slick deck of the drab grey British destroyer, Fleming discarded the remnants of a hand-rolled cigarette and pressed his binoculars to his eyes, adjusting the focus wheel to account for the darkness. In the distance, a series of fire-red, mushroom-shaped explosions, topped by the flickering silver glow from star shells, merged with the carnival of red, orange and green tracer fire that darted back and forth. Then came another round of staccato machine-gun and light cannon fire, punctuated at irregular intervals by the whiplash crack of larger-calibre naval gunfire. Something had gone wrong, and everyone on board realized that the carefully synchronized Operation Jubilee had begun—sixty-three minutes prematurely. Fleming, deeply concerned about the impact this encounter at sea might have on the crucial element of surprise, stood gazing at the spectacle, wondering how it would affect his IAU.

What Fleming and everyone aboard every ship in the raiding force were witnessing was the seemingly avoidable collision between Group 5 and the small German coastal convoy that the Naval Section had warned was making for Dieppe.* Group 5 was led by Commander

---

* Lacking any specific advance knowledge of the raid, Birch's Naval Section issued these messages as part of its routine daily work, which included

Derek Bathurst Wyburd in Steam Gun Boat 5 (SGB5), and it consisted of twenty ALCs carrying Lieutenant Colonel John Durnford-Slater's No. 3 Commando to Yellow Beach and their target—the Berneval coastal battery.

The German convoy—three converted deep-sea trawlers outfitted for anti-submarine warfare[*] and five coastal motor boats, or "flak detachments,"[†] indeed loaded with the desired signals materials—had appeared through low-lying mist and taken Wyburd by surprise. The sharp, wild firefight that ensued set the gunboat alight, knocking out her main guns and shearing off her antennae with a volley from the high-powered flak guns. The twenty landing craft were scattered in all directions, taking heavy fire, with some that carried extra petrol tanks exploding on the first hit. Group 5 now had little hope for a successful coordinated landing on Yellow Beach.

In Hughes-Hallett's after-action report and other accounts that followed, the collision between Group 5 and the German convoy was portrayed as a "chance" or "unfortunate" encounter. The Ultra messages prove, however, that the collision between Group 5 and the German coastal convoy was foreseen and that messages were dispatched to all the ships in the raiding force to warn them of the approaching threat. Apparently, all these messages were received, except by the headquarters ship *Calpe*, leaving Jock Hughes-Hallett and Ham Roberts in the dark, and the two destroyers, *Brocklesby* and the Polish vessel *Ślazak*, which had been ordered to protect that flank from marauding E-boats

---

reporting on almost every occurrence in the Channel. Although the commanders involved with the raid knew what to look for, the current evidence suggests that Birch remained in the dark.

* *UJ1404, UJ1411* and *UJ1410*

† *Ost-Vlanderen, Hydra, Iris, Spes-Salutis,* and the *Franz*

or U-boats. Astonishingly, Wyburd admitted later that he had in fact received the warning. However, he had decided even before the raid began that if his group was challenged by a German force on the way across the Channel, he would fight his way through in order to keep the delicate timing and synchronization of his portion of the raiding fleet intact. Clearly, he disregarded direct orders in the Jubilee plan which stipulated that, to maintain the essential element of surprise, captains should take evasive actions and avoid contact with enemy vessels during the crossing. Group 1 had followed those orders when informed of the approaching convoy. Wyburd, however, had compromised the entire raid by his insubordinate actions, and after he was finally rescued from his stricken ship, he was summoned aboard the *Calpe* to report to Hughes-Hallett. Inexplicably, the naval force commander did not reprimand him; in fact, he later lauded him for his "great gallantry and determination" and recommended him for a decoration! Something surely seems amiss here—but perhaps it can be explained by what happened next.

The German convoy took a serious beating as well, losing several ships. The first victim, the *Franz*, was hit repeatedly by British fire of unknown origin and eventually limped to shore, beaching herself on the rocks just below the Berneval battery, right between the two selected landing zones for Durnford-Slater's commandos. UJ1404 suffered a similar fate: with engines hit by armour-piercing shot, the converted trawler first slowed and then caught fire, forcing her crew to abandon ship, with twenty-five of the forty-four men falling into British hands. The remaining UJs fled towards the safety of Dieppe harbour, while the flak ships limped back to Treport harbour, where they augmented the port's anti-aircraft defences for the rest of the day.[28] Months later, a report on the capture of UJ1404, based on interrogations of the crew along with "supplementary" sources such as Ultra and "pinch sources," appeared in files from Birch's Naval Section. Something, it seems, although not of the golden variety the raiders were looking for in Dieppe, had been captured along with the crew. This outcome suggests that the "chance" contact with the convoy far off the coast was anything but incidental, and that perhaps Hughes-Hallett, at some distance from the coast, had gambled that he could seize what they were after well before they hit the beaches—just as Ryder had attempted before his raiding force appeared off the coast of St-Nazaire in March. At present, however, there is no direct evidence to support this theory, and it remains a seductive mystery.

This theory aside, many of the contemporary reports, and the historical works that followed, claim that this clash put the entire defences in Dieppe on alert, stripping the raid of the precious element of surprise and leaving the men about to land on the beaches at the mercy of a prepared opponent. The actual facts are somewhat different. Luckily for Hughes-Hallett, none of the escaping German ships realized that they had bumped into an amphibious landing force. Instead, they mistook the gunboat and landing craft for British MTBs, which periodically ventured across the Channel to prey on coastal convoys. At first, German naval headquarters reported: "At 0350hrs attack on our convoy by surface forces, 4 kilometres off Dieppe. Particulars not yet known. It is of the opinion of the Naval Command that it has been one of the usual attacks on convoys." Without any knowledge that amphibious craft or Allied troopships were involved, there was nothing to indicate to the Germans that they had encountered a very large raiding operation.[29]

Three-quarters of an hour later, less than fifteen minutes before the first boot was due to touch down on the flanks, the signal station at Dieppe observed vessels which, when challenged for a response, ignored it.[30] Again, there is nothing in the records to suggest that the Germans realized what was happening. Even after the raid began and fighting had started on the flanks, for instance, the German 15th Army, which was responsible for defence of this part of the French coast, still believed the flare-up had been nothing more than a mid-Channel squabble. All the same, it did warn the Kriegsmarine and the Luftwaffe, and ordered its lookouts to intensify their efforts.[31] The same could be said for the port of Dieppe, whose jetties were fully alight to guide the way for the fleeing trawlers and whose three guard ships stood ready just outside the mole entrance to escort them to the safety of the inner harbour. Although alerted to the clash off in the distance, the German defenders of Dieppe and its environs had no clue what was about to befall them. Even if the surprise was lost, the shock of the large raiding force suddenly descending on the shore might still have had its desired effect of initially sowing chaos and despondency among the enemy.

However, what British intelligence had failed to understand throughout the planning process was that the German army in 1942 was at its peak. The soldiers defending Dieppe, despite what the assault troops may have been led to believe, were well trained, professional and extremely good at what they did best—defence. British intelligence did not so much underrate the size of the force there as they did the quality of the men defending Dieppe, along with their doctrine, training and leadership. Once the first planes lit up their radar and pounced down to attack the headlands and the beach, followed closely by the naval bombardment from the destroyers, the Germans finally realized that they were facing a raid. At that point, they turned the full might of their defences against the invaders.

Despite the clash in the Channel, the surprise seemed to hold throughout the landing zones, except for one—and that was the result of plain bad luck. At exactly 0450 hours, the landings west of Dieppe, at Orange and Green Beaches, began with No. 4 Commando under Lieutenant Colonel Simon Fraser (Lord Lovat) storming ashore near their target, the coastal battery at Varengeville, while Lieutenant Colonel Cecil Merritt's South Saskatchewan Regiment landed on

Green beach at Pourville, tasked with securing the town and capturing the western headland overlooking the main beach. Lord Lovat's landing was stunningly successful; in just two hours, the sharp firefight ended with a classic bayonet charge and fierce hand-to-hand fighting that destroyed the battery guns, prompting the proud signal to Hughes-Hallett and Roberts on the *Calpe*: "Every one of the gun crews finished with bayonet, OK by you?"

That, however, would be the only clear-cut success for the raiding force that day. Although Merritt's South Saskatchewan Regiment achieved surprise, a navigational error by the landing craft flotilla put his battalion on the wrong side of the river Scie. This mix-up delayed their advance, forcing them to fight their way across the bridge in town, a narrow bottleneck where Merritt personally led them in an act of extreme valour that garnered him the Victoria Cross. Although the regiment established a small bridgehead in the town (for subsequent landings by the Queen's Own Cameron Highlanders from Winnipeg) and captured the radar station, they could not reach the top of the western headland overlooking the main beach, and it remained in German hands throughout the raid.

To the east of Dieppe, things were worse—much worse. Because of the convoy clash, only a handful of Durnford-Slater's No. 3 Commando made it to shore at Yellow Beach, and the ones who did ended up being killed or captured as they tried to rush the openings leading to the top of the cliff. The one exception was the intrepid platoon under Lieutenant Peter Young, whose small force of commandos managed to land, climb a steep cliff and creep up close to their target—the Goebbels coastal battery. After cutting the phone lines that connected it with Dieppe, Young ordered his vastly outnumbered platoon to snipe at the battery with mortar and rifle fire from an adjacent cornfield, in the hope of drawing the Germans' attention away from other targets. They succeeded for close to three hours before they ran short of ammunition, at which point Young ordered them to beat a hasty retreat back to the boats that had brought them ashore. Although Hughes-Hallett and Roberts were out of touch with events on the east flank of the bridgehead, Young would later boast about what he believed was his greatest success on the day: "I took 18 men ashore, did the job we had to do and brought 18 men back."[32]

Even though the landings on the outer flank had experienced some success, as had those on Green Beach to a lesser extent, it was a different story that developed at Puys, overlooking Blue Beach, to say nothing of the slaughter about to unfold on the main beach in Dieppe itself. At Puys, Lieutenant Colonel Douglas Catto's Royal Regiment of Canada had the crucial task of seizing the eastern headland and capturing the guns on Pollet Cliff overlooking Dieppe harbour—the armaments that controlled access to and from the harbour. Unlike in other parts of the defended zone around Dieppe, the convoy clash had initially led the German commander in that sector to put his men on full alert. Not expecting anything to come from what he too suspected was a routine clash, he was moments away from calling a stand-down when his enthusiastic second-in-command had a brainstorm. Seeing that his men were awake, alert and already at their guns, why not carry out an impromptu anti-raid drill? Reluctantly, the commander agreed, in complete ignorance of the scores of landing craft steaming towards Blue Beach, carrying the first wave of roughly five hundred men from the Royals, who were now running seventeen minutes late and would land in daylight rather than under the cover of darkness as originally prescribed in the plan.

From such lucky—or unlucky—chances are battles sometimes won or lost: arriving late on Blue Beach proved catastrophic for the Royal Regiment, and that in turn had a cascading effect on the entire plan for Operation Jubilee and the pinch itself.

The delay, however, was due not so much to the convoy clash as to human error. While loading into landing craft from their converted passenger liners, the *Queen Emma* and *Princess Astrid*, which acted as mother ships for the ALCs, the first wave of the Royals found themselves following the wrong steam gunboat towards Dieppe. Confusion ensued when they realized they were halfway to the Dieppe harbour mole rather than Puys. It was only when they saw the harbour lights flashing to assist the German trawlers escaping from the clash at sea that they realized their mistake, changed course and headed for Puys, now seventeen minutes behind schedule.

By that time, the pre-dawn darkness crucial for success had lifted, the early morning sun only intermittently obscured by haze. Within seconds of the landing craft coming into view of the defenders at Puys, the Germans opened fire in almost robotic fashion. The men aboard the landing craft who dared to sneak a peek could see flashes from the shore, announcing the projectiles that whizzed over their heads or smashed into the doors and walls of the boat. With touchdown on the beach only moments away, the tension soared, relieved only by the surge forward when the first craft contacted land. As the doors swung open, the slaughter on Blue Beach began.

German small-arms fire joined the staccato machine-gun bursts, the increasing thumps of mortars and the whine of artillery shells as the other craft closed on the shore. In some boats, when the ramps dropped or the doors swung open, the men exited in orderly fashion— right rank first, left rank second and middle rank last. In other craft, swept by gunfire, a frantic scrambling ensued as the living, laden with helmets, webbing, equipment and personal weapons, stepped over the dead and the dying to rush through the tight doors of the craft or plopped over the sides into the water. Almost immediately, the water off Blue Beach turned crimson.

Arriving in daylight, the men had no cover and few places to hide. They had no chance to take out the German defenders with the speed, dash and daring that Hughes-Hallett and Roberts had planned. The Germans, sitting in relative comfort on the cliffs above on three sides, saw hundreds of soldiers from the Royal Regiment clamber awkwardly out of landing craft into a hail of murderous fire as they attempted to cross a hundred yards of open beach. Only the Germans' cries for more ammunition proved louder than those of the wounded and dying below. Before long the full weight of mortar and artillery shells added to the carnage, while Wehrmacht soldiers casually dropped grenades onto the Canadians huddled below.

For Private Ron Beal, approaching in the third wave, with German tracer fire buzzing over his head, the sights and sounds from the beach ahead recalled an ominous discussion he had overheard hours earlier with his mates aboard the *Queen Emma*. When told of their destination, one soldier asked innocently, "How do you spell Dieppe?" He thought about it for a while before he said, "You know, the first three letters spell *die*." As Beal related to me years later, "When we got there, that's exactly what we did."[33] That exchange was foremost in his mind as his landing craft hit its mark and the doors swung open. Sprinting over bodies of wounded, dead and dying friends, wading through severed body parts and the discarded weapons and equipment of a battalion already torn apart, he saw flashes from German machine guns. Most of his comrades who had landed in the first two waves lay dead or writhing in pain on the beaches, or, like him, sat trapped along the seawall or under the cliff, hoping to avoid a needless confrontation with German fire from the flanks or from above.

At one point there was a glimmer of hope when Douglas Catto, using a gap in the firing while the Germans brought up more ammunition, managed to get to the top of the cliff with a small band of men and push on towards the eastern headland. The Germans were quick to realize what had happened and recommenced their deadly hailstorm onto Beal and his comrades, forcing them to surrender just a few hours after their inauspicious landing. Meanwhile, Catto, when the rest of his battalion failed to appear on the clifftop, ordered his men to hide out in a copse not far from their objective, the German gun battery atop Pollet Cliff, to await the reinforcements that never came. In the early afternoon, with the sounds of gunfire now a distant memory, he ordered them to lay down their weapons and surrender.

By 0520 hours—the moment the frontal assault had been scheduled to hit the main beach, following on the heels of the carefully timed air and naval bombardment—Ham Roberts and Jock Hughes-Hallett aboard the *Calpe* had nothing to rely on but the scraps of information pouring in over the dozen or so wireless sets, augmented by an occasional glimpse of the shore through the ship's naval binoculars. Everything— from the ships at sea to the units on land and afloat, from the air force above to Leigh-Mallory's No. 11 Group headquarters at Uxbridge and Admiral James's fort in Portsmouth—was patched in to the *Calpe* and the *Fernie*, offering Fleming and those fortunate enough to eavesdrop a vivid but incomplete account of the battle.

For the historian all these years later, the message logs kept by operators to record the conversations provide a unique testimony crucial for reconstructing events. Only some of the logs have survived, unfortunately, while others collected by Hughes-Hallett for his official after-action report were never seen again in their original form, only in the extracts he released with his official account. However, some messages compiled by 1st Canadian Corps Headquarters in England and by a few of the wireless operators on board *Calpe* and *Fernie* are available in the archives. This collection offers a unique, though partial, insight into what the force commanders faced as the raid unfolded—and, along with the contextual understanding of the pinch imperative as a driver for the operation, they provide a dramatic new understanding of decisions taken by Ham Roberts and Jock Hughes-Hallett that day.

Unlike commanders in the field, historians have the luxury of time: we can weigh and assess each message without the pressures of command or of life-and-death decisions hanging in the balance. Roberts and Hughes-Hallett, listening intently in real time to the radio chatter, were forced to play the role of coaches attempting to guide their side to victory from the remoteness of a dressing room rather than from the sidelines or behind the bench. In this case, moreover, the stakes were immeasurably higher than the outcome of a simple sporting match.*

At 0500 hours, the increasing drone of dozens of RAF attack aircraft announced the start of the main beach assault, with air attacks on the headlands on each side of Dieppe and a naval bombardment of the German positions on the beach. Up to this point, everything in this sector had proceeded like clockwork, with the assault troops lowered into landing craft from the troopships *Prince Charles*, *Prince Leopold* and *Glengyle* without incident and ten miles out, beyond the range of German radar. Unlike at Blue Beach, the landing flotillas formed up successfully and departed on time, providing the men with a near-perfect view of the fireworks ashore before the low-flying Boston bombers swooped in and the destroyers turned windward to lay down a thick smokescreen on the east headland and the beach ahead. The only hitch so far was the slow river gunboat *Locust*, which, having lagged

---

* The camaraderie and adventuresome spirit of military men were very much on display in the message logs. The plan called for the use of the first name or nickname of the formation commander as the code name for each unit. In this case, when the South Saskatchewans hit the shore at Pourville, the *Calpe* received word that at "0450 Cecil landed." Among the other code names were Bob (Labatt) for the Royal Hamilton Light Infantry, Fred (Jasperson) for the Essex Scottish, Ham (Roberts) for the Military Force Commander, Goose (Gostling) for the Cameron Highlanders, Doug (Catto) for the Royal Regiment of Canada, Joe (Ménard) for the Fusiliers Mont-Royal, Johnny for the Calgary Tanks, Tiger for Tiger Force, Robert for Robert Force, Bill (Southam) for the 6th Brigade and Sherwood (Lett) for the 4th Brigade.

behind the raiding force across the Channel, arrived forty-five minutes behind schedule—too late to participate in the Jubilee overture.

As prescribed in the plan, the landing craft slowed to a crawl about five hundred yards from shore to watch attack aircraft shift their attention from the headlands to the beachfront and the buildings on the boulevard de Verdun. Swarms of fighter bombers temporarily lifted the spirits of the infantry as aerial cannons pounded away at enemy positions, followed by the "crump, crump, crump" from sticks of bombs dropped by low-level bombers and the roar of engines at full throttle as they made good their escape over the Channel from the cascade of German anti-aircraft fire sweeping the skies. From their narrow viewpoint on the landing craft, the spectacle ahead suggested to the assault troops about to storm the main beach that the intricate Operation Jubilee was unfolding as it should. Then came touchdown.

Ordered to get off the beach and move as fast as possible over the promenade and into the town and port, they had no time to waste once the first landing craft opened its door. Captain Donald Fraser McCrae, attached to the Essex Scottish for the raid, recorded:

> At about four-thirty some of our aircraft began attacking shore targets and almost immediately the sea was lit up by flares and within a few minutes we were being fired upon. It was then light enough to see a little bit and while everyone kept their heads down in the assault craft, we were able to see some of the earlier air battles, and some of our bombers diving in to attack shore targets. As we continued to move in, visibility grew better and we came under fire of the shore weapons about five o'clock. The intensity of the fire increased and shells and long-range mortar bombers were bursting in the sea among the advancing craft. Some of the craft were hit and sunk but the majority of them were able to carry on. There was

no hesitation, flotillas retained their formation and despite the heavy fire, the assault wave of craft touched down on the beach at 0505hrs.[34]

Although both the Essex Scottish and the Royal Hamilton Light Infantry landing next to them on White Beach arrived on time and on target, along with the Canadian combat engineers, they were aghast to find the beach devoid of Churchill tanks. The first group of landing craft bringing the tanks was fifteen minutes behind schedule, leaving the men hopelessly exposed, with only the undulating rock beach or the low seawall for protection. Worse still, that delay gave the German defenders time to recover from the initial shock of the bombing and the naval gunfire. As McCrae continued:

> Immediately, the troops disembarked and ran up the shingle on the beach, where they were held up by the first row of barbed wire. They started to cross this immediately, some cutting a pathway through the wire to get through. The casualties were not very heavy at the first wire[,] and the bulk of the troops were able to take cover in the shingle while wire parties went on to cut the second fence of concertina wire. By this time, the enemy had begun shelling the beach very heavily with what seemed to be field artillery and heavy mortar.[35]

At first, the German fire was light, but as soon as the men crested the beach, they faced a torrent of steel and fire from carefully concealed machine-gun and sniper positions in the buildings on the boulevard de Verdun and the pillboxes and slit trenches on the promenade. Every move provoked a torrent of enemy fire and, despite the thick smoke-screen wafting across the beach, German shells of all calibres began to find their mark. The engineers, essential to clear the six-foot-high, barbed-wire-crowned concrete anti-tank obstacles placed in the tiny roads that led to the port and the town, began to fall by the score while attempting to drag their explosives ashore and up the beach.

Remaining on the beach was a guaranteed death sentence; pushing ahead offered a slightly better chance of survival. But with both headlands still in German hands and the smokescreens laid down by the aircraft and the ships offshore providing only intermittent cover at best, progress meant tackling pillboxes, barbed wire entanglements and German slit trenches while simultaneously dodging bullets and shellfire pouring down from three sides. Casualties soon became horrendous in number and, given the circumstances, gruesome in nature.

Howard Large, a twenty-two-year-old private in A Company of the Essex Scottish tasked with storming aboard the trawlers and seizing the signals material before their crews could destroy it, wondered what kept hitting him as he sprinted over the seawall to the second belt of wire. Once he reached it, he discovered to his horror that the projectiles were the severed body parts of comrades torn to pieces by sizzling shrapnel splinters or blown apart by high explosives. As he related his experience to me almost seventy years later to the day, nothing was more vivid or lasting than those moments on the beach. Next to him, an officer with one leg sheared off was still barking orders; another lay curled in the fetal position, his nerves fried by fear; a sergeant, writhing in pain as he tried to stuff his disgorged entrails back into his sliced abdominal cavity, was begging someone to finish him off. Further ahead, a friend, Everett McCormick, who had failed in his previous attempts to place a Bangalore torpedo to clear the barbed wire, decided instead to hold it in place as it detonated, ripping both the wire and the thirty-eight-year-old private apart. To the right, just yards away, Large watched in agony as another private, tangled in the wire, squirmed helplessly like a macabre marionette, yelping in high-pitched tones for his mother as the phosphorus grenades he carried on his webbing ignited and burned into his entire body, immolating him in seconds.[36]

At last, a quarter of an hour after the main landings went in, the Churchills from the Calgary Tanks arrived—but they struggled to get off the landing craft and up the chert-rock beach. Some, as expected, threw their tracks when the fist-sized stones clogged their sprocket holes, while others lumbered forward, attempting to make the steep grade to breach the seawall. Of the twenty-nine tanks that eventually landed during the course of the morning, just over half made it over the seawall and onto the promenade. Lacking support from the engineers, who lay scattered with the dead and wounded of the Royal Hamilton and the Essex Scottish regiments on the beach and promenade, the thirty-eight-ton beasts could not pierce the concrete roadblocks erected by the Germans in the narrow streets near the tobacco factory or in any alternative street leading to the port. So they roamed on their own up and down the formerly grassy promenade, ripping up the turf and crushing friend and foe alike under their treads, while the crews searched in vain for any exit that would lead to the harbour, or at least off the beach.

By 0600 hours, the four companies of the Essex Scottish were pinned down on Red Beach taking heavy casualties, as were the Royal Hamilton Light Infantry on White Beach. Some of the "Rileys" were forced to clear the casino and enter into close-quarter combat inside the walls of the dilapidated structure, including a dreaded hand-to-hand confrontation with its German defenders.[37] Right across the beach, cohesion at the battalion and company level began to break down, leaving the initiative to carry on in the hands of individual solders, platoons or even section-sized groups of intrepid but desperate men.

Although most of the Royal Hamilton Light Infantry remained trapped on the beach on either side of the casino, several men penetrated into the western part of the town through the walls of the local theatre (now a museum dedicated to the raid), about thirty yards beyond the boulevard de Verdun, reaching the post office, the Gestapo headquarters and Saint-Rémy church. This area was the only "bright spot" on the main beach—the obvious place for Ham Roberts to send reinforcements should he plan to exploit the success. Unfortunately, the Essex Scottish did not share the Rileys' relative good fortune on Red Beach.

Here, on the main beach, only two small parties, including Howard Large's group, crossed the promenade at full gallop while under heavy fire and reached the boulevard de Verdun, with the survivors disappearing into the buildings nearby that separated the beach from the port. The first party, led by the company sergeant major, Cornelius Stapleton, reached their objective: the structures overlooking the trawlers where the inner channel met the Quai Henri IV. The party that included Howard Large found itself trapped in a cellar somewhere between the beach and the harbour. But having suffered more than 75 percent casualties in little over an hour, the remnants of Lieutenant Colonel Fred Jasperson's 500-strong battalion were unable to continue organized fighting. Although they were but a stone's throw from the trawlers and less than a hundred yards from the Hôtel Moderne, they could go no farther. Without tank support, they did not possess the size, strength or firepower to achieve their objectives unless they received significant reinforcements.

When the *Locust* finally made it across the Channel to Dieppe, she was twenty minutes behind schedule and too late to contribute effectively to the Essex Scottish attack on the main beach. Given what transpired, though, it is doubtful that her four-inch guns would have made any difference. According to Jock Hughes-Hallett, not only was her lack of speed a factor but also, in the darkness, Red Ryder and her captain John Stride had her formed up behind the wrong landing group. Apparently "this mistake was not noticed until 0510hrs when she closed Red and White beaches at full speed arriving there about 0530hrs."[38]

When the smokescreen cleared, the entire Dieppe panorama came into view. To Douglas Bevan, the scene presented a paradox he never forgot: "It was a lovely day when we arrived there, early in the morning, beautiful blue sky. All Hell had been turned loose."[39] Indeed, the men on board saw smoke rising from the beachfront and the headlands, aircraft twisting and turning above to avoid German flak, the whole tableau accompanied by the constant sound of explosions in the distance. Meanwhile, the Royal Marines of Tiger Force remained on the upper deck, bodies pressed prone to avoid any stray bullets or shell fragments that might be flying around, preparing for their baptism of fire.

Due to the thick smokescreen and fires raging on the beach and in the town, Ian Fleming, located not far offshore on HMS *Fernie*, was able to see little of the actual fighting on the beaches. He could, however, hear the battle raging. The noise level provided hope that things would eventually proceed as planned, although the sight of returning landing craft, some shot up and already carrying wounded, suggested otherwise. For Red Ryder and his Cutting Out Force, the clock was now ticking. From the moment the first shot was fired, the chances for a successful pinch lessened with each passing minute. Despite the prevalent notion that the German defenders' "occidental attitude" of self-preservation would rule the day, they could still attempt to destroy the Top Secret signals material in their possession if they had enough time to recover from the initial shock.

As far as the records indicate, Ryder did not wait for the prearranged signal from the Essex Scottish, who in any event had bigger issues to worry about just then; at 0545 hours, he decided it was time for the *Locust* to play her part. Ordering Captain Stride to steer for the harbour entrance, Ryder recorded later that they made three headlong attempts to breach the mole. On each occasion, heavy fire rained down on the gunboat from the east headland—which, according to the plan, was supposed to be in the hands of the Royal Regiment of Canada. Instead, the Royals remained pinned down on Blue Beach at Puys, out of radio contact.

On the first attempt, neither Ryder nor Stride could locate the outstretched arms of the Dieppe jetties in the intense smoke, and after two near misses from large-calibre shells, Ryder ordered a quick about-face to prepare for another run. Sailing only eight feet above the waterline on the low-slung river gunboat's deck, Bevan recalled that, when the *Locust* unexpectedly turned hard following Ryder's command, the ship listed at such an angle that the men on the port side could scoop up the Channel water in their hands.[40] Below deck, Seaman John Parsons had little idea of what was happening above; all he knew was that the guns of *Locust* were blazing away, given the demands shouted down for a continuous stream of ammunition for the Chicago Piano and the other guns on deck.[41]

The second attempt met the same fate: the German guns were still active on the east headland, and those on the west headland were now reaching out for them too. This time Ryder asked Stride to reverse hard, backing away from the mole with all guns firing at whatever crevice tucked into Pollet Cliff belched fire and smoke at regular intervals. Undaunted, Ryder ordered yet another go at the harbour, hoping that in the intervening minutes the situation on the east headland had changed. However, in Ryder's words, "On the third occasion we were hit on the back of the bridge and two men were killed. We in the forward half of the bridge being saved by Stride's railway sleepers."[42]

Ernest Coleman, who had been designated to take the pinched material out of Dieppe on the motor launch, recalled:

> We came under heavy fire from a huge gun emplacement directly on the entrance to the harbour and by other shore batteries . . . the top deck of *Locust* was hit twice in quick succession . . . two were killed instantly and many more injured. I remember lying on the deck with no cover whatsoever, the speed of the shells coming over my head seemed to be parting my hair, they were that close. I saw one of the lads some short distance away from

me mumbling something or possibly praying, a few seconds later
I looked again, he was no longer with us.[43]

For Paul McGrath, the two hits on the *Locust* proved a pivotal moment
in his young life. "I was lying on the top deck . . . belly pressed hard
against the steel, rifle clutched in my right hand, my pulse at the double
and waiting with others of 10 platoon . . . for the moment to leap on
the quay side and go about our business."[44] Lifting his head for a brief
moment before the German shells hit home, he could see

> on the right, were the cliffs overlooking the shingle beaches and
> prominent waterfront. To the left were the lower escarpments
> dominating the harbour and the crooked channel leading to the
> inner harbour about a quarter of a mile from the entrance. Both
> heights were stiff with guns whose crews, relatively safe in their
> concrete bunkers, kept up a savage bombardment. They were
> having a field day.[45]

McGrath noticed his good friend "Ginger" Northern "some fifteen
feet away, not deigning to lie down" despite the obvious danger while
others lay prone beside him on the deck "adrenalin pumping and
primed for action."[46] Within seconds, another shell hit the *Locust* just
yards away from Coleman and McGrath. "The noise of the explosion
was gigantic," recalled McGrath.

> The shock of it blew all the fuses of my nervous system. I was
> petrified with such a terror it stunned my mind. I lay on the deck
> with a sort of premature rigor mortis, immobilized by the awful
> thought of an immediate and terrible death. The game of war,
> which I had been enjoying up to that point, had suddenly turned
> deadly serious. Of course, I had been aware that the game had its
> perils but getting killed was something that happened to other

chaps. Now, for the first time, it burst like a thunderbolt upon my consciousness that my life, too, was in danger of being abruptly snuffed out. The sods were actually trying to kill ME![47]

The air "thick with the smell of burnt explosives," McGrath noticed Sergeant John Kruthoffer, lying motionless on the deck.

> He was covered with small debris thrown up by the explosion and at first glance I thought he had been hit, but he grunted, stirred and expleted. He was shocked and unhurt, and like me, trying to collect his wits. Other members of the platoon lay nearby, some wounded and all in a state of shock.[48]

Not all of them escaped the wrath of the shells. Trying to collect himself, McGrath spotted the lifeless figure of Ginger Northern slumped against the bulkhead with one of the ship's crew rifling through his pockets. Prying himself from the deck, the nineteen-year-old corporal went over to inquire about this odd behaviour, only to be told by the petty officer in a gruff tone, "He's dead . . . and I'm taking his personal stuff to send back home . . . orders to throw the dead overboard . . . here, give me a hand." As they dumped the body overboard, McGrath wondered if his pal was the first member of the Royal Marine Commando to die on the raid. He was, but he would not be the last.

Red Ryder was under orders not to breach the harbour mole with the *Locust* if German artillery fire was still active, and the three futile and near-disastrous attempts to charge in had dramatically reinforced the wisdom of this provision in the plan. Losing the *Locust* while running the gauntlet was acceptable—the Royal Marines on board could "swim" to the stairs and fight on through the harbour if necessary— but nothing would be accomplished if she was sunk before reaching the inner channel. Now, having been denied on three occasions, Ryder received a direct order from Hughes-Hallett via radio at 0607 hours

A view of Dieppe on the day of the raid, showing British naval craft manoeuvring close inshore as fires burn in the background and the haze of the smokescreen billows around the landing zones. This is the perspective the men on HMS *Locust* would have had as they tried again and again to breach the harbour that morning.

An aerial image, captured by an RAF photo reconnaissance plane on the day of the raid, that reveals the outer harbour filled with German trawlers berthed at the Quai Henri IV, less than two hundred yards from the Hôtel Moderne to the left. In the background, smoke billows from the tobacco factory like a beacon marking the dividing line between Red and White Beaches—the shortest distance and most direct path from the main beach landing zones to the Hôtel Moderne and the trawlers in the harbour.

that the Locust should not "enter until the situation at Blue Beach clears."[49] Ryder pulled the gunboat back into the Channel but continued to exchange fire with the positions on the cliff, hoping that Catto's Royal Regiment would soon arrive from Blue Beach. For Jock Farmer, this respite was a welcome relief: "As there was very little protection on deck we dreaded the next salvo, but luckily Locust was still afloat. The skipper had already put her full astern and kept going until we were just out of range—for the time being."[50]

The force commanders aboard Calpe never had a clear idea about what was happening on the "sharp end"—on the beaches. Despite all the communications technology Mountbatten had installed on both command ships, the "fog of war" prevailed throughout the battle. Jock Hughes-Hallett and Ham Roberts were forced to make decisions based on a patchwork collection of information flowing in from numerous sources that was always incomplete, often contradictory and sometimes erroneous. The radio operators and forward observation officers tasked with relaying the events ashore had been cut down on the beach by enemy fire or had not even landed where expected. In the ensuing muddle, the commanders made some choices that, viewed through the safety of hindsight, seem wildly disconnected from reality.

By the time Hughes-Hallett ordered Ryder on the Locust to wait offshore, both he and Roberts knew that the landings on Orange Beach and Green Beach had scored some initial success, but they had no knowledge of the disasters on Yellow Beach and Blue Beach—only silence. With German gun positions on both headlands blazing away, they had to be aware that neither Doug Catto's Royal Regiment of Canada nor Cecil Merritt's South Saskatchewan Regiment had reached its prime objective and that the air attacks and naval bombardment had failed to deter the German gunners from raining fire down on the main beach or the seaward approaches to Dieppe. Most distressing for them was the news that the Calgary Tanks had arrived late, and that both the Royal Hamilton Light Infantry and the Essex Scottish, caught on the beach, were pinned down and reported to be taking heavy casualties. Despite the ominous news, in their view all was not yet lost.

The biggest decision for any commander in the heat of battle is whether to call in the reserve force—whether to reinforce the line or whether and when to call off an attack. There is no formula for the commander to follow in making this decision; rather, he trusts his instinct—what the Germans call *Fingerspitzengefühl*, or "fingertip feel." In this period of the war, some in the Anglo-Canadian high command held that commanders should not call off an attack before they had used the full extent of their force—an attitude particularly common in the cocky atmosphere of Combined Operations and among enthusiastic "thrusters" like Ham Roberts. Right from the start of the raid, Roberts and Hughes-Hallett had to weigh whether the losses incurred would justify the final result, and expectations at home were high: John Godfrey had classified the objectives of the pinch as A-1 targets—targets worth incurring heavy casualties to obtain. The dilemma was straightforward: if they embarked on an attack that incurred heavy casualties but in the process failed to achieve the main objective, then calling it off would be viewed as a waste of lives for no purpose; however, if they committed the rest of their force, in this case their reserves, and by so doing achieved their objective, then the extra cost would be considered worthwhile and justifiable.* [51] Despite the

---

* Lieutenant General Guy Simonds, who went on to lead the Second Canadian Corps in Normandy (and was Crerar's chief of staff at First Canadian Corps in 1942), summed up this philosophy in a speech to his officers in the summer of 1944: "As a Commander you must consider at the outset whether the losses incurred are going to be worth the final assault. You must determine where these losses are going to be the minimum you can afford in relation to the value of the objective. We can't fight the Boche without incurring casualties and every increasingly gloomy news pouring in over the radio, neither Ham Roberts nor Jock Hughes-Hallett would relent, and both seemed electrified by one pivotal but ultimately misleading message from the Essex Scottish. Within minutes of Hughes-Hallett's order for Red Ryder to wait, the command team learned that the "Essex Scottish R[egiment] crossed beaches and into houses at 604 [hours]."[52] That message marked the turning point in the Dieppe saga, and started a roller-coaster ride that ended in perhaps the most controversial set of decisions ever reached in Canadian military history—and one of the greatest blunders of the Second World War. Both Roberts and Hughes-Hallett assumed from the message that the whole battalion—all four companies and five hundred men, not just the remnants of two decimated and under-strength platoons—were in the town near the port and close to their targets. At this point, they decided to reinforce the Essex Scottish.

Minutes later, the news arrived that the Royal Regiment had failed to land on Blue Beach—but again the message was erroneous. The force commanders, thinking the Royals were still afloat rather than trapped on Blue Beach, immediately switched their landing zone, ordering them to come in over Red Beach and link up with the Essex

---

soldier must know this. My point of view is that if I can't embark upon an operation to take a certain feature, for example, unless it will be useful to me later, the operation is not worthwhile and I call it off with 50% casualties incurred, then I have achieved nothing but a waste of lives; if I continue, and incur a further 20% casualties and bring the operation to a successful conclusion, then the operation is worthwhile. I speak of casualties in grossly exaggerated figures. In no operations yet have I participated where casualties were not between 15% and 25% and even at that, 25% is still a grossly exaggerated figure." ("Report on the Address by Lt. Gen. G.G. Simonds, CBE, DSO, GOC 2nd Cdn. Corps, to Officers of 3 Cdn. Inf. Div. and 2nd Cdn. Armd Bde at the Château near Cairon by Major A.T. Sesia.")

as they tried to punch through to the port. Before long, Fred Jasperson's Essex Scottish began to report their true situation—that the battalion was pinned down on the beach and taking grievous casualties—but Hughes-Hallett and Roberts dismissed their cries, regarding them as the overexcited utterances of a green unit fighting its first battle. All they needed, they thought, was a little stiffening and reinforcement, either to consolidate their reported position in the town or to regain their momentum and push on into the port.

The force commanders also committed Lieutenant Colonel Dollard Ménard's Fusiliers Mont-Royal to the fray. At 0640 hours, Hughes-Hallett, no doubt in conjunction with Roberts, recorded that he issued orders for the FMR to land at Red Beach and link up with the Essex Scottish. That too was a disaster. The landing craft bringing them to shore lost their way in the dense smokescreen and scattered, landing parts of the five-hundred-man battalion at intervals all along Dieppe's shoreline, most of them near White Beach on both sides of the casino and at the foot of the western headland. Many of them were instantly gunned down or blown apart as they tried to cross the beach. Allegedly, a dozen men under the command of Sergeant Pierre Dubuc penetrated the town in the footsteps of the Royal Hamilton Light Infantry and made it as far as the two basins in the inner harbour. There, they apparently stormed aboard a set of barges, hoping to hand them over to the Royal Marines, but after a short firefight with the crews they ran short of ammunition and were forced briefly to surrender, before making their escape back to the beach.* [53]

---

* The account given by Sergeant Dubuc and entered in the official record was dismissed by his commanding officer, Lieutenant Colonel Labatt, as "absolutely preposterous from beginning to end." However, the Canadian Army Historical Unit under the legendary Canadian military historian Charles P. Stacey refused to dismiss the account in its entirety, although it included, as they said, "some embroidery."

At 0645 hours, Jock Hughes-Hallett summoned Red Ryder aboard the *Calpe* for a discussion—one that resulted in the most controversial decision of the entire deadly day. He met initially with Ryder alone, he wrote later in both his after-action report and his memoirs, while Roberts continued to monitor events from the bridge. After an emotionally charged exchange, he said, "with great moral courage, Ryder told me that he felt certain that any attempt to enter the harbour would be attended by the loss of all ships concerned, since they would have to run the gauntlet at point blank range of batteries of medium calibre guns concealed in the caves dug into the side of the cliff."[54] Given the fact that the orders had anticipated that result, Ryder's hesitation could have cost him his career, if not for his experience and his stature. Hughes-Hallett recorded that Ryder was "emphatic that this part of the operation was no longer on," and his "very forthright advice against carrying out his part of the operation showed as much moral courage in August as he showed physical courage when he won the VC in March at St. Nazaire. A lesser man might have felt it would be cowardly not to urge going ahead."[55]

With Ryder's position clear, they proceeded only then "to consult" with Roberts, who seems not to have been free to call the shots in the way Hughes-Hallett and Mountbatten would later claim. In his post-battle interpretation, Hughes-Hallett reluctantly followed Roberts's inexplicable order to commit the reserves to battle. However, in the words of the Australian journalist Wallace Reyburn, who spent hours observing the command team on board the *Calpe* during the battle, Roberts "had the look of someone in an office who had been given 'full authority' only to find that every time he turns around he finds the boss looking over his shoulder."[56] The evidence emerging in recently released documents shows that Hughes-Hallett was the main thread all through the raid—from conception to execution. This involvement, coupled with his confident and overtly ambitious personality, indicates that his account, supported in the postwar years by Mountbatten, is no more than an attempt to distance himself from the debacle by attributing their joint decision to Roberts alone. Both men in fact share full responsibility for the disaster about to unfold—what one Royal Marine called "the sea version of the Charge of the Light Brigade."[57]

While these decisions were being made, the Royal Marine Commando, including Ian Fleming's Intelligence Assault Unit (No. 10 Platoon), were waiting anxiously on the exposed decks of the *Locust* and the trailing French *chasseurs*. They had no clue what was about to befall them. For months they had trained intensively to run the gauntlet of Dieppe's inner channel, if necessary, in order to reach their targets in the outer harbour. Now, Red Ryder had wisely persuaded Jock Hughes-Hallett to cancel that axis of advance, but it is unclear whether he was in full agreement that they should be switched to an equally perilous course.

Less than thirty minutes after this crucial meeting, at 0708 hours, Hughes-Hallett, who had full authority to call off any naval action at any point during the raid, issued orders for a flotilla of landing craft to form up behind the *Locust*, and then at 0731 he commanded Ryder to "proceed as ordered."[58] Before his return to the river gunboat, Ryder shouted via megaphone to the men from Tiger and Robert Forces on *Locust* and the *chasseurs* to transship into the landing craft forming up behind the old river gunboat. Like the Fusiliers Mont-Royal, whose whereabouts were still unknown to Roberts and Hughes-Hallett, the Royal Marine Commando would go headlong onto the main beach with instructions to "exploit into the town and report to the Colonel of the Essex Scottish Regiment."* [59] The implications of these orders

---

* According to Captain Hellings, a Royal Marine officer riding on the *Locust*: "After the floating reserve had been landed there was no news, until Commander Ryder returned from *Calpe*, when he reported that Red and White beaches were clear of opposition and the General wished the Marines to go in and support the Essex Scottish through White Beach. The colonel (Picton-Phillips) gave his orders from

are now clear: The Royal Marines would not land as "simple rein-forcements," as many historical accounts claim. Rather, they would make one more attempt to reach their pinch targets in the harbour—albeit by different and distinctly desperate means.[60]

Within minutes of the order being issued, the men began their descent into an ad hoc flotilla of four ALCs and two tank landing craft (TLCs), some still smoking and battle-scarred from their earlier run. Once aboard the landing craft, Ernest Coleman noticed, as he recounts in his recently discovered memoir, that the battle surrounding them had whipped up to a feverish pace. "Dog fights were going on, German planes were also dive bombing the ships and small craft," he recorded. "How the cook on our boat managed to . . . make us some cocoa and sandwiches I will never know!"[61]

Jock Farmer, waiting impatiently to board one of the TLCs with the rest of No. 10 Platoon, could see and hear nothing but a cacophony of "explosions, tracer bullets and screams" from Dieppe's main beach. "Some of the landing craft," he noted, the half-wooden ones used by the Royal Hamilton Light Infantry, Essex Scottish and Fusiliers Mont-Royal before them, now burned "fiercely" like "death traps," while larger TLCs slowly sank on the shoreline. But even before they were all on board, the German gunners spotted them forming up through the intermittent gaps in the smokescreen. "Most of us managed to scram-ble aboard his craft," Farmer recalled. "Suddenly," he continued, "a

---

Locust THE IDEA BEING TO PASS THROUGH the beach to the town and there, reform and report to the Colonel of the Essex Scottish, the object of the force being to pass around the west and south of the town and attack the batteries on the eastern cliff from the south." However, B Company Commander Captain R.K. Deveraux reports, "I was told by Colonel Phillips that the whole force of the Royal Marine Commando was to go direct into the harbour." (Report Operation Jubilee Royal Marine Commando, 19 August 1942, statement by office commanding B Company, Captain R.K. Deveraux, TNA ADM 1/11986.)

couple of shells landed not far from us. The skipper of *Locust* immediately set us adrift."[62] Within minutes, the six landing craft were loaded and ready for their turn on Dieppe's main beach.

Meanwhile, reports flooded in from the Essex Scottish that shellfire was raining down on them from both headlands and that snipers were taking aim with machine guns from the tobacco factory and other buildings in front of them. These messages were quickly followed by desperate calls for immediate evacuation.[63] Then, starting at 0742 hours, a series of messages arrived that, to the over-optimistic force commanders, made it appear as if Operation Jubilee was finally coming together. Two messages confirmed that the Royal Regiment of Canada had indeed landed on Blue Beach, though they failed to indicate that Doug Catto's unit had already been wiped out there. Ham Roberts and Hughes-Hallett concluded there was still a slim chance that the Royal Marines could take the eastern headland. A message from Hunter Force, one of the Canadian combat engineer teams, indicated that they too were alive, after being out of touch for most of the morning.

Encouraged by these fragments, the force commanders decided to send in the remaining elements of the ungainly Calgary Tanks, to assist Jasperson, bolstered by the Royal Marines, in an attempt to punch through at the tobacco factory. Still they clung to the hope that they could grab their prime objectives in the port. In desperation, Brigadier Bill Southam, the commander of the 6th Canadian Infantry Brigade, which had just landed on the beach way behind schedule, exhorted the Essex Scottish to "go as far towards the trawlers as possible."[64] The final piece of this plan fell into place moments later when "elements" of the Calgary Tanks, after spending hours trapped on the beach and the promenade, reported that they had made "progress" in front of the tobacco factory.[65] To the commanders on *Calpe*, it seemed that the shortest and most direct route to the harbour and the Hôtel Moderne was about to open up—a hope that trumped any discouraging and realistic reports to the contrary.

At 0818 hours, with news that the situation on Red Beach was "out of control" and—erroneously—that White Beach was firmly in Canadian hands, the Essex Scottish and the Royal Marines began their death ride towards Dieppe.

FOURTEEN

ALL IN ON THE MAIN BEACH

Theirs not to reason why
Theirs but to do and die.

ALFRED, LORD TENNYSON,
"THE CHARGE OF THE LIGHT BRIGADE"

"**W**e are going in!" is the cry Corporal Paul McGrath remembers from that moment. As the order was passed quickly from man to man, one young Marine turned to Peter Huntington-Whiteley, standing next to Joseph Picton-Phillips at the back of the tank landing craft, and inquired, "For Christ sake, sir, where the fucking Hell are we?" For months the Royal Marines had trained in Portsmouth harbour for this moment, but for security reasons nobody except the officers had known the name of the port they planned to raid until the last moment; some, apparently, never knew. "I suppose I can tell you now," came the terse reply from the always correct lieutenant. "That," he said, pointing to the cloud of black smoke, "is Dieppe—and I want to see you in my office tomorrow morning for using improper language."[1]

Within seconds, all the boats, with the exception of one with mechanical trouble that trailed behind, were enshrouded in a smokescreen that muffled the sound of the engines. For some reason, only repetitive refrains of "Oh, Danny boy" raced through McGrath's mind. "For a while," he recalled, "we were in an eerie, fog-bound capsule of time," but as they drew near to the beach and the smoke cleared, shells of all calibres started to whizz overhead or fall between the craft. The closer they got to White Beach, the more intense it became, particularly from the western headland. Ernest Coleman, tucked along the starboard side of the landing craft nearest the cliffs, noted that "the noise from the machine gun was like somebody playing a kettle drum."[2]

For Bob McAlister, sitting with his Robert Force colleagues in a small landing craft that was following the TLC carrying members of Tiger Force, Picton-Phillips and No. 10 Platoon, the constant noise and explosions were "terrifying." He recalled:

> I couldn't see how I could summon up enough strength to lead my section into that inferno. I had a look behind me and what I saw gave me all the courage I needed and a great feeling of relief. The faces I looked at, including the officers sitting at the rear of the sections, were a mixture of my feelings. Their faces were white and drawn. I felt almost cheerful and could do anything.

Heading towards Dieppe at full speed, McAlister's boat was the first to be hit:

> There was a terrific bang at the rear of the craft. When I looked around the flames were shooting straight up for about 40 feet, like a blow torch. One man had just cleared the hatch and went straight into the water, another was climbing out through the flames, screaming in pain. He fell in the water and continued screaming. The first officer (naval) who was in the water was shouting to us to get off the boat at once as the petrol tanks could blow up. The third chap in the engine room of the boat

didn't make it. The naval chap kept shouting, "Get clear of the boat quickly, the tanks will catch fire." The smoke, fortunately for us, drifted across us as we piled out of the boat, hiding us from the guns on the cliff.[3]

With the German fire now increasing to fever pitch and the landing craft starting to drift apart in the smoke as they ran towards the beach, the futility of the charge began to dawn on Lieutenant Colonel Picton-Phillips, riding in the lead boat with the rest of Tiger Force and Fleming's IAU. Concluding that any effort to storm ashore would result in a useless waste of lives, the diminutive, eccentric but thoroughly determined Royal Marine commander embarked on a selfless and heroic action of the highest order—one witnessed by all aboard the landing craft, and one they could never forget. "The Colonel[,] realising the hopelessness of the situation," recorded Jock Farmer in his memoirs, "climbed on an ammunition box and, with Captain Comyn holding onto his legs as the boat was rocking heavily, put on white gloves so that other incoming craft would see him, and signalled them to turn back." In full view of the enemy on the shore and well above the protective steel walls, exposed to enemy fire, Picton-Phillips waved off the attack. "The next thing I noticed," a young Marine by the name of J.J. Dwan recalled, "was little puffs of green blanco coming off his equipment as he was being hit, then blood spurted from the left corner of his mouth and he slumped down on to the deck of the landing craft. Nobody could have lived through that fire doing what he did. It was the ultimate act of courage."[4]

The Intelligence Assault Unit history records that Huntington-Whiteley gave Picton-Phillips rum and comforted him in his last moments. His actions had saved some, but not all, of his Marines. Despite the signal, one or two other craft, and the TLC carrying the IAU, continued to plough their way to shore. As Paul McGrath, now standing next to the mortally wounded Picton-Phillips, recalled:

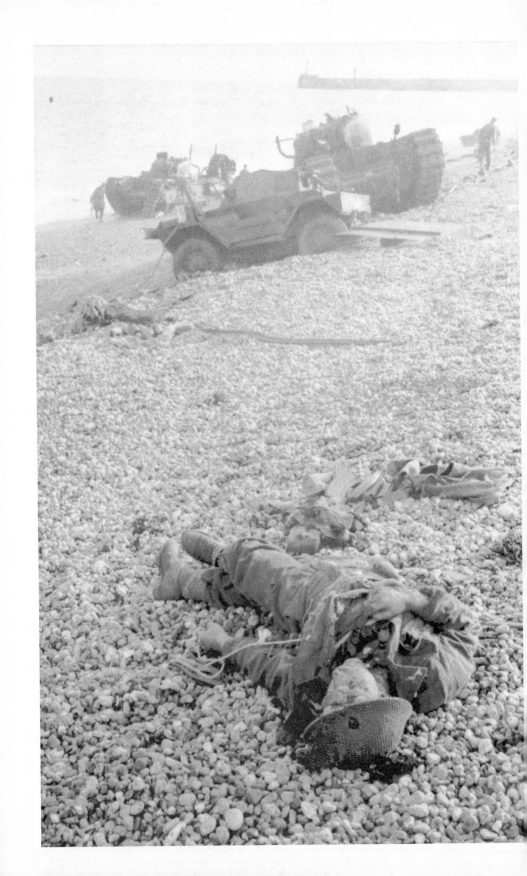

The Sub-Lieutenant who skippered our boat seemed unaware that the action had been called off. His job was to deliver us onto the beach at the designated point and he continued to drive forward at full throttle. The chaps at the bow were bracing themselves in the anticipation of the ramp falling in front of them, to be followed by a frantic scramble up the beach over potato-sized pebbles when, about thirty yards from the shore-line, the boat stopped abruptly. It was impaled on one of the many underwater obstacles that were submerged beneath the high tide.[5]

Then, suddenly, the vessel lurched to the starboard and righted itself. The quick spin gave some on board a glimpse of what lay ahead for them. As Sergeant John Kruthoffer noticed, the beach was

fireswept . . . occupied by prostrate bodies and a few desperate groups clinging to cover. A look in any direction showed only too clearly that along the whole stretch of beach the landing of tanks and infantry had been smashed to a standstill. For those of us who could see over the side, the feeling at that moment was not of panic or unreasonable fear—but sheer amazement and disbelief. Not a logical reaction, but a short space of a few seconds when the brain tries to reject what has been fed in. "Get out fast—spread out—and run like hell for cover."[6]

As much as Kruthoffer wanted to get off the ship, he could not: the ramp had been jammed by the grounding as well as a direct hit from a German gun concealed in a cave in the headland. They were hopelessly

―――――――――――――――――

OPPOSITE : A fallen Canadian soldier lies, almost as if at rest, on the rocky beach below the town of Dieppe. The large pebbles proved an unforeseen impediment to the Allies' tanks, stalling them on the beaches.

exposed to German fire, which now picked up in tempo and gave no signs of abating. McGrath watched in horror as "bombs and shells cascaded down around the boat and exploded in the sea[,] but some of the bullets struck home. There were gasps and groans and slumped bodies." Desperate to "get rid of us," the young naval sub-lieutenant in charge tried "to lower the ramp and finding it jammed, climbed up with a hammer. As soon as he showed himself he fell dead amongst us."[7] For Kruthoffer, the whole episode proved surreal, with only "parts of jigsaw" clearly remembered years later:

> A group at the front trying to kick the ramp down. The CO, the crewman and others hit and falling about; a scream at the back end trying to dodge small arms fire coming down amongst them. Those looking over the shore side or trying to climb out, getting it in the head or chest and crashing back on to those behind them. Some Bren-gunners at work—one immortal bawling for full magazines—another enthusiast firing from a sitting position, threatening to shoot the head off anyone moving sideways.[8]

There was no point in any attempt to return fire, but one Marine kept hammering away with his Bren gun in what McGrath called "a useless exercise." Hit again and again at the rear of the boat by German shells, some Marines died instantly while others found themselves hurtled into the sky and tossed overboard into the shallow surf.

Then, according to Coleman, "One of the naval ratings on the craft ignited a gas flare and tried to throw it over the side to give us some cover[,] but it hit the side and rebounded back into the craft."[9] The ALC, already covered with diesel oil from the engine and petrol from extra tanks that had been punctured by shell fragments, immediately erupted in flames. An alert regimental sergeant major ordered those sitting near the ammunition box to heave it overboard, even if alight. "We would have been blown to bits if the flames had reached it," a thankful Paul

McGrath reported. As more shells rocked the boat and the flames increased, the sergeant major, whom he never saw again, cried out, "I'm afraid it is every man for himself, try and make it back."[10]

But it was not easy to escape the flaming craft. "Being unable to disembark either through the front ramp or over the shore side," John Kruthoffer wrote,

> the start of a raging fire became a deciding factor even for those who had been slow in realising that their number was coming up. An effective smoke screen and very rapid movement meant that evacuation was carried out without many extra casualties. A quick check that those lying in the fire were dead—and then with anti-tank bombs and 36 grenades cooking and going off— instinct took over and saved the problem of planning the next move. Nobody made it ashore, except as POWs later, and the half-platoon which came back were those who were about to get out in one piece, and had the confidence to swim out towards home in the hope of being picked up.[11]

Once over the side, the survivors had a fateful choice to make: wade ashore to captivity and possible death or swim out to the Channel in the hope of being picked up before German fire or exhaustion got the better of them. For Paul McGrath and the rest of the IAU, the choice seemed obvious. "We crowded close to the boat's hull for protection against the bullets. I quickly inflated the Mae West and, not being a good long distance swimmer, its buoyancy encouraged me. Some voices were heard 'let's go to the beach.' Other voices, among them Sgt Kruthoffer's, urged 'Come on, let's make for the ships.'" Every man from Fleming's IAU decided to swim out to sea, hoping for rescue. Not all of them made it. The other craft that had not seen Picton-Phillips's frantic order to withdraw—the one carrying Major Titch Houghton—later landed its charges. All of them died on the beaches or fell into enemy captivity for the remainder of the war.

In 2007, John Barker, the son-in-law of Ernest Coleman, made an astonishing discovery: buried in secret beneath a dilapidated shed in the Coleman family's garden was his deceased father-in-law's account of the raid. Ernest Coleman was a Section leader in No. 10 Platoon, Company X of the Royal Marine Commando. His task, as he tells it, was to enter Dieppe to "secure . . . important documents" and bring them back to England. This famous photograph of a man whose trousers have been lost in the fighting is unidentified, but Ernest Coleman's account makes vivid sense of it for the first time:

> "At the promenade I met other prisoners who had been in the water, I sat down on the grassy bank on the edge of the promenade, I was not aware until this time that I had lost my underpants, they must have come adrift when I was in the sea. . . . The lads made me get in the centre of the column to save my embarrassment, I was still naked from the waist down, a bit later a Frenchman noticed me and handed me a pair of trousers, they were rather small for me but very much welcomed."

Ernest Coleman was now neck deep in water, huddled, as he tells the story, with the rest of the IAU alongside the burning landing craft, the fierce fire incinerating the bodies of the dead on board. "I was able to get around the side of the craft to get a little cover," he recalled,

> but we had few options open to us, some of the lads decided to swim out to sea, on seeing this I decided to join them, I stripped off my clothes except for my shirt and underpants, when boarding the landing craft I was given a Mae West, I also put this on, all the time we were still under heavy fire. I finally entered the water along with my weapons, swimming under water for as long as possible.[12]

About one hundred yards out, Coleman wrote, an explosion rendered him unconscious, and he awoke later having washed ashore. As he attempted to make a second break for the Channel, he crossed paths with two Germans, who took him prisoner.

Paul McGrath, floating out to sea on his back and using the Mae West for support, could see the landing craft still in flames. To his left, a motor speedboat suddenly catapulted out of the harbour at a frantic rate, in a desperate attempt to escape. Who was on it remains a mystery, but within three seconds a series of shells exploded as the Germans tried to find the range. "One behind, one in front, and one on target which disintegrated the boat," he noted. "The German gunners were on form that day."[13] Eventually, and near exhaustion, McGrath and the majority of his platoon (except for Coleman) were plucked from the English Channel and brought aboard *Calpe*, which by this time was conducting search and rescue and dodging the German bombers that were now appearing over the landing zone. Huntington-Whiteley, the man Fleming had chosen to lead what he hoped would be one of the most important missions of the entire war, was also missing. He had disappeared into the surf, and nobody had any idea what had happened to the commanding officer.

Although there is no record of any investigation, both Mountbatten's headquarters and John Godfrey's Naval Intelligence Division probably remained uneasy until Huntington-Whiteley's fate was established. With no knowledge of Bletchley Park or cryptographic methods or procedures, Huntington-Whiteley would not have seemed a prize intelligence catch. Unless German intelligence had some reason to suspect that there was more to him and his mission than his youthful demeanour betrayed, the secret would remain airtight. However, during the retreat from the beaches, Brigadier Bill Southam and his staff were taken prisoner and, in his abandoned landing craft, the Germans discovered an almost complete set of the highly intricate operational plan for Operation Jubilee—the document that Mountbatten had ordered his brigade commanders to take ashore. Contained in the surviving portions was Appendix L—the search plan for Dieppe—the same one I used to connect Huntington-Whiteley to the Hôtel Moderne and the naval headquarters. I had the luxury of knowing who he was and what he was after, but it would not have taken the Germans long to figure that out either: the German soldiers who discovered the documents belonged to MARES—the same German intelligence commando unit on which Godfrey and Fleming had styled their own Intelligence Assault Unit.* [14] Needless to say, when his interrogator plopped the captured search plan in front of him, Huntington-Whiteley would have had no place to hide. He would soon have been subjected to Nazi "enhanced interrogation," likely of the medieval sort.

Fortunately for all concerned, Huntington-Whiteley did make it out of Dieppe alive. Despite the burns he had suffered during the fire on board the landing craft, he had managed to swim out to sea rather

---

* The Germans were ruthless after they found the plans, rounding up several *Dieppois*, including the local printer, who had produced copies of the German maps for the local headquarters. The Germans accused him of giving copies to the resistance, who in turn gave them to the British for targeting purposes.

than fall into enemy hands and was picked up by a passing Royal Navy vessel, which brought him to the burn ward of the Brighton Municipal Hospital. In the description he wrote to John Kruthoffer from his hospital bed, he explained:

> It wasn't until Saturday that I learned that most of you had got back, and you can imagine my feelings, as for the previous three days I had been absolutely certain that I was the only survivor from our ill-fated [TLC]. I was picked up by a small flak ship manned by the royals who did some splendid shooting . . . I am right as rain now except for a peeling face, a couple of outsize lips and two brick-red legs which I consider very lucky remembering the amount of refuse that was flying about. I am going to write to the missing lads['] parents which will be very difficult as there is no definite news I can give them . . . In fact, the only one who I am certain about is poor [Ginger] Northern who, you may or may not know, was going to be married early in September.[15]

Finally, by mid-morning, after exhausting all the reserves and cancelling the landing of the remaining elements of the Calgary Tanks on the main beach, Ham Roberts and Jock Hughes-Hallett called off the operation just after 1000 hours.*

---

* The remaining two flights of PLCs, carrying the whole of A Squadron and three troops of C Squadron—a total of twenty-eight tanks—were never sent in. Although they did receive a signal at 0850 hours to land at White Beach, this order was countermanded ten minutes later during the approach. The two tank beach parties, instead of carrying out their planned initial tasks of directing the tanks to their objectives, spent most of their time in assisting wounded and in organizing tank cover for the general withdrawal. ("Extract of report from the Commanding Officer of 'B' LCT," app. 15 to encl. 13, p. 2, John Hughes-Hallett, "Naval Force Commander's Report No. NFJ 0221/92," 30 August 1942, LAC, RG 24/10872/232C2 [D48].)

Roberts sent a message by carrier pigeon back to England: "Very heavy casualties in men and ships. Did everything possible to get men off but in order to get any home had to come to sad decision to abandon remainder. This was a joint decision by Force Commanders. Obviously operation completely lacked surprise."

On the *Locust*, Red Ryder was also melancholy. Even years later he would be weighed down by the decisions made that day. "Coming back from Dieppe," he wrote in his memoirs,

> I had a nagging feeling that I had not lived up to my hopes and ambitions. We had made three attempts on the harbour entrance and received an explicit signal not to continue. And yet in view of what the Canadians suffered, should I not have pressed home our attack with more resolution? We would certainly have been sunk before reaching the entrance and one had to think of the many casualties it would have involved. It would have been a forlorn hope but might have helped others.[16]

On the *Fernie*, sitting at times just seven hundred yards off the main beach, Ian Fleming spent the day running between the bridge and the wardroom, trying to keep posted on the progress of the Royal Marines and his IAU. At times, according to his anonymous article in the *Weekly Intelligence Report*, he peered out through his binoculars. After the Royal Marines were dispatched to the main beach, he saw the *Locust* move towards the shore to take on the German guns in the east headland, "pumping 4-inch shells with incredible rapidity" while the tattered

---

OPPOSITE : Told to expect a one-day raid, a "return ticket" or "butcher and bolt" operation, the men of the raiding force were told to jettison their extra kit— including water bottles—in England, leaving many caught on the beaches or as prisoners in German hands thirsting for fresh water from any source.

landing craft went in. Off in the distance, he witnessed the British destroyer HMS *Berkeley* succumb to Luftwaffe bombs that crashed through its deck and exploded, leaving her to sink a stone's throw off the Dieppe coast. Then shells started to rip into the base of *Fernie's* funnel, killing and wounding a number of sailors.

As the wounded fleet headed back to England, Ian Fleming turned to catch one last glimpse of Dieppe through the smoke. Sporadically, through gaps in the smokescreen, he glimpsed the results of some of the heaviest fighting still going on in Dieppe. On the beach, he could now make out hundreds of small figures lying motionless in almost uniform pattern, punctuated by burning landing craft and the silhouettes of abandoned or trapped tanks. One landing craft that had ferried men and tanks to the shore only hours before was now crammed with the wounded and the bodies of the dead. The casino where he had fared poorly in his pre-war jaunts sat in near ruins. "It was a drunken mockery of a building," he wrote, confessing with "unholy delight" his satisfaction at seeing the "smile wiped off its face." "There was practically no movement, although heavy firing was still going on. It was a scene of utter desolation and destruction which one was glad to leave, though with a heavy heart."[17]

Two days after Fleming returned to England, he sat down at his desk in Room 39 and typed up a report addressed to Wing Commander Bobby de Casa Maury, Mountbatten's Chief Intelligence Officer. When Godfrey read it, he sent it directly to Mountbatten with a note: "I have read the attached notes by Commander Fleming who was present at Operation Jubilee in the course of his duties, and I generally agree with his remarks. I am forwarding the report personally to you as I think you may be interested to see what one of my staff has to say." Although most of Fleming's treatise revolved around issues of security, he concluded that the Germans had no advance knowledge of Operation Jubilee.

In these candid remarks, Fleming also addressed the real reason he had been on the *Fernie*. He admitted that he was not there as a simple observer, overseeing the debut of his new IAU, as many biographical treatments maintain, but because it was his job to participate actively in the raid. "I was accommodated in HMS *Fernie* with instructions to return to the nearest British port with any booty obtained by the IAU under the command of Lt. Col. Picton-Phillips, R.M. carried in HMS *Locust*. The IAU did not land and in consequence I remained in HMS *Fernie* throughout the operation and withdrawal." Here, in one document, is Ian Fleming's confession that has sat in the archives for years, but with the exception of one account that missed its significance, it has never before been published in any writing about Dieppe.[18] Fleming was to be the anchor man of the relay, with the Essex Scottish passing the booty to members of the IAU, who would then have Ernest Coleman whisked out of Dieppe harbour on a special motor launch to meet Fleming on *Fernie*. From there, with the battle still raging on shore, Fleming, perhaps accompanied by Ernest Coleman, would have headed directly to the nearest British port, bringing back what in cryptographic terms was the proverbial Holy Grail.

Less than two years after he had paced the shores of England's damp Channel coast waiting for Operation Ruthless to bear fruit, Fleming, unlike his legendary literary super-agent James Bond, had been foiled again. Nothing could be clearer: this intelligence pipeline was central to the Dieppe Raid, and Fleming was the final link in the chain designed to bring the pinched material home.

EPILOGUE

I n 1942, Ron Beal's war, like that of the overwhelming majority of the men who landed on Dieppe's beaches, was in essence fifty yards wide and fifty yards deep. As an infantry private in the Royal Regiment of Canada, he would not have been privy to the significance of the role his unit would play in relation to the overall plan. For the regular infantryman, the prevalent wisdom of the day dictated that he needed to know only just enough to get the immediate job done and nothing more. Such is the nature of military security, based on the strictest interpretation of the "need to know" principle. Without knowledge of the planning sessions in Richmond Terrace, or the ability to eavesdrop on radio traffic during the battle, or be a fly on the wall at Bletchley Park or in Room 39, Ron Beal's initial understanding of what he went through was as narrow as his job description. However, when he returned from the war, he began his life's journey, searching for the rationale behind what he and his comrades had experienced on August 19, 1942—something that seemed all too irrational. His quest translated into an advanced knowledge of all aspects of the raid—albeit knowledge based on the incomplete historical verdicts built up over the last seventy years.

For decades, his frustration and bitterness grew. The long litany of excuses, historical arguments and counter-arguments about what motivated the raid simply never made sense to him—or failed to satisfy his distinctly restless soul. Like many of the others who took part in the raid—and indeed like many in the generations that followed these veterans, including many of Beal's close friends—he felt they were, as he would say, "just thrown away." This was the Ron Beal I met with one spring morning in 2012 when I sat down to interview him for the documentary *Dieppe Uncovered*.

At first, I did not plan to reveal my years of research or my findings in a detailed way to the ninety-three-year-old veteran. However, my production partner on the film, producer/director Wayne Abbott, sensed Beal's profound angst and so we spent the afternoon with documents in hand, taking him step by step through the story that now appears in these pages. His response was both moving and profound.

Indeed, the new evidence, interwoven with the established historical record so thoroughly explored over the decades, fundamentally changes our understanding of Dieppe. But clearly, without that groundbreaking work of two previous generations of very talented historians, I would not have understood the potential of the initial discovery I made two decades ago in the British National Archives. Time too has been on my side, as the classified archives of the various intelligences services in England, Canada and the United States have slowly opened to the public. Such is the collective nature of history.

As the years passed, the new evidence fell into place like pieces of a jigsaw puzzle—and there will be more to come. These new documents have made a significant contribution to the Dieppe saga, demonstrating that the search for intelligence material was not *a* driver for the raid but indeed *the* driver. Certainly the four-rotor crisis was the most urgent problem facing British naval intelligence, and the beleaguered Allied war effort in general. After the failure of the Dieppe pinch, the crisis worsened. But just two months later, in October, pure luck—in this case a "pinch by chance" from a floundering U-boat off Port Said in Egypt by a group of heroic Royal Navy sailors—saved the day. That pinch, which included a four-rotor machine and its ancillary tables and code books, permitted the cryptanalysts in Frank Birch's

Naval Section to develop systems that, with a few exceptions, read this traffic for the remainder of the war. As the planners of the pinch raid at Dieppe certainly understood when they sanctioned the force commanders to go "all in" to obtain this objective, one good pinch could do the trick, as had happened in Norway. The evidence makes clear that they never doubted the importance of this material or the potential influence it would have on the course of the war.

We now know too what the main "targets" were. Until these were revealed, and their prime, urgent importance to the war effort contextually understood, their inclusion in the planning documents made little sense. That has changed, as it is now clear that both naval headquarters located in the Hôtel Moderne and the nearby trawlers were front and centre from the start, and remained constant imperatives throughout. The plans that Jock Hughes-Hallett and his team drew up for Dieppe—with, as is now apparent, crucial input from John Godfrey and Ian Fleming—saw all roads lead to the port and these targets. Even when the raid was postponed, these targets did not change; their centrality was, in fact, accentuated.

The resources devoted to the pinch and their coordination in the plan also provide compelling evidence. Nearly half the entire raiding force was committed to supporting the pinch (in both Operation Rutter and Operation Jubilee): two infantry battalions, the Royal Marine Commando containing Fleming's specially crafted IAU, one-third of the Calgary Tanks and the majority of the engineer units, not to mention the naval outlay that included "expendable" vessels such as the *Locust*. One must also consider the choice of Red Ryder—a recently minted Victoria Cross winner—to command the Cutting Out Force. Ryder, who had a passion for intelligence and would go on to command 30 Assault Unit after Dieppe, was one of very few men in the entire Royal Navy who possessed actual raiding experience. That rare commodity alone would have precluded risking him on a secondary objective such as a publicity stunt, a theory that has been promulgated over the years. If you were willing to risk losing Ryder, the potential payoff had to be significant.

The plan itself, now clarified after the discovery of Royal Marine Commando orders and the record of the coordinating meeting, is revealed to have a remarkable redundancy built right into it to ensure the objective was achieved. Three waves of troops, supported by tanks, engineers, a river gun boat, a sloop and half a dozen French *chasseurs*, were tasked with carrying out the pinch: first the Essex Scottish, Calgary Tanks and Royal Canadian Engineers; then the Royal Marines, broken down into two strike forces set to spring into action twenty minutes apart. Surely, the thinking went at the time, at least one of these three groups would succeed. If not, the "floating reserve" was standing by offshore, with the remaining Calgary Tanks and the Fusiliers Mont-Royal, which if necessary could form a fourth wave. No other objective in the Dieppe operation received such major attention or rivalled this effort in the slightest.

Compounding this evidence, the very way in which Jock Hughes-Hallett and Major General Ham Roberts handled the operation from their floating headquarters aboard the *Calpe* shows how firmly they were focused on the pinch. As the morning progressed, they continually tried to reinforce the Essex Scottish in their attempts to get to the trawlers and the Hôtel Moderne. Although more attractive opportunities for advancing inland appeared—in particular the relatively secure and tank-friendly Green Beach, and to a lesser extent White Beach after the casino fell—the commanders discounted these options. Yet each of these alternatives would have sufficed if their main objective had been to obtain a quick victory for public relations points, to bolster sagging morale, entice the Germans to fight, draw off German resources from the eastern front, build Mountbatten's reputation, or raid for the sake of raiding—all theories suggested over the past seventy years. Instead, on three separate occasions, the documents show that even when the operation did not unfold "according to plan," Ham

Roberts, no doubt with the support of Jock Hughes-Hallett, favoured a straight run down the middle of the main beach, over the shortest, most direct route to their targets in the port. Following Ryder's three futile attempts to breach the harbour mole under heavy fire, and after news reached them of the Essex's precarious position, they augmented the plan on the spot, ordering the Royal Regiment of Canada to land on Red Beach in direct support when it appeared they could not land on Blue Beach at Puys. This was soon followed by orders to land the Fusiliers Mont-Royal on the main beach and then send in the Royal Marines and the remaining tanks in their wake. The key here is that all had orders to link up with and reinforce the Essex Scottish, who, although pinned down and suffering heavily, seemed within inches of reaching the trawlers and the Hôtel Moderne.

In aerial photos taken during the raid, we can see there were indeed German trawlers berthed in the outer harbour; and from German records it is now known that sometime during the morning, when it became evident that the port might be overrun, the special security unit tasked with destroying sensitive documents went into action. As the battle raged, they proceeded to fill and drop overboard seven stuffed bags of Top Secret signals material in order to destroy their contents. The last bag, however, failed to sink, leading to a near-comical scene in which they used grenades to try to scuttle the floating sack. Instead of perforating it as expected, the explosion blew the contents sky-high, showering the dock with the very material they were trying to destroy— part of the proverbial pot of gold the raiders were after.

Despite the importance of the raid to the war effort, and although the commanders were operating in an atmosphere that condoned heavy casualties in order to achieve the pinch, by no means does the new evidence exonerate Ham Roberts or Jock Hughes-Hallett, or lessen their responsibility for the failure of the Dieppe Raid. However, it does cast their decision making in a fresh light that now raises a new set of questions for generations of Canadians and others—historians, military professionals and armchair generals—to consider. What must be factored in is the terrible human cost itself. In the end, it too forms a piece of compelling evidence.

On that one day in August, roughly one thousand Allied soldiers, sailors and airmen lost their lives for what appeared to be no real purpose, with approximately another three thousand wounded or taken prisoner. What is truly striking, and what has never been considered before, is the proportion of casualties incurred in pursuit of the pinch part of the raid. Of the 369 Royal Marines involved, one hundred—over a quarter—were either killed, wounded or captured. Had it not been for the selfless sacrifice made by their commanding officer, Lieutenant Colonel Joseph "Tiger" Picton-Phillips, that toll would have been dramatically higher. The cost to the other units involved was even more alarming. The Essex Scottish lost 530 men either killed, wounded or captured on Red Beach—96 percent of the total number they took into Dieppe. The Royal Regiment of Canada suffered similarly, losing 534 at Blue Beach (96 percent), with the Fusiliers Mont-Royal losing another 513 men (88 percent) and the Calgary Tanks 174 men and twenty-nine Churchill tanks. In total, after factoring in the casualties from the Canadian combat engineers, the naval officers and the ratings, the number of men lost whose involvement was specifically with the pinch reached over 1,800—of whom 500 were killed. All told, this accounts for over half of the casualties sustained and deaths suffered in the Dieppe Raid.

In sum, the evidence is irrefutable that the pinch formed the main driver for Operation Jubilee. Even a cynical interpretation of the raid would have to admit that, if the raid was a pinch by opportunity at its conception, it was a pinch by design at delivery. But the evidence is mounting that, as in other raids, Jock Hughes-Hallett and his planning syndicate had the pinch in mind right from the start: less than a month after the most successful pinch raid up to that time (at Vaagso and Lofoten), and just forty-eight hours after John Godfrey introduced a new pinch policy, Dieppe, long considered a possible raiding target due to its proximity to England, was added to the list of likely targets for the coming year. Because the planning for the raids at St-Nazaire and Bayonne were in their final stages, Dieppe sat on the back burner until early/late April. It exploded onto the scene, firmly supported by the NID, following the failure of those two raids to produce the coveted pinch material. And it provided a perfect opportunity to use the newly formed Intelligence Assault Unit.

With the Axis Powers on the offensive around the world, raiding proved the only way to access the desired material on land in a fashion that offered greater cover. To pinch effectively, the British had to overrun their targets and then cover their tracks, which meant using over-compensation, or the "sledgehammer to crack a nut" approach. In this case, the employment of disproportionately large forces to deflect suspicions not only brilliantly succeeded in blinding the enemy, but also generations of observers long after the war ended.

When I first read those two sentences at the British National Archives in 1995—"No raid should be laid on for SIGINT purposes only. The scope of the objectives should always be sufficiently wide to presuppose normal operational objects"—the implication was fantastic, moving, I thought, into the realm of speculation and conspiracy theories. Would they really mount a raid of that size and magnitude to cover a pinch? As more classified documents were released over time and the evidence started to build; slowly a new view of the raid emerged, with this passage now key. The Dieppe Raid was a natural extension of the earlier pinch raids, but it was coupled with a new policy for carrying them out—a new form of "special operations," albeit on a scale never witnessed before.

Generally speaking, there are no monocausal operations of the scale and complexity of Dieppe. In order to get a combined operation off the ground in 1942, planners needed to have objectives that would appeal to each of the players before they would agree to participate. For the War Office, Dieppe provided a chance for it to maintain its operational dominance over the Channel area in the face of the fast-rising Mountbatten and his Combined Operations; it was also an opportunity to take the offensive and get the Canadian Army some much-needed experience, placating their unyielding demands for action. For the Royal Air Force, Dieppe was an occasion to draw the Luftwaffe into battle and test various tactics and schemes, including harnessing Ultra and signals intelligence as an asset to be used in air battles. For the Royal Navy, in addition to the obvious benefits that would flow from a successful pinch, there were other attractions, such as testing out their ability to sneak a massive raiding fleet across the Channel under the cover of darkness and using cutting-edge technology to deceive the enemy, foil their radar and signals intelligence capabilities, and achieve surprise. Finally, both strategically and politically, Jubilee—had it been successful—would probably have drawn at least some German forces from the eastern front and would temporarily have placated both Stalin and the Americans in their calls for a second front in Europe.

There is no doubt that each of these imperatives was a driver, but not the main one. After the raid at St-Nazaire failed to strike gold by chance or opportunity, after the abortion of Operation Myrmidon at Bayonne and the cancellation of Rutter, Operation Jubilee looked like the only way of scoring a dramatic and potentially war-changing pinch. This was not just a naval intelligence problem, or simply an Admiralty or "British" problem; when the blackout hit, it quickly became an Allied problem, for the constant, uninterrupted flow of intelligence had been helping everyone. Everything depended upon control of the sea lanes, just as the body depends on blood in the veins to sustain life. And that meant that air, land, sea, industrial and domestic concerns— the very centre of gravity for the Allied war effort—were at stake.

And then there is Ian Fleming, whose important position as an intelligence officer began to surface a few years ago but whose true role in the raid remained shrouded in mystery. Fleming's actual inclusion in the raid was an enormous—and in hindsight irresponsible—risk to take if the stakes were not high. Fleming was, after all, Ultra indoctrinated and knew the inner workings of Bletchley Park; and as the DNI's personal assistant and main liaison officer, he had intimate knowledge of the landscape of British and Allied intelligence. He was privy to secrets that could prove highly damaging if he was captured. Even his presence on *Fernie* close by the main beach at Dieppe was either incompetent from a security perspective or a calculated roll of the dice undertaken because the stakes were high enough and the potential payoff deemed worth the risk—particularly for naval intelligence.

The inevitable question that will arise in light of all the new evidence is whether or not Dieppe was worth it in the end. No doubt that debate will rage on. Were the deaths of nearly a thousand men and the loss of three thousand others worth the potential, but unrealized, gain? Was there a better way to go about it than this? With hindsight, we might think so. But it is clear now that, at a moment when Britain's and the larger Allied war effort was in a most vulnerable state, what was at stake was—in the context of the time, wisely or unwisely—deemed worth the risk.

Perhaps the last voice on this should be that of Ron Beal, who, along with only a few comrades, not only survived the raid and German captivity but dedicated his life to finding the answer to a seemingly simple question: why?

That afternoon, after spending some time with him going through the recently declassified documents, I asked his opinion of them. At first, as could rightly be expected, all he was able to murmur was, "I'm in shock." On camera, he reiterated his original comment about his friends being thrown away for no reason. Then, in tears, he listed their names, apologizing for his sobbing, saying, "You'll have to forgive an old man, but I guess I am like a lot of the other ones, that carry very heavy loads about their friends that didn't make it." The old soldier gathered himself abruptly, and after a pause to reflect he said, "It gave me a different perspective on why there was a Dieppe Raid . . . there was a reason behind it. Despite the fact that it was never accomplished, that doesn't mean anything. There was an objective, and I know in my heart that my comrades did not die for nothing; that there was an absolute reason and purpose to the raid."

At that point, we shut the cameras off and took a much-needed break. Ron Beal turned back towards his wife, who had stood by his side throughout his post-war ordeal. Then, as if finally liberated from shackles he had worn for seven decades, he looked at me and uttered the line that made all the years of research worthwhile. "Now," he said, the tears welling up again, *"now I can die in peace. Now I know what my friends died for . . ."*

The redoubtable Essex Scottish veteran, Private Howard Large, survived the carnage on Red Beach and actually made it into the town and as close to the trawlers and the Hôtel Moderne as anyone did on that day. Like many of his comrades, he was forced to surrender. He lost his leg as a result of a wound he received in Dieppe. He spent the next few years in a prisoner-of-war camp in eastern Poland before being marched across much of east and central Europe in the dead of winter in 1945, as part of Hitler's "forced march."

Private Ron Beal of the Royal Regiment of Canada spent several horrifying hours pinned to the bottom of the cliff after landing under intense fire as his comrades fell around him on Blue Beach. After the real reasons behind the raid were revealed to him in 2012, he was moved to say: "Now I can die in peace. Now I know what my friends died for."

ABBREVIATIONS

ALC	assault landing craft
CIA	Central Intelligence Agency (United States)
CCO	Chief of Combined Operations
CMHQ	Canadian Military Headquarters (London)
COHQ	Combined Operations Headquarters
COI	Co-ordinator of Information (United States)
DDNI	Deputy Director of Naval Intelligence
DNI	Director of Naval Intelligence
FBI	Federal Bureau of Investigation (United States)
GC&CS	Government Code and Cypher School
GHQ	General Headquarters
IAU	Intelligence Assault Unit
ISIS	Inter-Services Information Series
ISSB	Inter-Services Security Board
ISTD	Inter-Services Topographical Department
JIC	Joint Intelligence Committee
MEW	Ministry of Economic Warfare
MI6	Secret Intelligence Service
MTB	motor torpedo boat
NID	Naval Intelligence Division
OIC	Operational Intelligence Centre
OSS	Office of Strategic Services (United States)
PWE	Political Warfare Executive
RAF	Royal Air Force
RDF	Radio Direction Finding
RFP	Radio Finger Printing (see Glossary)
RNVR	Royal Naval Voluntary Reserve
SIS	Secret Intelligence Service (or MI6 as it is popularly known)
SIGINT	signals intelligence (see Glossary)
SOE	Special Operations Executive
TLC	tank landing craft

GLOSSARY

BLOCK SHIP: a ship purposely sunk to render a port or waterway unusable

BOMBE: a high-speed electromechanical device designed specifically to decipher Enigma-encrypted messages, originally designed by Polish cryptographers in the 1930s and perfected by the British at Bletchley Park

"C": the name by which the Chief of the Secret Intelligence Service was known, his or her actual identity being top secret until only recently. Stewart Menzies was "C" at the time of the Dieppe Raid.

CIPHER: a disguised writing system in which individual letters are replaced by other letters. Enigma was a cipher machine. To decipher an enciphered message requires knowledge of the cipher key. Second World War German cipher keys included *Offizier* (officer), *Stab* (staff), *Triton* (for U-boats), *Heimisch* (for German home waters; later called *Hydra*, or *Dolphin* by the British), *RHV* (a hand cipher) and *Werftschlüssel*, a dockyard hand cipher.

CODE: a disguised writing system in which groups of letters, or entire words, or even groups of words, are replaced by symbols (which might be letters, numbers or words). WW (*Wetterkurzschlüssel*), for example, was a weather code used by the Germans.

CRUISER: a warship that is smaller than a battleship but larger than a destroyer. Types of cruisers used in the Second World War include the heavy cruiser, the anti-aircraft cruiser and the German pocket battleship.

CRYPTANALYSIS: the process of decoding/deciphering codes and ciphers using analysis

CRYPTOGRAPHY: the process of writing or decoding/deciphering codes and ciphers. Cryptanalysis is a form of cryptography.

DIRECTION FINDING, or DFING: the process of establishing the direction from which a received signal was transmitted. Methods included HF/DF (Huff Duff), or high-frequency direction finding, and VHF/DF, or very high-frequency direction finding.

E-BAR: a type of German short signal

E-BOAT: the English name for a German motor torpedo boat, which the Germans called S-boot (*Schnellboot*, "fast boat" or "speedboat")

KRIEGSMARINE: the name given to the German navy between 1935 and 1945

MARES (*Marine Einsatzkommando*): the German naval commando unit

M-BOAT (*Minensuchboote*): large German minesweeping vessels

PINCH: a military operation in which sensitive material, such as intelligence material, is stolen (or "pinched") from the enemy

POCKET BATTLESHIP: a form of heavily armed cruiser peculiar to the Kriegsmarine. There were only three pocket battleships: the *Deutschland*, the *Admiral Scheer* and the *Admiral Graf Spee*.

RADIO FINGER PRINTING, or RFP: a technology that was capable of identifying the particular wireless set from which a message was transmitted by photographing its wave form

R-BOAT (*Räumboote*): small German minesweeping vessels

RHV (*Reservehandverfahren*): an emergency hand cipher used by vessels as a backup for Enigma when it broke down or on vessels not yet outfitted with the machine

S-BOAT: see E-boat

SHORT SIGNAL: a coded wireless message of fewer than twenty-two characters. German short signals included E-bars and Z-bars.

SIGINT: signals intelligence, which included cryptography, direction finding, radio finger printing and traffic analysis

SPECIAL INTELLIGENCE: see Ultra

SUPER-BATTLESHIP: an unofficial classification used to denote the very largest German battleships, such as the *Bismarck* and *Tirpitz*, as opposed to the pocket battleships

SURFACE RAIDER (also known as merchant raider): an armed military vessel disguised as a non-combatant commercial vessel

TINA: see *traffic analysis*

TRAFFIC ANALYSIS (code-named TINA): a form of intelligence in which the patterns in wireless communication are analyzed (even if the messages themselves cannot be decrypted)

TRIBAL-CLASS DESTROYER: a type of destroyer constructed for the Royal Navy and Royal Canadian Navy before and during the Second World War, including HMS *Bedouin* and HMCS *Haida*

U-BOAT (*Unterseeboot,* "undersea boat"): the English name for a German military submarine, specifically those used during the First and Second World Wars

UJ BOAT (*U-Jäger,* "submarine hunter"): a German anti-submarine vessel

ULTRA: a security classification for intelligence derived from tapping into enemy communications, via cryptanalysis or signals intelligence. The cryptographic component of this was known in the Royal Navy as Special Intelligence.

WRENS: members of the Women's Royal Naval Service (WRNS)

ENDNOTES

ABBREVIATIONS USED IN THESE NOTES:

ADM, Admiralty; CAB, Cabinet Office (U.K.); CAFO, Confidential Admiralty Fleet Order; CANUKUS, Canada–U.K.–U.S.; DEFE, Ministry of Defence (U.K.); DHH, Directorate of History and Heritage (Department of National Defence, Canada); DU, *Dieppe Uncovered* (Northernsky Entertainment, 2012, producer/director Wayne Abbott, for History Television in Canada and UKTV in the United Kingdom, first aired August 19, 2012); FO, Foreign Office (U.K.); GOD, Godfrey Papers; GRO, Baillie-Grohman Papers; HW, Government Communications Headquarters; LAC, Library and Archives Canada; MG, Manuscript Group; NMM, National Maritime Museum (Greenwich, U.K.); RG, Record Group; RMM, Royal Marine Museum Archives (Portsmouth, U.K.); TNA, National Archives (United Kingdom).

ONE: THE CANADIAN ALBATROSS

1.   Ronald Atkin, *Dieppe 1942: The Jubilee Disaster* (London: Macmillan, 1980), 252.
2.   Juno Beach Centre, "The Dieppe Raid," http://www.junobeach.org/e/2/can-eve-mob-die-e.htm (accessed February 18, 2013).
3.   Jock Gardner, "Admiral Sir Bertram Ramsay," in Stephen Howarth, ed., *Men of War: Great Naval Leaders of World War Two* (London: Weidenfeld and Nicolson, 1992), 360.
4.   Sir Harry Hinsley, "The Influence of Ultra in the Second World War" (lecture, Cambridge University, 19 October 1993).

TWO: A VERY SPECIAL BOND

1.   The nickname "Blinker" came from Hall's chronic facial twitch, which caused one of his eyes to "flash like a navy signal lamp."
2.   Nicholas Rankin, *Ian Fleming's Commandos: The Story of 30 Assault Unit in WWII* (London: Faber and Faber, 2011), 29.

Endnotes

3. Donald McCormick, 17F: The Life of Ian Fleming (London: Peter Owen, 1994), 47. Donald McCormick was a historian and journalist who served with Fleming in the NID and later alongside him as a journalist on the foreign desk of the Sunday Times in the postwar years.

4. Ibid., 48.

5. Ben Macintyre, For Your Eyes Only (London: Bloomsbury, 2012), 231–33. Kindle edition.

6. Ibid.

7. Ibid., 123–25. According to Macintyre, Ian Fleming kept a signed, framed copy of the eulogy as a personal treasure throughout his life.

8. J.H. Godfrey, "The Naval Memoirs of Admiral J.H. Godfrey," Vol. V, 1947–1950 NID, Part II, 284 and 387, NMM GOD/171. Godfrey's memoirs (called "Naval Memoirs" in these notes) and the hundreds of pages he either penned or had produced for what he hoped would eventually form a definitive history of the NID have remained in their unpublished form at several archival repositories, including the British National Archives, the National Maritime Museum and the Churchill College Archives in Cambridge.

9. William Plomer, "Ian Fleming Remembered," in Encounter (January 1965), quoted in Godfrey, "Naval Memoirs," 397.

10. Macintyre, For Your Eyes Only, 160–62.

11. Plomer, "Ian Fleming Remembered," 400.

12. Charles Babbage, The Writings of Charles Babbage (Alvin, TX: Halcyon Press, 2009), Kindle edition; Bruce Collier and James MacLachlan, Charles Babbage and the Engines of Perfection (New York: Oxford University Press, 1999); Abdul Montaqim, Pioneers of the Computer Age: From Charles Babbage to Steve Jobs (London: Monsoon Media, 2012).

13. McCormick, 17F, 40.

14. Ibid., 41. Fleming wrote a paper on Babbage's work on cryptography for Godfrey, which apparently has never been found.

15. Ibid., 30.

16. J.H. Godfrey, "Ian Fleming," NMM GOD/177.

17. Godfrey Papers, 10 November 1966, NMM GOD/161.

18. Ibid.

19. Godfrey, "Ian Fleming."

20. William Plomer, address given at the Memorial Service for Ian Fleming, 15 September 1964, NMM (Papers of Vice Admiral Sir Norman Denning 2/4).

21. J.H. Godfrey, "Room 39," 10 July 1948, 1–3, NMM GOD/93.

22. Godfrey, "Naval Memoirs," Vol. 5, Part II, 386.

23. "Ian Fleming: The Playboy Interview," in *50 Years of the Playboy Interview*, Kindle 2012.

24. NMM GOD/161.

25. Godfrey, "Ian Fleming."

26. Nigel West, *Historical Dictionary of Ian Fleming's World of Intelligence: Fact and Fiction* (Lanham, MD: Scarecrow Press, 2009), 67.

27. J.H. Godfrey, "The Significance of British Naval Intelligence during WWII, and Post War Security," 6 April 1965, NMM GOD/97; Naval Section miscellaneous papers, TNA HW 8/23.

28. NMM GOD/161. Italics are underlined in original.

29. NMM GOD/161.

30. J.H. Godfrey to Donald McLachlan, 5 April 1965, NMM GOD/97.

31. Godfrey, "Significance of British Naval Intelligence."

32. Godfrey, "Ian Fleming."

33. Godfrey, "Naval Memoirs," Vol. 5, Part II, 387.

34. Personnel file of John Henry Godfrey, TNA ADM 196/92/39.

35. Patrick Beesly, *Very Special Admiral: The Life of Admiral J.H. Godfrey, CB* (London: Hamish Hamilton, 1980), 84.

36. NMM GOD/170.

37. ADM 196/92/39.

38. Godfrey, "Naval Memoirs," Vol. 5, Part II, 271.

39. NMM GOD/161/2.

40. Ibid.

41. Godfrey, "Naval Memoirs," Vol. 5, Part I, 105.

42. NMM GOD/161/2.

43. Ibid.

44. Ibid.

45. McCormick, 17F, 53.

46. NMM GOD/161/2.

47. Ibid.

48. J.H. Godfrey, "History of Naval Intelligence Division 1939–1942," 12, TNA ADM 223/464.

49. Godfrey, "Naval Memoirs," Vol. 5, Part II, 207.

50. Ibid.

51. Ibid.

52. NMM GOD/161/2.

53. Godfrey, "Naval Memoirs," Vol. 5, Part II, 207.

54. NMM GOD/161/2.

55. Godfrey, "Naval Memoirs," Vol. 5, Part II, 387.

56. "Madrid: the Claire Case," TNA FO 1093/225.

57. NMM GOD 171. Quoted in Robert Harling, "Where Bond Started," *Sunday Telegraph* (London), August 16, 1964.

58. NMM GOD/161/2.

59. J.H. Godfrey, "Afterthoughts: Naval Propaganda," 87, TNA ADM 223/619.

60. Godfrey, "History," 146, ADM 223/464.

61. Rankin, *Ian Fleming's Commandos*, 106.

62. Godfrey "History," 146.

63. Quoted in McCormick, 17F, 51.

64. Godfrey, "Naval Memoirs," Vol. 5, Part II, 278.

65. NMM GOD/170.

66. McCormick, 17F, 71.

67. Quoted in ibid., 55.

68. Alan N. Scheider, "Ian and I," *Naval Intelligence Professionals Newsletter* (Fall 1987).

69. "Ian Fleming, 007—James Bond," TNA Sefton Delmer Archive (accessed online August 11, 2013).

70. McCormick, 17F, 96.

71. Donald McLachlan, "Room 39: Top Secret Birthplace of Bond," quoted in Godfrey, "Naval Memoirs," Vol. 5, Part II, 394.

THREE: A RUTHLESS START

1. NMM GOD/161.

2. Naval Section GC&CS, memo, 7 September 1940, TNA HW 25/18.

3. Note by P.R. Chambers ADI, 17 October 1940, TNA AIR 20/5238.

4. "Air Ministry Instructions for Operation 'Ruthless,'" 17 October 1940, 3, TNA AIR 20/5238.

5. J.H. Godfrey, "History of Naval Intelligence Division 1939–1942," 263, TNA ADM 223/464.

6. Ibid.

7. Winston Churchill, speech to House of Commons, 21 January 1941.

8. Old Mersey Times, "Loss of the *Athenia* 1939," http://www.old-merseytimes.

co.uk/ATHENIA.html (accessed August 12, 2013).

9. Godfrey, "History," 264.

10. Ibid.

11. "CANUKUS Joint Services SIGINT discussions held in Washington, 6–17 April 1942," HW 14/46.

12. Jak P. Mallmann Showell, *Enigma U-Boats: Breaking the Code* (Birmingham, U.K.: Ian Allan, 2009), 86. Kindle edition.

13. The original Enigma machine, used by the German army and air force, offered only five wheels.

14. B. Jack Copeland, *Turing: Pioneer of the Information Age* (Oxford: Oxford University Press, 2013), 644–46. Kindle edition.

15. David Kahn, *The Codebreakers: The Story of Secret Writing* (London: Macmillan, 1966).

16. A.P. Mahon, "History of Hut 8," 18, TNA HW 25/2.

17. Mavis Batey, *From Bletchley with Love* (Bletchley, U.K.: Bletchley Park Trust, 2008).

18. Copeland, *Turing*, 976–80.

19. I.G. Good, "From Hut 8 to the Newmanry," in B. Jack Copeland, *Colossus: The Secret of Bletchley Park's Codebreaking Computers* (New York: Oxford University Press, 2006). Kindle edition.

20. Godfrey, "History," 264.

21. Head of Naval Section to Denniston, 19 October 1940, TNA HW 8/46.

22. Godfrey, "History," 264.

23. GC&CS, "The Handling of Naval Special Intelligence," app. B to ch. XIII "Activities of German Naval Units in the Channel," 10 September 1940, TNA HW 8/46.

24. Ibid.

25. Ibid.

26. Ibid., 5 December 1940.

27. Ibid.

28. Birch to Denniston, 21 December 1940, TNA HW 8/22.

29. Ibid.

30. Ibid.; Birch to Denniston, 27 December 1940, TNA HW 8/22.

FOUR: ANNUS MIRABILIS

1. J.H. Godfrey, "History of Naval Intelligence Division 1939–1942," 246, TNA ADM 223/464.

2. Dönitz had "absolute commitment to victory, absolute belief in his men and the

force he commanded, absolute hatred of the enemy creed, indeed of the enemy, absolute commitment to his own country and creed. He was a convinced Nazi." P. Padfield, "Grand Admiral Karl Donitz," in S. Howarth, ed., *Men of War: Great Naval Leaders of World War II* (London: Weidenfeld and Nicolson, 1993), 178.

3. Lord Hankey, *Diplomacy by Conference: Studies in Public Affairs 1920–1946* (London: E. Benn, 1946), 148.

4. Bernard Edwards, *Attack and Sink: The Battle of the Atlantic 1941* (New York: Brick Tower Press, 2006), 80–81. Kindle edition.

5. "Evidence as to the Use of SIGINT in certain Naval Operations," TNA HW 50/95.

6. Ibid.

7. Christopher M. Bell, *Churchill and Sea Power* (Oxford: Oxford University Press, 2013), 203. Kindle edition.

8. Bell, *Churchill and Sea Power*, 215.

9. "Admiralty Use of Special Intelligence in Naval Operations," 56, TNA ADM 223/88.

10. Ibid.

11. Ibid.

12. Intelligence from intercepted German, Italian and Japanese radio communications, ZTP 819 (2355hrs, 25 May 1941), ZTP 820 (1925hrs, 25 May 1941), ZTP 822 (0111 hrs, 26 May 1941), TNA DEFE 3/1.

13. "Admiralty Use of Special Intelligence," 66.

14. Tom McGowen, *Sink the Bismarck: Germany's Super-Battleship of World War II* (Brookfield, CT: Twenty-First Century Books, 1999).

15. William H. Garzke, Jr., and Robert O. Dulin, Jr., *Battleships: Axis and Neutral Battleships in World War II* (Annapolis, MD: Naval Institute Press, 1985).

16. "Admiralty Use of Special Intelligence," 76.

17. Marc Milner, *Battle of the Atlantic* (Stroud, Gloucestershire, U.K.: History Press, 2011).

18. "Technical Intelligence and the Processing of Captured Documents," 56, TNA HW 43/23.

19. Grand Admiral Karl Doenitz, *Memoirs: Ten Years and Twenty Days* (New York: Da Capo Press, 1997).

20. TNA HW 8/103.

21. "Handling of Naval Special Intelligence," 171, TNA HW 8/46; "Report on British Procedure for Capturing and Exploiting Captured Enemy Naval Documents," 2, HW 8/103.

22. "German Ciphering Machines Quoted in Handling of Naval Special Intelligence," CAFO 1544, 184, TNA HW 8/46.

23. TNA HW 8/103.

24. TNA HW 8/46.

25. "Technical Intelligence and the Processing of Captured Documents," 65, TNA HW 43/23.

26. J.H. Godfrey, "Churchill and Combined Operations," MM/GOD/161.

27. "Handling of Naval Special Intelligence," TNA HW 8/46.

28. Ibid.

29. Operation Claymore, TNA CAB 121/447.

30. Most Secret memo to the Prime Minister, Operation Claymore, from Colonel Hollis, 27 January 1941, TNA CAB 121/447.

31. Godfrey, "History," 163.

32. Ibid.

33. TNA DEFE 2/142. As an example of the type of report that appeared in Allied papers, the *Singleton Argus* from New South Wales, Australia, ran the headline TEN GERMAN SHIPS SUNK: EFFECTIVE RAID ON LOFOTEN ISLAND on Friday, March 7, 1941. In the short article that followed, they stressed the ship sinkings, the destruction of the fish-oil plant, the rescue of Norwegian patriots and the capture of prisoners.

34. "Handling of Special Naval Intelligence," 175, TNA HW 8/46.

35. Ibid.

36. Ibid.

37. Ibid.

38. Ibid.

39. U-boat Archive, http://www.uboatarchive.net/U-110-3rdEscortGroupLTBalmeReport.htm.

40. "Handling of Special Naval Intelligence," 176, TNA HW 8/46.

41. David Kahn, *Seizing the Enigma: The Race to Break the German U-Boat Codes, 1939–1943* (Houghton Mifflin, 1991), 173.

42. "Handling of Special Naval Intelligence," 177, TNA HW 8/46.

43. Ibid.

44. Ibid., 175.

45. Ibid., 177.

46. Ibid.

47. J.H. Godfrey, "The Naval Memoirs of Admiral J.H. Godfrey," Vol. V, 1947–1950

NID, Part II, MM GOD/170.

48. Although no current financial statements have been made public, it is a long-held view that GCHQ, the successor to GC&CS, maintains the largest budget of all the intelligence services in Great Britain, something echoed in the United States with the NSA and in Canada with the CSEC.

FIVE: SWIMMING WITH SHARKS

1. Ralph Erskine, "Naval Enigma: the Breaking of Heimisch and Triton," *Intelligence and National Security* 3(1) (1988): 162–83.

2. "History of Hut 8," 74, TNA HW 25/2; and Schlüssel M (Form M4) c. 22 January 1942, HW 8/24.

3. In fact, the "four-rotor" did not have a fully functioning fourth wheel but rather a set half-wheel that did not move with the others when the machine was in operation. Although this restriction theoretically reduced the machine's efficiency, it still massively increased the odds against decryption.

4. TNA HW 1/118; HW 1/122.

5. Ibid.

6. Short signals used a code book to make up messages that were then enciphered on Enigma. There were three editions of the book. Edition 1: 1939–20 January 1941, indicator taken from first letter of transmitted message. Edition 2: 20 January 1942–10 March 1943, indicating tables used: Weimar 20 January 1942–25 October 1942, Eisenach 25 October 1942–11 January 1943, Naumburg 11 January 1943–10 March 1943. Edition 3: 10 March 1943–8 May 1945, indicating tables changed on the first of every month.

7. Naval Section memorandum, "A survey of 'Werftschlüssel,'" 23 November 1941, TNA HW 8/23.

8. Adrian Smith, *Mountbatten: Apprentice Warlord* (London: IB Tauris, 2010). Kindle edition.

9. *Life* magazine, 17 August 1942, 64.

10. TNA ADM 196/93/0/56; ADM 196/123/0/346; ADM 196/147/0/425.

11. Mountbatten's alleged homosexuality was a source of constant debate before and after his assassination in 1979. His most recent biographer, Adrian Smith, has found no direct proof of any homosexual relations between the Chief of Combined Operations and Coward or any of the other openly gay men whom he kept as friends. Smith states categorically that "no correspondence held by

the University of Southampton contains any obvious suggestion of a homo-erotic relationship," though he does caution that "this is scarcely surprising as any intimate letters would remain firmly under lock and key at Broadlands [Mountbatten's home]." Smith, *Mountbatten*, 23.

12. Elizabeth Nel, *Winston Churchill by His Personal Secretary: Recollections of the Great Man by a Woman Who Worked for Him* (Bloomington, IN: iUniverse, 2007), 1045–46. Kindle edition.

13. Donald McLachlan, *Room 39: Naval Intelligence in Action, 1939–45* (London: Atheneum, 1968), xi.

14. TNA ADM 196/93/0/56; ADM 196/123/0/346; ADM 196/147/0/425.

15. McLachlan, *Room 39*, xi.

16. Quoted in David Reynolds, *In Command of History: Churchill Fighting and Writing the Second World War* (Harmondsworth: Penguin Books, 2005), 12528–29. Kindle edition.

17. "Brigade 115 Force Operation Order 1," 6 December 1941, TNA ADM 202/352.

18. For Anklet, see TNA CAB 121/455; ADM 116/4381; ADM 202/351; ADM 202/352.

19. For Operation Archery, see TNA WO 231/5; WO 199/3057; AIR 20/1050; WO 32/10535.

20. Ken Ford, *Operation Archery: The Commandos and the Vaagso Raid 1941* (Oxford: Osprey Publishing, 2011), 18.

21. Hugh Sebag-Montefiore, *Enigma* (London: Weidenfeld and Nicolson, 2000).

22. Ibid.

23. Ibid.

24. *London Gazette*, 16 August 1940.

25. John Hughes-Hallett, "Before I Forget," Hughes-Hallett Papers, LAC MG30-E463.

26. Lieutenant Commander A. de Costobadie, DSC, RN, "Report on Operation Archery," in Niall Cherry, *Striking Back: Britain's Airborne and Commando Raids 1940–1942* (Solihull, U.K.: Helion & Co., 2010), app. XIII.

27. Ibid.

28. Ibid.

29. Ibid.

30. Ibid.

31. "Handling of Naval Special Intelligence," 177, TNA HW 8/46.

32. Ibid.

33. Ibid.

34. Ibid.

35. Naval Section Memorandum No. 12, "State of Work Report, February 1942," 3 January 1942, Naval Section Miscellaneous Papers, TNA HW 8/24.

36. William Manchester and Paul Reid, *The Last Lion: Winston Spencer Churchill: Defender of the Realm, 1940–1965* (New York: Little, Brown, 2012), 10408–10. Kindle edition.

37. Naval Section memorandum, 9 March 1942, Naval Section Miscellaneous Papers, TNA HW 8/24.

38. Naval Section Memorandum No. 6, 31 January 1942, TNA HW 8/24.

39. Naval Section Miscellaneous Papers, TNA HW 8/24.

40. Schlüssel M (Form M4), c. 22 January 1942, HW 8/24.

41. "History of Hut 8," 74, TNA HW 25/2; and Schlüssel M (Form M4) c. 22 January 1942, HW 8/24. The date of the message referring to the outfitting of two destroyers was January 14, 1942.

42. TNA HW 8/24 S.

43. Naval Section Miscellaneous Papers, 20 January 1942, TNA HW 8/24.

44. J.H. Godfrey, "History of Naval Intelligence Division 1939–1942," 46, TNA ADM 223/464.

45. Cavanaugh Report, 7, TNA HW 8/103.

46. Ibid., 16–17.

47. Ibid., 8; and Schlüssel M (Form M4), TNA HW 8/24.

48. A glossary of German naval technical terms was also of paramount importance. When the cryptographers managed to break into the German messages, they were confronted by the plain-language technical terms that could be almost as daunting as a cipher itself.

49. Cavanaugh Report, 8, TNA HW 8/103.

50. Ibid. According to the historian at GCHQ, these cards were destroyed at the end of the war as they were considered "ephemeral" and therefore not for historical preservation.

51. Ibid.

52. Ibid.

53. Godfrey to Mountbatten, 13 May 1942, University of Southampton Mountbatten Papers, MB1/B15.

54. Mountbatten to Godfrey, 15 May 1942, University of Southampton Mountbatten Papers, MB1/B15.

55. Frank Birch, "Our Intentions," 11 April 1942, TNA HW 8/24.

56. Ibid.

57. Frank Birch to Captain Haines, 7 April 1942, TNA HW 8/24.

58. TNA ADM 196/93.

59. Baillie-Grohman to Mountbatten, 14 September 1942, NMM GRO/29.

60. Ibid.

61. Ibid.

62. Mountbatten to Baillie-Grohman, 17 September 1942, NMM GRO/29; TNA ADM 196/93. A further assessment of Hughes-Hallett from 1942 related that "he had a forceful personality and much self-confidence and is generally right, but not quite always."

63. Hughes-Hallett, "Before I Forget," 117.

64. Ibid.

65. Ibid., 106.

66. TNA ADM 196/149/615.

67. Hughes-Hallett, "Before I Forget," 118.

68. COHQ, "War Diary, Operation Bludgeon," TNA DEFE 2/2.

69. Hughes-Hallett, "Before I Forget," 117; "Operation Myrmidon," TNA DEFE 2/366.

70. Hughes-Hallett, "Before I Forget," 117.

71. Ibid., 118.

72. Ibid.

SIX: FADE TO BLACK

1. Grand Admiral Karl Doenitz, *Memoirs: Ten Years and Twenty Days* (New York: Da Capo Press, 1997), 202

2. Gudmundur Helvason, "U-109," http://uboat.net, http://uboat.net/boats/u109.htm (accessed August 11, 2013).

3. The Wrecksite, "SS *Tacoma Star*," http://www.wrecksite.eu/wreck.aspx?31352 (accessed August 11, 2013).

4. U-boat Archive, "Report of 4th War Patrol U-109," http://www.uboatarchive.net/AdmiraltyMessage1942-MAY-Frame.htm (accessed August 11, 2013).

5. Gudmundur Helvason, "Tacoma Star," http://uboat.net/allies/merchants/ships/1307.html (accessed August 11, 2013).

6. U-boat Archive, "Report of 4th War Patrol U-109."

7. Ibid.

8. Ibid.

9. "U-Boat Tracking and Anti-U-Boat Warfare" NID 8S, 3, TNA ADM 223/284; John

Godfrey, NID 8S "U-Boat Tracking," 24 April 1947, ADM 223/284.

10. "U-Boat Tracking and Anti-U-Boat Warfare" NID 8S, 3, TNA ADM 223/284.

11. Ibid.

12. "History of Hut 8", TNA HW 25/2.

13. Ibid., 65.

14. Michael Smith, *The Secrets of Station X: How the Bletchley Park Codebreakers Helped Win the War* (London: Biteback, 2011), 2624–29. Kindle edition.

15. Ibid., 2666–69.

16. Jim DeBrosse and Colin Burke, *The Secret in Building 26* (New York: Random House, 2004).

17. "U-Boat Tracking and Anti-U-Boat Warfare."

18. Naval Intelligence Division and Operational Intelligence Centre, Intelligence Reports and Papers. Operational intelligence: special intelligence monographs, TNA ADM 223/294.

19. TNA ADM 223/464; Memorandum No. 65, RFP and TINA, 8 September 1942, HW 8/24; Naval Section Analysis of RFP/TINA on U/B W/F, July–August 1942, HW8/24.

20. Godfrey to Rear Admiral Willis, 19 January 1942, TNA ADM 223/285.

21. Ibid.; TNA ADM 223/464.

22. Godfrey to First Sea Lord and Vice Chief Naval Staff (VCNS), 9 June 1942, TNA ADM 223/285.

23. Ibid.

24. TNA ADM 223/464; Hervie Haufler, *Codebreakers' Victory: How the Allied Cryptanalysts Won World War II* (New York: New American Library, 2003), 1488–90. Kindle edition.

25. Naval Air Requirement, 27 February 1942, ADM 205/15; T.D. Statistical Section, "Note on Annual rate of loss of Merchant tonnage (Required for the First Lord)", 18 March 1942.

26. Naval Air Requirement, 27 February 1942, ADM 205/15.

27. First Sea Lord's Records 1939–1945, "Merchant Tonnage Sunk by Enemy Action as Reported up to 22nd December 1942" (Thousands gross tons), TNA ADM 205/14.

28. "Requirements in Aircraft to Regain Command at Sea," c. October 1942, TNA ADM 205/15.

29. Naval Air Requirement, 27 February 1942, ADM 205/15; T.D. Statistical Section, "Note on Annual rate of loss of Merchant tonnage (Required for the First Lord)",

18 March 1942.

30. Ibid.

31. Ibid.

32. Ibid.

33. William Manchester and Paul Reid, *The Last Lion: Winston Spencer Churchill: Defender of the Realm, 1940–1965* (New York: Little, Brown, 2012), 10935–44. Kindle edition.

34. DeBrosse and Burke, *Secret in Building 26*, Prologue.

35. T.D. Statistical Section, "Note on Annual rate of loss of Merchant tonnage (Required for the First Lord)", 18 March 1942.

36. Director of Plans, "Memorandum: Sea and Air Power in Future Developments," 27 February 1942, ADM 205/15.

37. Naval Air Requirement, 27 February 1942, ADM 205/15.

38. Ibid.

39. "Imports into United Kingdom 1942," ADM 205/14.

40. Memo for First Sea Lord, 25 June 1942, TNA ADM 205/20.

41. Ibid.

42. Director of Plans, "Memorandum: Sea and Air Power in Future Developments," 27 February 1942, TNA ADM 205/15; "Requirements in Aircraft to Regain Command at Sea," c. October 1942, ADM 205/15; Naval Air Requirement, 27 February 1942, ADM 205/15.

43. Laurence Paterson, *2nd U-Boat Flotilla* (Annapolis, MD: Naval Institute Press, 2003), 139.

44. Elizabeth Nel, *Winston Churchill by His Personal Secretary: Recollections of the Great Man by a Woman Who Worked for Him* (Bloomington IN: iUniverse), 1403–11. Kindle edition.

45. Naval Air Requirement, 27 February 1942, TNA ADM 205/15.

46. Sir Dudley Pound to Vice Chief Naval Staff (VCNS) et al., 24 February 1942, TNA ADM 205/15; Christopher M. Bell, *Churchill and Sea Power* (Oxford: Oxford University Press, 2013), 259. Kindle edition.

47. Martin Gilbert, "Churchill and Bombing Policy" (Fifth Churchill Center Lecture, Washington, D.C., 18 October 2005).

48. WSC memorandum, "A Review of the War Position," 21 July 1942, CAB 66/26/41WP (42) 311, quoted in Bell, *Churchill and Sea Power*, 385.

49. Tovey to Pound, 7 June 1942, ROSK 7/210, quoted in Bell, *Churchill and Sea Power*, 262.

50. National Security Agency, Early Papers Concerning U.K.–U.S. Agreements, "Aide Memoire for the President," 8 July 1940.

51. Herbert Osborn Yardley, *The American Black Chamber* (New York: Bobbs-Merrill, 1930).

52. "History of Liaison with OP-20-G (Washington)", 4, TNA HW 8/49.

53. Robert L. Benson, "Origins of British-American Intelligence Cooperation (1940–1941)", U.S. National Security Agency web page.

54. David O'Keefe interview with Professor Sir Harry Hinsley, Cambridge University, Cambridge, 13 February 1996.

55. Ibid.

56. Ibid.

57. Benson, "Origins of British-American Intelligence Cooperation."

58. J.H. Godfrey to Ted Merrett, 19 February 1965, NMM GOD/68.

59. Message for C.S.S. from Tiltman Washington, 27 November 1941, TNA HW 57/10.

60. Godfrey to Hastings, 23 January 1942, TNA ADM 223/285; and Message for Naval Attaché, 5 March 1942, TNA ADM 223/285. In March 1942, the British had yet to deliver upon their promise to provide a captured naval Enigma to OP-20-G. With the Ultra pipeline now dry and unable to aid in reducing the slaughter off the Eastern Seaboard, the U.S. Navy fired off a message direct to its naval attaché in London that not only violated proper channels and normal protocol but reinforced Britain's two greatest fears concerning American insecurity and impatience: "Urgently desire the Admiralty furnish Navy Department one captured German Naval Enigma Cipher Machine, even if damaged and inoperative, plus all available keys, even though out of date. This in accordance agreement mutual exchanges all cryptographic information of Axis Powers under which U.S. Government furnished Japanese Purple Machine and other Japanese naval and diplomatic codes and ciphers to British Government. Also request all available captures or solutions of weather report, contact report, and other minor systems."

61. Quoted in Stephen Puleo, *Due to Enemy Action: The True World War Two Story of USS Eagle* (San Francisco: Untreed Reads, 2013), 56.

62. DeBrosse and Burke, *Secret in Building 26*.

63. "Enigma Policy," 5 May 1942, TNA HW 57/9.

64. Ibid.

65. Colin Burke, "Agnes Meyer Driscoll vs. the Enigma and the Bombe," http://userpages.umbc.edu/~burke/driscoll1-2011.pdf (accessed March 27, 2013).

66. DeBrosse and Burke, *Secret in Building 26*, ch. 4.

67. Burke, "Agnes Meyer Driscoll."

68. Ronald Lewin, *Ultra Goes to War* (Barnsley, U.K.: Pen and Sword Books, 2008), 144.

69. Tiltman to Travis, 6 April 1942, TNA HW 57/9.

SEVEN: KICK AT THE DARKNESS

1. Originally known as NID6.

2. Godfrey to Menzies, 13 January 1942, TNA ADM 223/285.

3. Obituary of Margaret Godfrey, *Independent* (London), November 1, 1995.

4. J.H. Godfrey, "The Naval Memoirs of Admiral J.H. Godfrey," Vol. 5 1947–1950 NID, Part II, 284, MM GOD 171.

5. Ibid., 365.

6. Ibid., 284.

7. Ibid., 284.

8. J.H. Godfrey, "Churchill and Strategy," 16 June 1966, NMM GOD 177.

9. J.H. Godfrey, "Working with Churchill," 1966, NMM GOD 177.

10. Godfrey, "Naval Memoirs," Vol. 5, Part II, 288.

11. Ibid., 284. As Godfrey himself noted years later, the concept was truly profound and displayed foresight that he later argued served as a basis for the creation of the modern MOD structure in the United Kingdom.

12. J.H. Godfrey, "Afterthoughts: 'Total Intelligence,' the ISTD and Geographical Handbooks," 87, TNA ADM 223/619; Patrick Beesly, *Very Special Admiral: The Life of Admiral J.H. Godfrey* (London: Hamish Hamilton, 1980).

13. Godfrey, "Naval Memoirs," Vol. 5, Part II, 211.

14. "Inter-Services Topographical Department—The Early Days," TNA ADM 223/466.

15. Ibid.

16. Godfrey, "Naval Memoirs," Vol. 5, Part II, 285.

17. Nicholas Rankin, *Ian Fleming's Commandos: The Story of 30 Assault Unit in WWII* (London: Faber and Faber, 2011).

18. Bassett and Wells, "Inter-Services Topographical Department"; Beesly, *Very Special Admiral*, 205.

19. Beesley, *Very Special Admiral*, 205.

20. Godfrey, "Naval Memoirs," Vol. 5, Part II, 286.

21. Ibid., 289.

22. Ibid.

23. TNA WO 252/469.

24. Godfrey, "Naval Memoirs," Vol. V, Part II, 383.

25. C.E. Lucas Phillips, *The Greatest Raid of All* (London: Heinemann, 1958); and Jeremy *Clarkson: Greatest Raid of All Time* (BBC television documentary, 2007).

26. This dry dock had been specially built to service the passenger liner *Normandie*, hence its name.

27. Interestingly, Charles Lambe, the deputy director in the Plans Division and, after March 1942, the director, was one of Mountbatten's trusted confidants. Earlier, in 1936, Mountbatten had used his connections to secure Lambe an appointment as a royal aide-de-camp, partly as a career boost for his old friend, but primarily to ensure that the Royal Navy was permanently represented inside Buckingham Palace. In 1959, Lambe succeeded Mountbatten as First Sea Lord and Chief of the Naval Staff.

28. TNA DEFE 2/131.

29. Winston S. Churchill, *The Second World War*, vol. 4, *The Hinge of Fate* (Boston: Houghton Mifflin, 1950).

30. J.H. Godfrey, "History of Naval Intelligence Division 1939–1942," 56, TNA ADM 223/464.

31. TNA CAB 121/364. Although the citation has March 25 noted on it, this date is a mistake. According to Alan Brooke's diary, the meeting to discuss the outline plans for the raids took place on the morning of February 25. On March 25, he wrote, "no points of great importance" occurred. Considering that Chariot went in on March 28 and Myrmidon a week after that, there is no way that an outline plan for an operation of this size could gain approval and move into full operation in such a short space of time.

32. "Myrmidon Outline Plan," n.d., TNA DEFE 2/367.

33. "Myrmidon Summary," 22 February 1942, TNA DEFE 2/367.

34. Minutes from COS meeting, 25 February 1942, TNA CAB 121/364.

35. "Naval Orders Operation Myrmidon," TNA DEFE 2/367.

36. Ibid.

37. Ken Ford, *St. Nazaire 1942: The Great Commando Raid* (Oxford: Osprey Publishing, 2001), 63.

38. Richard Hopton, *A Reluctant Hero: The Life of Captain Robert Ryder VC* (Havertown, PA: Casemate Publishers, 2012), 4253–54. Kindle edition.

39. This road, however, was not without its bumps. On March 5, Godfrey sent a message that can only be described as a "rocket" to Mountbatten, complaining about a comment he had made at a Chiefs of Staff Committee meeting in which

Mountbatten claimed they did not have sufficient intelligence in the Bayonne area for Operation Myrmidon. "Actually, our intelligence on this part of the world is not at all bad and could easily be worked up . . . I do suggest in common fairness that it would be better to bring us into the picture as early as possible and, of course, you will appreciate how discouraging it is for my junior intelligence officers to see such a remark when they are simply longing to do all they can to help you and, incidentally, working very hard on our behalf. I am sure you won't mind my calling your attention to this, but Intelligence is a two-way traffic business. One's got to push and pull and not be content to sit down and let the stuff come to him." (Godfrey to Mountbatten, 5 March 1942, TNA ADM 223/90)

40. Quoted in Philip Ziegler, *Mountbatten: The Official Biography* (London: Collins, 1985), 170.

41. "Confidential Report on Operation Myrmidon," 9 April 1942, TNA DEFE 2/366.

42. Jock Gardner, "Admiral Sir Bertram Ramsay," in Stephen Howarth, ed., *Men of War: Great Naval Leaders of World War Two* (London: Weidenfeld and Nicolson, 1992), 360.

43. Mountbatten to Major General F.H.N. Davidson, Director of Military Intelligence, 14 May 1942, TNA DEFE 2/366.

44. Quoted in Ziegler, *Mountbatten*, 165. The actual motto was "United We Conquer."

45. On the occasion of Ryder's investiture, Mountbatten wrote: "I have never had more pleasure in writing to congratulate anybody than in writing to you for your grandly earned Victoria Cross. Alas, so few of the V.C.s of this war have been given to living people and it is essential for the younger officers and men coming along to have a few heroes to look up to who are still in the land of the living. I consider your V.C. will have achieved a double purpose: firstly, it is the greatest compliment that could be paid to the whole of your force; secondly, it will centre round it all the enthusiasm for the fighting spirit which is only awaiting an outlet in this country." (Hopton, *Reluctant Hero*, 4372–77)

46. Hopton, *Reluctant Hero*, 4399.

47. Phillips, *Greatest Raid of All*, xvii.

EIGHT: "AUTHORIZED LOOTERS"

1. "History of 30 AU," TNA ADM 223/500.

2. The only time the commandos came under Mountbatten's control was when they were attached to his headquarters for operational purposes by the War Office under orders from the chiefs of staff.

3. After Dieppe, the title for A Commando was changed to No. 40 Royal Marine Commando.

4. Dr. Anthony King, "The Ethos of the Royal Marines: Precise Application of Will" (report, Department of Sociology, University of Exeter, May 2004).

5. Ibid.

6. *Globe and Laurel*, August 1942, 75, quoted in King, "Ethos of the Royal Marines."

7. No. 40 Royal Marine Commando, "War Diary," TNA ADM 202/87.

8. Jock Farmer, *JOCK of 40 Royal Marine Commando: My Life from Start to Finish* (Shanklin Chine: Shanklin Chine Publishers, 2007).

9. R.E.D. Ryder, unpublished memoirs, courtesy of Mr. Lisle Ryder.

10. Farmer, JOCK.

11. Ibid.

12. Ibid.

13. Ibid.

14. Robin Neillands, *By Sea and Land* (Barnsley, U.K.: Pen and Sword, 2004), 20.

15. Ibid.

16. King, "Ethos of the Royal Marines."

17. "A History of 30 Commando (Latterly Called 30 Assault Unit and 30 Advanced Unit)," TNA ADM 223/214, ch. 2; Paul McGrath interview for DU.

18. Farmer, JOCK.

19. John Kruthoffer to Robin Neillands, 25 March 1986, Robin Neillands Papers, RMM.

20. I.G. Aylen, "Recollections of 30 Assault Unit," *Naval Review* 65, no. 4 (1977): 318.

21. "Proposal for Naval Intelligence Commando," 20 March 1942, TNA ADM 223/500.

22. The unit was also known during the war by several cover names, such as the Special Engineer Unit, No. 30 Commando and 30 Advanced Unit.

23. "Proposal for Naval Intelligence Commando."

24. Ibid.

25. "A History of 30 Commando (Latterly Called 30 Assault Unit and 30 Advanced Unit)," ch. 2, TNA ADM 223/214.

26. "Proposal for Naval Intelligence Command," 20 March 1942, TNA ADM 223/500; "A History of 30 Commando (Latterly Called 30 Assault Unit and 30 Advanced Unit), ch. 2, ADM 223/214.

27. "A History of 30 Commando." What the report missed was that this unit was part of a larger group of intelligence commandos that the Germans had

employed since the invasions of Poland and later France, where they scored great success capturing material left behind by the fleeing Allied armies in Paris and in naval facilities all along the coast.

28. It was Godfrey's successor, Admiral Edmund Rushbrooke, who coined this telling phrase. Memo "No. 30 Commando," 4 November 1942, TNA ADM 223/500.

29. "Proposal for Naval Intelligence Command."

30. Ibid.

31. Ben Macintyre, *For Your Eyes Only* (London: Bloomsbury, 2012), 259. Kindle edition.

32. "A History of 30 Commando."

33. Adrian Smith, *Mountbatten: Apprentice Warlord* (London: IB Tauris, 2010). Kindle edition.

34. Casa Maury to Fleming, 1 April 1942, TNA ADM 223/500.

35. Godfrey to Campbell, Drake and Fleming, 13 April 1942, TNA ADM 223/500.

NINE: DARKNESS TO DAYLIGHT

1. There is no evidence of the Gare Maritime in Dieppe today; it was demolished in 1995 to make way for a promenade and a series of quayside restaurants and cafés.

2. The streets were named in honour of First World War field marshal Ferdinand Foch, who commanded the French army at the end of the war, and Verdun, the site of a ten-month bloodletting battle of attrition in 1916 that had a profound effect on France and its culture. As historian Stéphane Audoin-Rouzeau suggests, "You can't understand France without understanding Verdun." Community Television of Southern California, "The Great War and the Shaping of the 20th Century: Verdun—'The Battle of France,'" http://www.pbs.org/greatwar/historian/hist_audoin_03_verdun.html (accessed May 5, 2013).

3. J.H. Godfrey, "Formation of the Situation Report Centre of the JIC," 18 August 1942, TNA ADM 223/107.

4. Ibid.

5. Robin Neillands, *The Dieppe Raid: The Story of the Disastrous 1942 Expedition* (London: Aurum Press, 2005), 163.

6. Naval Section Memorandum No. 75 "State of Work," 25 September 1942, TNA HW 8/158.

7. TNA HW 18/13; HW 18/35; ADM 223/94.

8. TNA DEFE 2/550. Although "NID" (Naval Intelligence Division) appears at the top of the document, subsequent messages make reference to "DNI" (Director of Naval Intelligence) as the originator of the message. Given the fact that both are acronyms, I assumed that the latter was a mistake until subsequent documents spelled it out in no uncertain terms. In other words, the Director of Naval Intelligence—in this case Godfrey, or Fleming on his behalf—was the author of the special inquiry. See DEFE 2/542.

9. Addendum No. 1, TNA DEFE 2/550. Although this document lists the originator as NID, a subsequent mention spells out that it came from the "Director of Naval Intelligence," precluding any typographical confusion over DNI/NID.

10. Addendum No. 9, TNA AIR 8/896.

11. "Naval Commander Channel Coast: First Report on Dieppe Operation," 20 August 1942, LAC RG 24, vol. 20,488.

12. "Intelligence Control Station France: Evaluation of Dieppe Operation," 12 September 1942, LAC RG 24, vol. 20,488.

13. Combined Operations, Intelligence Section, Report CB 04157 F (I) Addendum No. 9, TNA AIR 8/896.

14. "Minutes of a Meeting Held at Combined Operations Headquarters at 1100 hrs 14/4/42 to Discuss Operation Rutter," TNA DEFE 2/546. For Haydon, see TNA WO 373/93.

15. TNA DEFE 2/542.

16. Battle Summary No. 33: "Raid on Dieppe, August 19th 1942" (1946), 2, TNA ADM 234/354.

17. Ibid.

18. Ibid.

19. Built in 1938 in Scotland, the vessel was commissioned in spring 1940 and went straight into battle with De Costobadie at the helm during the Dunkirk evacuation, an action in which he earned the Distinguished Service Cross for bravery.

20. TNA ADM 223/479.

21. Special Information Centre, Offensive Operations, 1942 COS (42) 144th, TNA CAB 121/368.

22. Special Information Centre, Offensive Operations, "1942 Report by CinC Home Forces, AOC-in-C Fighter Command and Chief of Combined Operations," 28 March 1942, TNA CAB 121/368.

23. TNA AIR 20/5429.

24. Naval Section Memo No. 26, 20 August 1942 and 24 August 1942, TNA HW 8/26.

25. Field Marshal Lord Alanbrooke, *War Diaries 1939–1945* (Berkeley: University of California Press, 2001), 257; Adrian Smith, *Mountbatten: Apprentice Warlord* (London: IB Tauris, 2010). Kindle edition.

TEN: ALL THE KING'S MEN

1. Shane B. Schreiber, *Shock Army of the British Empire: The Canadian Corps in the Last 100 Days of the Great War* (Santa Barbara, CA: Praeger, 1997).

2. Peter Henshaw, "The Dieppe Raid: A Product of Misplaced Canadian Nationalism?" *Canadian Historical Review* 77, no. 2 (1996): 250–66; John Nelson Rickard, *The Politics of Command: Lieutenant General A.G.L. McNaughton and the Canadian Army, 1939–1943* (Toronto: University of Toronto Press, 2010); Paul Douglas Dickson, *A Thoroughly Canadian General: A Biography of General H.D.G. Crerar* (Toronto: University of Toronto Press, 2007); Dean Oliver, "Historiography, Generalship and Harry Crerar," in Lieutenant-Colonel Bernd Horn and Stephen Harris, eds., *Warrior Chiefs: Perspectives on Senior Canadian Military Leaders* (Toronto: Dundurn Press, 2001); J.L. Granatstein, *The Generals: The Canadian Army's Senior Commanders in the Second World War* (Toronto: Stoddart, 1993).

3. "Notes on a Conference Held on 6 Mar 42," LAC RG 24, vol. 10,765; Crerar to Lieutenant General B.L. Montgomery, 5 February 1942; "Memorandum on Visit of Lt-Gen B.C.T. Paget, GOC, SE Command, to Comd Cdn Corps, at 1500hrs, 6 Sept 1941," LAC RG 24, vol. 10,765.

4. Mountbatten to Guy Simonds, 4 February 1969, LAC Hughes-Hallett Papers.

5. Ibid.

6. Ibid.

7. Terence Robertson, *Dieppe: The Shame and the Glory* (London: Pan Books, 1965), 55.

8. Wade Davis, *Into the Silence: The Great War, Mallory, and the Conquest of Everest* (Toronto: Knopf, 2011). Mallory's body remained undiscovered for seventy-five years, until 1999, when an expedition that had set out to search for the climbers' remains found clothing they could identify on a slope eight hundred vertical feet from the summit. Whether Mallory and his climbing partner, Andrew "Sandy" Irvine, reached the summit before they died remains a subject of continuing speculation.

9. TNA ADM 196/92.

10. Adrian Smith, *Mountbatten: Apprentice Warlord* (London: IB Tauris, 2010), 207. Kindle edition.

11. Baillie-Grohman to Mountbatten, 14 September 1942, NMM GRO/29.

12. Memo from Baillie-Grohman to Mountbatten, 10 July 1942, NMM GRO/29. Unfortunately, there is nothing in the files so far released to confirm or dispel the suggestion that Baillie-Grohman was indeed referring to Ian Fleming.

13. Dickson, *A Thoroughly Canadian General*, 203.

14. Granatstein, *The Generals*, 32.

15. Admiral William James, *Portsmouth Letters* (London: Macmillan, 1946), 173–74.

16. John Hughes-Hallett, "Before I Forget," 155, Hughes-Hallett Papers, LAC MG30-E463.

17. Ibid., 135.

18. CMHQ Report No. 159, "Operation Jubilee, The Raid on Dieppe, Aug. 19: Additional Information on Planning," 4, DHH.

19. CMHQ Report No. 100, "Operation Jubilee, Part I: Preliminaries of the Operation," DHH.

20. Ibid.

21. Ibid.

22. George Ronald, interview with General Hamilton Roberts, c. 1962, George Ronald Papers, LAC MG30-E507.

23. Battle Summary No. 33: "Raid on Dieppe, August 19th 1942" (1946), 5, TNA ADM 234/354.

24. CMHQ Report No. 101, 34, DHH.

25. Richard Hopton, correspondence with author, August 2012.

26. R.E.D. Ryder, unpublished memoirs.

27. Ibid.

28. Ibid.

ELEVEN: DIEPPE BY DESIGN

1. J.H. Godfrey, note, "30 AU," 5 September 1970, TNA ADM 223/214.

2. Rear Admiral Godfrey DNI to Brig. Kirkman, AVM Medhurst, Brig. Menzies, Brig. Petrie with copy to JIC, 2 June 1942, TNA ADM 223/500.

3. Ibid.

4. Ibid. The pinch aspect of Operation Rutter seems to have been in place right from the start: Godfrey had been interested in the Hôtel Moderne as soon as Dieppe came under consideration. His request in this letter was not operational but, rather, administrative. In other words, the wheels were already in motion to

include a force like this one on the raid as an "experiment." Godfrey was looking for official "logistical" sanction to create a standing unit, and his request should not be confused with one for an operational nod.

5. "A History of 30 Commando (Latterly Called 30 Assault Unit and 30 Advanced Unit)," ch. 1, TNA ADM 223/214.

6. Ibid. Very little, if anything, is known of these units except for a brief passage that appears in this history.

7. "RM Commando Exercise Operational Order No. 8," 22 June 1942, No. 40 Royal Marine Commando War Diary, TNA ADM 202/87.

8. Ibid.

9. Paul McGrath, *The Dieppe Raid, Wednesday 19th August 1942: Recollections of W.P. McGrath DSM*, self-published.

10. "RM Commando Exercise Operational Order No. 8."

11. "History of 30 AU," Part II, Section 3, Intelligence Briefing and Planning for 30 Commando/30 Assault Unit, TNA ADM 223/500. Although the Royal Marine Commando was known only as A Commando at this time, it was re-designated as No. 40 Royal Marine Commando immediately after the raid—a name it still has today. Thereafter, all paperwork, war diaries and references to A Commando were changed to reflect its new name, No. 40 Royal Marine Commando, although technically it did not exist as such at the time.

12. On the fiftieth anniversary of the Dieppe Raid, McGrath wrote a short memoir about his exploits for the Royal Marine Association. He later self-published it under the title *The Dieppe Raid, Wednesday 19th August 1942: Recollections of W.P. McGrath DSM*.

13. McGrath, *Dieppe Raid*.

14. No. 40 Royal Marine Commando, "War Diary," February 1942, TNA ADM 202/87.

15. Miles Huntington-Whiteley, interview for DU.

16. Paul McGrath, interview for DU.

17. "History of 30 AU," Part II, Section 3.

18. "Technical Intelligence and the Processing of Captured Documents," 67–68, TNA HW 43/23.

19. Godfrey Edward Wildman-Lushington to Chiefs of Staff, 8 June 1942, TNA CAB 121/364.

20. "CCO/SOE Liaison Officer's Report No. 78 date 4/5/42 0900hrs," TNA HS 8/819. In his report, the liaison officer notes that as of this date, no firm plan has been made, no assistance from SOE has been asked for with the exception of targeting intelligence, and that "a great deal hangs on the tank exits from the main beach of the town."

21. Search Plan, app. L, TNA WO 252/108.

22. "Considerations affecting Operation Rutter and the Clarification of this plan to be known as Rutter II," 7 July 1942, LAC RG 24, vol. 10,750.

23. Ibid.; "Raids 2nd Canadian Division RUTTER II: Considerations affecting Operation Rutter and the Modification of this plan to be known as Rutter II," LAC RG 24, vol. 10,750.

24. "Notes on Meeting Held Inf[orming] Bde [Brigades] about Forthcoming Operation 'Rutter,'" 27 June 1942, LAC RG 24, vol. 10,872, File 252C2 (D37) Rutter—Generally.

25. "Operation Rutter Detailed Military Plan Phase IIB Attack on Trawlers," LAC RG 24, vol. 10,765.

26. "War Diary Essex Scottish," August 1942, app. VI, LAC RG 24, vol. 17,513.

27. "Operation Rutter Detailed Military Plan Phase IIB Attack on Trawlers."

28. "Notes on a Conference of Navy, Essex Scot, Tanks, Engrs and RM Commando 28/'06/42," LAC RG 24, vol. 10,872, file 252C2 (D37) Rutter—Generally.

29. Ibid.

30. "Royal Marine Commando Operational Orders No. 8 Operation Rutter June 30 1942 and No. 9 Operation Jubilee August 15 1942," TNA ADM 1/11986.

31. Ibid.

32. Ibid.

33. Ibid.

34. "Operation Rutter: Section III—Special Instructions June 22, 1942," TNA ADM 179/220. This portion, hastily pencilled in, called for the R-boat to rendezvous with *Calpe*, but this seems to be an error for *Fernie*.

35. "Operation Rutter, Minutes of 1st Meeting of the Combined Force Commanders at Combined Operations Headquarters on June 1st 1942," TNA DEFE 2/546.

36. Ibid.

37. "Notes on Meeting Held Inf[orming] Bde [Brigades] about Forthcoming Operation 'Rutter.'"

38. Ibid.

39. Ibid.

TWELVE: ALL ESSENTIAL FEATURES

1. R.E.D. Ryder, unpublished memoirs.

2. Ibid.

3. Parsons, correspondence with author.

4. Ibid.

5. TNA ADM 202/87; Parsons, correspondence with author.

6. Beth Crumley, "A Roomful of Military Historians," Marine Corps Association & Foundation, http://www.mca-marines.org/blog/beth-crumley/2011/06/20/ roomful-military-historians-0 (accessed August 12, 2013).

7. "Brit spymaster reveals tensions with 'gangster' Hoover in WW2," Windsor Star, October 27, 2012, http://www2.canada.com/windsorstar/news/story. html?id=c6c72f15-311c-4f51-9f6b-a013f6d2f178 (accessed August 13, 2013).

8. David Stafford, Roosevelt & Churchill: Men of Secrets (London: Thistle Publishing, 2013), 1296–99. Kindle edition.

9. Joseph E. Persico, Roosevelt's Secret War: FDR and World War II Espionage (New York: Random House, 2001), 1648–51. Kindle edition.

10. Center for the Study of Intelligence, Central Intelligence Agency, "COI Came First," https://www.cia.gov/library/center-for-the-study-of-intelligence/ csi-publications/books-and-monographs/oss/art02.htm (accessed August 12, 2013).

11. Thomas F. Troy, "Donovan's Original Marching Orders" (originally published 1973), Center for the Study of Intelligence, Central Intelligence Agency, https:// www.cia.gov/library/center-for-the-study-of-intelligence/kent-csi/vol17no2/ pdf/v17i2a05p.pdf (accessed August 12, 2013).

12. Sig Rosenblum, Spymaster: "Wild Bill" Donovan, Father of the CIA (Hampton Hill, 2008), 639–43. Kindle edition.

13. Ibid., 1414.

14. Crumley, "A Roomful of Military Historians."

15. Ibid.

16. Ibid.

17. Thomas E. Ricks, The Generals: American Military Command from World War II to Today (New York: Penguin Press, 2012), 26. Kindle edition.

18. Telegram from Joint Staff Mission Washington to General Ismay, 9 April 1942, TNA DEFE 2/908.

19. Ismay to Mountbatten, 9 April 1942, TNA DEFE 2/908.

20. Birch to DD(s), 1 August 1942, TNA HW 57/9.

21. "OIC and NID Summaries Naval Section German Effort Against North Russian Convoy Routes," TNA ADM 223/3.

22. Winston S. Churchill, The Second World War, vol. 4, The Hinge of Fate (Boston:

Houghton Mifflin, 1950), 237.

23. Hinsley to OIC, "Comments on ZTPG Series of German Naval Messages 0115hrs 04/07/42," HW 18/158.

24. Ibid.; and Hinsley to OIC, "Comments on ZTPG Series of German Naval Messages 0305hrs 04/07/42," HW 18/158.

25. Brian Loring Villa, *Unauthorized Action: Mountbatten and the Dieppe Raid*, 2nd ed. (Oxford: Oxford University Press, 1994).

26. Extract from COS (42) 355, 23 December 1942, TNA ADM 223/299.

27. "Memorandum of meeting for Operation J_____ on July 16, 1942," 25 July 1942, LAC RG 24, vol. 10,584.

28. Ibid.

29. At the time, the security classification for this history read Ultra Secret, which included not only signals but also the histories written after the war. They all came under one great Ultra umbrella.

30. "Naval Intelligence Division History, 1939–1942," Manuscript II, Royal Navy Historical Branch, Portsmouth, U.K.

31. Ibid.

32. Message from McNaughton to Stuart, 18 August 1942, LAC RG 24, vol. 10,584.

33. For an excellent treatise on the bureaucratic manoeuvring by Mountbatten, see Stephen Prince, *The Royal Navy and the Raids at St. Nazaire and Dieppe* (London: Frank Cass, 2002).

34. Martin H. Folly, "Seeking Comradeship in the 'Ogre's Den': Winston Churchill's Quest for a Warrior Alliance and his Mission to Stalin, August 1942" (research paper, Brunel University, 2007), http://bura.brunel.ac.uk/handle/2438/5738 (accessed May 1, 2013).

35. Alexander Cadogan to Lord Halifax, "War: Soviet Union. Account of Stalin/ Churchill Meeting in Moscow," 29 August 1942, TNA FO 1093/247.

36. Ibid.

37. TNA PREM 3/463.

38. David Wragg, *Sacrifice for Stalin: The Cost and Value of the Arctic Convoys Re-assessed* (Havertown, PA: Casemate, 1105–6). Kindle edition.

39. Alexander Hill, "British Lend-Lease and the Soviet War Effort June 1941–June 1942," *Journal of Military History* 71, no. 3 (July 2007): 773–808.

40. CHUR 4/ 25A/ 21– 3.

41. David Reynolds, *In Command of History: Churchill Fighting and Writing the Second World War* (Harmondsworth: Penguin Books, 2005), 7422–24. Kindle edition.

42. Ibid., 7426–27.

43. Ibid.

44. Winston S. Churchill, *Memoirs of the Second World War* (Boston: Houghton-Mifflin, 1959), 636.

45. TNA CAB 120/66.

46. TNA CAB 120/69 (italics added).

47. TNA CAB 120/69.

THIRTEEN: THE CROSSING

1. "Anonymous member of Special Branch, Newhaven–Dieppe," *Weekly Intelligence Report* [NID] no. 129, 28 August 1942, 11–20, DHH; Fleming to Casa Maury, 21 August 1942, DEFE 2/333.

2. Memorandum for CCO from Brigadier Truscott, n.d., *c*. Aug.–Sept. 1942, TNA DEFE 3/335.

3. "Anonymous member of Special Branch," 11.

4. No. 40 Royal Marine Commando, "War Diary," TNA ADM 202/87.

5. Jock Farmer, *JOCK of 40 Royal Marine Commando: My Life from Start to Finish* (Shanklin Chine: Shanklin Chine Publishers, 2007), 59.

6. "Memorandum on interview at Navy Office of Canada, on October 14th with Sto. I Pearson, V10685, and Ldg. Stm Cline, N.W., LAC RG 24, vol. 3951.

7. McAlister memoirs, courtesy of the McAlister family and Phillip Lloyd of No. 40 Royal Marine Commando Association.

8. Farmer, *JOCK*, 59.

9. Paul McGrath, *The Dieppe Raid, Wednesday 19th August 1942: Recollections of W.P. McGrath DSM*, self-published, 1.

10. Farmer, *JOCK*, 59.

11. Douglas Charles Bevan, interview, Imperial War Museum (IWM 14882), 1995.

12. McGrath, *Dieppe Raid*, 1.

13. Bevan, interview.

14. John Kruthoffer to Robin Neillands, 25 March 1986, Robin Neillands Papers, RMM.

15. McGrath, *Dieppe Raid*, 1.

16. John Hughes-Hallett, "Before I Forget," 177, LAC Hughes Hallett Papers.

17. Ibid.

18. Ibid., 178.

Endnotes

19. Jock Hughes-Hallett, "Naval Force Commander's Narrative," Hughes-Hallett Papers, DHH 78/492.

20. R.E.D. Ryder, unpublished memoirs.

21. Ibid.

22. ZIP/ZTPG 68844 and ZIP/ZTPG 68845, DEFE 3/187.

23. Battle Summary No. 33: "Raid on Dieppe, August 19th 1942" (1946), 13, TNA ADM 223/354.

24. Ibid.

25. ZIP/ZTPG 68850, TNA DEFE 3/187.

26. Fleming to Casa Maury, 21 August 1942, DEFE 2/333.

27. Enclosure 13 "Extract of Report from HMS Locust," app. 20, LAC RG 24, vol. 10,872; NMM GRO/24.

28. "Combat Report of four Coastal Motor Ships," 22 August 1942, DHH Steiger Papers SGR II/285.

29. Battle Summary No. 33.

30. Dieppe Operation Naval Commander Channel Coast, "Lessons Learnt August 30 1942," DHH Steiger Papers SGR II/280.

31. Ibid. "According to information from 81st Army Corps, one of our convoys has been attacked by fast British ships at 0400hrs, at about 20 kilometres off the port of Dieppe. Troops have intensified their lookout. Navy and Air authorities have been advised."

32. Robin Neillands, The Dieppe Raid: The Story of the Disastrous 1942 Expedition (London: Aurum Press, 2005), 129.

33. Interview with author for DU, 3 March 2011.

34. "Action of the Essex Scottish (Red Beach), Statement by Capt D.F. McCrae," TNA DEFE 2/339.

35. Ibid.

36. Author's interview with Howard Large for DU, 3 October 2011.

37. Denis W. Whitaker and Shelagh Whitaker, Dieppe: Tragedy to Triumph (Toronto: McGraw-Hill Ryerson, 1992), 253.

38. Jock Hughes-Hallett, "Naval Force Commander's Narrative," Hughes-Hallett Papers, DHH 78/492.

39. Bevan, interview.

40. Ibid.

41. John Parson, correspondence with author.

42. R.E.D. Ryder, unpublished memoirs.

43. Ernest Coleman, unpublished memoirs, courtesy of John Barker.

44. McGrath, *Dieppe Raid*, 5.

45. Ibid.

46. Ibid.

47. Ibid., 6.

48. Ibid.

49. Naval Force Commander's Narrative, encl. no. 5, "Operation Jubilee List of Important Signals," LAC Hughes-Hallett Papers.

50. Farmer, JOCK, 60.

51. LAC RG24, vol. 17,506.

52. Naval Force Commander's Narrative, encl. no. 5.

53. "Operation Jubilee: The Raid at Dieppe 19/08/42, Part II: The Execution of the Operation, Section 2, The Attack on the Main Beaches, Report Battle Account of St. Pierre Dubuc, Fusiliers de Mont-Royal," DHH CMHQ 108.

54. Hughes-Hallett, "Before I Forget," 185.

55. "Lord Mountbatten's Comments on Dieppe Chapter," c. 1970, LAC Hughes-Hallett Papers. In this case, it is Mountbatten quoting Hughes-Hallett back to Hughes-Hallett.

56. Wallace Reyburn, letter to the editor, *Sunday Telegraph* (London), 17 September 1967, LAC Hughes-Hallett Papers.

57. Quoted in Neillands, *Dieppe Raid*, 238.

58. Naval Force Commander's Narrative, encl. no. 5, "Operation Jubilee List of Important Signals," LAC Hughes-Hallett Papers.

59. "Report Operation Jubilee Royal Marine Commando 19/08/42," TNA ADM 1/11986; Capt. P.W.C. Hellings RM DSC, "Report on Events of 19/08/42 off Dieppe of A Coy Royal Marine Commando," TNA ADM 1/11986.

60. Ernest Coleman, unpublished memoirs.

61. Farmer, JOCK, 61.

62. Naval Force Commander's Narrative, encl. no. 5. Hughes-Hallett's only response was to order Ryder, who had remained on *Locust*, to pick up the wounded on the beach once the Royal Marines landed.

63. Naval Force Commander's Narrative, encl. no. 5.

64. Hugh G. Henry, "The Planning, Intelligence, Execution and Aftermath of the Dieppe Raid, 19 August 1942" (Ph.D. dissertation, St. John's College, University of Cambridge, October 1996).

FOURTEEN: ALL IN ON THE MAIN BEACH

1. Paul McGrath, *The Dieppe Raid, Wednesday 19th August 1942: Recollections of W.P. McGrath DSM*, self-published, 1.

2. Ernest Coleman, unpublished memoirs.

3. McAlister, unpublished memoirs.

4. Jock Farmer, *JOCK of 40 Royal Marine Commando: My Life from Start to Finish* (Shanklin Chine: Shanklin Chine Publishers, 2007), 61.

5. J.J. Dwan to Neillands, 7 November 2002, Robin Neillands Papers, RMM.

6. McGrath, *Dieppe Raid*, 9.

7. Kruthoffer, quoted in Robin Neillands, *By Sea and Land* (Barnsley, U.K.: Pen and Sword, 2004), 29.

8. McGrath, *Dieppe Raid*, 8.

9. Kruthoffer, quoted in Neillands, *By Sea and Land*, 29.

10. Ernest Coleman, unpublished memoirs.

11. McGrath, *Dieppe Raid*, 8.

12. Kruthoffer, quoted in Neillands, *By Sea and Land*, 29.

13. Ernest Coleman, unpublished memoirs.

14. McGrath, *Dieppe Raid*, 11.

15. "A History of 30 Commando (Latterly Called 30 Assault Unit and 30 Advanced Unit)," ch. 2, TNA ADM 223/214; "Camp 020 Interim Report on the case of Erich Pfeiffer," TNA KV 2/267.

16. Huntington-Whiteley to Sergeant Kruthoffer, n.d., c. 26 August 1942; quoted in Neillands, *By Sea and Land*, 33-34.

17. R.E.D. Ryder, unpublished memoirs.

18. *Weekly Intelligence Report* [NID] no. 129, 28 August 1942, DHH.

19. The exception was John Campbell's masterful *Dieppe Revisited*, in which he cites the document but fails to understand its true significance. Rather, he focused on the security issues and on Fleming's veiled references to his own Ultra indoctrination.

EPILOGUE

1. DU.

2. Mountbatten to Godfrey, 29 August 1942, BNA DEFE 2/955. As Mountbatten would later tell Godfrey after the DNI petitioned for the VC winner's services to head the new 30 Assault Unit following Dieppe: "I know you will agree it will

not be much use having the most perfect Intelligence Assault Unit unless the operations on which they are sent are properly planned and carried out."

3. Of course, if Jock Hughes-Hallett did not agree, he had the power as naval force commander—not to mention the cocksureness—to call off any attempts to land further reinforcements simply by refusing to provide the boats or by turning for home. Despite their difference in rank, for the raid Roberts and Hughes-Hallett were equals, masters of their own military and naval domains respectively.

4. Intelligence Control Station France, "Evaluation of Dieppe Operation," 14 September 1942, LAC RG 24, vol. 20,488.

The classic photo taken by a German propaganda cameraman of the carnage on Blue Beach at Puys, where over five hundred men from the Royal Regiment of Canada (including Ron Beal) and the Black Watch of Montreal landed, suffering close to 95 percent casualties in just a few hours. In the distance, below the white house on the escarpment, are three of the five bunkers and pillboxes that housed the German machine guns, which took such a heavy toll on the Canadians.

Happy to be home: Two unidentified infantrymen of the Essex Scottish Regiment, relieved to be home after surviving the hell on earth on Red Beach, in England on August 23, 1942.

ACKNOWLEDGEMENTS

The research for this book unfolded over a period of nearly two decades, and I would like to begin by thanking everyone who helped to make it possible. One of the best aspects of this historical research journey has been meeting a wide range of people who have influenced my work and become colleagues—and some, lifelong friends.

Without the work of at least two generations of historians before me, this book could not have been written. Starting with C.P. Stacey's pioneering work in the days following the raid, through Terence Robertson's work in the sixties that embedded Dieppe in the Canadian consciousness, to the stellar and seminal offerings of Brian Villa and John Campbell in the late eighties, followed by historians such as Ben Greenhous, Steve Prince, Peter Henshaw, Hugh Henry, Denis and Shelagh Whitaker and more recently Beatrice Richard and Timothy Balzer, all these historians have made dramatic and lasting contributions to our understanding of the darkest day in Canadian history. Contextually, the many publications by J.L. Granatstein, David Bercuson, Holger Herwig, Desmond Morton and Terry Copp have been invaluable to my research.

In the area of cryptography, the work of Ralph Erskine continues to inspire, as do the lasting contributions by David Kahn, David Syrett and Richard Aldrich. Likewise, Hugh Sebag-Montefiore's excellent study on the early days of pinch operations is clearly groundbreaking, as is Nicholas Rankin's book on 30 Assault Unit, Richard Hopton's on Robert "Red" Ryder, Robin Neilland's on the Royal Marines, Jack Copeland's on Alan Turing, and Jock Gardner's on Ultra and the Battle of the Atlantic.

I am grateful to Dr. Stephen Harris, who recruited me some twenty years ago, when I began my graduate studies, to work at the Directorate of History and Heritage in Ottawa. That appointment not only gave me a job but laid the path for a career. Likewise, there were many others at DHH who have generously helped me over the years: Serge Bernier, Alec Douglas, Bill McAndrew, Bob Caldwell, Bill Rawling, Donna Porter, Isabelle Campbell, Mike Whitby, Richard Gimlett, Sean Hunter, Ken Reynolds, Michelle Litalien, Jean Morin, Greg Donahy, Bill Johnston, Yves Tremblay and the late Ben Greenhous, among others. This list also includes a historian's best friend—the archivist. In this case, without the support and expertise of Owen Cooke, Warren Sinclair and Valerie Casbourn at DHH and the wisdom, friendship and advice of Paul Marsden at Library and Archives Canada, this research would never have been possible.

Although he has moved on from DHH to greener pastures at the Laurier Centre for Military and Disarmament Studies in Waterloo, I must thank Dr. Roger Sarty, who was a friend, mentor and boss all those years ago when I was a very small cog in the machine that created the official history of the Royal Canadian Navy in the Second World War. In addition, I would like to thank Mike Bechthold and Professor Emeritus Terry Copp at Wilfrid Laurier University, who gave me sage research advice that I have never forgotten.

Equally, I would like to thank Brian Villa, Peter Henshaw and Hugh Henry, whose scholarship and encouragement kept me on my toes, constantly posing a battery of salient questions throughout this process. Similarly, I am grateful to Beth Crumley at the United States Marine Corps Historical Center for information on the USMC commitment to the Dieppe Raid. I am indebted to Ralph Erskine and, at Bletchley Park, to Bob Horner and the late Brian Oakley for their insights on British cryptography. In addition, I must thank Bob Hanyok for his generous help with the American cryptographic landscape, and Adrian Smith at the University of Southampton for his assistance with Mountbatten. This research could not have been completed without "bird dogs" on the ground—the researchers at various archival facilities, particularly Simon Cawthorne, Bob O'Hara, Gregor Murbach and Greg Hill, who fulfilled that role with remarkable skill.

I would also like to thank the staff at the National Maritime Museum in Greenwich, the Imperial War Museum in London, the University of Toronto

Acknowledgements

Archives (in particular Eric McGeer), the Royal Marine Commando Museum and Archives in Portsmouth, and Hugh Alexander and Mark Dunton at the British National Archives (fondly remembered as the PRO).

I am grateful to Stephen Prince and his staff at the Royal Navy's Naval Historical Branch in Portsmouth, and especially to Jock Gardner and Mark Bentinck (who put me on to Paul McGrath), for their generous help with numerous naval queries from this all too "military" of historians. None of this could have come to fruition without the help of the historian at GCHQ who, when presented with the evidence, immediately provided key technical advice and judiciously expedited the release of key documents that helped take my research to a new level.

A special note of appreciation goes out to the veterans and their families who generously gave of their time to talk to me and granted permission to quote from their letters, diaries, journals and unpublished memoirs—all of which add to the drama and human reality of this story. They include Ron Beal, Howard Large, Ted Bennett, John Parsons, Paul McGrath, the family of Ernest "Lofty" Coleman, Edward Peter Yard-Young and Andy Wilkinson, Simon McAlister and the family of Robert McAlister, Miles Huntington-Whiteley and Leo Huntington-Whiteley, Barry Batterton and the family of Roy Batterton Jr., David McKellar and the family of Bob McKellar, Lisle Ryder and the family of Red Ryder, and David Lloyd of No. 40 Commando Association. I would like to thank the Honourable Stephen Blaney, Kelly Power and Andrew Bernardo from Veterans Affairs Canada for their help in locating veterans and for all they have done to help promote the research.

One of the bonuses of conducting historical inquiries such as this one is having a reason to visit the site in question. In this case, I was most fortunate to spend close to six months over an eighteen-month period in Dieppe. The City of Dieppe Archives proved crucial to establishing the whereabouts of the Hôtel Moderne, as were the owners of the Hôtel Les Arcades, Karine and Mathieu Leducq, who energetically joined in the search. I also want to thank Nicola Bucourt, Frederick Jeanne, Mathieu Masson, Hervé Fihue, and Heimdal publications in Caen for their help.

What took me over to Dieppe on a regular basis was the filming of the documentary *Dieppe Uncovered* for History Television in Canada and UKTV in England. This project would never have happened without the support of Sarah Jane Flynn, Nick Crowe and Cameron Mask at History Television. I have happily worked in conjunction with them for fifteen years, and they continue to support groundbreaking historical research on their network. Special thanks go to my "partner in crime" in several documentary productions, the talented producer/director Wayne Abbott—who has traipsed across many a battlefield with me, from Hong Kong to Europe, in our effort to bring history to life on the small screen.

Having taught history at the university, college and high school levels for close to twenty years, I was most fortunate to sign on with Marianopolis College in Westmount a few years ago. There, I have always received tremendous support for my research endeavours. In particular, I want to thank Len Even and Norma Raimondo for their visionary approach to professional development and Kareen Latour, my incredible and supportive department chair, for making everything work out smoothly. I must also thank a fantastic faculty and staff who truly value excellence and the spirit of collegiality, especially my office mate, Dr. Maria Salomon, who listened with great patience as I droned incessantly about all things Dieppe. Thanks for being a friend.

To put a complex book together requires a team of experienced and talented professionals. My literary super-agent, Rick Broadhead, went beyond the call of duty to ensure that everything came together and that it stayed on the rails. The excellent group at Knopf Canada—especially copy editor John Sweet, proofreader Doris Cowan, designer Andrew Roberts and indexer Barney Gilmore—deserve special mention, along with Deirdre Molina, Kate Icely, Tracey Turriff, Shona Cook, Matthew Sibiga and Nina Ber. My picture researcher Avril McMeekin overcame many obstacles and, like the rest of the team, worked long hours and gave up weekends with friends and family to complete the book on time. They all have my deep respect and admiration for a job well done.

Acknowledgements

Certainly this tribute extends to the incomparable Rosemary Shipton, whose editing prowess and historical training allowed this rather convoluted story to unfold with energy and grace, and who gave my usual impenetrable academic prose the space to breathe. Above all, this project would not have got off the ground without the vision and drive of my publisher and co-editor Louise Dennys, who, captivated by what this story means for Canadians, pulled out all the stops to acquire the rights and then provided the guiding hand and consummate leadership needed to bring this project to fruition. It is due to her genuine commitment that my time in the trenches writing the text will be one of the most memorable and rewarding experiences of my life.

To the friends and family I have put on hold for the last year—Earl Chapman, Lionel Chetwynd, Greg Hill, the Black Sox, the Knights, my former colleagues at LBP and the Black Watch, John, Liette, Pat, Lorina, Dave, Carly, Stephanie and all the nieces and nephews—I thank you for your patience, understanding and friendship.

I also want to mention my mother and my late father, who, during a European trip in 1962, stopped by Dieppe to pay their respects to the many friends lost on the morning of August 19, 1942, and who filmed a thirty-second segment of the harbour and Pollet Cliff with their 8 mm camera. They could never have realized the supreme irony of that moment: despite better vantage points, they chose, for whatever reason, to take the photo from the front steps of the Hôtel Moderne. Pure coincidence, of course—but history can move in mysterious ways.

Finally, to my wife, Carolyn, my children, Jessica, Andie and Kevin, and our big yellow Lab, Maya, thank you so much for your support throughout this remarkable journey. I love you all.

PHOTO CREDITS

page 26. Old Admiralty Building, London
© David Iliff

page 32. John Godfrey
© Imperial War Museums (A 20777)

page 36. Admiral Sir William "Blinker" Hall
date and photographer unknown

page 44. Winston Churchill
© Imperial War Museums (MH 26392)

page 66. Three-wheel Enigma machine
Crown Copyright. Used by permission, Director GCHQ

page 67. Enigma wheels
Crown Copyright. Used by permission, Director GCHQ

page 72. Alan Turing
date and photographer unknown

page 76. The Bombe
Crown Copyright. Used by permission, Director GCHQ

page 77. Close-up view of Bombe
Crown Copyright. Used by permission, Director GCHQ

page 77. Women seated at Bombe machines
Crown Copyright. Used by permission, Director GCHQ

page 84. Karl Dönitz
© Bundesarchiv Bild 146-1976-127-06A

page 98. Harry Hinsley
Photo courtesy of Hugo Hinsley

page 98. Workers at Bletchley Park
Crown Copyright. Used by permission, Director GCHQ

page 102. Lofoten Islands Raid
© Imperial War Museums (N 397)

page 106. Canadian seamen boarding U-744
© Canada. Dept. of National Defence / Library and Archives Canada /
PA-139427

page 108. Enigma machine with code books
Photo courtesy of Wayne Abbott

page 108. Wireless control room
© Bundesarchiv Bild 101II-MW-4222-02A

page 117. Four-wheel Enigma machine
© Bletchley Park Trust

page 123. Louis Mountbatten
©Yousuf Karsh/Maclean's Magazine/Library and Archives Canada /
PA-215000

page 132. Vaagso Island Raid
© Imperial War Museums (N 530)

page 144. John Hughes-Hallett
Photo courtesy of Frederick M. Jeanne

page 244. "New Objectives list"
© The National Archives, Kew / DEFE 2/550

page 262. Hamilton Roberts
© Canada. Dept. of National Defence/Library and Archives Canada / PA-153531

page 284. No. 10 Platoon, X Company
Photo courtesy of Paul McGrath.

page 285. Ian Fleming's commandos
Photo courtesy of Paul McGrath.

page 286. Paul McGrath and No. 10 Platoon members
Photo courtesy of Paul McGrath.

page 292. Peter Huntington-Whiteley
Photo courtesy of Huntington-Whiteley family

page 293. NID intelligence search document
© The National Archives, Kew / WO 252/108

page 345. Landing craft en route to Dieppe
© Canada. Dept. of National Defence / Library and Archives Canada / PA-171080

page 346. HMS Fernie
© Imperial War Museums (FL 1677)

page 346. HMS Locust
© Imperial War Museums (FL 10250)

page 372. View of beaches smoking
© The National Archives, Kew / DEFE 2/338

page 373. Aerial photo with tobacco factory
© The National Archives, Kew / DEFE 2/338

page 386. Fallen Canadian soldier
© Bundesarchiv Bild 101I-291-1209-26

page 390. Prisoners of war
date and photographer unknown

page 394 and jacket back panel. Soldier drinks from helmet
© Bundesarchiv Bild 101I-291-1238-37A

page 408. Howard Large
© Nick Brancaccio/the *Windsor Star*

page 409. Ronald Beal
© Colin McConnell/Getstock.com

page 414. Carnage on Blue Beach

page 415. Essex Scottish soldiers
© Capt. W.G. Abel / Canada. Dept. of National Defence / Library and Archives Canada / PA-189474

PERMISSIONS

Every attempt has been made by the author to trace the copyright or permissions holders of images used or works quoted in this book. I welcome any information or clarification in the few instances where such information was untraceable or unavailable to me.

Pages 15, 16, 103: Permission to reproduce from *The Girl From Station X: My Mother's Unknown Life*, Copyright ©Elisa Segrave, published by Union Books, an imprint of Aurum Press Ltd, September 2013, is granted by permission of the author.

Page 82: Permission to reproduce from *Turing: Pioneer of the Information Age*, p. 64, Copyright © B. Jack Copeland, published by Oxford University Press, November 2012, is granted by permission of Oxford University Press.

Page 342: Permission to reproduce lyrics from "Privateering," written by Mark Knopfler, is granted by permission of Universal Music Publishing Group, a division of Universal Music Canada Inc.

Pages 348, 371: Permission to quote from the IWM's interview with Douglas Charles Bevan (IWM 14882) is granted by permission of the Imperial War Museums.

Pages 372–73, 394: Permission to reproduce from Ernest Coleman's unpublished memoirs, Copyright © Ernest Coleman, 2013, is granted by permission of John Barker.

INDEX

DAVID R. O'KEEFE is an award-winning historian, documentarian and professor at Marianopolis College in Westmount, Quebec. He served with the The Black Watch (Royal Highland Regiment) of Canada in Montreal and worked as a Signals Intelligence research historian for the Directorate of History and Heritage (DND). He has also created and collaborated on over 15 documentaries for History Television and appeared on CBC Radio, Global Television, and the UKTV Network in Great Britain. In 2002 he joined forces with Emmy award-winner producer Wayne Abbott; among the television documentaries they have made is *Dieppe Uncovered*, which aired simultaneously on History Television in Canada and Yesterday TV in the U.K. on 70th anniversary of the raid, to major acclaim.